Heroin Addiction: Theory, Research and Treatment *by Jerome J. Platt and Christina Labate*

Children's Rights and the Mental Health Profession *edited by Gerald P. Koocher*

The Role of the Father in Child Development *edited by Michael E. Lamb*

Handbook of Behavioral Assessment *edited by Anthony R. Ciminero, Karen S. Calhoun, and Henry E. Adams*

Counseling and Psychotherapy: A Behavioral Approach *by E. Lakin Phillips*

Dimensions of Personality *edited by Harvey London and John E. Exner, Jr.*

The Mental Health Industry: A Cultural Phenomenon *by Peter A. Magaro, Robert Gripp, David McDowell, and Ivan W. Miller III*

Nonverbal Communication: The State of the Art *by Robert G. Harper, Arthur N. Wiens, and Joseph D. Matarazzo*

Alcoholism and Treatment *by David J. Armor, J. Michael Polich, and Harriet B. Stambul*

A Biodevelopmental Approach to Clinical Child Psychology: Cognitive Controls and Cognitive Control Theory *by Sebastiano Santostefano*

Handbook of Infant Development *edited by Joy D. Osofsky*

Understanding the Rape Victim: A Synthesis of Research Findings *by Sedelle Katz and Mary Ann Mazur*

Childhood Pathology and Later Adjustment: The Question of Prediction *by Loretta K. Cass and Carolyn B. Thomas*

Intelligent Testing with the WISC-R *by Alan S. Kaufman*

Adaptation in Schizophrenia: The Theory of Segmental Set *by David Shakow*

Psychotherapy: An Eclectic Approach *by Sol L. Garfield*

Handbook of Minimal Brain Dysfunctions *edited by Herbert E. Rie and Ellen D. Rie*

Handbook of Behavioral Interventions: A Clinical Guide *edited by Alan Goldstein and Edna B. Foa*

Art Psychotherapy *by Harriet Wadeson*

Handbook of Adolescent Psychology *edited by Joseph Adelson*

Psychotherapy Supervision: Theory, Research and Practice *edited by Allen K. Hess*

Psychology and Psychiatry in Courts and Corrections: Controversy and Change *by Ellsworth A. Fersch, Jr.*

Restricted Environmental Stimulation: Research and Clinical Applications *by Peter Suedfeld*

Personal Construct Psychology: Psychotherapy and Personality *edited by Alvin W. Landfield and Larry M. Leitner*

Mothers, Grandmothers, and Daughters: Personality and Child Care in Three-Generation Families *by Bertram J. Cohler and Henry U. Grunebaum*

Further Explorations in Personality *edited by A.I. Rabin, Joel Aronoff, Andrew M. Barclay, and Robert A. Zucker*

Hypnosis and Relaxation: Modern Verification of an Old Equation *by William E. Edmonston, Jr.*

Handbook of Clinical Behavior Therapy *edited by Samuel M. Turner, Karen S. Calhoun, and Henry E. Adams*

Handbook of Clinical Neuropsychology *edited by Susan B. Filskov and Thomas J. Boll*

The Course of Alcoholism: Four Years After Treatment *by J. Michael Polich, David J. Armor, and Harriet B. Braiker*

Handbook of Innovative Psychotherapies *edited by Raymond J. Corsini*

The Role of the Father in Child Development (Second Edition) *edited by Michael E. Lamb*

Behavioral Medicine: Clinical Applications *by Susan S. Pinkerton, Howard Hughes, and W.W. Wenrich*

(continued on back)

A DEVELOPMENTAL APPROACH
TO ADULT PSYCHOPATHOLOGY

A Developmental Approach to Adult Psychopathology

Edward Zigler
Yale University

Marion Glick
Southern Connecticut State University

A WILEY-INTERSCIENCE PUBLICATION

JOHN WILEY & SONS

New York • Chicester • Brisbane • Toronto • Singapore

Library of Congress Cataloging-in-Publication Data:

Zigler, Edward, 1930-
  A developmental approach to adult psychopathology.

  (Wiley series on personality processes)
  "A Wiley-Interscience publication."
  Bibliography: p.
  Includes indexes.
  1. Psychology, Pathological. 2. Developmental
psychology. I. Glick, Marion. II. Title.
III. Series. [DNLM: 1. Psychopathology. WM 100 Z685d]

RC454.4.Z55 1986   616.89   85-31447
ISBN 0-471-81268-4

Printed in the United States of America

10 9 8 7 6 5 4 3 2 1

This book is dedicated to Jon and Scott,

two young men who taught us much about human development

and made the learning a pleasure.

Foreword

As Aristotle noted, one cannot claim to possess a thorough grasp of a particular phenomenon unless one is totally aware of its genesis and ultimate outcome. Etiological and teleological questions have been two of the primary issues that have captured the attention of developmental theorists. As Werner (1948), Werner and Kaplan (1963), and Cicchetti and Pogge-Hesse (1982) among others have stated, the term "developmental" is not merely a synonym for the study of youngsters or the field of child development. Rather, these theorists have suggested that a developmental orientation is best depicted as a "world view" (Pepper, 1942). Accordingly, it follows that one can take an adevelopmental approach to the study of children, or a developmental approach to any unit of behavior, discipline, culture, or person—either "normal" or deviant in some capacity or capacities. Developmental contributions to virtually every discipline have been with us since the inception of Western thought (Cicchetti, 1984; Kaplan, 1966).

In their book *A Developmental Approach to Adult Psychopathology*, Edward Zigler and Marion Glick present the theoretical and empirical efforts of more than 25 years of work conducted by Zigler and a large number of his colleagues on the development of adult psychopathology. In this yeoman work, Zigler and Glick cover a large array of topics that are essential to a complete understanding of the processes underlying the diagnosis, causes, course, prognosis, sequelae, treatment, and ultimate adaptation or maladaptation across a variety of adult dysfunctions.

THE DEVELOPMENTAL PERSPECTIVE

Unlike most works on descriptive adult psychopathology, which necessitate viewing the various psychiatric syndromes as discrete entities, in this book a developmental orientation is applied to this diverse group of disorders. Influenced by the thinking and writing of many developmentalists, most notably Heinz Werner, Bernard Kaplan, and Jean Piaget, Zigler and Glick utilize an "Organizational" (Cicchetti & Braunwald, 1984; Cicchetti &

Schneider-Rosen, 1986; Cicchetti & Sroufe, 1978; Sroufe, 1979) or "organismic-developmental" (Werner & Kaplan, 1963) conceptualization of development. According to the organizational viewpoint, development may be conceived as a series of qualitative reorganizations which take place by means of differentiation and hierarchical integration. Variables at many levels of analysis determine the character of these reorganizations: genetic, constitutional, neurobiological, biochemical, behavioral, psychological, environmental, and sociological. Moreover, these variables are conceived as being in dynamic transaction with one another.

"Normal" or "healthy" development is not defined in terms of the average level of functioning, since it is not necessarily the case that the mean defines mental health. Rather, it is defined in terms of a series of interlocking social, emotional, and cognitive competencies. Competence at one period of development, which tends to make the individual broadly adapted to his or her environment, prepares the way for the formation of competence at the next period (Sroufe & Rutter, 1984). Moreover, normal development is marked by the integration of earlier competencies into later modes of functioning. It follows then that early adaptation tends to promote later adaptation and integration.

Pathological development, in contrast, may be conceived of as a lack of integration of the social, emotional, and cognitive competencies that are important to achieving adaptation at a particular developmental level (Cicchetti & Schneider-Rosen, 1986; Kaplan, 1966, Sroufe & Rutter, 1984). Because early structures often are incorporated into later structures, an early deviation or disturbance in functioning may cause much larger disturbances to emerge later on.

However, just as early competence may lead to later adaptation and incompetence to later maladaptation, this isomorphism in functioning may not be the only expectable outcome. Consequently, it is necessary to engage in a comprehensive evaluation of those factors that may influence the nature of individual differences, the continuity of adaptive or maladaptive behavior patterns, and the different pathways by which the same developmental outcomes may be achieved. It is important to map out the processes whereby the normal course of development in the social, emotional, and/or cognitive domains, in dynamic transaction with the "inner" (i.e., biological) constitutional and "outer" (i.e., familial conditions, stresses, support systems, peer groups) environmental characteristics, may lead to outcomes that either inhibit or exacerbate early deviations or maintain or disrupt early adaptation.

In the "organizational" approach, the qualitative reorganizations characteristic of development are conceived as proceeding in accordance with the *orthogenetic principle* (Werner, 1948), which states that the developing organism moves from a relatively diffuse and globally undifferentiated state, by means of differentiation and hierarchical integration, to a state of greater articulation and organized complexity. The orthogenetic principle may be seen as a solution to the problem of the individual's continuous adaptation to the environment and the question of how integrity of function may be maintained in the face of change. Continuity in functioning can be maintained via hierarchical integration despite rapid constitutional changes and biobehavioral shifts (Block & Block, 1980; Sroufe & Rutter, 1984).

Utilizing such a developmental orientation, Zigler and Glick provide a conceptual framework in which various adult disorders can be compared and contrasted to each other, with a focus on both the similarities and differences underlying these psychopathological processes and outcomes. Uniquely and most importantly, Zigler and Glick illustrate how these groups of disturbances may be viewed and understood within the framework of normal development, utilizing general "regulative" developmental principles (Werner, 1948). As such, significant advances in the understanding of social competence and adjustment, psychiatric classification and diagnosis, schizophrenia, alcoholism, self-image disparity, and prognosis have been made.

CONCEPTUAL SHIFTS IN UNDERSTANDING THE CAUSES AND CONSEQUENCES OF PSYCHOPATHOLOGY

In recent years, linear models of causality and development have fallen into increasing disfavor in the biological, psychological, and sociological sciences (e.g., see Cicchetti & Schneider-Rosen, 1984; Engel, 1977; Marmor, 1983; Reese & Overton, 1970; Sameroff & Chandler, 1975; Zubin & Spring, 1977). Increasingly, transactional systems-theory approaches are being adopted by theoreticians, researchers, and practitioners from a diverse array of disciplines (Bertalanffy, 1968; Cicchetti & Rizley, 1981; Engel, 1977; Sameroff, 1983). One important outcome of this conceptual shift has been an increased, more sophisticated search to understand the etiology, course, sequelae, prognosis and treatment of both normal and pathological processes (Ainsworth, Blehar, Waters, & Wall, 1978; Block & Block, 1980; Cicchetti, 1984; Main, Kaplan, & Cassidy, 1985; Schneider-Rosen, Braunwald, Carlson, & Cicchetti, 1985; Sroufe & Rutter, 1984).

A major outgrowth of this new mode of thinking has been the emergence of a new field of scientific inquiry—the domain of developmental psychopathology (Cicchetti, 1984; Rutter & Garmezy, 1983; Sroufe & Rutter, 1984). Sroufe and Rutter (1984) have defined the domain of developmental psychopathology as *"the study of the origins and course of maladaptation, whatever the age of onset, . . . the causes, . . . the transformations in behavioral manifestation, and however complex the course of the developmental pattern may be"* (p. 18).

As its name denotes, developmental psychopathology must draw upon the results of many different areas of research and expertise gathered from many disciplines: in particular, general developmental psychology, traditional academic psychology, the clinical sciences of psychiatry and clinical psychology, the neurosciences, and sociology. Developmental psychopathology is a new science in part because it is the product of an integration of various disciplines, the efforts of which have previously been separate and distinct. Moreover, by virtue of its interdisciplinary nature, the field of developmental psychopathology necessitates that multiple domains of development be studied, including cognitive, linguistic, socioemotional, and biological processes.

Although developmental psychopathology may be characterized as a new science or an emergent discipline, it nonetheless has historical roots within psychology as well as other scientific disciplines. Most of the great systematizers in psychology have argued that we can learn more about the normal functioning of an organism by studying its pathology and, likewise, more about its pathology by studying its normal condition. Furthermore, workers in other scientific domains, including neurophysiology (Jackson, 1884/1958; Sherrington, 1906), embryology (Waddington, 1966; Weiss, 1969), physiological psychology (Teitelbaum, 1971), neurobiology (Jacobson, 1978; Rakic & Goldman-Rakic, 1982), and developmental neurochemistry (Wiggins, McCandless, & Enna, 1985) have proffered similar viewpoints. Zing-Yang Kuo captures the essence of this multidisciplinary, multidomain approach to the study of human behavior quite nicely in his book *The Dynamics of Behavior Development: An Epigenetic View (1967).*

> *The study of behavior is a synthetic science.* It includes comparative anatomy, comparative embryology, comparative physiology (in the biophysical and biochemical sense), experimental morphology, and the qualitative and quantitative analysis of the dynamic relationships between the organism and the external physical and social environment. (p. 25)

Kuo further states that one of the major goals to accomplish in this venture is to obtain a comprehensive understanding of the behavioral repertoire of the person and to ascertain the causal factors that occur from stage to stage during ontogenesis.

OUTGROWTH OF HISTORICAL AND CONTEMPORARY FACTORS UPON CHANGES IN THE ZEITGEIST TOWARD THE DISCIPLINE OF DEVELOPMENTAL PSYCHOPATHOLOGY

During the past few years several prestigious journals, including *Child Development, The American Journal of Psychiatry, The Journal of Consulting and Clinical Psychology, The Journal of the American Academy of Child Psychiatry, The Journal of Child Psychology and Psychiatry, and New Directions for Child Development*, have devoted special issues or sections to the domain of developmental psychopathology. Within the next few years, I will be the editor of a journal devoted exclusively to the field of developmental psychopathology.

In addition, the most recent edition of the archival reference in the field of child development, Mussen's (1983) *Handbook of Child Psychology*, contained the first chapter on the topic since the publication of its first edition approximately 40 years ago (Rutter & Garmezy, 1983). While chapters dealing with childhood psychopathology, behavior disorders, and mental retardation appeared in earlier editions of the *Handbook*, these contributions, though comprehensive and very scholarly, often lacked an explicit developmental focus.

Not surprisingly, several textbooks and scholarly volumes have been published which utilize the term developmental psychopathology in their titles. While many are fine abnormal psychology, clinical child psychology, or child psychiatry books, almost none can be classified as a legitimate work in the domain of developmental psychopathology.

This book by Zigler and Glick, in sharp contrast, is one of the best exemplars of a true *developmental* approach to psychopathology. Guided by the organizational/organismic-developmental approach, Zigler and Glick beautifully illustrate many of the defining characteristics of the field as delineated by some of today's major theorists (e.g., Sroufe & Rutter, 1984). Moreover, they demonstrate that *adult* psychopathology may be studied developmentally. Through careful theoretical and empirical work, they underscore how a developmental approach may help elucidate our understanding of the organization of psychopathology from within a normative framework. Accordingly, our knowledge of normal development, especially the complexity underlying *individual* adaptive and maladjustive processes and outcomes as well as the factors that may either inhibit or exacerbate such patterns of organization, is enhanced as well. Furthermore, the common theoretical threads running through their work as well as that of organizational theorists studying the sequelae of early adaptation in normal or "high risk" children (e.g., Lewis, Feiring, McGuffog, & Jaskir, 1984; Main, Kaplan, & Cassidy, 1985; Sroufe, 1983), the precursors or prototypes of later psychopathology (e.g., Cicchetti & Aber, 1986; Cummings & Cicchetti, in press; Garmezy, 1975; Sameroff, Seifer, & Zax, 1982; Schneider-Rosen et al. 1985), the causes, course, and sequelae of childhood psychopathology (e.g., Cicchetti & Schneider-Rosen, 1984; Robins, 1966), and the factors, both intraorganismic and extraorganismic, that promote or inhibit the development of competence in children (Garmezy, 1981; Garmezy & Rutter, 1983; Rutter, 1979), can help build an empirically and theoretically sound developmental psychopathology. Such a science should bridge disciplines, span the life cycle, and aid in the discovery of important new truths about the processes underlying adaptation and maladaptation as well as the best means of preventing or ameliorating psychopathology.

In summary, this book is a magnum opus—a definitive work that sets the standard for the field. It illustrates the importance of theory and of a broad-based perspective for understanding psychopathological processes and outcomes. It also focuses on the development of strengths and coping in dysfunctional adults without relegating all adults with a pathological disorder to a deleterious outcome. Consequently, I believe that this book is necessary reading for clinical and developmental psychologists, developmental psychopathologists, psychiatrists, sociologists, practitioners, and policy makers.

Although some may doubt that any one scholarly work could have impact on such diverse areas of academic and therapeutic life, anyone who knows Ed Zigler will not be surprised. For over 30 years, Zigler and his colleagues have done ground-breaking work in many areas of clinical and developmental psychology. His work on mental retardation, child abuse, social policy, child development, and Head Start, among many others, is characterized by a breadth and depth of knowledge that are echoed in the work he and Marion Glick report here. Moreover, Zigler's work is always conspicuously marked by a love and concern for the people he studies. My bet is that his genuine passion and caring for the topics he researches—the *affective* components of his mind—set him apart from most "intellects" and contribute greatly to his spanning dualisms that are too frequently inherent between clinical study of and research into childhood and adult disorders, between basic and applied research, and between developmental psychology and psychopathology. Zigler is an unusually creative, compassionate, well-integrated being. I eagerly await the completion of the future studies as well as their clinical application that Zigler and Glick have suggested in this monumentally important scientific and sociopolitical work.

Acknowledgment: I would like to thank Jennifer White for her enthusiasm, help, and support during the preparation of this manuscript. In addition, the writing of this foreword was supported by a grant from the National Institute of Mental Health (1-R01-MH37960-01).

DANTE CICCHETTI
University of Rochester
Associate Professor
Department of Psychology and
Psychiatry
Director, Mount Hope Family Center

REFERENCES

Ainsworth, M., Blehar, M., Waters, E., & Wall, S. (1978). *Patterns of attachment.* Hillsdale, N.J.: Erlbaum.

Bertalanffy, L. von (1968). *General systems theory.* New York: Braziller.

Block, J. H., & Block, J. (1980). The role of ego control and ego resiliency in the organization of behavior. In W. A. Collins (Ed.), *Minnesota symposium on child psychology* (Vol. 13). Hillsdale, N.J.: Erlbaum.

Cicchetti, D. (1984). The emergence of developmental psychopathology. *Child Development, 55,* 1–7.

Cicchetti, D., & Aber, J. L. (1986). Infant precursors to later affective disorder: An organizational perspective. In L. Lipsitt (Ed.), *Advances in infancy,* Vol. 4. Norwood, N.J.: Ablex.

Cicchetti, D., & Braunwald, K. (1984). An organizational approach to the study of emotional development in maltreated children. *Journal of Infant Mental Health, 5,* 172–183.

Cicchetti, D., & Pogge-Hesse, P. (1982). Possible contributions of the study of organically retarded persons to developmental theory. In E. Zigler & D. Balla (Eds.), *Mental retardation: The developmental-difference controversy.* Hillsdale, N.J.: Erlbaum.

Cicchetti, D., & Rizley, R. (1981). Developmental perspectives on the etiology, intergenerational transmission, and sequelae of child maltreatment. *New Directions for Child Development, 11,* 31–55.

Cicchetti, D., & Schneider-Rosen, K. (1984). Toward a transactional model of childhood depression. *New Directions for Child Development, 26,* 5–27.

Cicchetti, D., & Schneider-Rosen, K. (1986). An organizational approach to childhood depression. In M. Rutter, C. Izard, & P. Read (Eds.), *Depression in children—Developmental perspectives.* New York: Guilford.

Cicchetti, D., Sroufe, L. A. (1978). An organizational approach to affect: Illustration from the study of Down syndrome infants. In M. Lewis & L. Rosenblum (Eds.), *The development of affect.* New York: Plenum.

Cummings, M., & Cicchetti, D. (in press). Attachment, depression, and the transmission of depression. In M. Greenberg, D. Cicchetti, & M. Cummings (Eds.), *Attachment in the preschool years.* Chicago: University of Chicago Press.

Engel, G. (1977). The need for a new medical model: A challenge for biomedicine. *Science, 196,* 129–135.

Garmezy, N. (1975). The experimental study of children vulnerable to psychopathology. In A. Davids (Ed.), *Child personality and psychopathology: Current topics* (Vol. 2). New York: Wiley.

Garmezy, N. (1981). Children under stress: Perspectives on antecedents and correlates of vulnerability and resistance to psychopathology. In A. Rabin, A. Barclay, & R. Zucker (Eds.), *Further explorations in personality.* New York: Wiley, 1981.

Garmezy, N., & Rutter, M. (Eds.) (1983). *Stress and coping in childhood.* New York: McGraw-Hill.

Jackson, J. H. (1884/1958). Evolution and dissolution of the nervous system. In J. Taylor (ed.), *The selected writings of John Hughlings Jackson* (Vol. 2). New York: Basic Books.

Jacobson, M. (1978). *Developmental neurobiology.* New York: Plenum.

Kaplan, B. (1966). The study of language in psychiatry: The comparative developmental approach and its application to symbolization and language in psychopathology. In S. Arieti (Ed.), *American handbook of psychiatry.* New York: Basic Books.

Kuo, Z. Y. (1967). *The dynamics of behavior development*. New York: Random House.

Lewis, M., Feiring, C., McGuffog, C., & Jaskir, J. (1984). Predicting psychopathology in six-year-olds from early social relations. *Child Development, 55,* 123–136.

Main, M., Kaplan, N., & Cassidy, J. (1985). Security in infancy, childhood and adulthood: A move to the level of representation. *Monographs of the Society for Research in Child Development, 50,* 66–106 (serial no. 209).

Marmor, J. (1983). Systems thinking in psychiatry: Some theoretical and clinical implications. *American Journal of Psychiatry, 140,* 833–838.

Mussen, P. (Ed.) (1983). *Handbook of child psychology* (4 Vols.; 4th ed.). New York: Wiley.

Pepper, S. (1942). *World hypotheses*. Berkeley, CA: University of California Press.

Rakic, P., & Goldman-Rakic, P. (1982). Development and modifiability of the cerebral cortex. *Neuroscience Research Program Bulletin, 20,* 433–438.

Reese, H., & Overton, W. (1970). Models of development and theories of development. In L. R. Goulet & P. Baltes (Eds.), *Life-span developmental psychology: Research and theory*. New York: Academic Press.

Robins, L. (1966). *Deviant children grown up*. Baltimore: Williams & Wilkins.

Rutter, M. (1979). Protective factors in children's responses to stress and disadvantage. In M. Kent & J. Rolf (Eds.), Primary prevention of psychopathology, Vol. 3: *Social competence in children*. Hanover, N.H.: University Press of New England.

Rutter, M., & Garmezy, N. (1983). Developmental psychopathology. In E. M. Hetherington (Ed.), *Handbook of child psychology,* Vol. 4: *Social and personality development*. New York: Wiley.

Sameroff, A. (1983). Developmental systems: Contexts and evolution. In P. Mussen (Ed.), *Handbook of child psychology*. New York: Wiley.

Sameroff, A., & Chandler, M. (1975). Reproductive risk and the continuum of caretaking casualty. In F. Horowitz, M. Hetherington, S. Scarr-Salapatek, & G. Siegel (Eds.), *Review of child development research* (Vol. 4). Chicago: University of Chicago Press.

Sameroff, A., Seifer, R., & Zax, M. (1982). Early development of children at risk for emotional disorder. *Monographs of the Society for Research in Child Development* (serial no. 199).

Schneider-Rosen, K., Braunwald, K., Carlson, V., & Cicchetti, D. (1985). Current perspectives in attachment theory: Illustration from the study of maltreated infants. In I. Bretherton & E. Waters (Eds.), *Growing points in attachment theory and research. Monographs of the Society for Research in Child Development, 50,* 194–210 (serial no. 209).

Sherrington, C. (1906). *The integrative action of the nervous system*. New York: Scribners.

Sroufe, L. A. (1979). Socioemotional development. In J. Osofsky (Ed.), *Handbook of infancy*. New York: Wiley.

Sroufe, L. A. (1983). Infant caregiver attachment and patterns of adaptation in preschool: The roots of maladaptation and competence. In M. Perlmutter (Ed.), *Minnesota symposium on child psychology* (Vol. 16) Hillsdale, N.J.: Erlbaum.

Sroufe, L. A., & Rutter, M. (1984). The domain of developmental psychopathology. *Child Development, 55,* 17–29.

Teitelbaum, P. (1971). The encephalization of hunger. In E. Stellar & J. Sprague (Eds.), *Progress in physiological psychology* (Vol. 4). New York: Academic Press.

Waddington, C. (1966). *Principles of development and differentiation.* New York: Macmillan.

Weiss, P. (1969). *Principles of development.* New York: Hafner.

Werner, H. (1948). *Comparative psychology of mental development* (2nd ed.). Chicago: Follett.

Werner, H., & Kaplan, B. (1963). *Symbol formation.* New York: Wiley.

Wiggins, R., McCandless, D., & Enna, S. (Eds.) (1985). *Developmental neurochemistry.* Austin: University of Texas Press.

Zubin, J., & Spring, B. (1977). Vulnerability: A new view of schizophrenia. *Journal of Abnormal Psychology, 56,* 103–126.

Series Preface

This series of books is addressed to behavioral scientists interested in the nature of human personality. Its scope should prove pertinent to personality theorists and researchers as well as to clinicians concerned with applying an understanding of personality processes to the amelioration of emotional difficulties in living. To this end, the series provides a scholarly integration of theoretical formulations, empirical data, and practical recommendations.

Six major aspects of studying and learning about human personality can be designated: personality theory, personality structure and dynamics, personality development, personality assessment, personality change, and personality adjustment. In exploring these aspects of personality, the books in the series discuss a number of distinct but related subject areas: the nature and implications of various theories of personality; personality characteristics that account for consistencies and variations in human behavior; the emergence of personality processes in children and adolescents; the use of interviewing and testing procedures to evaluate individual differences in personality; efforts to modify personality styles through psychotherapy, counseling, behavior therapy, and other methods of influence; and patterns of abnormal personality functioning that impair individual competence.

IRVING B. WEINER

University of Denver
Denver, Colorado

Preface

The developmental approach to adult psychopathology represents an effort of more than 25 years by Edward Zigler and many colleagues to apply the principles of organismic–developmental theory to the problems of psychopathology. This approach to understanding the behavior of disturbed individuals has evolved over the course of many empirical studies and theoretical papers and has led to expansions, refinements, and, in some instances, reformulation of the initial assumptions.

Until now, the developmental approach to adult psychopathology has been presented only in discrete papers scattered throughout a variety of sources. This volume brings the work together. All of the major studies that have served to advance or explicate the developmental formulation are reviewed. Researchers who want to be more fully acquainted with the developmental position will no longer be forced to undertake a rather tedious literature search. Even more important, the evolving theoretical formulation, which has hitherto been presented piecemeal, is consolidated. Not only should this provide greater clarity but it should also permit a closer theoretical scrutiny of the developmental formulation. The theoretical and empirical efforts representing the developmental approach to psychopathology are examined in relation to the empirical efforts of other workers.

This programmatic effort to interpret psychopathology within the framework of general developmental principles has allowed for a unified approach to diverse phenomena of major clinical interest. The development formulation has provided theoretical coherence for work on premorbid social competence and premorbid adjustment. It has led to new ways of looking at the symptom pictures patients present and the processes underlying diagnosis. Paranoid–nonparanoid differences in schizophrenia have been interpreted within the developmental framework, and this has given rise to an alternative formulation about underlying processes in paranoid schizophrenia. A developmental interpretation of self-image disparity has been advanced as well. Efforts have been directed at deriving a developmental typology of alcoholism. Further, the developmental position has led to a broader view of prognosis, and various indicators of developmental level have been found to be related to the course and outcome of disorder in schizophrenic patients and in patients with such other diagnoses as affective disorder and personality disorder.

In contrast to positions that necessitate a piecemeal view of the various disorders as discrete entities, the developmental formulation provides the conceptual framework in which various forms of disturbance can be viewed in relation to each other and in accordance with the positive and active strivings that characterize normal development.

The developmental approach to psychopathology presented here originally took root and grew in the intellectual climate of the Worcester State Hospital–Clark University complex. In the early 1950s, with the organismic––developmental concepts of Heinz Werner serving as the major theoretical impetus, workers at Clark and Worcester State Hospital began the task of applying developmental principles to phenomena of interest in psychopathology. While our work derives most closely from the organismic–developmental position of Werner, the formulations of many developmental theorists have influenced our approach. The first two chapters present the theoretical assumptions that underlie our work.

In the early years, Zigler conducted a series of studies with Leslie Phillips as his primary collaborator. These studies utilized premorbid competence as a broad gauge of the individual's developmental level. It was held that the individual's developmental level represented no less than the total information-processing system utilized by the person in mediating all behaviors. A further assumption was that the individual's developmental level would continue to influence behavior after the person was designated "pathological," just at it did prior to this designation, during the individual's premorbid period. Chapter 3 presents the original version and a recently revised scaling of the Zigler-Phillips premorbid competence index. The rationale underlying the construction of the measure is considered, together with data concerning its reliability, validity, and factorial structure.

Beginning with the work of Phillips and Rabinovitch (1958) and extending into the 1980s, a number of principles have been employed to order the symptoms patients present along developmental continua. Chapter 4 presents these developmental orderings of symptoms (on the basis of role orientation, expression in action vs. thought, and the distinction between delusions and hallucinations) and reviews findings concerning the relationship of these orderings to premorbid competence and outcome. Relationships discovered between our developmental measures and broad categories of psychiatric diagnosis (schizophrenia, affective disorders, personality disorders) are considered in Chapter 5. Conceptual issues regarding the nature of diagnosis are also discussed.

With Jacob Levine as primary collaborator, the developmental formulation was extended to considerations of the paranoid–nonparanoid distinction in schizophrenia and the essential–reactive distinction in alcoholism. Chapter 6 reviews data supporting the position that paranoid schizophrenia represents a higher developmental form than nonparanoid schizophrenia. The authors of this book recently extended this formulation and proposed an unorthodox view of paranoid schizophrenia. This view, that at least some forms of paranoid schizophrenia represent a defense against underlying depression, is presented in Chapter 7. The developmental interpretation of the essential–reactive distinction in alcoholism is considered in Chapter 8.

Chapter 9 examines relationships discovered between premorbid competence as well as other indicators of developmental level and prognosis broadly conceptualized as including age of onset of disorder as well as outcome following treatment. Considerable data support the assumption that higher developmental functioning is associated with a more favorable prognosis both for schizophrenic patients and for patients in other diagnostic groups. While developmentally higher functioning is not presumed to prevent the occurrence of psychopathology, individuals at higher developmental levels should possess greater adaptive resources, resulting in improved prognosis.

The developmental interpretation of self-image disparity is presented in Chapter 10. In contrast to positions that view a sizable self-image disparity as a sign of maladjustment, the developmental position interprets increased self-image disparity as the natural concomitant of normal growth and development. Chapter 10 reviews a broad body of data that supports the developmental position and proposes an expansion of the original developmental position.

Chapter 11 considers gender and social class differences in psychopathology, particularly as these relate to the developmental formulation. Finally, Chapter 12 briefly summarizes our efforts to date on the developmental approach to psychopathology and indicates some areas in which further research or theoretical elaboration is needed.

Preparation of this book owes much to the financial support of grant HD 03008 from the National Institute of Child Health and Human Development and to the help of many people. We are grateful to Roger Weissberg, who provided a thoughtful critical reading of the manuscript and valuable suggestions for improvements. We are indebted to Maren Jones for her careful editing of the manuscript. The advice, support, and encouragement of Dante Cicchetti are very much appreciated. Mary Acunzo deserves special thanks for her help in the preparation of this manuscript. We also thank Victoria Czernicki, Sandra Masterson, and Rebecca Murray for their assistance. Several other people provided valuable advice and support whenever we needed it; particular thanks go to Robert Hodapp and Victoria Seitz. Finally, we would like to extend our thanks to the staff of John Wiley & Sons for their skills, dedication, and support.

EDWARD ZIGLER
MARION GLICK

New Haven, Connecticut
February 1986

Contents

A DEVELOPMENTAL APPROACH TO ADULT PSYCHOPATHOLOGY

CHAPTER 1

A Point of View:
Assumptions About Human Behavior
and Its Understanding

This book presents a developmental approach to adult psychopathology, a formulation that has been evolving over more than 25 years. Central to this formulation is the thesis that there is a process of growth underlying psychological functioning. Individuals can be viewed as functioning at different levels along this underlying developmental continuum. Equally fundamental to our approach is the assumption that the individual's developmental level continues to influence behavior after the person has been designated "pathological" just as it did prior to this designation during the patient's premorbid period. Like adaptive behavior, therefore, manifestations of disturbance should reflect underlying differences in developmental level. Psychopathology may be seen as a consequence of using inappropriate methods in coping with the various demands confronted by the individual. Within this context, the pathological syndromes may be conceptually ordered and viewed as corresponding to different inappropriate resolutions, each of which is tied to a different developmental level.

Within our approach, the individual's developmental level is seen as representing no less than the total information-processing system utilized by the individual in mediating all behaviors. This developmental-level construct is thus a very broad one, presumed to be applicable not only to cognitive but also to social and emotional realms of functioning. The major dimensions employed in our work to define developmental differences will be presented in the next chapter. At the outset, it is nevertheless important to point out that, because the work concerns developmental differences in adult functioning, a series of discrete stages that delineate qualitatively distinct modes of organizing experience is not specified. Stage sequences of this type have primarily characterized work that focuses on development during childhood and adolescence (e.g., Kohlberg, 1969; Loevinger, 1976; Piaget, 1951; Selman, 1980). Central to these various stage formulations are the dramatic changes in cognitive organization that have been found to occur between infancy and adolescence (Piaget, 1960). Whether the concern is with concepts of object, justice, self, or social interaction, the levels that distinguish the functioning of younger from older children and adolescents primarily reflect distinct differences in modes of cognitive organization. Research has not uncovered any such dramatic changes in cognitive organization beyond the adolescent period. As will be discussed in Chapter 3 (see Figure 3.1 in that chapter), intellectual growth as assessed by most major measures asymptotes at about 16–20 years of age. However, adults differ in the level at which intellectual growth becomes asymptotic. Different degrees of cognitive complexity thus characterize different adults. Furthermore, aspects of functioning other than cognitive change (e.g., experience in coping with a widening variety of circumstances) seem more pertinent to adult development. Perhaps, then, as one moves beyond the major changes in cognitive organization that occur from infancy to adolescence, development rather than being marked by discrete stages may more fruitfully be conceptualized along continua reflecting such dimensions as degree of differentiation, intricacy or complexity in organization, or behavioral expression in action versus thought. Among the major developmental theorists, Heinz Werner was most concerned with extending developmental principles to domains other than ontogenesis. (These domains included anthropology, comparative psychology, and adult psychopathology.) As Chapter 2 will especially emphasize, Werner's organismic–developmental formulation provides the theoretical cornerstone for our work. While he conceptualized development as discontinuous (involving qualitatively distinct levels of organization) as well as continuous, Werner's emphasis was upon certain dimensions (continua) of change. Prominent among his dimensional principles are those mentioned above, differentiation and integration and expression in action versus thought. (While the latter principle designates qualitatively distinct modes of response, Werner treats it primarily as a dimension defined by the two poles of action vs. thought.)

The application of developmental principles to adult psychopathology has considerable theoretical and practical significance both for research and ultimately for treatment programs. First, it allows the various forms of psychopathology to be considered in relation to each other. Despite differences in particular forms of behavioral expression, underlying similarities can be discerned. Second, it permits a classification system based on a coherent, theoretically derived, interrelated set of categories. Third, by viewing psychopathology within the context of normal maturation, it allows for an emphasis on the adaptive potential of the individual and provides a framework whereby the movement between pathological and nonpathological conditions can be understood. Finally, implicit in a developmental formulation is the view that different treatments will be required for individuals who are themselves at different developmental levels.

The evolution, the empirical studies addressing, and the present status of this developmental approach to psychopathology will constitute the substance of the subsequent chapters. First, however, it is necessary to clarify certain of our fundamental assumptions about the nature of human behavior and about what is required for an adequate theory of psychopathological functioning. On the surface, it would seem that our basic approach conforms to the generally held psychodynamic assumption that developmental experiences bear a fundamental relation to the nature of psychopathology. However, it is our view that, although a general concept of maturation pervades most psychodynamic orientations, the major implications of this concept have never been fully or rigorously applied to psychopathology. Within these orientations, maturation is often employed as a backdrop against which particular psychodynamic events are chronologically ordered. These events are then organized around a central theme (e.g., unresolved dependency needs, the threat of abandonment, oedipal or sibling rivalries), and the patient's behavior is then explained on the basis of this theme. If the validity of such a conceptualization is questioned, the clinician may support it on the grounds that it conforms to a particular "theory" of human behavior. Inasmuch as the ordering is chronological, the explanation typically is seen as developmental.

However, our position is that this type of approach, although somewhat maturational in basis, does not constitute a developmental interpretation since it ignores certain fundamental precepts of developmental theory. Furthermore, we suggest that the psychodynamic interpretations that one frequently finds in the clinical sphere do not adequately qualify as theories inasmuch as these views have as their ultimate test the inner coherence imposed on the case material with little or no stress being placed on the predictable consequences of such organization. The remainder of this chapter will present our point of view as to what constitutes development, what is the nature of adaptive and maladaptive functioning, and what is required for the adequate understanding of behavior. This statement of our general philosophy and goals of necessity precedes the presentation of the specific constructs from developmental theory utilized in our approach. These developmental constructs will be the subject of the second chapter.

HUMAN BEHAVIOR, DEVELOPMENT, AND ADAPTATION: FUNDAMENTAL ASSUMPTIONS

Human behavior has been interpreted from radically different perspectives that entail fundamentally different assumptions about the nature of the human organism. In effect, the underlying metatheoretical assumptions determine the course of any theoretical and empirical enterprise. The perspective from which behavior is viewed determines what categories are appropriate for theoretical analysis, what problems are seen as meaningful for investigation, and what types of interpretations are given to empirical data (comprehensive discussions of the nature of competing worldviews and their implications have been presented by Kuhn, 1962; Langer, 1969; Overton & Reese, 1973; Pepper, 1942). As such, it is necessary at the outset to present our view of the nature of human functioning and to discuss the implications of this view both for the conceptualization of development and for the interpretation of psychopathology.

The developmental approach advanced here is based upon an organismic perspective. Three fundamental and interrelated assumptions lie at the core of this view and distinguish it from other models of human behavior, and thus of development. These are (a) that the individual is an organized entity whose behavior and development can be understood only on the basis of organizational constructs; (b) that the individual is an active agent who mediates and constructs experiences; and (c) that development is a positive process involving the emergence of ever greater adaptive abilities.

The Organizational Perspective

Within the organismic model, the individual is viewed as an organized entity and particular responses are seen as part processes whose meaning is derived from the organization of the whole. Concern, therefore, is with the discovery of principles or patterns of organization whereby large behavioral units and whole response systems (e.g., cognition, social functioning) are interrelated. Within this framework, personality can never be viewed as the additive accumulation of discrete traits, abilities, or experiences. Development is conceptualized as an orderly sequence of structural changes or internal reorganizations in response systems. At each successive level or developmental stage, new functional integrations, new patterns of cognitive and personality organization emerge. As such, qualitative rather than quantitative change is emphasized, although quantitative changes are acknowledged as well. The task of the developmentalist is one of constructing principles or constructs to make such qualitative change comprehensible, by discovering the modes of organization that characterize each successive developmental stage and by uncovering the transition rules that govern these developmental changes. The change itself rather than the content of change is the central issue.

In viewing development as a series of structural or formal changes, the organismic position relegates temporal sequence and chronology to a minor and nonessential role. As Zigler (1963, 1969) has emphasized, time is not a psychological variable. The developmentalist is interested in change not as a function of time but rather as a group of organismic processes that take place over time. Thus developmental psychology is not seen as limited to the study of childhood. Neither chronological age nor chronological history is a defining aspect of developmental analysis (Kaplan, 1967; Werner, 1957; Wohlwill, 1970; Zigler, 1963, 1969).

This definition of development as a formal rather than a historical or chronological sequence distinguishes our position from other maturational approaches in general psychology and especially in the field of psychopathology. The term *developmental psychopathology* has frequently been employed to indicate a concern with disordered functioning in childhood with no reference to structural change. Clinicians have not been alone in equating the study of development with the study of childhood. This has been the general tendency in psychology, which has only recently been mitigated by a growing emphasis on life-span developmental psychology (e.g., Baltes & Schaie, 1973; Goulet & Baltes, 1970; Levinson, 1978; Nesselroade & Reese, 1973; Neugarten, 1979; Schaie & Gribbin, 1975). However, even this concern with adult development does not necessarily imply a structural rather than a temporal view of the developmental process. Much attention in life-span work has necessarily focused on methodological issues (e.g., the problem of distinguishing age from generational differences). Other work on the adult life cycle has concentrated more on what happens to the individual than on internal modes of structuring experience. Erikson's (1950) conceptualization of the adult life cycle has been seminal for later work. Nevertheless, although his stages are broadly defined as reflecting successive levels of ego mastery, the actual definitions of the three adult stages focus more upon changing demands made upon individuals as age increases than upon internal changes resulting from these demands. Levinson's (1978) delineation of life stages for adult men draws upon Erikson's work. His stages are, however, closely tied to age and the particular life demands of our culture. When particular life experiences are emphasized, questions can be raised about the universality of the developmental sequence defined. Gilligan (1982) has questioned the degree to which Erikson's stages apply to women. And the applicability of Levinson's work either to women[1] or to individuals in other cultures cannot be presupposed. As Loevinger and Knoll (1983) noted, "Levinson writes of structure-building at each stage, but the connotations appear different from the hierarchical structures of the cognitive developmentalists" (p. 206). In contrast to these approaches, Kohlberg (1969), Loevinger (Hauser, 1976; Loevinger, 1976; Loevinger & Wessler, 1970), and Selman (1980) have delineated successive stages involving internal structural reorganizations. The stages defined by these theorists emphasize changes that occur during childhood and adolescence, and the majority of research related to their work has likewise concentrated on this age range. As we indicated at the outset of the chapter, qualitatively distinct levels of organization seem to characterize development through adolescence and to be related to dramatic developmental changes in modes of cognitive organization. As we did, Vaillant (1971, 1977) considered adults. The development he observed in a longitudinal study of adult men appeared to be continuous rather than stepwise. Nevertheless, Vaillant's delineation of developmental changes, particularly with respect to adaptive ego mechanisms, focused on internal restructuring. The approaches of Kohlberg, Loevinger, Selman, and Vaillant are particularly compatible with our own, and they will be discussed at greater length in sections of the book to which they are relevant. Nevertheless, while these approaches share our organismic perspective, few attempts have been made to extend this work to the analysis of maladaptive functioning (Noam et al., 1984).

Freud in his delineation of psychosexual stages gave little attention to the concept of developing structures. He emphasized the id rather than ego development and presupposed few changes in the superego after this form of functioning emerged at the end of the third psychosexual stage. As we noted earlier, the chronological ordering of significant psychodynamic events, often with particular emphasis on early experience, remains a common practice in clinical thinking. A central theme that cuts across maturational levels is noted and case history materials are then organized around this theme. The similarity of experiencing across developmental levels is emphasized with little recognition that at different stages in development apparently similar events may be both experienced differently and responded to differently due to changing modes of organization. What is presented is a continuity of content rather than a logical sequence of structural reorganizations.

Yet the continuity of specific behavioral traits over time appears to be a highly questionable assumption. This issue has been very thoughtfully reviewed by a number of theoreticians and investigators (Bowers, 1973; Cicchetti & Pogge-Hesse, 1982; Garber, 1984; Kagan, 1980; Kohlberg, LaCrosse, & Ricks, 1972; Loevinger & Knoll, 1983; Santostefano & Baker, 1972). In the field of personality, the issue of the consistency of behavior has generally been framed in terms of the relative contributions of traits versus situations as determinants of behavior. The argument for situational determination was advanced forcefully by Mischel (1968), who noted that the "small (about .30) albeit statistically significant relations between individual difference measures and behavior . . . become understandable when the enormous variation due to situationally specific variables that determine the consequences for behavior in any particular context is recognized" (pp. 82–83).

As Loevinger and Knoll (1983) indicated, the current consensus emphasizes the interaction between intrapsychic and situational determinants (Bem & Funder, 1978; Bowers, 1973; Magnusson & Endler, 1977). Particularly relevant to our work has been the emergence of an organizational perspective. "Trait theory is most impressive . . . when it displays not literal consistency from one situation to another but predictability or coherence in what appear to be different behaviors" (Loevinger & Knoll, 1983, p. 209). As these authors noted, trait stability is more likely to be found when defined by broad measures (Block et al., 1981; Epstein, 1980) and with respect to personality characteristics that are important to the individual (Kenrick & Stringfield, 1980) and socially valued (Brim & Kagan, 1980).

The value of the organizational perspective for developmental psychopathology has been documented in many careful reviews (Cicchetti & Pogge-Hesse, 1982; Garber, 1984; Kohlberg et al., 1972; Santostefano & Baker, 1972; Sroufe & Rutter, 1984). Isomorphic relationships have not been discovered between childhood and adult symptomatology (Kohlberg et al., 1972; Santostefano & Baker, 1972; Sroufe & Rutter, 1984) or between behaviors at various ages during childhood (Garber, 1984; Kagan, 1971). However, when the search has been for patterns of organization underlying specific symptoms and behaviors, continuity between childhood and adult symptomatology has been demonstrated and coherence achieved. Highly significant relationships have appeared between the presence of acting-out symptomatology in childhood and adult antisocial and/or impulsive behavioral disorders (for cogent reviews of the research see Garmezy & Streitman, 1974; Kohlberg et al., 1972; Santostefano & Baker, 1972; Sroufe & Rutter, 1984). For example, in a follow-up study of children treated in child guidance clinics, Robins (1966) found that the 96 percent of those who later became sociopathic were originally referred for antisocial behavior.

Of particular importance for the developmental formulation is evidence reviewed by both Kohlberg et al. (1972) and Santostefano and Baker (1972) that indicates that the long-term consistency in acting-out symptomatology is not due to the unchanging presence of specific symptoms. What appears to remain constant is a broad class of behaviors reflecting an immediate and relatively unmodulated mode of responding to external stimuli and internal need states, that is, a relatively immature mode of responding. Thus, for example, antisocial aggressive behavior and school truancy in childhood have been related to adult alcoholism (Gomberg, 1968; Robins, 1966). The shift from response in direct action to mediated verbal or symbolic modes of expression defines a major dimension of developmental change (Werner, 1948; Werner & Kaplan, 1963). This fundamental tenet of developmental theory is discussed in Chapter 2, and it constitutes a major dimension in our analyses of developmental differences in symptom expression (see Chapter 4).

This applicability of the organizational perspective for understanding sequelae of acting out and aggressive symptomatology in childhood is brought into clear focus by relationships that have been discovered between such childhood symptoms and adult schizophrenia (Michael, Morris, & Sorokur, 1957; Morris, Escoll, & Wexler, 1956; Pollack et. al, 1966; Robins, 1966; Watt & Lubensky, 1976; Watt et al., 1970; Woerner et al., 1972). Employing follow-up and follow-back research strategies, these studies have yielded a consistent body of data to indicate that the children who later became schizophrenic were more likely than others to have been characterized as antisocial, negativistic, irritable, or delinquent in school reports and child guidance clinic records. In noting as well that "milder forms of antisocial behavior are relatively good predictors of all forms of maladjustment," Kohlberg et al. (1972) concluded:

> The predictive power of antisocial behavior does not depend on specific types of antisocial behavior or upon particular levels of aggressive, sexual, or other motives but seems to reflect the fact that distortions of ego development and distortions in the child's relation to his environment are necessary conditions for relatively frequent or severe forms of antisocial behavior. (p. 1253)

What are being described then are failures in childhood adaptation or competence. As Garber (1984), Kohlberg et al. (1972), and Sroufe and Rutter (1984) emphasize, the continuity between childhood and adult functioning reflects a general pattern of organizing experience and interacting with the environment that is adaptive or maladaptive. Supporting the positions of these authors are findings by Prentky et al. (1980) that childhood developmental variables (e.g., childhood school behavior) were "at least as discriminating as adult psychiatric symptoms in predicting long-term outcome" (p. 139) for adult inpatients with various psychiatric diagnoses. Lewine, Watt, and Fryer (1978) further found that adult schizophrenics with different subtype diagnoses (undifferentiated, paranoid, schizoaffective) differed significantly in childhood interpersonal competence assessed through ratings of school records. Moreover, the schizophrenics had significantly lower childhood interpersonal competence scores than patients in other diagnostic groups (Lewine et al., 1980). Finally, the ratings of childhood competence indicated a stability in this trait between younger and older school age years (Lewine et al., 1980). Other authors have likewise reported significant associations between poor peer relations in childhood and later psychopathology (John, Mednick, & Schulsinger, 1982; Roff & Ricks, 1970). In sum, then, when an organizational approach is taken and the view is toward patterns of adaptive or maladaptive behavior that are progressively restructured at different developmental levels, long-term coherence can be found. Although this principle has been exemplified here in terms of the continuity between childhood and adult symptomatology, it seems equally applicable in the analysis of adult symptomatology, as the research described in Chapter 4 will indicate.

The Individual as Active Processor

A corollary to the emphasis on internal structuring is the view of the individual as an active processor of experience, the source of acts rather than one who is merely activated. Possessing important inherent characteristics, the individual actively organizes experience, transacting with the environment rather than merely being a reactor or even an interactor (Zigler & Child, 1969, 1973). As Inhelder (1957) has noted, the structures of thought help shape experience itself. A further assumption, having important implications for psychopathology, is that the capacity to structure actively and thereby control experience increases as a function of developmental level. At lower stages, where response systems are globally organized with few mediating structures, the organism is more reactive, stimulus bound, impelled by external forces and internal need states. In the course of development, with greater capacities to organize experience, the individual becomes ever more able to plan, to control and respond selectively to internal and external forces, and to initiate interactions with the environment. Thus the developmental process is characterized by an increasingly active role on the part of the organism and the emergence of ever greater adaptive capacities.

This fundamental emphasis within the organismic perspective contrasts sharply with the mechanistic model of human functioning that not only characterizes behavioristic analyses derived from classical stimulus–response (S–R) tension-reduction models of learning but that frequently inheres also in psychodynamically oriented clinical analyses. Within the mechanistic model (see Langer, 1969; Overton & Reese, 1973; Pepper, 1942) the organism is viewed as reactive, passive, and empty. Behavior is seen as a function of external forces applied to the individual. The organism does not structure, but is structured. The basic information-acquiring processes are assumed to be qualitatively the same at every developmental level with the essential passivity of the organism remaining unchanged.

When the continuity of particular psychodynamic events occurring at different stages in the life cycle becomes the organizing principle for clinical analysis, an implicit assumption is a view of the individual as a passive reactor. By contrast, the organismic perspective assumes not only that there will be sequential qualitative changes with development in the manner in which experience is organized, but also that these changes permit greater flexibility and a wider variety of modes for the adaptive handling of experience at higher developmental levels. In exerting less active control over the environment and their responses to it, persons functioning at developmentally lower levels might be expected to experience difficulty in meeting even the common expectancies of everyday life, for example, making friends, dating and selecting a mate, or obtaining a job and keeping it. When adaptive resources are few, the pressures encountered in dealing with such expectancies could be sufficient to precipitate psychopathological disorder. By contrast, the developmentally higher-level individual, in possessing greater capabilities for active control and mastery, would be expected to deal with these minimal societal expectations. While developmentally higher functioning does not prevent the occurrence of psychopathology, precipitating factors would be expected to involve either unusually stressful events (e.g., the death of a spouse, major role losses) or symbolic constructions of the individual's own making (e.g., the person's own view of the self as a failure, overriding guilt for minor transgressions).

Development as a Positive Process

Our final assumption, the view of development as a positive process, derives directly from a perception of the individual as an active processor whose capabilities for active control increase with development. Growth, therefore, is conceptualized as the continuous emergence of ever greater adaptive abilities with the growing organism demonstrating and fulfilling this greater potential at successive stages in development. The individual is viewed as a positive, striving, adaptive being, and a changing potential with growth is seen as the essence of maturation.

In contrast to this position, a negative view of human nature was for a considerable time dominant in American psychology. As Zigler and Child (1969) have indicated, several variables in the conception of human functioning can be treated together because they do tend to be correlated. A thinker's position on one dimension is somewhat predictive of his or her position on the others. Furthermore, each of these variables has similar implications for a view of human nature and development. One variable has to do with whether human beings are thought of as inherently evil or whether they are thought of as inherently good. This is obviously a question that the scientific temper might want to regard as irrelevant. Yet a position on it is frequently implicit in research. A second variable is whether the individual is thought of as innately motivated only by biological drives arising out of physiological need states or whether the individual is thought of also as innately motivated by personal and social motives. A third variable is whether human goal states are thought to consist only of the reduction of drives (of tension or stimulation) or whether human behavior is assumed to be purposive and thus to involve goals that also include the production or creation of something (e.g., an object, a social relationship, or an understanding). What is common to these variables is that each contrasts a negative with a positive view of human functioning. In one instance, the implication is that human nature is inherently passive or evil while in the other it is that human nature is essentially good.

The focus on the negative and maladaptive is clearly exemplified in the classical Freudian interpretation of social functioning. Freud believed that society existed primarily to protect individuals from each other and that culture was established to assist in preventing the breakthrough of primitive, selfish, or destructive needs. Thus all human endeavors and social institutions become ultimately the product of immature and negative needs. The development of such a viewpoint is understandable in a theory that so largely derives from the observation of the tortured thoughts and aberrant behavior of disturbed individuals, the raw data of that acute observer, Freud. However, this sensitivity to the negative and symptomatic has been widely accepted in clinical thinking as the appropriate basis for understanding all human behavior. Normal functioning is described with reference to the abnormal, and all persons are evaluated in terms of their success in harnessing their essentially negative drives and desires. The only positive aspect of functioning is the degree to which the individual has been able to reduce the tensions created by these appetitive needs in a socially acceptable manner. Furthermore, inasmuch as these drives are presumed to be universal and continuously to bombard the functioning psyche, everyone is viewed as being potentially if not imminently psychopathological. Mental illness is seen as lurking everywhere. Such a pervasively negative orientation does not allow for the adequate description, delineation, and differentiation of the adjustments that individuals make.

The inadequacies of negative tension-reduction views of motivation to explain exploration, curiosity, mastery, and attempts to deal competently with one's environment have been widely recognized in both academic (e.g., Harter, 1978; Harter & Zigler, 1974; White, 1959) and clinical psychology. Behavior theory has become increasingly concerned with curiosity, manipulation, exploration, and other features of positive adaptation that are viewed as essentially independent of biological drives. More pertinent to clinical thinking have been the positions of those personality theorists who consider growth, self-fulfillment, and self-actualization to be the defining human motives (e.g., Allport, 1955, 1961; Jahoda, 1958; Maslow, 1968; Rogers, 1951, 1961) and the emphasis within psychoanalytic ego psychology on the developing capacities of the individual for adaptation and mastery (e.g., Erikson, 1950; Fairbairn, 1954; Hartmann, 1958, 1964; Loevinger, 1976; Loevinger & Wessler, 1970; Rapaport, 1960).

On the face of it, no more positive view of human functioning seems possible than that of the self-actualization personality theorists. The drive toward self-fulfillment is seen as the only intrinsic motivating force for all behavior, and individual self-fulfillment is assumed invariably to improve society. The healthy coping capacities of the individual are emphasized and mental health is defined in terms of such qualities as positive attitudes toward the self, personality integration, creativity, and potential for growth. In relation to the outside world, mentally healthy individuals maintain their own autonomy, are realistic in their assessments of the external environment, and are capable of mastering or coming to terms with it.

While we find ourselves in essential agreement with this orientation, which evaluates the functioning of the individual in terms of its positive aspects, we find ourselves in disagreement with the actual criteria established to define the self-actualizing or psychologically healthy individual. Even a cursory examination of these criteria indicates that they are so stringent that almost no one qualifies as a healthy person. In establishing such demanding criteria, this definition of normality has in essence reinforced the assumption of a pervasive presence of psychopathology among the general population. The ideals associated with self-actualization do not describe the typical behavior or psychological state of most people who, burdened with concerns and difficulties, behave in a far less godlike manner. Thus a position that should have provided a positive orientation toward human functioning has in actuality fostered the opposite view.

This paradoxical situation appears to rest on two implicit assumptions of the self-actualization theorists: namely, that the potential for growth is almost unlimited and that this potential is the same for every individual. Although such an egalitarian view is in keeping with certain social and moral value systems, it runs counter to our knowledge about individual differences. It is our premise that people differ in their potential for adaptation just as they differ on any number of other significant continua. Thus self-actualization, in the extreme form in which it is often defined, seems more appropriately viewed as the idealized upper end of a continuum rather than as a definition, and thus a criterion, for normality. To insist that all individuals conform to and be judged by their ability to live up to such idealized social requirements is to do them an injustice. Moreover, such a position carries its own dialectic negation. It comes full circle to the older, more entrenched position in the field of psychiatry. It implies that the common assumptions about people who manifest psychopathology need to be extended to the vast majority of the population at large. It suggests that people generally are emotionally "sick," and that nearly all individuals stand in need of therapeutic help. Such a view can be avoided by simply asserting that there are various modes or styles of potential adaptation. Thus individuals at different developmental levels can be seen as functioning adaptively although the particular style may vary according to the person's developmental level.

This assertion brings us to what appears to be a fundamental weakness in the self-actualization theorists' emphasis on the positive direction of growth. They define the direction of development without linking this direction to organizational constructs. The developmental view of growth as a positive process derives directly from and is immutably tied to the nature of the structural reorganizations that define development. The teleological aspect of the developmental position is regulative, not ontological (Reese & Overton, 1970). Because each successive level of organization carries with it a greater adaptive potential, development is seen as a positive process. That different levels of adaptation both are possible and can be specified is thus axiomatic for the developmentalist. By contrast, in the absence of such organizational constructs, the self-actualization position lacks the means for specifying levels of potential adaptation. Only an idealized end point of adaptive accomplishment can be specified, and little can be said about the individual who does not reach that goal. Vague dimensional statements can be made that the individual's functioning is less than ideal, but no clear qualitative description of the actual level of functioning is possible. This limitation is serious for the study of the normal population and becomes critical when applied to psychopathology.

Though most people do not lead social movements nor create lasting works, they do meet the demands of society, gain much satisfaction in the process, and often contribute to the welfare of others. We must continually remain aware of how complex and difficult it can be for the typical individual to meet such demands of society as earning one's living and caring for one's self, forming appropriate social relationships, and marrying and taking on responsibilities for the lives of other individuals. Particularly in regard to pathological populations, the ability to deal with the basic problems of life seems to be a more pertinent issue than the achievement of behavior patterns that typify the lives of society's paragons.

The positions of the ego psychologists (e.g., Erikson, 1950; Loevinger, 1976) are more compatible with our own in that they emphasize both the positive adaptive nature of development and changing modes of organization as constituting the essence of development. These theoreticians have made it clear that the lifelong efforts of individuals toward adaptation and mastery cannot be explained only in terms of the satisfaction of base (libidinal and aggressive) drives. The striving toward competence, mastery, and creative production is given an independent existence and viewed as fundamental in human nature rather than as merely the appendage or derivative of primitive instinctual forces. The concern with specifying successive levels of mastery, so central in Erikson's (1950, 1968) work, has culminated in Loevinger's (Loevinger, 1976; Loevinger & Wessler, 1970; Loevinger, Wessler, & Redmore, 1970) formulations, which have been particularly valuable for their specification of intermediate levels of organization in the development of adaptive functioning. With only a few exceptions (Noam et al., 1984; Vincent & Vincent, 1979), the formulations of ego psychology have been applied to the functioning of nonpsychopathological individuals and have had limited impact in the investigation of maladaptive behavior. What must be remembered is that in virtually all individuals who manifest pathological phenomena we see so much in the way of adaptive mechanisms. Even in the midst of abnormality, the patient is a functioning individual. Yet the healthy aspects in psychopathological behavior have tended to be minimized, not only in formulations derived from ego psychology but in general. For instance, little concern has been expressed over the extent to which psychotics retain the potential for positive adaptation.

In this book we will stress the major significance of adaptive potential for the understanding of psychopathology. This emphasis derives from the definition of development as a series of structural changes in response systems, changes that by their very nature progressively facilitate active coping and adaptation. It is important to make it clear, however, that in stressing the positive in development and the active role of the individual in processing experience we are not denying the existence of negative behavioral propensities nor are we asserting that behavior is influenced only by internal structuring processes. There is no need to choose between the active and passive views of human functioning; we need them both. The active mediational cognitive characteristics of the individual are important in adaptation, but they are not the only determinants of adaptive functioning. In addition to being an active processor, every individual is a passive recipient in regard to internal physiological and/or genetic predispositions and environmental influences. That we need not choose between the positive and negative should also be evident. The assertion that coping potential expands with development does not preclude the operation of more primitive and negative drives nor the possibility of tension reduction as a goal in some human functioning.

It is our view that people do have emotional difficulties and problems but that everyone possesses some potential for coping with these and desires to come to terms with them. We have outlined the differences that exist between ourselves and others who have stressed the positive in development and adaptation. Central to our position is the hypothesis that people can be placed along a continuum of constructive adaptation. In this book we shall develop the argument that the recognition of differences between individuals in this adaptive potential is vital for the prediction of the occurrence of mental disorder, the types of pathological phenomena that will be manifested, and the likely outcome of the disordered state.

What we are saying is that psychopathology cannot be understood in isolation but rather must be investigated within the context of normal development. In adopting this position, we intend to imply not that all people are creatures of blooming psychic health, but rather that each individual can be placed somewhere on a continuum of effectiveness in dealing with the goals and tasks set by society and in meeting personal standards and values.

AUTOCHTHONOUS AND EXPERIENTIAL DETERMINANTS IN DEVELOPMENT AND PSYCHOPATHOLOGY

In emphasizing invariant patterns of sequential change across individuals, developmentalists have given little attention to the problem of individuality or uniqueness of functioning and to the question of what factors inherent in the organism or the environment may give rise to individual differences (Zigler, 1963). The application of developmental principles to psychopathology involves the consideration of two types of variations between individuals. In the first place, individual differences in the rate of development and in the upper levels achieved require explanation inasmuch as these differences in maturity level are presumed to be associated with coping potential. Secondly, if psychopathology is viewed as the consequence of using ineffective and inappropriate coping mechanisms tied to different developmental levels, the factors that may lead one individual to adopt inappropriate mechanisms while another individual at the same developmental level functions appropriately must ultimately be identified.

In regard to factors that may be considered to be inherent in the organism, two very different classes of variables must be distinguished: (a) a variety of biological, constitutional, and genetic predispositions; and (b) the modes of internal organization by means of which the individual structures experience. Frequently, in discussions of the influence of internal or autochthonous factors, these two classes of variables have not been sufficiently differentiated.

The importance of innate determinants or genetic predispositions has been recognized in regard to normal cognitive and personality development (Escalona, 1968, 1972; Lenneberg, 1967; Nash, 1970; Schaffer & Emerson, 1964; Thomas & Chess, 1977; Thomas, Chess, & Birch, 1968). Moreover, the evidence for the existence of a genetic factor in the transmission of schizophrenia (Cancro, 1979; Gottesman & Shields, 1972, 1976; Hirsch, 1973; Heston, 1966; Kety et al., 1975; Tsuang et al., 1978) as well as other forms of psychopathology (Guze, 1976; Winokur, 1979; Winokur & Clayton, 1967) has become increasingly compelling. Genetic predisposition must be regarded as a major etiological factor in any accounting of mental disorder. However, as Cancro (1979) has stressed, what is transmitted genetically may not be a predisposition specific to pathology. In regard to schizophrenia, the literature on vulnerability suggests that genetic variables may be necessary but not sufficient etiological preconditions. The determining factor may be how the individual copes with these predispositions and life experiences.

Situationism stresses the environment as the primary determinant both in the acquisition of behavior and in subsequent learned responding (e.g., Bandura, 1969; Kanfer, 1970; Mischel, 1968). Although this view has been modified to give greater emphasis to cognition as a determinant of behavior (Bandura, 1978; Mischel, 1973), the organism is still considered relatively passive in an active environment (Mischel, 1977).

The developmental position that emphasizes the individual's role in actively structuring the environment and thus in creating and determining experience has been clearly explicated by Bowers (1973) and Wachtel (1973). Primary concern is with developmental changes in the organization of internal response systems and with the sequential emergence of new structures and operations. Environmental or situational influences are acknowledged. Yet, as Zigler and Child (1969) have noted, developmentalists of this persuasion, though giving considerable lip service to the importance of the experiences of the organism, nevertheless treat experience and learning as a constant, giving their primary theoretic attention to internal factors in the developmental process. For example, while Piaget and Chomsky both regard environmental stimulation as a necessary prerequisite for development, neither specifies the types of environmental stimulation that may foster particular developments. The environment is, in fact, treated as an amorphous surrounding nutrient that the individual acts upon in fostering his or her own development. The criticism most frequently leveled against Piaget and other developmentalists is that their approach underemphasizes the importance of cultural and experiential factors in determining the nature of thought and that with proper emphasis on these factors cognitive development would no longer be seen as moving through a series of stages. All too often the developmental view has, in practice, been one of an active organism in a passive environment.

An adequate theory of human behavior must take into account: (a) the activity of the organism in structuring experience both with regard to the internal interpretation of experience and in terms of active manipulation of environmental circumstances; and (b) the activity of the environment in determining the content of experience and quite probably also in contributing to internal structuring processes. What is required is a view of an active organism in an active environment (Riegel, 1973). Not only must reciprocal influences of the individual and the environment on each other be acknowledged, but this interactionist view must be translated into research practice. The work of Bem and his associates (Bem & Allen, 1974; Bem & Funder, 1978) is important to this effort in the field of personality. As Zigler and Child (1969) have suggested, considerable theoretical gains could be made if attention were turned to the solution of two major problems: (a) the degree to which and the process by which environmental factors influence the rate of development; and (b) the determination of those aspects of behavior that are little influenced by environmental factors and those that are almost completely the product of environmental influences.

Furthermore, just as the relationship between the individual and the environment must be viewed from an interactionist perspective, it seems appropriate to consider the internal structuring processes of the individual and the person's genetic, constitutional, and biological endowment as reciprocally interrelated. While genetic vulnerabilities may influence the development of coping mechanisms, the individual's level of coping should be equally influential in determining the degree to which a particular vulnerability actually handicaps functioning. Thus an individual's developmental level should influence responses both to environmental conditions and to constitutional variables and genetic predispositions. In regard to both classes of variables, developmentally higher functioning is presumed to entail more effective coping capabilities.

CONCEPTS, FRAMES OF REFERENCE, AND THEORIES

Let us now turn to a consideration of the requirements involved in constructing a theory of human functioning. It has long been Zigler's contention (e.g., Zigler, 1963) that what have passed for theories in the fields of both normal and disordered development are in fact no more than grand designs or frames of reference, collections of interrelated concepts that by attempting to explain everything succeed in explaining very little. While such frames of reference may constitute a legitimate first stage in theory construction, a shortcoming of many formulations has been a reluctance to move on to more circumscribed and refined theoretical efforts.

There appear to be three discernible stages involved in moving from the observation of gross behavior to the construction of a theory dealing with such behavior. The first stage is the formation of concepts, an activity that appears to be primarily inductive in nature. It involves the necessary process of grouping phenomena together on the basis of similarity. The similarity attributed to the diverse phenomena represents the conceptual entity.

As such the groupings are necessarily abstractions and are arbitrary. Given the number and diversity of unique events that comprise experience, such groupings are required if order, regularity, and structure are to be given to experience and the world of everyday living is to be made comprehensible. However, the choice of particular attributes to serve as the basis for the commonality is discretionary.

The diversity and complexity of human behavior have, in general, required the construction of multiple-concept systems in order to satisfy the need for organizing and explaining. Such conceptual systems will be referred to in this presentation as frames of reference. Thus any collection of interrelated concepts that allows for the explanation of a behavioral event qualifies as a frame of reference. The utilization of such frames of reference involves both advantages and difficulties. The primary advantage lies in the organizing and explanatory aspects of the schemata. Frames of reference not only give structure to the world but allow the person to act on the basis of this structuring. When one is armed with a frame of reference, the world becomes a comprehensible place in which to live, and one avoids the disquiet of ambiguity. (This explains why an individual's frame of reference assumes such personal importance, and why it must be continually guarded and defended.)

Although frames of reference are obviously necessary for the everyday functioning of individuals, certain difficulties arise from their use. Not the least of these is the choice between two competing frames of reference. Since any present-day frame of reference worth its salt possesses enough concepts to explain any bit of behavior that presents itself, some criterion of validity must be established independent of the particular conceptual system. Without such a criterion, each competing system remains an encapsulated entity, and all systems become equally true in that they satisfy the explanatory needs of those who subscribe to them. As a result, frames of reference proliferate and exist side by side. It is only to the extent that one employs some criterion of truth other than explanatory ability that one can evaluate the respective merits of two competing systems. One such criterion, often employed in science, is whether empirical statements or predictions derived from a conceptual schema are validated. However, it is our view that legitimate hypotheses or predictions can be derived not from frames of reference but only from theories. Thus, it becomes necessary to differentiate clearly the characteristics of a theory from those of a frame of reference.

If we forgo the more subtle distinctions, the primary prerequisites for transforming a frame of reference into a theory are that each concept in the system be defined through reference to events or operations that take place in the physical world, distinguished from the conceptual world, and that the exact relationship between each concept and every other concept within the system be specified. Only when both these requirements are met is legitimate prediction possible.

Theory construction begins with the somewhat arbitrary process of selecting the concepts to be included within the system. The concepts can be chosen from a myriad of preexisting concepts, or the theory constructor can draw upon his or her own experience to form new concepts. The process of concept selection involves both inclusion and exclusion, and the criteria may involve not only the assumed explanatory merits of the particular concepts employed but the breadth of the behavior that the theory is to encompass. Once the concepts to be included are identified, each must be connected to events or operations that take place in the physical rather than the conceptual world.

Let us examine the necessity for such definition more closely. Due to the very nature of its construction, a concept is obviously applicable to the behavioral events from which it was induced. The problem lies in deciding what other events shall be included within the domain of the concept. Since the concept's primary value lies in its explanatory features, it is soon applied to a multitude of events that occur outside the concept's proper domain. In the clinical realm, for example, we can be faced with a situation in which such diverse phenomena as stuttering and the overprotectiveness of a mother toward her child are conceptualized as being due to hostility. While concepts of this sort have value in explaining phenomena once they have occurred, it is difficult to envisage how such ambiguously defined conceptual entities could possibly be included in a predictive system. Prediction requires that the exact observable referents of the concept be specified. For instance, hostility might be defined in terms of certain carefully prescribed behaviors (e.g., verbal or physical assault), or by the scores an individual obtains on a test of hostility, or by a combination of measures. What is important is that, whatever measures are employed, they are all specified, so that the definition of the concept comes at last into the public domain.

This is not to suggest that the theoretician must forever remain content with the arbitrary referents initially chosen to define the concepts. One may legitimately assert that, for the time being, the concept shall be defined by a particular set of referents, but that the meaning attributed to the concept is not exhausted by the referents employed. At this stage in theory construction, hypothetical constructs as well as intervening variables are appropriate. Although initially the theoretician must be given considerable leeway in developing the definitions of concepts, the need for a full and exhaustive definition of concepts cannot forever be held in abeyance. In the theoretical enterprise, one must continually examine both one's own experience and one's conceptual formulations, reshaping the concepts and as a result adding to or subtracting from the collection of defining referents until one is satisfied that for the purposes intended the referents accurately and completely particularize the concept. It should thus become apparent that any final theoretical system would consist of a collection of intervening variables rather than hypothetical constructs.

Although this metamorphosis from hypothetical constructs to intervening variables reflects the increased refinement and specificity of the system, the pragmatic consequences of employing systems composed of either type of concept are not as different as one might imagine. The predictions derived from either type of system would always be couched in terms of those particular referents being employed to define the concepts. If the system is one of intervening variables, the theoretician is indicating a final satisfaction with the definitions of the concepts. If the system is one of hypothetical constructs, the theoretician is saying that the final definition of the concepts is not yet formulated. However, in both instances, the theoretical formulations advanced are tested by the degree of validity of the predictions derived from the system, with the predictions always being spelled out in terms of the definitions being employed at that time.

A collection of concepts, each of which is carefully defined, still does not constitute a theory. A theory must allow for the derivation of hypotheses or predictions that are open equally to disproof as to proof, and for this to be accomplished, the exact relationship of each concept to every other concept in the system must be delineated. The necessity for such delineation can be illustrated in the following example. Let us assume that we have constructed a hypothetical three-concept system involving frustration, hostility, and fear, and let us also assume that we have carefully defined each of these concepts in terms of observable measures. In order to test the hypothesis that hostility increases as a function of frustration, and employing specific referents to define the concepts, it might be predicted that when a group of subjects is confined to a room and not allowed to eat for a considerable period of time (frustration) the number of negatively toned remarks (hostility) the subjects make to one another will increase. Let us assume that the experiment was actually conducted. If the prediction was confirmed, the temptation would be to assert that we were dealing with a legitimate theoretical derivation that was confirmed. Our original statement that hostility increases as a function of frustration certainly appears to be open to confirmation, but is it equally open to disconfirmation? What would the typical user of our three-concept system do if disconfirmatory findings were obtained? A likely response would be to save the formulation, even in the face of negative findings, by introducing the third concept, fear. Thus our hypothetical investigator might continue to assert that hostility increases as a function of frustration but might add that in the experimental situation the subjects were afraid to express hostility and therefore negatively toned remarks decreased even as hostility increased. The observant reader will be aware that a concept or two has been implicitly added to the system, but, as indicated earlier, this is exactly how such frames of references operate. Again, while one does not have a truly predictive system when such schemata are employed, one is never at a loss to explain any behavior one may encounter.

What is lacking is an explanatory edifice to clarify why and under what conditions a particular behavior occurs rather than another. In order for either inter- or intraindividual differences in behavior to become theoretically comprehensible, the relationship of each concept to every other concept in the system must be designated. For this to be accomplished, constructs of the middle range are needed. These constructs serve to bridge the distance between very specific and very broad concepts. In both developmental psychology and psychopathology, however, such concepts of the middle range are rare. Instead, two types of concepts predominate: (a) lower-level concepts that are so closely tied to observables that they represent little more than shorthand expressions for the empirical observations they encompass; and (b) broad assumptive concepts that are so far removed from observables that the empirical operations that give these concepts meaning cannot be delineated. Constructs of the middle range are required to provide the bridge between the two, illuminating the empirical content the system seeks to encompass.

In our illustration above, if we were to designate exactly how fear interacts with frustration and hostility, our frame of reference would evolve into a theory. Under such circumstances, we could generate a legitimate hypothesis that would probably take the form that frustration would be followed by no increase in hostile remarks when fear of making such remarks is high, but that hostile remarks would follow frustration when fear of making such remarks is low. If such a statement precedes our experiment, we cannot take refuge in our theory when faced with negative findings. Indeed, we would be forced to assert unequivocally that our theory has generated an erroneous prediction. But this has value. What has been missing in the field of psychopathology is the steady increase in knowledge resulting from the cumulative effects of data collection interspersed with ever-evolving theoretical formulations.

The preceding discussion has made it apparent that, before legitimate hypotheses can be derived from a conceptual system, each concept in the system must be defined, and the exact relationship of each concept to every other concept must be specified. There can be little argument that these requirements must be met before the conceptual schema qualifies as a theory since they are essential to the hypothetic–deductive enterprise that constitutes the very essence of theory usage. Inasmuch as the real criterion for understanding phenomena is not a personal but a public one, the system that does not allow for testable predictions, open to disproof as well as to proof, is useless. One can only claim understanding when legitimate predictions made about phenomena are confirmed. Based on these criteria, it should be evident that there is presently no comprehensive theory of psychopathological functioning. Instead we find a collection of frames of reference. It is not our purpose, however, to indict such frames of reference, for a frame of reference is a mandatory stage in theory development lying between the generation of single concepts on the one side and a legitimate theory on the other. What is being indicted is the tendency of so many to be satisfied with such inadequate systems.

A question that naturally arises at this point is whether our proposition constitutes a theory or a frame of reference. An examination of the position will reveal that we too are presenting a frame of reference. What then distinguishes this effort from the efforts of others? There is, of course, the difference in the particular concepts we have decided to employ, but this is just a matter of content and would have little to recommend it over other conceptual schemata presently available. The distinguishing feature of this effort appears to be our dissatisfaction with it. The aim is to construct a comprehensive theory of psychopathology, and the work of more than 25 years that is summarized in this book represents significant steps in that direction. Nevertheless, we are still dealing with hypothetical constructs rather than intervening variables. Furthermore, although the work encompasses a broad range of phenomena and issues in psychopathology, many interrelationships between concepts remain to be specified. The reader will discover that certain concepts have been clearly related to other concepts, but to date these relationships serve as bridges between some relatively isolated theoretical islands. A finished theory demands that all of these islands and bridges be joined together into one comprehensive nomological network. Thus, while an extremely kind evaluator of this body of work might insist that a miniature theory or two has been built, as a totality the work must still be considered a frame of reference. However, we have worked and will continue to work toward a theory. Therefore, the particular statement of the position presented in this book should be considered neither fixed nor final. It represents the present stage in our evolution toward a theory.

REFERENCE NOTE

1. Here it is important to note that Levinson's group is currently studying adult development in women (Levinson, 1985).

CHAPTER 2

Developmental Principles
and Their Application
to Psychopathology

The fundamental assumptions presented in Chapter 1 define the metaphysical and metatheoretical context within which our developmental approach to psychopathology must be viewed. With these assumptions delineated, the present chapter examines the specific tenets of developmental theory and the issues involved in the application of these principles to psychopathology. Rorschach developmental-level scoring represents a major early effort to apply organismic–developmental principles to psychopathology. Thus this work is considered in some detail. The chapter then presents the developmental formulation of psychopathology evolved by Zigler and his colleagues. This formulation does not presuppose that psychopathology represents a general regression to developmentally lower forms of functioning. Our view is that different individuals can be characterized as functioning at different levels along a developmental continuum and that the person's characteristic level of functioning continues to influence behavior after the person has been designated "pathological" just as it did prior to the onset of disorder. In line with our position, an alternative interpretation of regression is advanced.

BASIC DEVELOPMENTAL CONSTRUCTS

The developmental approach to psychopathology presented in this volume owes a primary theoretical debt to Heinz Werner (Werner, 1937, 1948, 1957; Werner & Kaplan, 1963), although the influence of many other developmentalists of both psychoanalytic (e.g., Hartmann, 1952; Kris, 1950; Rapaport, 1951) and nonpsychoanalytic persuasion (Lewin, 1936, 1946; Piaget, 1951, 1960) must be acknowledged. Inasmuch as they all derive from an organismic perspective, these various positions display considerable commonality in the types of organizational constructs employed. Similarly, the formulations of Loevinger (Loevinger, 1976; Loevinger & Wessler, 1970) and of Luria (1961) and Vygotsky (1962) are both compatible with and relevant to our approach to psychopathology. Nevertheless, it was Werner and his students who expended the greatest effort in applying developmental principles to phenomena of interest in psychopathology. Werner's orthogenetic principle, his delineation of progressive levels of organization, and his assumptions about the multiformity and the multilinearity of development are central to our categorizations of psychopathological behavior. Because analogous constructs have been formulated by other developmentalists and because our developmental approach is traceable to these various conceptual roots, the presentation of the conceptual underpinnings of our developmental approach to psychopathology will be organized around the salient constructs rather than the separate positions of the various developmentalists. Most central to our work are Werner's (1957) orthogenetic principle and the assumption that expression in unmediated action characterizes lower developmental functioning whereas at higher levels responses are mediated by thought.

Within the organismic framework, development is defined as both a continuous and a discontinuous process. As Langer (1970) has indicated, the dialectic issue is how the organism can change qualitatively with development and at the same time preserve its integrity and inner stability. The continuity of development is expressed in Werner's orthogenetic principle, which states that "wherever development occurs it proceeds from a state of relative globality and lack of differentiation to a state of increasing differentiation, articulation, and hierarchic integration" (1957, p. 126). This definition of the basic structural nature of developmental change is shared by Lewin, and, although they emphasize it less, by the ego psychologists. Moreover, the orthogenetic principle finds a functional equivalent in Piaget's eqilibration principle.

Of greatest relevance to psychopathology are the implications of the orthogenetic principle in regard to self–world relationships. At immature levels, subjective experience and external events tend to be fused, and neither the boundaries nor the point of view of the self can be adequately distinguished from the boundaries or the point of view of the other. In psychodynamic terms, this condition is described as the relative lack of boundary articulation and reality testing. Inasmuch as clear distinctions are not made between imagining and perceiving, an individual's own thoughts, wishes, and fantasies can be confused with external reality. Thus, as is the case with hallucinations, internal images may be given the status of tangible external events.

By contrast, at more mature levels, not only are self and world distinguished, they are also reintegrated in complex and relatively stable ways. Furthermore, with development each realm becomes itself differentiated and hierarchically organized. In terms of personal and social functioning, a sense of personal identity can be achieved, the individual can perceive the separateness and the distinct needs and point of view of the other, and self and other can be reintegrated so that the individual perceives himself or herself as a member and a participant in social interactions. As was indicated previously, the ability to view subject and object as differentiated entities, each organized in its own right and interrelated with the other, allows for greater planning and active control over both external events and internal need states. Gratification can be delayed, goals can be envisioned, and it becomes possible to employ substitutive means and alternative ends in order to achieve these goals. Adaptive capacities, therefore, increase as a function of the structural changes that define development. Our use of premorbid competence as a broad though imperfect benchmark of an individual's developmental level (see Chapter 3) rests upon this assumption that higher developmental forms of functioning provide a basis for greater coping effectiveness. The orthogenetic principle likewise provided much of the conceptual basis for the work on self-image described in Chapter 10.

In regard to the discontinuity of developmental change, successive stages are presumed to be marked by the emergence of new properties that render them qualitatively different from and not reducible to developmentally earlier forms. Werner and other developmentalists (e.g., Piaget, Lewin, and many ego psychologists) have suggested that primitive, developmentally early behavior is marked by immediate, direct, and unmodulated responses to external stimuli and internal need states. By contrast, higher levels of development are characterized by the appearance of indirect, ideational, conceptual, and symbolic or verbal behavior patterns. Thus developmental psychology suggests that a shift in emphasis from action to thought is an expression of the developmental sequence. As will be discussed in Chapter 4, the distinction between expression in action and thought constitutes a major dimension in our developmental analysis of symptomatology.

In developmental transformations, the earlier forms are presumed not to be lost but to be subordinated to and integrated within the higher forms of functioning. The developmentally advanced individual, therefore, possesses a wide range of modes of responding that are both differentiated from each other and hierarchically organized. The lower forms of functioning are both available to the individual and controlled by the more abstract conceptual processes. This provides an increased flexibility as well as stability at higher levels. Multiple means become available for the achievement of a particular goal, and multiple goals can be served by a single means. The greater adaptability and control that this provides has been stressed by Santostefano and Baker (1972):

> The availability of multiple means and alternative ends frees the individual from the demands of the immediate situation, enabling him to express behavior in more delayed, planned, indirect, organized . . . terms and to search for detours which acknowledge both opportunities and limitations of the environment but still permit successful adaptation. (p. 117)

This availability of multiple means also requires that, in the interpretation of behavior, underlying processes must be distinguished from the surface appearance or material form of the behavior. One cannot assume that two behaviors have the same meaning because they are physically identical; neither can one assume that two dissimilar behaviors have different meanings. The developmental position is that a particular behavior can only be understood through an examination of the processes underlying it and thus of the function that it serves in the total organization of behavior. In psychopathology, for example, particular symptomatic behaviors have not been found to be consistent over time or to have much predictive value (Kohlberg et al., 1972; Santostefano & Baker, 1972; Strauss, Carpenter, & Bartko, 1974). By contrast, however, when the surface symptoms have been grouped on the basis of the underlying processes they reflect, such as developmental differences in modes of organization, longitudinal consistency and prediction have become possible (Cicchetti & Pogge-Hesse, 1982; Kohlberg et al., 1972; Phillips, Broverman, & Zigler, 1966; Prentky et al., 1980; Santostefano & Baker, 1972; Sroufe & Rutter, 1984; Zigler & Phillips, 1961c).

As a formal regulative principle, the orthogenetic law defines a universal, unilinear developmental sequence. In actual manifestation, development is multilinear. Just as individuals may differ in their rate of development and in the final level of maturation attained (Zigler, 1969), they also differ in the specialized directions development may take. For example, as Werner (1957) has indicated, the physiognomic perception of the artist is not analogous to the young child's perception but represents the culmination of a horizontal growth process, a branching out or specialized horizontal development within a particular mode of organization. Given the multilinearity in conjunction with a unilinearity in development, one would expect that within any individual there would be some correspondence but also considerable variation in the rate of development of different response systems. Thus while one would expect some correspondendence between an individual's cognitive maturity and his or her social maturity, one would not expect an identity between these developmental forms. Due to the specialization in development, in any particular individual, cognitive growth might outstrip social maturation or vice versa.

The principles just summarized greatly influenced the developmental interpretation of psychopathology first formulated by Zigler in collaboration with Leslie Phillips. Also influential to this work was research ongoing at the time directed toward the application of developmental principles to Rorschach scoring. Therefore, this research will be reviewed prior to the presentation of Zigler's formulation.

THE EARLY APPLICATION OF DEVELOPMENTAL PRINCIPLES TO PSYCHOPATHOLOGY: RORSCHACH DEVELOPMENTAL SCORING

The programmatic research on the developmental scoring of the Rorschach, which was undertaken in the 1950s at Clark University and Worcester State

Hospital, represents a prominent early effort to extend systematically the organismic–developmental framework to major phenomena in psychopathology. Goldfried, Stricker, and Weiner (1971) and Lerner (1975) have provided careful reviews of this work.

As was stated in Chapter 1, the organismic position does not equate development with ontogenesis. Organismic–developmental principles can equally be applied in comparative animal psychology, in ethnopsychology, and in psychopathology (Werner, 1948). However, a major problem in extending developmental principles to areas other than childhood development is the question of how to assess maturity level in adult samples, an issue that can be sidestepped in the study of child development by using chronological age as an indirect indicator of developmental status. It must be remembered that neither chronological age nor the passage of time is a psychological variable (Kaplan, 1967; Werner, 1957; Wohlwill, 1970; Zigler, 1963, 1969). Thus neither can serve as a defining aspect for developmental analyses. The developmental scoring of the Rorschach, originally devised by Friedman (1953), represented one solution to this problem in the area of psychopathology. Based upon Werner's orthogenetic principle, the structural aspects or form qualities of Rorschach percepts were analyzed for degree of differentiation and hierarchic integration. Responses that were characterized as developmentally immature (amorphous, vague, minus, confabulatory, and contaminated responses as well as perseverations and fabulized combinations) were seen as reflecting a perceptual organization that was diffuse, syncretic, indefinite, rigid, and labile. Developmentally high responses were seen as reflecting the opposite, an integrated pattern of perceptual organization characterized as discrete, articulated, definite, flexible, and stable.

Central to this work was a conceptualization of psychopathology as representing a regression (Friedman, 1953; Goldman, 1962; Siegel, 1953). As such, the Rorschach percepts of severely disturbed psychiatric patients (e.g., schizophrenics) were expected to be similar to, but not identical with, the percepts of young children. "Just as any developmental stage preserves vestiges of the earlier stages from which it has emerged, so will any degeneration bear signs of the higher level from which it has retrogressed" (Werner, 1948, quoted in Friedman, 1953).

Pioneering this effort, Friedman (1953) compared the Rorschach responses of three groups: (a) normal adults; (b) schizophrenic patients with hebephrenic and catatonic symptoms; and (c) children between the ages of 3 and 5. As predicted, the resonses of the schizophrenic patients were less mature than those of normal adults and in some aspects of their structural organization resembled the responses of the young children. In other aspects of the perceptual organization of their responses, the patients appeared to occupy an intermediate position between the normal adults and the preschool children.

In a closer examination of ontogenetic changes in Rorschach developmental level, Hemmendinger (1953) noted what appeared to be a three-stage progression in the organization of Rorschach percepts. Whereas the percepts of children between 3 and 5 were global and diffuse, the Rorschach responses of children between 6 and 9 years of age emphasized detail at the expense of integrated structuring. Beginning at about age 9 and most evident in adulthood was an integrated and articulated structuring of Rorschach percepts. Utilizing these age norms, Siegel (1953) observed a correspondence in structure between the Rorschach responses of paranoid schizophrenics and "the more differentiated but little integrated perception of children between six and ten years of age" (p. 161). The paranoid schizophrenic group, then, occupied an intermediate position between the global amorphous structuring characteristic of hebephrenic and catatonic patients and the more integrated perceptual organization of normal adults. A further diagnostic differentiation was noted by Frank (1951, cited by Hemminndinger & Schultz, 1977), who found the developmental-level scores of psychoneurotics to be intermediate between those of paranoid schizophrenic patients and those of normal adults.

In a series of studies carried out at Clark University and reviewed by Phillips, Kaden, and Waldman (1959), Rorschach developmental level was found to be predictably related to symptom expression, ordered along an action–thought continuum. As indicated previously, direct expression in action is presumed to reflect a less mature form of functioning than is mediated representation in thought. Accordant with this assumption, assaultive patients were found to obtain lower developmental scores than patients who merely threatened assault (Misch, 1954). Similarly, patients who had made actual suicidal attempts or whose sexual behavior was overtly deviant evidenced more global organization on the Rorschach than did patients who threatened suicide or who exressed concern about sexual deviation in the absence of overt behavioral expression (Kruger, 1954). Moreover, children characterized as hyperactive obtained lower developmental scores than a comparison group whose symptoms were classified as underactive (Hurwitz, 1954).

Further validation of the Rorschach developmental scoring was provided by findings that developmental-level scores (a) increased during microgenesis (Phillips & Framo, 1954); (b) were predictably related to mental age or IQ in both normal (Lane, 1955) and mentally retarded samples (Rosenblatt & Solomon, 1954); and (c) were associated with a variety of measures reflecting maturity in cognitive and perceptual functioning (Lipton, Kaden, & Phillips, 1958; Lofchie, 1955; Phillips et al., 1959). Additional corroborative findings were later reported by Blatt and Allison (1963) and by Kissel (1965).

Linking perceptual organizations with processes relevant to social judgment, Feffer (1959) observed significant relations between developmental level as evidenced by Rorschach scores and the ability to take the perspective of another. Associations between Rorschach developmental level and social effectiveness or maturity were also reported by Lane (1955) and

Fowler (1957, cited in Phillips et al., 1959), using both normal and schizophrenic samples.

In research carried out beyond the confines of the Clark University–Worcester State Hospital complex, Rorschach developmental-level scoring was applied to the process–reactive distinction in schizophrenia. Consistent with his argument that process and reactive schizophrenia represent points along a developmental continuum, Becker (1956) reported developmentally higher Rorschach scores for reactive than for process schizophrenic patients. This finding was subsequently replicated by other investigators (Steffy & Becker, 1961; Ullmann & Eck, 1965; Zimet & Fine, 1959), although nonsignificant findings were occasionally reported (Judson & Katahn, 1964). Especially relevant to this volume are the highly significant relationships reported by Lerner (1968) between Rorschach developmental level and premorbid social competence as measured by the Zigler-Phillips index. Moreover, in addition to the association with premorbid adjustment, Rorschach developmental level has been found to be related to adjustment during hospitalization, likelihood of discharge, and posthospital adjustment (Hunter, Schooler, & Spohn, 1962; Kaden & Lipton, 1960; Levine, 1959; Wilensky, 1959).

The remarkable consistency of these findings would seem to attest to the value of Rorschach scoring as a broadly applicable measure of developmental level. At the beginning of the 1960s, however, the Rorschach fell out of favor as a research instrument. As Hemmendinger and Schultz (1977) documented, this was due mainly to the emphasis given in much of the research to content rather than structural analyses. When content was emphasized (e.g., oral vs. anal themes), reliability in scoring was problematic and little evidence was provided to support the validity of the measure. By contrast, structural analyses of Rorschach responses have been highly reliable (between scorers and over time) and have produced substantial evidence for the validity of the instrument (e.g., Blatt et al., 1976; Goldfried et al., 1971; Holt, 1963; Schimek, 1974). Also contributing to the much diminished use of the Rorschach in research was the emergence of a variety of psychometrically sophisticated self-report measures for assessing personality variables (e.g., the MMPI). More recently, the value of developmental Rorschach scoring has been reaffirmed. As Goldfried et al. (1971) concluded in their review:

> Friedman's scoring of the Rorschach results in a good measure of developmental level of functioning. . . . The research failures with the developmental scoring have been comparatively few . . . as it has been shown to be a valuable research tool, Friedman's scoring of the Rorschach should receive greater use as a dependent variable. (pp. 54–55)

Rorschach developmental-level scoring has again found its way into the research literature, and the relationships noted earlier between Rorschach developmental scores and the following variables have been reconfirmed: (a) chronological age, mental age, and IQ (Gerstein, Brodzinsky, & Reiskind, 1976; Greenberg & Cardwell, 1978; O'Neill, O'Neill, & Quinlan, 1976; Weisz et al., 1978); (b) premorbid adjustment (Harder & Ritzler, 1979); and (c) diagnosis (Donnelly, Murphy, & Scott, 1975; Harder & Ritzler, 1979; Schaeffer, 1977), although some discrepancies between current and earlier findings in regard to diagnosis merit further investigation.

However, despite the promise of the developmental scoring of the Rorschach as a vehicle for assessing developmental variations in adulthood, Zigler looked for a more practical approach to assessing developmental differences. The reasons for moving beyond Rorschach scoring were that: (a) childlike responses on the Rorschach are emitted too infrequently by adults to make this a very sensitive indicator of developmental variations among adults; (b) the perceptual –cognitive realm assessed by the Rorschach is too narrow to be employed as a total indicator of developmental level, whose effects permeate the individual's personality (including traits and systems of defense) and social functioning; and (c) collecting developmental Rorschach scores is too laborious easily to permit research with relatively large samples of individuals. In regard to the first of these reasons, data reported by Harder and Ritzler (1979) also suggest that Rorschach developmental scores may not allow for sufficiently fine-tuned differentiations within adult samples. In Harder and Ritzler's investigation, Rorschach developmental-level scores were found to differentiate psychotic from nonpsychotic patients and to be moderately correlated with premorbid adjustment. However, in contrast to earlier findings (Siegel, 1953), finer diagnostic differentiations (i.e., between schizophrenic and nonschizophrenic psychotic patients, and between paranoid and nonparanoid schizophrenics) could not be made on the basis of Rorschach scores. The discrepancy between the two studies may reflect sampling differences. Whereas Siegel's nonparanoid schizophrenic patients were all diagnosed as hebephrenic or catatonic, this severity of disturbance was not matched in Harder and Ritzler's nonparanoid schizophrenic subsample. Thus, although there are limitations in the Rorschach approach, this research provides an important demonstration of the applicability of organismic–developmental principles to psychopathology.

ZIGLER'S POSITION AND THE ZIGLER-PHILLIPS DEVELOPMENTAL APPROACH TO PSYCHOPATHOLOGY

Given the limitations of the developmental scoring of the Rorschach, Zigler's efforts, begun in collaboration with Leslie Phillips, were directed toward a broader application of developmental principles to the field of psychopathology. In keeping with the formulations of Werner and the other developmentalists discussed earlier in the chapter, developmental level was conceptualized as representing no less than the total information-processing system utilized by the individual in mediating all behaviors (Zigler, 1963). As such, the developmental-level construct was presumed to be as pertinent to analyses of emotional, motivational, and social functioning as to behavior in the perceptual–cognitive domain. Although such constructs as level of cognitive organization, intelligence, and cognitive complexity represent very broad dimensions or traits in the assessment of individuals, the developmental-level construct is far broader, being presumed to mediate all behavior and to pertain equally to adaptive and maladaptive functioning.

Fundamental to the Zigler-Phillips approach to psychopathology is the assumption that disordered functioning can best be understood within the context of normal development. The developmental position takes as its given the level of maturity attained by the individual, and this maturity level is presumed to be reflected in both intellectual and social functioning and to underlie both normal and pathological behaviors. Thus an inherent continuity between adaptive and maladaptive functioning is stressed, and mental disorder is seen as a continuous process in which premorbid, disordered, and postmorbid modes of functioning are meaningfully interrelated.

Just as modes of adaptive functioning can be isolated and ordered along a developmental continuum, the various forms of psychopathology can be ordered and viewed as representing inadequate resolutions at different levels of development. As such, the Zigler-Phillips approach was aimed at the discovery of dimensions whose applicability extended beyond individual disorders to all of psychopatholgy. The concern, therefore, was to apply developmental principles to the analysis of adaptive functioning and to the illumination of major variables of interest in psychopathology (e.g., overt symptomatology, case history, treatment, and outcome).

However, one issue has remained problematic since Zigler and Phillips began their work. That is the question of how organismic–developmental principles can be meaningfully and precisely extended to the analysis of personal and social functioning, especially in adulthood. Despite its holistic intent and the conceptualization of mental operations as including feelings, motives, and social judgments, the organismic–developmental framework has primarily been applied to cognitive–perceptual phenomena. The extension of these principles to personal and social functioning, even in regard to the investigation of normal development, remains incomplete (Langer, 1970), although important inroads are being made (e.g., Gurucharri, Phelps, & Selman, 1984; Kohlberg, 1969; Kohlberg & Zigler, 1967; Loevinger, 1976; Selman, 1980; Selman & Demorest, 1984; Vaillant, 1971).

While some degree of relationship is to be expected between an individual's level of cognitive organization and the level of maturity demonstrated in personal and social functioning, such a relationship should, at best, be imprecise. Given the assumptions about the multilinearity of development discussed earlier, one might expect that within any particular individual specialized directions in development might lead to accentuated and/or accelerated development in certain areas of functioning with a corresponding deceleration in other areas. As imperfect reflections of that broader construct, developmental level, cognitive, personal, and social maturity would be expected to be only partially interrelated.

The need for measures that more specifically tap dimensions of personal and social maturity is pressing (Zigler & Trickett, 1978). As Kohlberg et al. (1972) observed, the current state of affairs in which intelligence test scores continue to be the most consistent longitudinal predictors of personal and social adjustment attests more to the inadequacy of present measures of personal and social functioning than to the superior importance of cognitive ability as a determinant of overall functioning and adjustment. Research on the effectiveness of early childhood intervention programs, discussed in the next chapter, and on predictors of adult occupational success (e.g., Jencks, 1979; Seitz, Rosenbaum, & Apfel, 1985; Zigler & Trickett, 1978) clearly indicate that social competence and not just cognitive ability per se is a major contributor to successful functioning even in educational and occupational realms. That measures of cognitive development predict as well as they do, even in regard to personal and social functioning, would seem to attest to the power of the developmental approach. It has been argued that the broader the dimension of personality being measured the greater the predictive utility of the measure. Thus the predictive potential of the developmental-level construct would seem to be very strong indeed.

Faced with the problem of how to assess an individual's developmental level as manifested in personality (including traits and systems of defense) and social adaptation, Zigler, together with Phillips and other colleagues, has over the course of years developed a variety of means for assessing developmental level that are applicable not only to disordered functioning but to adaptation in nondisordered individuals. These indicators of developmental level include the Zigler-Phillips Premorbid Social Competence Index, characterizations of symptomatology as involving expression in action versus thought, the role-orientation formulation that has been extended to nonpsychopathological individuals, and self-image disparity as a reflection of developmental level. This work therefore has implications not only for psychopathology but for developmental psychology in general. These efforts represent only a beginning in the ongoing attempt to operationalize the developmental-level construct as broadly conceived. Nevertheless, because of its programmatic nature and because of the attention that has been paid to interrelationships among the various developmental measures, this work has contributed to the enlarged understanding of that most ubiquitous construct in developmental thought, developmental level.

Of particular relevance to adult psychopathology is the issue of individual differences in development, an issue that has attracted relatively little attention in developmental thought. The concept of developmental level or stage is more concerned with general laws of responsiveness and addresses itself to the sequentiality in which various systemic organizations make their appearance rather than to the problem of individuality or uniqueness of experience. Yet, as Zigler (Kimble, Garmezy, & Zigler, 1980; Zigler, 1969) has

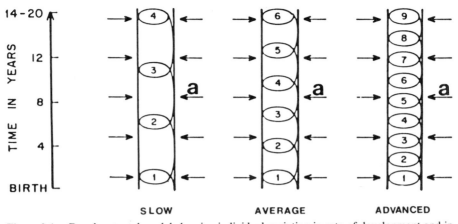

Figure 2.1. Developmental model showing individual variation in rate of development and in final level attained. The single vertical arrow represents the passage of time. The horizontal arrows represent environmental events impinging on the individual, who is represented as a pair of vertical lines. The individual's development appears as an internal ascending spiral, in which the numbered loops represent successive stages. The number of stages characterizing the three illustrated courses of development has been selected arbitrarily. The actual number of stages that can be identified varies with the particular processes being examined.

asserted, while the sequence of developmental change is seen as invariant, individuals may vary in both the rate of development and the level of development to which the developmental curve finally becomes asymptotic. This model is graphically presented in Figure 2.1.

Represented in Figure 2.1 are three individuals, each of whose development is taking place at a different rate and becomes asymptotic at a different level. The discontinuity in development is represented by the successive spirals, each indicating a qualitatively different stage. Continuity in development can also be represented. If we add to the model presented in Figure 2.1 certain aspects of the model suggested by Lewin (1936), it will express the view that each stage of development is more differentiated than the one preceding it (Figure 2.2).

The approach to development represented by this model is essentially an interactionist one in which experience (represented by the horizontal arrows in both figures) impinges on or interacts with a variety of indigenous factors over the course of development. Important to notice here is that an externally similar experience or event (which can be represented by similar horizontal arrows occurring at a given point in time, as for example the arrows marked "a" in Figure 2.1) interacts with markedly different qualities in individuals whose developmental characteristics differ. As was indicated in

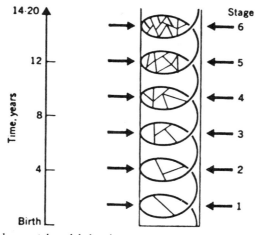

Figure 2.2.   Developmental model showing greater differentiation, or an increasing number of "regions," as Lewin called them, at each successive stage. Although equally important, the increasing hierarchization with development is not represented graphically. From *Principles of General Psychology* (5th ed.) by G. A. Kimble, N. Garmezy, and E. Zigler, 1980, New York: John Wiley & Sons.

Chapter 1, these differences within individuals can radically alter the nature of the experience itself.

The model represented in Figure 2.1 is admittedly overly simplistic, arbitrary, and in many ways ambiguous. It does not go very far in resolving some of the most important general issues concerning cognitive development. Left unanswered are such questions as: Is the sequentialitity in cognitive development inevitable or does it only reflect the experiential programming of the organism? Exactly how do environmental events interact with nativistic factors in the development of any single process? Precisely what precipitates the movement from one developmental level to the next? Is development essentially the growth of a variety of highly related processes and thus best represented by a single progression (as in the figures here) or is it better viewed as a collection of relatively independent processes developing at different rates as a function perhaps of quite different environmental and nativistic factors?

Despite these problems, this model appears to have considerable value. We certainly need not await the resolution of the issues noted above before employing such a model. In keeping with most thought in the area of the philosophy of science, the question that must be raised is not whether a model is "true" or "untrue" but rather whether it is useful or not. That is, does the model help organize knowledge obtained up to this point in time and, more importantly, does it generate hypotheses capable of being disproved as well as proved the testing of which can lead us to greater knowledge?

Our view of the relationship between pathological and nonpathological functioning can also be represented graphically, and this model is presented in Figure 2.3.

As Figure 2.3 illustrates, the movement between normal and pathological conditions does not assume a shift in the developmental status of the individual's behavior. Central to the Zigler-Phillips formulation is the view that the individual's developmental level continues to influence the person's functioning after the person is designated "pathological" just as it did prior to this designation, during the individual's premorbid period. In becoming symptomatic, the individual does not appear to change habitual modes of responding. For every maturity level there exist effective patterns of adaptation as well as pathological deviations from these patterns. Thus both the normal and the pathological aspects of the individual's functioning can be seen as reflecting the maturity level attained.

The view that individuals continue to maintain their position on the developmental continuum even after they are adjudged pathological stands in opposition to the psychodynamic view that pathology represents a general regression to an immature or developmentally low level of functioning. In light of the central position that the concept of regression has occupied in thinking about psychopathology, and given the conflicting and often ambiguous conceptualizations of the regressive process, a closer examination of this concept seems warranted.

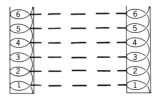

Mode of Functioning

Nonpathological ——— Psychopathological

Figure 2.3. Model showing the continuity in developmental level between nonpathological and psychopathological functioning. Psychopathological and nonpsychopathological modes of functioning are viewed along a continuum. The pair of ascending spirals represent developmental levels in nonpathological functioning during the premorbid period (left spiral) and after psychopathology becomes manifest (right spiral). The broken horizontal lines illustrate our view that the developmental level at which the individual typically functions is not radically altered when psychopathology becomes manifest. For each developmental level, there exist effective patterns of coping as well as pathological deviations from these patterns.

THE CONCEPT OF REGRESSION: ALTERNATIVE VIEWS

In both psychoanalytic (e.g., Cameron, 1963; Fenichel, 1945) and developmental thinking (e.g., Goldman, 1962), a common assumption has been that psychopathology reflects a regression to ontogenetically lower forms of functioning and/or a fixation at these levels. A corollary to this premise is that as the severity of the pathology increases so do the magnitude of the regression and consequent level of fixation (Glatt & Karon, 1974). This assumption was fundamental in the Rorschach research discussed previously, and it has also been basic to many studies of schizophrenic thought (e.g., Andreasen & Powers, 1976; Gottesman, 1964; Rashkis, Cushman, & Landis, 1946; Youkilis & DeWolfe, 1975). According to this view, degree of psychopathology becomes reducible to developmental level.

However, this view is at variance with the fact that individuals display so many different forms of pathology and with the fact that even within a single nosological category a variety of levels of functioning can be displayed (Akiskal & McKinney, 1975; Miller, 1976; Zigler, Levine, & Zigler, 1976). More disturbed patients have not uniformly been found to function at developmentally lower levels than their less disturbed or even normal counterparts (Blatt et al., 1976; Russell & Beekhuis, 1976; Zigler, Glick, & Marsh, 1979). Furthermore, the strength of the drive toward growth and development posited and exemplified in a number of ways by various theorists (e.g., Angyal, 1941; Rogers, 1951) argues against any assumption that development can stop or be fixated. Several observations further mitigate against the view that severity of psychopathology is mirrored by the degree of regression to and fixation at earlier forms. Observations of schizophrenic patients reveal that their speech and reality testing differ markedly from the speech patterns and playful fantasies of children (Brown, 1973). Further, conceptual groupings imposed by schizophrenics may be more abstract (open) albeit more idiosyncratic (private) than the groupings of either organic patients or normal control subjects (McGaughran & Moran, 1956, 1957). Finally, a given patient can be observed to function at a variety of levels and to cope even in the midst of pathology. An additional limitation to the view that pathology represents a common regression is the relative lack of supporting longitudinal data (Buss & Lang, 1965).

Nevertheless, severely pathological and especially schizophrenic thought and behavior are frequently disorganized, primitive, and even childlike in some of their aspects. An alternative formulation of the nature of regression can encompass both the similarities and the differences that have been observed in the speech and thought of severely disturbed patients and children. Regression as a change in the content of responses, as a return to earlier modes of operation, or as retrogression (Lewin, 1946) can be distinguished from a conceptualization of regression as involving some disintegration of superordinating structures.

A basic principle in developmental thought is that, in the course of development, earlier structures or modes of operation are not lost but become reorganized within and subordinated to higher structures. Thus for every individual a variety of modes or developmental levels of functioning are ever present. Moreover a mark of the developmentally advanced individual is a flexibility of functioning. Possessed of multiple modes of operation, the mature individual can select that level of functioning most appropriate to particular situational demands (Santostefano, 1978; Sroufe & Rutter, 1984). In psychopathology, therefore, the distinguishing feature is not that lower forms are present but that these forms are insufficiently integrated with and subordinated to higher forms. In being less under the control of higher mediating structures, the lower forms break through.

This conceptualization of psychopathology as involving a weakening of integrating structures with the consequent uncontrolled breaking through of lower forms contrasts substantially with the view of psychopathology as a common regression to earlier levels of functioning. The two views of regression depend upon different conceptualizations of the developmental process—conceptualizations that are illustrated in Figure 2.4.

In its more common connotation, regression can be represented as a backward or downward movement through a stepwise series of stages. This view is represented as Model A in Figure 2.4. Here development is schematized as a simple stepwise movement from one stage to the next. Although prior experience and thus earlier stages remain a part of the organ-

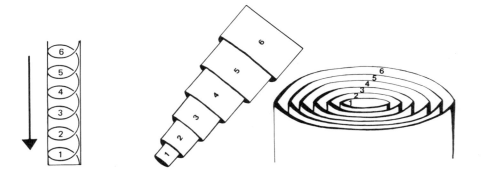

Model   A   Model   B

Figure 2.4. Developmental models of two alternative conceptualizations of the relationship between developmental stages or levels of organization, each entailing a different view of regression. The downward arrow in Model A represents the view of regression as a downward movement to successively earlier stages. In Model B, development is represented as a telescope of expanding structurally interrelated circles. The view of regression associated with this model cannot be rendered pictorially but entails a weakening of the structural ties between levels of organization.

ism's experience, the earlier stages are not systematically and structurally incorporated within the higher forms of organization. Given this view of development, regression becomes a simple downward movement from one stage to the next lower stage and so on. Inasmuch as Freud did not define the sequence of psychosexual stages in terms of the structure of mental operations, this view of development and thus of regression coincides with Freud's general position.

An alternative view of development with different implications regarding the nature of regression is represented in Model B of Figure 2.4. Rather than being rendered as a series of discrete steps or stages, development is represented in this model as a telescope of expanding circles. The earlier stages or the inner circles in this telescope model do not disappear or become of minor relevance as later stages (the expanding outer circles) emerge. They are structurally contained within and subordinated to the higher modes of functioning. Regression, therefore, involves not the abandonment of higher modes of operation, but a weakening of the structural ties whereby earlier forms are integrated with, and function in the service of, higher modes of operation. In regard to psychopathology, this alternative model seems preferable in that it not only recognizes the disorganization in psychosis but provides a framework that more easily allows the mature functioning displayed even by severely symptomatic patients to be recognized and accounted for. Moreover, by employing this model, the primitive thought evidenced in psychosis can be related to the mental operations of other individuals and to aspects of the creative process.

This view of psychotic disorganization as reflecting a disintegration in hierarchical structuring is highly consistent with Werner's (1957) position and especially with his view of development as involving the progressive integration of multiple modes of operation. Both Werner (1948, 1957) and his students (e.g., Langer, 1969) have at times conceptualized psychopathology as involving a "breaking down of superordinative regulative centers, thereby admitting genetically lower systems into independent activity" (Langer, 1969, p. 180). This model has also been applied to the issue of creative expression through the assumption that the creative individual is distinguished by a "wider . . . range of operations in terms of developmental level" (Werner, 1957, p. 145). Despite these assertions, however, Werner has, in the same writings (Werner, 1948, 1957), discussed regression as the backward movement to developmentally earlier forms that are similar to, but not identical with, children's mental operations. This latter model is the one primarily adhered to in the Rorschach research reviewed previously, and it has also been extended to psychopathology more generally (Goldman, 1962).

Thus, while we are in complete agreement with one model of regression suggested by Werner, we are in disagreement with the other. Werner simultaneously discussed regression in terms of two models whose implications differ. As a result of this confusion and given the connotations of the term *regression,* people have frequently interpreted Werner's meaning as reflecting only the simpler and older view of regression as a movement backward to ontogenetically prior states.

In addition to its manifestations in psychopathology, primitive cognition has been regarded as an intrinsic mechanism in the creative process. Among the similarities that have been noted (e.g., Arieti, 1976; Barron, 1969; Kris, 1952) between schizophrenic thinking and aspects of the creative process are: (a) manifestations of primary-process thinking; (b) the frequent expression of ideas and feelings in imagery; (c) what Arieti (1976) has described as the assumption of identity based upon similarity, that is, based upon identical predicates rather than identical subjects; and (d) a dedifferentiation of the word as symbol from the object it represents. These similarities and also some evidence of a genetic link between predisposition to schizophrenia and creativity have raised intriguing questions about the relationship between schizophrenia and creativity.

However, the differences between the two conditions are substantial. Unlike schizophrenia, creative expression involves discipline and appropriate adaptation to reality. Creative work is often accompanied by a sense of social responsibility (Arieti, 1976; Barron, 1969; Rosner & Abt, 1970), and ultimately it must be publicly communicable, "something that . . . ordinary thinking will understand, accept, and appreciate" (Arieti, 1976, p. 4). "The artist familiarizes us with our own being and reveals experiences we share with others. The world of the schizophrenic is not beyond anything; it is a closed frame of internal references without prospective truth value" (Muscari, 1979, p. 377). Finally, while the schizophrenic may display limited competence even in everyday functioning, "great creativity is responsible for humanity's greatest achievements and social progress" (Arieti, 1976, p. 10).

Inasmuch as both these conditions, despite vast dissimilarities, involve the noticeable presence of primitive mechanisms in adult thought, an explanatory principle that extends to both seems desirable. The concept of regression as a backward movement or return to ontogenetically prior modes of operation does not seem adequately to fit current thinking about the nature of the creative process. Far more fitting appears to be the view of development as involving the progressive reintegration and thus subordination of earlier modes of functioning to higher structures. The simultaneous operation of lower and higher forms of functioning (or of primary- and secondary-process mechanisms) has been widely described as the distinguishing feature of the creative process. Koestler (1964) refers to this concurrent operation of multiple levels of functioning as bisociation. Barron (1969) describes this multilevel functioning in terms of shifting patterns of defusion and integration sustained by enduring attention, while Arieti (1976) describes the tertiary process, which involves a "magic synthesis" of primary- and secondary-process mechanisms. Kris's (1952) concept of regression in the service of the ego expresses a somewhat similar view. Nevertheless Arieti (1976) criticizes the psychoanalytic approach for its emphasis on motivation and insufficient attention to structure, and he questions Kris's use of the term *regression:* "The use of the primary process is not necessarily to be viewed as a manifestation of regression but as an emerging accessibility or availability which is connected with regression only occasionally" (Arieti, 1976, p. 24). While Arieti acknowledges that his differences with Kris may be semantic, this only underscores the confusion about the meaning of the term *regression* that we discussed earlier.

When development is viewed as involving the availability of multiple modes of operation subordinated to and thus under the control of higher functions, the creative process can be understood as involving the "simultaneous activation" (Arieti, 1976, p. 51) of various levels of functioning. The very substantial differences between creativity and schizophrenia can be accounted for, while at the same time the similarities in the two forms of functioning are recognized. In creativity, the earlier forms are integrated with, subserve, and enhance higher functioning, whereas in schizophrenia the earlier forms break through, become dislodged from higher structures, and thus serve no purpose beyond their own expression.

Findings reported by Hersch (1957) utilizing the developmental scoring of the Rorschach are consistent with this position. In comparison with a normal sample, highly creative artists were found to be characterized both by the greater availability of relatively primitive cognitive–perceptual operations and by a much greater emphasis on more mature cognitive forms. This work, which was carried out within the Clark University–Worcester State Hospital complex, appears to reflect Werner's alternative emphasis regarding regression.

Observations concerning the functions of imagery and developmental changes in the use of imagery are also consonant with the model of development as a progressive reintegration of multiple modes of operation. There is an imaginativeness in the artistic expression of preschool children that bears a resemblance to the work of creative artists but that tends to disappear at about the time the child enters school. Gardner (1980) has suggested that this disappearance may be due to the burgeoning of linguistic skills that occurs at this point in development. With greater linguistic resources, the nonverbal medium is less necessary as a means of expression and communication. Yet, creative art utilizes similar forms of expression. "Once I drew like Raphael, but it has taken me a lifetime to draw as a child" (quoted from Picasso, by Gardner, 1980). Similarly, synesthesia, which is common in early childhood, tends to be lost with age and to be largely vestigial in adulthood except for its appearance in schizophrenic thought and creative expression. Why should such imagery and iconic representation become submerged during ontogenesis? And if, in addition to childhood thought, it tends to appear in schizophrenic thought and creative expression, how are these various uses of imagery to be distinguished? Marks (1975) has proposed an explanation in regard to synesthesia that corresponds closely with Gardner's (1980) suppositions concerning children's art. Synesthesia represents one mode of information processing. "One of its special roles is to summarize important cognitive distinctions in a convenient and economical way. . . . The cross-modal corresondences between and among the senses serve to highlight, in a convenient manner, important dimensions held in common" (Marks, 1975, p. 325). Nevertheless, synesthetic cognition represents a primitive mode of organization that is diffuse or imprecise, inflexible, and concrete. Thus Marks suggests that it is superseded by a more flexible mode of organization, namely, abstract language and symbolic thought, and becomes somewhat vestigial in adulthood. Eidetic imagery represents another example of visual concrete information processing that is found more frequently in young children and tends to disappear as development progresses. Again, however, vestiges of this form of functioning can be seen in adulthood when, for example, a person has a clear image of where on a page a passage is to be found. Recall of the passage is not visual, but recall of the location is.

However, in conjunction with higher integrating functions, the special characteristics of image representation play a crucial role in the creative process. Whereas conceptual thought functions to classify and regularize events and, in making the world predictable, has necessary survival value, such functioning by its very nature precludes that awareness of the unique and the novel that is essential in creativity. Imagery not only provides a fresh view of the object unencumbered by "ready-made associations and worn-out meanings" (Barron, 1969, p. 172), but allows a rapid shifting of focus and a flow of associations whereby new possibilities become open to thought (Arieti, 1976). Unlike schizophrenic thinking and image representation in childhood, the new views and possibilities that imagery provides are in the creative process integrated with and scrutinized by the more abstract, rational, or secondary-process cognitive modes. Findings (e.g., Kinsbourne, 1982; Milner, 1974) that information is processed differently in the right (visual–spatial) and left (verbal–conceptual) cerebral hemispheres underscore the permanence throughout life of both modes of information processing. What changes with development is the manner in which the two modes of functioning are organized and integrated.

Research on individuals vulnerable to schizophrenia has provided some evidence of a possible genetic link between predisposition to schizophrenia and creativity (Bleuler, 1974; Heston & Denney, 1968; Karlsson, 1966, 1974; McNeil, cited in Garmezy, 1971). While this evidence is suggestive rather than conclusive (Garmezy, 1971), Cancro (1979) has advanced an interesting formulation that by extension points to attentional regulation as a possible mediating characteristic in the relationship between schizophrenia and creativity.

In reviewing the evidence for the existence of a genetic factor in the transmission of schizophrenia, Cancro has argued that what is transmitted is probably a general psychological characteristic and not a specific predisposition to schizophrenia. The psychological characteristic that he nominates as the more likely candidate is an unusual form of attentional regulation. Such a characteristic does not predispose the individual to psychosis, but if the person becomes psychotic, it suggests that the psychosis will be manifested in a particular way. "People who are different in health are very likely to be different in psychosis" (Cancro, 1979, p. 457). By way of extending this formulation, the divergent thinking that has generally been recognized in creative individuals may reflect a mode of attentional regulation that is also manifested in the overinclusive thinking that characterizes certain forms of schizophrenia. Again, while schizophrenic and creative thought may reflect a common propensity to rapidly shifting associations, the distinguishing feature appears to be the degree to which these earlier genetically predetermined forms are integrated within higher conceptual operations. The speculation that a similar combination of genetic factors may predispose individuals to a style of thinking that on the one hand may be manifested in the disordered attention of schizophrenia but on the other hand might give rise to the divergent thinking that characterizes the creative process has relevance also to the Darwinian evolutionary view. In light of the assumption that adaptive forms tend to be perpetuated in the evolutionary process, why has schizophrenia, which seems so clearly maladaptive, continued to be so prevalent? If the genetic underpinnings are not for a specific disorder but rather ones that permit highly creative thought and expression, what has been perpetuated is not a maladaptive form but a characteristic that has been central to the development of the species.

SUMMARY

The developmental approach to psychopathology derives most directly from the organismic–developmental position of Heinz Werner, although other developmental theorists also influenced the work. In the individual's transactions with the world, the greater differentiation and hierarchical organization, presumed to characterize all development, should lead to greater flexibility, more capacity for planning, and a wider range of response alternatives. In this sense, then, greater coping potential should characterize developmentally higher functioning. Development is also characterized by a shift from expression in direct action to mediated verbal and symbolic responses. As development proceeds, earlier modes of functioning are presumed not to be lost but to be subordinated to and integrated within higher-level structures.

Work on developmental-level scoring of the Rorschach represents an early application of organismic–developmental principles to psychopathology. While this work yielded important findings, the use of Rorschach scores to assess developmental variations in adulthood has a number of limitations. Rorschach scoring concentrates on cognitive–perceptual functioning and focuses on structural similarities between the responses of young children and those of disordered adults.

Within the developmental approach to psychopathology, developmental level is broadly defined as representing no less than the total information-processing system utilized by the individual in mediating all behaviors. This developmental-level construct is presumed to apply to both adaptive and maladaptive functioning. In contrast to interpretations that view psychopathology as representing a general regression to earlier forms, we assume that individuals continue to maintain their position on the developmental continuum even after they are adjudged psychopathological. For every maturity level, there are presumed to exist both effective patterns of adaptation and pathological deviations from these patterns.

Our interpretation of regression is that it represents a weakening of the structural ties by means of which developmentally lower forms are subordinated to and controlled by developmentally higher levels of functioning. This view of regression can be contrasted with positions that define regression as involving the abandonment of higher modes of operation. Consistent with our views are observations that mature forms of functioning can be found even in severely disordered patients. Furthermore, the view of regression as involving a dislodging of developmentally earlier forms from developmentally more advanced and superordinate structures provides a framework that can encompass both the similarities and the essential differencess between schizophrenic thought and creative expression.

CHAPTER 3

Premorbid Social Competence

The fundamental tenets of the organismic view of development have now been presented. In applying these principles to adult psychopathology, the issue is how to translate the broad organismic perspective into a concept system that both is relevant to major phenomena of clinical interest and permits the derivation of hypotheses that are as open to disproof as to proof.

A persistent problem has been the question of how to measure developmental level when the construct is broadly conceptualized as including social, emotional, and motivational as well as cognitive components and when the differentiation of levels of adult functioning is of primary concern. When one is applying the developmental approach to adult behavior, measurement issues cannot be bypassed by using chronological age as an external, albeit indirect, referent for the developmental-level construct. Although Piaget, Werner, and other developmentalists have provided us with a number of measures to gauge developmental level in cognitive and perceptual functioning occurring between early infancy and adolescence, these measures are only minimally relevant to the developmental tasks of adulthood. The Rorschach research previously described reveals the difficulties encountered when behaviors characteristic of young children are employed as developmental indictors in adulthood. It is this practice applied to pathological adults that appears to have given rise to the common view that pathology is best conceptualized as a general regression to an immature or developmentally low level of functioning (Goldman, 1962; Lidz, 1978).

THE ZIGLER-PHILLIPS PREMORBID SOCIAL COMPETENCE INDEX

Rationale

Central from the outset of the work on the developmental approach to adult psychopathology was the commitment to a positive view of development with emphasis placed on adaptive processes even in the midst of pathology. This commitment required that the developmental measures employed be pertinent to coping effectiveness in everyday functioning. Yet, given the negative view that has pervaded much clinical thinking, conceptions of adaptive behavior were and tend to remain vague, abstract, and insufficiently tied to observable behavior. Greater progress seems to have been made in operationalizing maladaptive functioning than in defining those behaviors that characterize adaptive functioning in the typical adult.

Recent efforts particularly by Loevinger (for thoughtful and informed reviews of her work as well as that of other stage theorists such as Kohlberg see Hauser, 1976; Loevinger & Knoll, 1983; Loevinger & Wessler, 1970; Loevinger, Wessler, & Redmore, 1970) and Vaillant (1971, 1977) represent important advances in the application of developmental principles to adaptive functioning in adulthood. The developmental views embodied in these efforts are in many ways compatible with our own. Vaillant's findings (e.g., 1975, 1978) with a sample of men selected for psychological health will, in fact, be considered later in this chapter because of the parallels between his measures and findings and our own work. At the outset of the work on the developmental approach to psychopathology, such gauges of developmental level were not available. Furthermore, the efforts of Loevinger and Vaillant, while they clearly emphasize adaptive functioning, have to date been seldom applied to the study of disordered groups (Noam et al., 1984). Finally, the work on the developmental approach to adult psychopathology required that a measure be devised that would permit reliable scoring for large numbers of individuals based on case record data. As Strauss and Harder (1981) pointed out, if problems in reliability can be minimized, the case record method is particularly valuable for initial steps in hypothesis testing because of the large amount of information provided.

Zigler and Phillips (1960, 1961c) felt that the developmental-level construct was too broad and contained too many facets to permit a direct, simple, and practical single measure. For reasons discussed in Chapter 2, Rorschach developmental scores were rejected as too narrow to be employed as a total indicator of developmental level whose effects permeate the individual's personality (including traits and systems of defenses) and social functioning. Zigler and Phillips chose to measure instead the individual's premorbid social competence, which was conceptualized as a broad though imperfect benchmark of maturity level.

In devising the index, Zigler and Phillips attempted to establish molar measures whereby various dimensions important to effective coping in adult life could be assessed. The selection of particular indexes to serve as broad though imperfect benchmarks of personal and social maturity was guided by a number of considerations. As Phillips (1968a) indicated, it was important that the tasks chosen be fairly universal-in our society and thus applicable to the majority of individuals. A second criterion was that the behaviors be overt and thus able to be assessed in a relatively objective, easily quantifiable manner. In order to be able to rate as many individuals as possible along these dimensions, it was also necessary that the indexes measure aspects of functioning that are routinely recorded in psychiatric case histories. Finally the behaviors chosen had to be ones that could reasonably be taken to reflect personal and social maturity. Based on these criteria, six variables thought to be indicative of the individual's cognitive, interpersonal, and social functioning were selected. The premorbid competence score was obtained by examining the patient's placement on each of the variables of age, intelligence, education, marital status, occupation, and employment history. Each of these six variables was divided into three categories with each category conceptualized as representing a step along a social competence continuum. Zigler felt that each of these measures had a considerable margin of error and none taken in isolation would be a particularly good indicator of developmental level. The hope was that the general pattern of scores as reflected in the mean of the six variables would be a broadly derived, reliable assessment of that most ubiquitous construct in developmental thought, developmental level. Table 3.1 presents the scoring categories for each premorbid competence variable. The rationale for the selection and scoring of each variable is discussed in the following section. It should be noted, however, that some of the premorbid competence categories have recently been rescaled. This rescaling is discussed later in the chapter and summarized in Table 3.2.

The Component Variables of the Premorbid Competence Index

Age

While age is admittedly an indirect measure of developmental status, development does proceed over time. In terms of personal and social functioning, the average 40-year-old must be seen as more mature than the average 20-year-old. An exception concerns cognitive development as traditionally measured. For nonretarded individuals, IQ scores asymptote at about 16–20 years. Similarly, on Piagetian and other cognitive reasoning tasks, improved functioning has seldom been noted beyond adolescence. The absence of measurable cognitive changes in adulthood and the traditional emphasis of developmental stage theories on cognition may have contributed to the historical focus by developmental psychology on childhood and adolescence.

The emerging emphasis on life-span development has led to the more prominent consideration of noncognitive tasks. As Loevinger and Knoll (1983) and Neugarten (1979) pointed out, some theorists (e.g., Levinson, 1978) have given greater emphasis to changes with age in the nature of life demands that then require internal redefinitions, while others (e.g., Kohlberg, 1969; Vaillant, 1971, 1977) have concentrated more on internal changes. Despite some differences in emphasis, common themes can be stated. New and more complex demands are made on the individual at each successive stage in the life cycle. From adolescence through adulthood, less is done for the individual and more is expected, in terms of an increased responsibility first for the self and then for a widening circle of others. Certainly this is the sequence underlying Erikson's (1950) delineation of life crises from adolescence through much of adult life (identity, intimacy, generativity). A similar succession of stages involving person independence, commitments to others, and the progressive assumption of responsibility for others has been identified by Levinson (1978). Vaillant's (1975, 1978) longitudinal study of males selected for high potential for success provided particlarly compelling evidence for the broadening of generativity and the widening of responsibilities in individuals of 45 or older, the highest age category employed by Zigler and Phillips.

TABLE 3.1. The Premorbid Competence Index, Original Version

Variable	Categories Ordered from Low to High
1. Age	24 years and below; 25–44 years; 45 years and above
2. Intelligence	IQs obtained on a standard intelligence test of 84 or less; 85–115; 116 and above
3. Education	None or some grades including ungraded or special classes; finished grade school, some high school, or finished high school; 1 year of college or more
4. Marital Status	Single; separated, divorced, remarried, or widowed; single continuous marriage
5. Occupation[a]	Unskilled or semiskilled; skilled and service; clerical and sales or professional and managerial (categorized using the *Dictionary of Occupational Titles*, U.S. Government Printing Office, 1965)[b]
6. Employment history[a]	Usually unemployed; seasonal, fluctuating, frequent shifts, or part-time employment; regularly employed

Note: For each variable, placement in the lowest category results in a score of 0 for that index; in the middle category, a score of 1; and in the highest category, a score of 2. Only patients who receive ratings on at least three of the six premorbid competence variables are included in any sample. The overall premorbid competence score for each person is the mean of the scores obtained on the individual variables. Thus the final premorbid competence score for any patient can range from 0 (the patient falls into the lowest category on every variable for which information is available) to 2 (the patient falls into the highest category on every variable for which information is available).

[a]Occupation and employment history scores are based upon a period of at least 2 years and up to 10 years prior to hospitalization, depending upon the person's availability for employment. If a person has been available for work for less than 2 of these years (e.g., the person kept house full time, was a student or in military service), occupation and employment history are not scored.

[b]In the earliest version, the *Dictionary of Occupational Titles*, U.S. Government Printing Office, 1949, was used.

In addition to the changing and progressively more challenging nature of life demands that confront individuals as they move through the adult life cycle, internal changes involving greater maturity in adaptive ego mecha-

TABLE 3.2.   The Premorbid Competence Index, Rescaled

Variable	Categories Ordered from Low to High
Age	Unchanged from original version (see Table 3.1)
Intelligence	IQs obtained on a standard intelligence test of 84 and below; 85–114; 115 and above
Education	Less than high school graduation; high school or trade school graduate; 1 year of college or more
Marital status	Single; separated, divorced, or remarried; single continuous marriage, including widowed individuals if the marriage ended with the death of the spouse and the individual either did not remarry or remarried without later separation or divorce
Occupation[a]	Unskilled or semiskilled manual work requiring no specific prior training; skilled manual, service, or clerical–sales work requiring specific prior training; skilled technical, major or minor professional, or managerial, based on the previous 5 years
Employment history[a]	Employed less than 50% of the time; employed more than 50% but less than 90% of the time; employed at least 90% of the time, based on the previous 5 years

Note: As in the original version, for each variable placement in the lowest category results in a score of 0; in the middle category, a score of 1; and in the highest category, a score of 2. The overall premorbid competence score is the mean of the scores obtained on the individual variables. A patient must receive ratings on at least three of the six premorbid competence variables to be included in a sample.

[a]Time spent as a student is included for scoring employment history but not occupation. If a person has not been available for work during the entire 5-year period (e.g., the person kept house full time), neither occupation nor employment history is scored. If a person has been available for work for only part of the 5-year period, the scoring of occupation and employment history is based only upon the time actually spent in the job market.

nisms and a wider perspective occasioned by more varied role taking have been described by Vaillant (1977) and Kohlberg (1969). In a sample examined longitudinally, more differentiated perceptions of humans were found to characterize Rorschach resonses at age 30 as compared with those given in the late teenage years (Blatt et al., 1976). With respect to psychopathology, we have found striking differences in the characteristic symptom pictures displayed by younger and older psychiatric inpatients (Glick, Zigler, & Zigler, 1985). Along with other investigators, we have found paranoid status in schizophrenia to be associated with older age upon first hospitalization (Zigler & Levine, 1981a).

Intelligence

Intelligence has been defined as adaptation (Piaget, 1951). As Zigler and Trickett (1978) indicated, IQ scores are most fruitfully viewed as polyglot samples of behavior that are influenced by a variety of motivational and/or personality variables rather than as pure measures of formal cognition. It is this conception of intelligence that explains the success of IQ test performance as a longitudinal predictor of personal adjustment (Haan, 1963; Kohlberg et al., 1972). Moreover, whatever combination of motivational factors and cognitive capacities is reflected in IQ scores, findings that schizophrenic patients with higher IQs are first hospitalized at an older age, remain hospitalized for shorter periods of time, and are rehospitalized less frequently than their lower-IQ counterparts (Heffner, Strauss, & Grisell, 1975; Offord & Cross, 1971) are consistent with the view that IQ scores reflect capacities that are related to coping effectiveness. Accordingly, an estimate of intellectual functioning comprises the second variable in the social competence index. IQs obtained on standard intelligence tests are divided into three categories representing below-average (84 or less), average (85–115), and above-average (116 or above) functioning.

The categorization of intelligence on the Zigler-Phillips index is thus psychometric rather than being based on qualitative measures of levels of cognitive organization of the type employed by Piaget. The use of a psychometric gauge of intellectual functioning was necessitated both by the relative absence of qualitative measres (e.g., Piagetian tests) applicable to adult functioning and by the requirement that the social competence indexes be derivable from routine case history records in a mental hospital. Nevertheless, substantial correlations have consistently appeared between IQ scores and Piagetian measures. The commonalities between the two approaches have been cogently discussed by Elkind (1969). Particularly pertinent is the observation that qualitatively different levels of functioning are reflected in the succession of items on IQ tests. Mental age (MA) serves as a psychometric indicator of attained level of cognitive performance, reflecting the level of mental ability of the average child at a particular chronological age (CA). The IQ score is a measure of the rate of mental growth rather than of the level of cognitive functioning attained. At the same CA level, MA and IQ are perfectly correlated. Inasmuch as intellectual growth becomes asymptotic at about 16–20 years, individuals over the age of 16 are considered similar in CA for purposes of IQ scoring. Thus for adults IQ can serve as a benchmark of MA. Although intellectual growth becomes asymptotic at 16–20 years, the level at which mental growth approaches a plateau varies across individuals. These differences in cognitive complexity are reflected in IQ scores (Zigler, 1969). As Figure 3.1 illustrates, the level of the asymptote is higher for individuals whose rate of mental development was more rapid prior to ages 16–20.

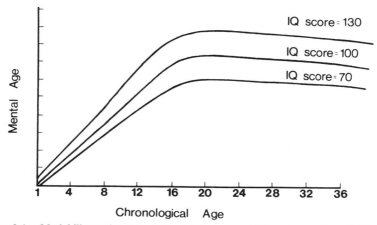

Figure 3.1. Model illustrating the relationship between childhood mental age (MA), rate of intellectual growth during childhood, and IQ score after intellectual growth asymptotes at 16–20 years.

Finally, it is important to note that, although IQ was originally included as one of the six premorbid competence variables, this variable has frequently been omitted in calculating premorbid competence due to the unavailability of IQ scores (e.g., Glick & Zigler, in press; Levinson & Campus, 1978; Turner & Zabo, 1968; Zigler, Glick, & Marsh, 1979; Zigler & Levine, 1981b; Zigler, Levine, & Zigler, 1977).

Education

The third variable, education, further reflects the adaptive use of intelligence, presupposing a stronger motivational component than would be expected to be reflected in IQ test performance. The continuation of education requires a degree of perseverance and some ability to delay gratification. As Zigler and Trickett (1978) note, the correlation between IQ and educational performance tends to be about .70. For these reasons, Zigler and Trickett recommended that molar measures such as high school graduation be interpreted as reflecting social competence and employed to evaluate the long-term effectiveness of Head Start and other intervention programs for economically disadvantaged preschool children. A number of findings concerning the effects of such intervention programs attest to a degree of separability between measured intellectual capacity and commonly achieved levels of educational attainment. For example, few studies have reported long-term gains in IQ scores or on standard measures of linguistic ability for children participating in Head Start or other preschool intervention programs. By contrast, a number of investigators have reported that in comparison to control subjects Head Start graduates are more likely to be in the correct grade for their age and less likely to be in special classes (U.S Department of Health and Human Services, 1980). Similar findings were reported by Seitz, Rosenbaum, and Apfel (1985), who also noted substantially higher school absenteeism for control children who had not been involved in the early intervention program. In addition, these investigators observed that, whereas low IQ primarily determined the later need for special services for children who had been in the early intervention program, control subjects, even of average IQ, were likely to receive such services, due to behavioral and motivational problems. One conclusion from these early intervention studies is that the attainment of expected levels of education reflects not only intellectual endowment but also motivational and personality variables associated with social competence. Lower educational levels, school failure, and truancy have been associated with poor adjustment in longitudinal studies of delinquent or predelinquent youth (Glueck & Glueck, 1968; Robins, 1966). The importance of motivational factors in the education measure is underscored by the robust relationship discovered between school truancy and adult maladjustment (Robins, 1970) as well as by Robins's observation that "truancy was as powerful a deterrent to high school graduation as was low IQ" (p. 237). Furthermore, in psychiatric samples, a consistent finding has been that patients with higher levels of education are more likely to utilize and persevere in outpatient treatment (Brandt, 1965; Luborsky et al., 1971; Salokangas, 1978).

The three levels of education originally employed by Zigler and Phillips (1960) in the scoring of premorbid competence are presented in Table 3.1. Because high school graduation is now commonplace, the education variable has been rescaled. This revised scaling is presented in Table 3.2 of this chapter.

The final three social competence variables, marital status, occupation, and employment history, reflect the major dimensions of adult functioning designated by Freud as *lieben* and *arbeiten*, which have subsequently been utilized in almost all definitions of adult adjustment.

Marital Status

The selection of marital status as a statistical indicator of interpersonal maturity was based on a number of considerations. Marital status constitutes an objective criterion that can be reliably scored from case history records. Marriage is a major task and event in adult life that despite changing values and life-styles is a widely endorsed and socially valued behavior. Most individuals expect to marry and do so. Finding a spouse requires a degree of social participation and interpersonal competence. Finally, marriage carries with it the intention of intimacy and of commitment in an enduring and responsible relationship. These qualities of stability and commitment and of intimacy and personal responsibility for the other have long been considered to be hallmarks of interpersonal maturity.

Empirical relationships between marital status and other aspects of interpersonal competence have consistently appeared in both pathological and nonpathological samples. Furthermore, for both types of individuals, marital status has been found to be a potent prognostic indicator. In schizophrenic samples, marital status has been found to be highly correlated with total scale scores on measures of premorbid adjustment whose items include a variety of aspects of interpersonal functioning, for example, the Elgin (Wittman, 1941, revised by Becker, 1956), the Phillips (Phillips, 1953), the Kantor (Kantor, Wallner, & Winder, 1953), and the Ullmann-Giovannoni (Ullmann & Giovannoni, 1964) measures (Garfield & Sundland, 1966; Meichenbaum, 1966). More favorable outcomes for married patients have been consistently demonstrated in schizophrenia research (e.g., Klorman, Strauss, & Kokes, 1977), and similar findings have been noted in samples that have included nonschizophrenic psychiatric patients (Crago, 1972; Ferber et al., 1967; Fulton &Lorei, 1967; Lewinsohn, 1967; Mannino & Shore, 1974; Orr et al., 1955). Even for patients with certain medical diseases (e.g., tuberculosis), married status has been associated with more rapid recovery (Berle et al., 1952; Holmes et al., 1961).

Even more pertinent to the developmental formulation are longitudinal findings obtained with normal subjects (Harvard undergraduates) selected on the basis of their apparently good adjustment and high potential for success (Vaillant, 1974, 1975, 1976, 1978). In this research, not only were marital stability and satisfaction related to later mental health status and work adjustment, but, even more important, the men with stable marriages demonstrated more extensive friendship patterns and more mature defensive structures. The finding that in this sample the majority of second marriages also ended in divorce was seen as a further indication that "divorce, however understandable it may be in an individual case, provides a statistical indicator of impaired capacity for object relations" (Vaillant, 1978, p. 657).

Whatever variables may determine a particular individual's marital status, there is considerable evidence to support the use of marital status as a statistical indicator of interpersonal competence. Nevertheless, one course for further development of the premorbid competence index would be to include other items that also assess social participation (e.g., friendships and social activities). As it now stands and as has been noted previously (Zigler et al., 1979; Zigler & Levine, 1981b; Zigler & Phillips, 1960), the Zigler-Phillips index tends to emphasize competence in instrumental role functioning to the relative neglect of items reflecting interpersonal competence.

A closer examination of the intermediate marital status category presented in Table 3.1 (separated, divorced, widowed) is also recommended. One change has been made regarding the category. Widowed individuals, if they do not experience a later separation or divorce, are now included in the highest marital status category (see Table 3.2). This change is consistent with Odegaard's (1953) finding that the rates of first hospital admission for married and widowed schizophrenics were similar and substantially lower than admission rates for either never-married or divorced schizophrenic patients. The adjustment status of divorced individuals also requires closer scrutiny. As Klorman et al. (1977) noted, the recent changes in sexual conventions may mean that divorced status is less valuable as an indicator of either maladjustment or a lack of involvement in heterosexual relationships. Earlier findings are contradictory regarding the adjustment status of divorced individuals. Crago (1972) reported a higher incidence of mental disturbance in divorced persons than in any other marital status group, and Garfield and Sundland (1966) found single and divorced women to be comparable on length of hospitalization measures. By contrast, Overall (1971) and Pokorny and Overall (1970) noted less severe disturbance (except on factors related to depression) in divorced patients than in other marital status groups and an even greater diminution of disturbance in multiple-divorce patients as compared with patients divorced only once. The contradictory nature of these findings, the changed cultural attitudes toward divorce, and the delineation by Overall (1971) and Pokorny and Overall (1970) of subgroups within the divorced category (e.g., single- vs. multiple-divorce) necessitate the empirical reexamination of correlates of divorced status. Any further alteration of the marital status scale would depend on results obtained from this reexamination.

Occupation

In normal samples, work adjustment has been found to be significantly correlated not only with measures of social adjustment, including marital status and marital satisfaction, but also with such indicators of personal adjustment as ego functioning, maturity of defenses, and absence of psychopathological disorder (Haan, 1969; Vaillant, 1974, 1975, 1976). The prognostic significance of work adjustment has been similarly established for psychiatric patients (e.g., Miller & Willer, 1976; Salokangas, 1978; Strauss & Carpenter, 1974b, 1977; Turner & Zabo, 1968) and for such other groups as clients in outpatient psychotherapy (Luborsky et al., 1971), individuals suffering from certain physical disorders (Berle et al., 1952), and delinquents (Glueck & Glueck, 1968).

Two aspects of work functioning were selected by Zigler and Phillips for inclusion in their index. These were (a) occupational level and (b) regularity of employment or employment history. Although they are interrelated, each aspect was assumed to be partially independent. Based upon Roe's (1956) analysis, occupational level appears to reflect the individual's skill and capability applied in the economic sphere and, even more centrally, the degree of responsibility demanded by the work. By contrast employment history appears to reflect more directly the individual's persistence in the application of skills (Phillips, 1968a) and to be less tied to the education variable (Roe, 1956).

The classification of occupational level was based primarily on Roe's (1956) research. As Roe indicated, failure in work (the inability to obtain or hold a job) is easy to assess. The difficulty lies in establishing criteria of occupational success. Roe originally categorized occupations into six levels with each level reflecting an increase in the skills required and the degree of personal responsibility demanded. Ordered from low to high these levels were (a) unskilled; (b) semiskilled; (c) skilled; (d) semiprofessional and small business; (e) lower-level professional and managerial; and (f) higher-level professional and managerial. These categories were combined and modified by Zigler and Phillips to yield the following three levels of classification: (a) unskilled or semiskilled; (b) skilled and service; and (c) clerical and sales or professional and managerial. The *Dictionary of Occupational Titles* (U.S. Government Printing office, 1949) was employed to place each occupation into the appropriate category.

With the collapsing of the distinctions between the higher occupational levels designated by Roe, the dependence of occupation on educational level could be somewhat diminished, and the scale was also rendered more appropriate to psychiatric populations that would be expected to contain fewer individuals of high occupational attainment. The inclusion of clerical and sales positions in the highest category in the Zigler-Phillips measure was intended to render the scale more applicable to women inasmuch as their educational and occupational opportunities were, at the time of the scale's construction, severely limited.

The attainment of higher occupational levels is certainly dependent upon education, and these two variables define socioeconomic status as traditionally measured. (The intercorrelations between education and occupation and the relationship of both to SES will be discussed later in the chapter.) Nevertheless, an individual with ample educational opportunities may not translate these into adult occupational achievement. In contrast to educational achievement where responsibility is primarily toward the self, higher levels of occupational attainment (e.g., physician, business manager, scientist) require a commitment, or at least an extension of the self toward the external world. The things produced and the tasks performed are directed toward others. Work involves cooperating with others and, at higher levels, frequently entails a high degree of responsibility for others. Finally, it is important to note that the recent rescaling of the Zigler-Phillips index (see Table 3.2) has involved a number of changes in the scoring of occupational level. Whereas the original scoring, described here, makes a clear distinction (in level 1 vs. 2) between blue-collar and white-collar work, the revised scaling places skilled technical work in the highest category. Thus emphasis is given to using skilled training in the work world rather than to the type of training received (e.g., technical school vs. liberal arts college). Individuals can come from a wider variety of educational backgrounds and still be placed in the highest occupational category. The downgrading of clerical and sales positions in the revised index both is consistent with a scaling that emphasizes the application of prior training and reflects the societal change in women's work opportunities from the time the scale was first developed.

Employment History

The second aspect of work functioning, employment history, is less tied to the education variable, as the factor-analytic results to be reported later in the chapter will indicate. An individual can be highly trained but display a sporadic work history due to limited motivation and lack of perseverance. By contrast an individual with limited educational opportunities can display steady employment due to perseverance, motivation, and reliability. A major characteristic of higher developmental functioning involves the incorporation of societal expectations and values, and a consequent social guilt if one fails to live up to these expectations. Although societies may differ in the amount of work expected, all societies expect that adults will work. Thus a major aspect of adult role definition is that one works and in so doing contributes to the society. People's accounts of their work, while they may include descriptions of negative aspects, also underscore the importance of work in defining the self as productive, contributing, and socially valued (Terkel, 1974). Strauss et al. (1981) have presented evidence of the importance of employment for psychiatric inpatients who derive a number of intrinsic rewards from employment, including the enhancement of self-esteem. In comparison with occupation, then, employment history implies a stronger motivational component. Given a greater internalization of societal standards, the developmentally advanced individual would be expected to display greater commitment in seeking and maintaining employment and to experience unemployed status as unacceptable. Employment history is not solely determined by the individual. However, across the vicissitudes of economic conditions, the developmentally advanced person should be more likely to get a job and remain employed.

The Rescaled Premorbid Competence Index

In the previous section, we discussed the rationales underlying each of the recent changes in the scaling of the component variables of premorbid competence. The revised scaling follows the procedure of Turner and Zabo (1968) and is presented in Table 3.2. This revised scale has been employed in two recent studies (Glick & Zigler, in press; Glick et al., 1985), both discussed in Chapter 9. Further research will continue to employ and examine the revised scale. In the two studies that have used this scaling, the relationships discovered between premorbid competence and other variables have been similar to those obtained with the original index. A task for future research will be the direct comparison of the original version and the revised premorbid competence index. As will be discussed later in the chapter, schizophrenic women have been found to obtain higher premorbid competence scores than men. This finding has been obtained using a variety of premorbid competence measures in addition to the Zigler-Phillips scale. One question that arises is whether the premorbid competence scores of schizophrenic women will remain as high, in comparison to those of schizophrenic men, since under the new scaling clerical and scales positions (traditional female occupations) have been downgraded.

Reliability and Validity of the Premorbid Competence Index

In light of the straightforward nature of the demographic variables comprising the premorbid competence index, it is not surprising that they can be reliably scored. With respect to the original version, interjudge agreement on age, education, marital status, occupation, and employment history has been reported at 99, 92, 94, 86, and 84 percent, respectively (Zigler et al., 1979). Similarly high rates of interjudge agreement have been found in other studies (e.g., Zigler & Levine, 1973, 1981b). With respect to the revised scaling, interjudge agreement assessed by means of the weighted kappa (Cohen, 1968) has been found to be 1.00, .95, .91, .88, and .87 for the variables of age, education, marital status, occupation, and employment history, respectively (Glick & Zigler, in press). Also of note is an apparent advantage in using case record data as compared with patient self-reports, at least for low competence individuals. Mylet, Styfco, and Zigler (1979) compared two sources of biographical data from which premorbid competence was rated—clinical charts and self-reports on a biographical information form. No conflicting information was found for high competence patients, but low competence patients tended to give inaccurate information about themselves. The inaccurate information given on the self-report measure was invariably in the direction of self-enhancement (e.g., claiming more years of education than actually achieved).

The overall premorbid competence index appears to have some face validity. Most would agree that a 45-year-old, high-IQ college graduate who is married and regularly employed in a profession represents a more mature person than a 22-year-old, low-IQ elementary school dropout who is unmarried and irregularly employed in an unskilled job. The construct validity of the overall premorbid competence index (which invariably proves to be a better predictor than any one of the component variables alone) has now been demonstrated in numerous studies. This premorbid competence measure has been found to be positively correlated with Rorschach developmental-level scores (Lerner, 1968) and with maturity in moral reasoning as assessed by Kohlberg's test (Quinlan, Rogers, & Kegan, 1980). The heuristic value of the scale has been firmly established by findings of significant relations between the level of premorbid competence and variables derived from the developmental formulations underlying the scale. Some of the variables that have been found to be associated with developmental level as measured by the Zigler-Phillips index include diagnosis (Glick & Zigler, in press; Glick et al., 1985; Zigler et al., 1979; Zigler & Phillips, 1961a), symptomatology and defenses employed (Draguns et al., 1970; Mylet et al., 1979; Phillips, Broverman, & Zigler, 1966; Phillips & Zigler, 1964; Sanes & Zigler,

1971; Zigler & Levine, 1973, 1983b; Zigler & Phillips, 1960, 1962), prognosis and psychiatric outcome (Glick & Zigler, in press; Glick et al., 1985; Marsh, Glick, & Zigler, 1981; Phillips & Zigler, 1964; Zigler et al., 1979; Zigler & Levine, 1981a; Zigler & Phillips, 1961b), the essential–reactive distinction in alcoholism (Blum & Levine, 1975; Levine & Zigler, 1973, 1981; Sugerman, Reilly, & Albahary, 1965), the paranoid–nonparanoid distinction in schizophrenia (Zigler & Levine, 1973, 1981a; Zigler, Levine, & Zigler, 1976; Zigler et al., 1977), magnitude of the individual's self-image disparity (Achenbach & Zigler, 1963; Mylet et al., 1979), and humor responses (Levine & Zigler, 1976). These studies will be reviewed in subsequent chapters devoted to each topic. Scores on the Zigler-Phillips index have also been found to be significantly correlated with total scale scores on a variety of other measures of premorbid adjustment (Held & Cromwell, 1968; Levinson & Campus, 1978; McCreary, 1974). Included in these studies have been the Elgin Prognostic Scale (Wittman, 1941, revised by Becker, 1959), the Phillips Prognostic Rating Scale (Phillips, 1953), the Defining Frame of Reference Scale (Kantor, Wallner, & Winder, 1953), the Zigler-Phillips Premorbid Social Competence Index (Zigler & Phillips, 1960), the Ullmann-Giovannoni Scale (Ullmann & Giovannoni, 1964), the Premorbid Asocial Adjustment Scale (Gittelman-Klein & Klein, 1969), and the UCLA Premorbid Adjustment Scale (Evans, Goldstein, & Rodnick, 1973), although each study considered only some scales and thus not all combinations of the scales listed have been compared.

Also consistent with the developmental position is mounting evidence that suggests (a) that premorbid social competence is best conceptualized as reflecting a unitary dimension rather than dichotomous (process and reactive) conditions (Becker, 1959; Garmezy, 1970; Higgins, 1964; Kantor & Herron, 1966; Zigler & Phillips, 1962) and (b) that this dimension is not uniquely applicable to schizophrenia but is predictably related to outcome and to other personality variables over a range of diagnoses that include affective disorders, personality disorders, and neuroses as well as certain physical illnesses (Achenbach & Zigler, 1963; Garmezy et al., 1979; Klorman et al., 1977; Mylet et al., 1979; Phillips, 1968a; Phillips et al., 1966; Zigler et al., 1979; Zigler & Phillips, 1961c, 1962).

What Does Premorbid Competence Measure?

While considerable support can be garnered for the developmental interpretation of premorbid social competence and despite the empirical success of the Zigler-Phillips scale (and of other indexes of premorbid adjustment as well), there is little consensus about what these scales measure and why they predict as well as they do. Reviewers have been unanimous in calling for far greater theoretical elaboration of the premorbid competence construct (Garmezy et al., 1979; Gittelman-Klein & Klein, 1969; Kokes, Strauss, & Klorman, 1977; Zigler et al., 1976; Zigler & Trickett, 1978). Social competence appears to be one of those constructs that are definable only in terms of other constructs whose own definitions are vague.

A number of interrelated issues require clarification. In the first place, as Held and Cromwell (1968) have suggested, the global construct of premorbid competence must be replaced by a more specific understanding of the component variables in premorbid adjustment measures. A broader question is whether premorbid competence is best conceptualized as defining a single dimension or, alternatively, more than one. The dimensionality issue takes on considerable significance in view of the fact that the Zigler-Phillips scale includes such conventional measures of socioeconomic status (SES) as education and occupation. The possibility has been raised (Nuttall & Solomon, 1965, 1970; Raskin & Golob, 1966; Turner & Zabo, 1968; Zigler & Child, 1973) that the predictive efficacy of the scale rests solely on its SES component. The studies to be reviewed in the next section will consider this dimensionality issue. The relationship of SES to premorbid competence will be considered both in that section and later in the chapter.

A far greater specification of the underlying conceptual dimensions assessed by premorbid competence measures is also required. The component indexes of social competence are themselves the outcomes of successful coping (Sundberg, Snowden, & Reynolds, 1978). "Educational achievements, friendships, sexual attachments and employment history record the statistics of one's adaptation" (Garmezy et al., 1979, p. 36). Much more needs to be known about the processes that underlie these attainments and thus mediate the relationships discovered between premorbid competence scores and other major variables of interest in psychopathology. Related to this issue is the question of how the social competence construct as it is employed in psychopathology relates to the usage of the construct in other areas of developmental research: in compensatory education, in the field of mental retardation, and in research on the developmental etiology of effectance motivation (Zigler & Trickett, 1978).

A final issue requiring clarification concerns the gender differences that have repeatedly appeared in premorbid competence scores, both with respect to the Zigler-Phillips index and on other measures of premorbid adjustment. This issue will be discussed later in this chapter.

INTERRELATIONSHIPS AMONG COMPONENT INDEXES OF PREMORBID SOCIAL COMPETENCE

In order to examine more closely what is being measured by the Zigler-Phillips scale, Zigler and Levine (1981b) investigated the interrelationships among the five most commonly employed indexes in the Zigler-Phillips measure—age, education, marital status, occupation, and employment history—using the case histories of three samples of schizophrenic patients: 295 (173 paranoid, 122 nonparanoid) VA hospital male, 300 (150 paranoid, 150 nonparanoid) state hospital male, and 300 (150 paranoid, 150 nonparanoid) state hospital female schizophrenic patients. Social competence was scored in the manner described previously and presented in Table 3.1.

Correlational analyses examined the relationship of each component index of the Zigler-Phillips measure to overall premorbid competence scores. Inasmuch as each of the premorbid competence variables was conceptualized as reflecting, although in an indirect and incomplete manner, the individual's underlying developmental level, the expectation was that scores on each component would be positively correlated with overall premorbid competence scores. This expectation was confirmed. Highly significant positive correlations appeared between each of the five component indexes and overall premorbid competence scores in each of the three samples examined (all 15 p's < .001).

In order to address the issue of whether the scale is best conceptualized as defining a single dimension or more than one, a principal components factor analysis was performed on each of the three groups' social competence score intercorrelations. The factors were submitted to an orthogonal varimax rotation, and the results of this rotation are presented in Table 3.3. For each of the three groups, the social competence scores were found to reflect three orthogonal factors. In all three groups, education and occupation (conventional measures of SES) were heavily loaded on a single factor. For both the VA male sample and the state hospital female sample, age and marital status heavily loaded on a second factor and employment history on a third factor. For the state hospital males, marital status and employment history loaded together while age comprised the third factor.

These results are consistent with the view of premorbid competence as multidimensional (Kokes et al., 1977; Salokangas, 1978), and they lend support to the assertion of Zigler and Phillips (Phillips, 1968a; Zigler & Phillips, 1960) that this premorbid social competence measure, while including social class (the education–occupation factor), is broader than SES (the other two factors discovered in each of the three samples). This issue will be discussed more fully later in the chapter.

To assess how much each of the five social competence indexes contributed to the unique variance in the overall social competence score, Zigler and Levine performed a stepwise multiple regression analysis on the inter correlations of the three groups combined. (Combining groups was dictated by highly similar findings when the groups were examined separately.) The contribution made by each of the five variables proved to be highly significant. The standardized coefficients (beta weights) for the five variables were .39, .38, .38, .34, and .23 for occupation, marital status, employment history, age, and education, respectively. The unique variances contributed to the overall score by the variables were .117, .117, .133, .102, and .041, respectively. Although significant, the contribution of the education score was markedly less than that of the other four scores. The smaller contribution of the education measure to overall competence appeared to have been due

TABLE 3.3. The Component Indexes of Premorbid Social Competence: Rotated Factor Loadings of Factors 1, 2, and 3 for Three Groups of Schizophrenic Patients

Index	VA Males			State Hospital Males			State Hospital Females		
	1	2	3	1	2	3	1	2	3
Age	.205	-.847	-.120	.107	.065	-.955	-.083	.810	-.188
Education	.857	.130	-.030	-.082	.874	.119	.813	-.123	.038
Marital status	-.247	-.753	.287	.727	-.172	-.380	.066	.784	.260
Occupation	.803	-.144	.167	.207	.830	-.205	.833	.102	.009
Employment history	.115	-.054	.957	.870	.233	.059	.028	.027	.967
Percent of total variance	30.8	28.0	18.4	35.4	28.2	16.6	27.9	26.3	19.8

Source: "Premorbid Competence in Schizophrenia: What Is Being Measured?" by E. Zigler and J. Levine, 1981b, *Journal of Consulting and Clinical Psychology 49.* Copyright 1981 by American Psychological Association. Adapted by permission of the authors.

to the relatively restricted range of the education scores. Given the increased amounts of schooling that have become typical in recent years, a rescaling of the educational variable was recommended. This rescaling has been accomplished and was presented in Table 3.2 earlier in the chapter.

A study by Glick, Marsh, and Zigler (1984) continued Zigler and Levine's (1981b) effort to illuminate the inherent nature of the Zigler-Phillips scale. As will be discussed in Chapter 9, a continuing controversy centers around the issue of whether the premorbid competence construct applies only to schizophrenia or whether, as the developmental position holds, premorbid competence reflects a general dimension of underlying coping effectiveness applicable to patients with various psychiatric diagnoses and even to nondisordered groups. Glick et al. (1984), therefore, examined the factorial structure of premorbid competence scores for nonschizophrenic as well as schizophrenic psychiatric patients.

This study was based upon an examination of the case history records of 381 male state hospital patients in four diagnostic groups: schizophrenia ($N = 92$), affective disorder ($N = 89$), neurotic ($N = 98$), and personality disorder ($N = 102$). Social competence was scored according to the criteria presented in Table 3.1. For the total patient sample and for each diagnostic group examined separately, principal components factor analyses were performed on each group's premorbid competence score intercorrelations. The factors were submitted to an orthogonal varimax rotation, and the results of this rotation are presented in Table 3.4.

Consistent with the results of Zigler and Levine (1981b), the premorbid competence scores of each of the four diagnostic groups were found to reflect three orthogonal factors. For schizophrenic and affective disorder patients as well as the total sample, the three factors discovered were identical to those found by Zigler and Levine in two of their three samples. That is, age and marital status loaded heavily on one factor, education and occupation on another, and employment history on the third factor. As can be seen in Table 3.4, slight deviations from this general pattern appeared for both nonpsychotic groups.

In a reanalysis of the Zigler and Levine (1981b) data, Tanaka and Bentler (1983) reported a two-factor social competence model based upon analysis of covariance rather than correlational matrices. Despite differences in the methods employed, the factorial structure obtained by Tanaka and Bentler is in many respects similar to the ones reported by Zigler and Levine (1981b) and Glick et al. (1984). One factor discovered by Tanaka and Bentler was again defined by the variables of education and occupation while the second factor was identified as a general social competence factor.

Over a range of diagnoses, a quite consistent factorial pattern has emerged that accords with the original proposal of Zigler and Phillips (1960) that the social competence measure may be conceptualized as reflecting at least two dimensions: a factor involving instrumental role functioning and the striving for personal advancement (education and occupation), and a

TABLE 3.4. Rotated Factor Loadings of Factors 1, 2, and 3 for the Total Patient Group and for Each Diagnostic Subgroup

Index	Total Patients			Schizophrenia			Affective Disorder		
	1	2	3	1	2	3	1	2	3
Age	.852	−.078	.156	−.034	.878	−.097	.852	.132	.122
Education	−.083	.902	−.072	.903	−.114	−.031	−.089	.876	−.081
Marital status	.865	.104	.085	.018	.835	.200	.860	.150	.049
Occupation	.134	.783	.320	.822	.111	.287	.108	.870	.080
Employment history	.176	.115	.957	.146	.057	.967	.123	.002	.989
Percent of total variance	37.8	28.2	14.8	34.6	30.3	16.6	32.8	31.1	17.6

Index	Neurotic Disorder			Personality Disorder		
	1	2	3	1	2	3
Age	.226	−.020	.917	.709	−.165	.422
Education	.200	.649	−.507	−.043	.946	.096
Marital status	.873	−.051	.118	.928	.080	.008
Occupation	.052	.935	.052	.124	.446	.693
Employment history	.769	.254	.075	.137	−.007	.882
Percent of total variance	34.7	29.8	14.1	39.8	24.9	14.8

factor of social participation (the marital status variable, most frequently paired with age).

UNRESOLVED ISSUES

Premorbid Social Competence and Socioeconomic Status

The factor-analytic research does not appear to support the possibility raised by some workers (Nuttall & Solomon, 1965, 1970; Raskin & Golob, 1966; Turner & Zabo, 1968; Zigler & Child, 1973) that the predictive efficacy of the premorbid competence scale derives solely from its overlap with socio-economic status (SES). More compatible with the data is the position that the premorbid competence measure while including a factor of social class is broader than SES.

Also mitigating against the argument that premorbid competence is reducible to SES are the inconsistent relations that have appeared between premorbid competence scores and measures of SES. Whereas Chapman and Baxter (1963) found that low SES was related to good premorbid adjustment, neither McCreary (1974) nor Raskin and Golob (1966) obtained significant relations between premorbid competence and SES. In contrast to these investigators, Allon (1971) employed the patient's own SES rather than parental SES to measure social class and found that low social class status was related to poor premorbid adjustment. Yet, since paternal or parental SES is less contaminated by the effects of the patient's psychiatric disorder, it may be the more appropriate measure (Klorman et al., 1977). Consistent with this assumption is McCreary's finding that, whereas the occupational levels of reactive schizophrenic patients were comparable to the occupational levels of their fathers, there was a significant downward drift in the occupations of process schizophrenics in comparison with their fathers. Wing (1978, 1980) has also discussed findings that suggest that the lower occupational status of disordered individuals rather than causing the disorder may reflect a downward drift arising as a consequence of the disorder. Also relevant is evidence cited by Phillips (1968a) for a higher correspondence between the patient's own SES and both the degree of psychiatric impairment and outcome than between paternal SES and these variables.

Furthermore, less consistent relationships have been found between SES and other variables of interest in psychopathology than between premorbid competence and the same variables. Unlike social competence, SES has not generally been found to predict either symptomatology (Raskin & Golob, 1966) or outcome (Klorman et al., 1977). The exception to this general pattern of findings concerns social class V. In contrast to membership in the other levels of SES, membership in this lowest group has been found to be highly discriminating both in terms of degree of impairment (Dohrenwend & Dohrenwend, 1965, 1974; Hollingshead & Redlich, 1958; King, 1978; Srole,

1975) and with regard to a host of other variables (Strauss, Kokes, Ritzler, Harder, & Van Ord, 1978). Finally, as will be discussed more fully in Chapter 11, SES has been found to be a moderator variable in premorbid competence–outcome relations (Farina, Garmezy, & Barry, 1963; Raskin & Golob, 1966) and in other predictor-criterion relationships in psychopathology (Clum, 1975).

A broader issue concerns the psychological meaning of social class. As Zigler and Child (1973) noted, when a psychologist is confronted with evidence that a sociological variable (e.g., social class or a particular dwelling zone within a city) is related to a psychological variable (e.g., particular forms of disturbed behavior), the psychologist does not feel that the relationship has been explained until it has been conceptualized as a set of psychological events that could cause the behavior being examined. At a psychological level of analysis, social class membership or residence within a particular zone of a city cannot be viewed as the cause of a higher prevalence of a particular form of disturbed behavior. Instead, some social–psychological concomitants of these sociological variables, such as particular forms of family interactions (e.g., Myers & Roberts, 1959) or the individual's personal isolation or lack of sufficient intimacy (e.g., Brown & Harris, 1978; Rose, 1955), are advanced as psychological mechanisms moderating the relationship between social status variables and resultant psychological events. A similar position was elaborated recently by Strauss (1979). Inasmuch as findings to be discussed in a number of subsequent chapters pertain to the relationship of socioeconomic status to psychopathology, this issue will be considered more broadly in Chapter 11.

Given the apparent complexity of social class influence, the routine analysis of SES has been recommended for research on premorbid competence (Klorman et al., 1977; Raskin & Golob, 1966). As regards the Zigler-Phillips index, future studies could easily employ factor scores to determine how much of the variance in correlates of interest is due to the SES factor (education and occupation) and how much to factors (e.g., age and marital status) we now know to be relatively independent of SES. Furthermore, such research could employ measures of parental SES rather than relying on the patient's social class alone.

In addition, research should focus specifically on social class V. In the studies concerned with the premorbid competence–SES relationship cited previously (Chapman & Baxter, 1963; McCreary, 1974; Raskin & Golob, 1966), membership in social class V was not separately categorized. Thus a potential relationship between social class V membership and premorbid social competence may have been obscured. In addition, differences across studies in the proportion of patients in the lowest social class may have contributed to the inconsistent findings. Differences in the premorbid adjustment measures employed also render the results of these various investigations noncomparable. Inasmuch as premorbid adjustment appears to be multidimensional, with the different scales emphasizing different facets of the construct (Kokes et al., 1977), relationships to social class might be expected to differ as a function of the premorbid social competence measure employed.

In inquiring into the relationship between premorbid social competence and SES, the question has been raised as to whether the individual's sociocultural nexus, as reflected in SES, primarily determines the level of premorbid competence achieved or vice versa (Held & Cromwell, 1968; Zubin & Spring, 1977). Based on the findings reviewed, an interactionist position seems most tenable. Within this framework, rather than viewing premorbid social competence as antecedent and social class as the product (or vice versa), both sets of variables would be assumed to interact continually. Thus both sets of variables would be both antecedents and products, rendering the search for an unidirectional influence of one variable upon the other inappropriate.

In keeping with this position, the appropriate research question becomes: To what degree does premorbid social competence vary, and what is the predictive efficacy of this variable when social class is held constant (or conversely, when premorbid social competence is held constant, to what degree does SES vary, and what is the predictive efficacy of this variance)? Phrasing this question another way, one can ask: What is the predictive value of premorbid social competence at different levels of SES? Inasmuch as social competence may be multidimensional, a further question is: Which components of premorbid competence vary as a function of SES and which components predict at different levels of SES?

Gender Differences in Premorbid Competence

The interpretation of gender differences in behavior remains highly problematic for developmentalists. Yet, as will become evident as the reader progresses through this book, highly consistent gender differences have been observed with respect to many major variables of clinical interest, for instance, symptoms, diagnosis, and prognosis. In order to incorporate these findings, the broader discussion of gender differences will be reserved for Chapter 11. Only the issue of social competence will be considered here.

Almost without exception and across a variety of scales, female schizophrenic patients have been found to obtain higher premorbid competence scores than males (DeWolfe, 1973; Farina, Garmezy, & Barry, 1963; Farina et al., 1962; Gittelman-Klein & Klein, 1969; Goldstein, 1978; Klorman et al., 1977; Lane, 1968; Lewine, 1981; Raskin & Golob, 1966; Rosen, Klein, & Gittelman-Klein, 1971; Salokangas, 1983; Zigler & Levine, 1981b, 1983a, 1983b; Zigler et al., 1977; Zigler & Phillips, 1960). Few studies have examined gender differences in the premorbid competence scores of nonschizophrenic patients. Lewine et al. (1980) and Phillips and Zigler (1964) found that women obtained higher premorbid competence scores than men in diagnostically heterogeneous samples that included schizophrenic, affective disorder, neurotic, and personality disorder patients selected with no gender restrictions. However, this finding was not replicated within particular diagnostic categories (e.g., affective disorder, personality disorder) when equal numbers of male and female patients were examined in each diagnostic category (Glick & Zigler, in press; Glick et al., 1985). Thus whether the gender difference found for schizophrenic patients holds within other specific diagnostic categories is not known and requires investigation.

The differential meaning of marital status and heterosexual activity for males versus females has been proposed as one explanation for the gender differences in the premorbid competence of schizophrenic patients. It has been argued (most forcefully by Farina and his colleagues—Farina et al., 1963; Farina et al., 1962) that compared to females, males must be more assertive in heterosexual relations, including getting married. The implication here is that there is a greater likelihood for low competence females to be married than for equally low competence males. As such, women's superiority in premorbid competence would be expected to be confined primarily to the marital status variable and marital status would be expected to be less highly correlated with overall competence scores in women than in men. Neither was found to be the case by Zigler and Levine (1981b). Compared to men, the women in their sample were older and had higher-level occupations and better employment histories. Furthermore, the marital status score for men was not more highly correlated with either the overall score or with scores on the other component variables than it was for women.

One potentially artifactual reason for the elevated premorbid competence scores of women resides in the questionable practice in the original Zigler-Phillips scale of assigning the highest occupation score to clerical and sales positions—occupations frequently held by women. Since this aspect of the occupation scale has now been revised, a critical test will be whether women's premorbid competence scores will contine to be higher than those of men. With regard to the early research, it is also possible that, because many of the women were housewives and thus not scored on either occupation or employment history, the premorbid competence measure was less sensitive to variations in women's functioning. Inasmuch as the majority of women are now employed outside the home, this difference in the applicability of the scale to men and women should be reduced.

The reason(s) that women have higher premorbid competence scores than men, therefore, remains a mystery. The different socialization experiences of women and men may contribute to the gender differences in premorbid competence scores (Rosen, Klein, & Gittelman-Klein, 1969; Zigler & Levine, 1981b; Zigler et al., 1977; Zigler & Phillips, 1960). With the exception of age, the variables in the Zigler-Phillips scale appear to be sensitive to the fulfillment of societal expectations by the individual. As Zigler and Phillips (1960) noted, women in our society may be subjected to far greater pressure for social conformity than men. These differences in socialization may be such that even when suffering from the schizophrenic process women display less overall disintegration and thus make a better social adjustment.

On the biological side we are aware that all women are genetically different from all men. Biological differences are most vividly seen in the longer life span of women. Although still somewhat controversial, considerable evidence has now been presented indicating differences in brain function between males and females (Bornstein & Matarazzo, 1982; Inglis & Lawson, 1982; MacLusky & Naftolin, 1981; McGlone, 1980). The possibility must be raised that the genetic differences between the two genders are such that women are genetically buffered against the insidious effects of the schizophrenic process and perhaps other disorders as well. A parallel to such a state of affairs may be found in the area of mental retardation. In a comprehensive investigation of the variations in intelligence, Pauls (1972) concluded that the same genotypes for intelligence resulted in different phenotypes in the two genders, with females displaying better phenotypes than males.

Underlying Personality Variables

Of utmost concern in every area of psychology in which the social competence construct has been employed is the need to specify the processes that underlie social competence and contribute to the predictive efficacy of the construct. The problems in accomplishing this have been the subject of many recent reviews (Garmezy et al., 1979; Sundberg et al., 1978; Zigler et al., 1976; Zigler & Trickett, 1978). When one moves beyond the demographic variables so commonly employed in the assessment of social competence, measurement often becomes difficult and conceptualization vague. The list of personality variables that could potentially contribute to the outcome of effective coping in life becomes unwieldy (e.g., Anderson & Messick, 1974), and it becomes difficult to determine a logical cutoff in an almost endless chain of potentially relevant factors.

Nevertheless a number of personality characteristics have quite consistently been put forward as factors that may influence competence functioning as defined by the attainment of both social and personal goals. These include: the self-image (Anderson & Messick, 1974; Garmezy et al., 1979; Sundberg et al., 1978; Zigler & Trickett, 1978); locus of control (Baumrind, 1975; Sundberg et al., 1978; Zigler & Trickett, 1978); formal cognitive ability and cognitive complexity (Phillips, 1968; Sundberg et al., 1978, Zigler & Trickett, 1978); a sense of effectance versus learned helplessness (Garmezy et al., 1979; White, 1959; Zigler & Trickett, 1978); impulse control (Jacobs et al., 1973; Sundberg et al., 1978); and a sense of social or moral responsibility (Baumrind, 1975; Phillips, 1968a). Each of these variables can be interpreted developmentally, and, for most, reliable measurement seems possible.

SUMMARY

Early in the work on the developmental approach to psychopathology, Zigler and Phillips (1960) chose premorbid competence as a molar indicator of the individual's underlying developmental level. The premorbid competence index comprises six component variables: age, intelligence, education, marital status, occupation, and employment history. While each of these variables has a considerable margin of error and none taken in isolation could be considered a particularly good indicator of developmental level, the hope was that in combination these variables could provide a broadly derived reliable assessment reflecting developmental differences between adult patients.

Premorbid competence continues to be employed as a major variable in our work. This chapter presented the original measure and the rationale for its construction as well as the revised scaling we have recently begun to employ. The premorbid competence measure has been found to be reliable and to have predictive validity. The issue of whether the premorbid competence scale is best conceptualized as defining a single dimension or more than one has been addressed in factor analyses of the premorbid competence scores of schizophrenic patients and patients in other diagnostic groups (affective disorder, neurotic, personality disorder). Over this range of diagnoses, a quite consistent factorial pattern has emerged that supports the original position of Zigler and Phillips (1960). The premorbid competence measure may be conceptualized as reflecting at least two dimensions: a factor involving instrumental role functioning and the striving for personal advancement, and a factor of social participation.

Despite the empirical success of the Zigler-Phillips scale and other premorbid competence instruments, there is little consensus about what these scales measure and what accounts for their predictive validity. The possibility has been raised that the predictive efficacy of the premorbid competence scale derives solely from its overlap with socioeconomic status (SES). However, factor analysis suggests that the premorbid competence measure, while including a factor of social class, is broader than SES. Other findings regarding premorbid competence and social class are reviewed, and the gender differences consistently found in premorbid competence research are discussed. A final issue is what personality variables may underlie differences in premorbid competence and contribute to the predictive validity of premorbid competence measures.

The developmental-level construct is very broad and difficult to operationalize, particularly in relation to adult behavior. The premorbid competence measure represents one effort to operationalize this construct. Another approach that involves the application of developmental principles for categorizing symptomatology will be discussed in the next chapter. Because of the difficulty in operationalizing the developmental-level construct, particularly as it applies to adult psychopathology, our work has emphasized interrelationships among the various measures, each of which is presumed to tap imperfectly the broad underlying construct of developmental level. These measures include premorbid competence, developmental categorizations of symptomatology, and self-image disparity (to be described later in the book).

CHAPTER 4

Developmental Level
and Symptom Expression

An issue of continuing controversy has been whether the symptoms employed in conventional psychiatric diagnosis are meaningful and interpretable variables for the understanding of psychopathology or whether, as many have argued, symptoms represent peripheral phenomena whose study is more likely to distract than to guide investigators and clinicians. Since after many decades of work investigators have not yet resolved numerous perplexing issues in psychopathology, several workers have become disenchanted with the central role that symptom manifestation has occupied in conceptualizations about mental disorder. This chapter will begin with the consideration of the positions of these workers. In opposition to the view of these workers, the research to be presented in this chapter provides considerable evidence that, if organized conceptually and interpreted as indicators of major underlying dimensions (e.g., the individual's developmental level), symptoms are meaningfully related to major variables in psychopathology. Given these findings, it would appear that, rather than disregarding the symptom-oriented descriptive efforts that have evolved over almost a century, workers in the field should put forth renewed efforts to conceptualize symptoms and symptom clusters in meaningful ways that can further the understanding of important processes in psychopathology.

DISENCHANTMENT WITH SYMPTOM ANALYSIS

Symptom Analysis Versus Laboratory Measures

The disenchantment with symptom analysis has been forcefully expressed by Cromwell (1975, 1984), who has argued that research in schizophrenia should forgo utilizing symptoms, substituting laboratory measures (e.g., attention directing) in their place. Cromwell's position is that, whereas symptom manifestation is "inextricably confounded with the nonpathological factors of personality, socioeconomic status and level of cognitive functioning" (Cromwell, 1975, p. 594), "schizophrenic deficit may well be studied and better understood during the few seconds and fractions of seconds which follow carefully constructed novel, ambiguous, decision demanding or otherwise difficult stimuli'' (Cromwell, 1975, p. 614). Cromwell buttresses his argument with findings that the laboratory measures whose use he recommends have been consistently related to the process–reactive distinction in schizophrenia. He further maintains that this distinction appears to be the most effective predictor of major variables of clinical interest (e.g., outcome). Others, however, have pointed to the somewhat tenuous relationship between laboratory measures and premorbid adjustment scores (see Sarbin and Mancuso, 1980, for a review of this research). Moreover, even in schizophrenia, the relationship of premorbid adjustment (reflecting the process–reactive distinction) to outcome has not been found to be especially robust (Zigler et al., 1979) or even always significant (Lewine, Watt, Prentky, & Fryer, 1978).

Cromwell's position represents a recent expression of a longstanding disenchantment with symptom analysis in the field of psychopathology. Positions taken by earlier workers in this regard have been reviewed by Phillips and Draguns (1971) and Zigler and Phillips (1961b) and are also discussed later in this chapter. A question that arises then is why this view of Cromwell and others has remained a minority position, inasmuch as workers in the field continue to rely heavily on symptoms to classify individuals into pathological groupings. The commitment to the importance of symptom manifestation can be traced to at least three factors:

1.   The dramatic and compelling nature of symptoms makes them a focal point of attention in psychopathology.

2.   Psychological thought in general and the field of psychopathology in particular are committed both implicitly and explicitly to a deterministic view of human behavior. The impact of Freud's work gave impetus to the acceptance of determinism in psychopathology. Certainly if a slip of the tongue could be analyzed and the underlying causes discovered, then there would be considerable hope for discovering the determinants of the more striking gross dramatic symptoms encountered in psychopathology.

3.   Psychopathology occurs in a social context. For the patient and/or interested others, symptoms are the problem; if only the symptoms were alleviated, the patient would be considered nonpathological and would no longer be within the purview of mental health professionals. This concern of the patient and others represents an ecological rather than a substantive argument for the continued focus on symptomatology.

Physical medicine has long distinguished between symptoms (defined as subjective experiences of abnormality) and signs (considered to be objective indicators of dysfunction). And in physical medicine, signs (e.g., blood pressure) that can be considered quite esoteric and beyond the immediate awareness of the patient and family members have been established as central indicators of the cause of disorder and indicated treatment. The ambiguity in diagnosing psychopathological disorders was exemplified by Buchsbaum and Haier (1983). In contrast to a traditional medical complaint, they note that "in schizophrenia, the physical sign is absent, no laboratory test is available, and validation of the symptom or diagnosis uncertain" (p. 403).

A longstanding hope in the field of psychopathology has been that for each of the major forms of disturbance some unambiguous indicator could be found that would be truly pathognomonic for that disorder. Efforts to establish psychophysiological or biological signs of disturbance have been accelerating rapidly, especially with respect to psychotic disorders. Underlying this work has been the hope of uncovering a central nervous system dysfunction as the fundamental abnormality (Zubin et al., 1975). A variety of such signs have been proposed and examined, each time with the hope that finally an unequivocal test for a particular disorder had been discovered. Each time, however, continued research suggested that the particular indicator was neither sufficiently sensitive nor specific to the particular disorder. In schizophrenia research, many laboratory tests of behavioral responsiveness have been explored. Yet, as Neale and Oltmanns (1980) indicated, relationships between laboratory tests and psychiatric diagnosis have been found to be too weak to be of practical value. With respect to pursuit eye movements, for example, not only are eye-tracking dysfunctions frequent in schizophrenia (Holzman & Levy, 1977), but they appear in substantial numbers of affective disorder and organic patients (Baloh & Honrubia, 1979; Buchsbaum & Haier, 1983; Iacono et al., 1982; Shagass, Roemer, & Amadeo, 1974). Neither have classifications based solely on laboratory measures been found to be fruitful (Neale & Kopfstein, 1973). With respect to depression, the dexamethasone suppression test (DST) represents a recent embodiment of the hope for an unequivocal diagnostic method. Yet as Baldessarini, Finklestein, and Arana (1983) concluded, "The DST and other endocrinologic tests being developed for use in evaluating depression are limited in sensitivity, and their specificity, when applied to acutely, severely ill psychiatric patients, is not secure" (p. 573). With respect to both the DST and biological marker research in schizophrenia (platelet monoamine oxidase), Buchsbaum and Haier (1983) concluded that "many patients with a diagnosis fail to show the marker, and some normals and patients with other diagnoses do show the marker" (p. 415).

The longstanding hope for unequivocal diagnostic methods is expressed in the search for laboratory signs of disorder, and is also embodied in efforts in schizophrenia research to define the syndrome by a small subset of symptoms that would be truly pathognomonic for the disorder (e.g., Bleuler, 1950; Langfeldt, 1969; Schneider, 1959). Underlying these efforts has been the view that certain symptoms are basic to the disorder, while others reflect at best a camouflaging overlay to the basic symptoms. None of these attempts to define schizophrenia with a small number of basic symptoms has won wide acceptance.

Whether signs or symptoms serve as the criteria, no simple unequivocal diagnostic test has yet been found for the major functional disorders in psychopathology. The forms of disorder appear complicated and intertwined. As will be discussed in the next section, many appear to be multiply caused. While the longstanding hope may have been for the equivalent of a series of diagnostic litmus tests, one specific to each disorder, such a hope is unlikely to be realized. Those measures, whether signs or symptoms, that are found to be most strongly associated with the major variables of concern (i.e., the onset, course, treatment, and outcome of disorder) will finally be employed as the major criteria for defining disorder. At present, the empirical relations discovered between signs of disorder and the major variables of concern in psychopathology do not appear sufficiently strong to warrant the substitution of these measures, as Cromwell (1975, 1984) suggests, for the symptom criteria traditionally employed to define psychopathology.

At this point in the work on psychopathology, it seems reasonable to assume that our understanding of mental disorders will be enhanced by the use of more rather than less information about the patient in our classification procedures. Symptom-based and non–symptom-based approaches are certainly not mutually exclusive. Many studies adopt both, as in those instances where paranoid and nonparanoid schizophrenics are compared on a variety of laboratory measures (Cromwell & Pithers, 1981; Magaro, 1980; Neale & Oltmanns, 1980; Swanson, Bohnert, & Smith, 1970) and with respect to such others aspects of functioning as premorbid social competence and course of illness (Gift et al., 1981; Winokur et al., 1974; Zigler & Levine, 1973, 1981a; Zigler et al., 1976, 1977). That this multidimensional approach to unraveling the mysteries of mental disorder has become the consensus of the field may be seen in DSM-III (American Psychiatric Association, 1980), where multiple axes, employing symptom-based and non–symptom-based variables, are used in diagnosis.

Symptom Analysis and Etiological Preconception

In line with Cromwell's concern that symptoms may be too infused with experiential and social variables to be of much value in discerning underlying processes, Rotter (1954) also argued for the incidental, and perhaps random, nature of symptom manifestation. For example, although pencils are frequently yellow, this characteristic, while striking, provides no useful information about the inherent nature of the implement. Unlike Cromwell, however, Rotter was concerned that an emphasis on symptom description inevitably leads to a disease model of mental disorder. Rotter's (1954) concern has likewise been expressed by other learning theorists (Kanfer & Saslow, 1969; Ullmann & Krasner, 1965) and by adherents to a variety of positions that stress societal contributions to mental disorder (e.g., Albee,

1969; Smith, 1974), including the view that the devalued status implied in labeling the patient actually creates the disorder (e.g., Braginsky, Braginsky, & Ring, 1969; Sarbin & Mancuso, 1980; Scheff, 1974; Szasz, 1961). Our view that psychiatric conditions are real circumscribable phenomena and not merely the product of labeling will be discussed in the next chapter. At this juncture, what is important to note is that the description and analysis of symptoms and symptom clusters do not presuppose any particular etiological view. As behaviors, symptoms can as easily direct attention to psychological and social variables as they can to somatic ones.

The careful observation and classification of signs and symptoms have been central in physical medicine and have frequently led to the isolation of separate disease entities that were later discovered to be etiologically distinct as well. In the field of psychopathology, the history of our understanding of paresis represents a longstanding model of efforts in this direction (Zilboorg & Henry, 1941). First one isolates the manifestations, that is, symptoms and signs, of the disorder. One is then able to diagnose the disorder and thus identity a homogeneous group of afflicted patients. Finally, through examination of their life histories and a close physiological analysis, the cause (i.e., syphilitic spirochete) is discovered. Once the causal agent is known, methods of treatment and prevention quickly follow. In being derived from this model, Kraepelin's classificatory efforts had two major characteristics: a commitment to a detailed description of the manifest symptomatic behaviors of the individual and an underlying assumption that such a descriptive classification would be transitory, eventually leading to and being replaced by a system whose classificatory principle was the etiology of various mental disorders.

Kraepelin's basic concern with the problem of etiology has remained a focus of effort in the clinical area. As important as the discovery of etiology is, it is only one of a multitude of variables of interest in psychopathology. Further, as Zigler and Phillips (1961b) noted, etiology is typically the last characteristic of a disorder to be discovered. Inasmuch as the amount of descriptive effort required before etiological factors are likely to be discovered has been underestimated (Zigler & Phillips, 1961b; Zubin & Spring, 1977), the pursuit of etiology should represent an end point rather than a beginning for descriptive classification. In recognizing this, we can regret but need not be unduly alarmed by the fact that even after decades of work there are still no widely accepted cause–effect formulations for most mental disorders.

However, approaching the problem of description with assumptions as to the necessary correlates of such descriptions leads to circularity (Brown & Harris, 1978; Zigler & Phillips, 1961b). For example, in his preoccupation with etiology, Kraepelin refused to accept as cases of dementia praecox individuals who recovered, since he assumed irreversibility as a necessary concomitant of the hypothesized neurological base of the disorder. As Zigler and Phillips (1961b) observed more than two decades ago, it is not "the descriptive approach itself which is open to criticism, but description contaminated by preconception" (p. 615).

It has become increasingly apparent that the model of discrete disease entities, each with a distinctive course following from a single etiological agent, represents an insufficient conceptualization for most major mental disorders. Models specifying multiple processes that may ultimately implicate multiple causative factors appear to provide the most appropriate framework (Strauss et al., 1981). For both schizophrenia and depression, manifest symptoms have been conceptualized as representing final common pathways arising from various etiologies (Akiskal & McKinney, 1975; Zubin & Steinhauer, 1981).

There thus appear to be no shortcut solutions to the problem of etiology. The attempt to illuminate the variables associated with the myriad maladaptive behaviors called symptoms in no way mitigates against the view of mental disorders as multiply caused. What continues to be required is a systematic empirical attack on the problem of mental disorders. Inherent in this program is the employment of symptoms, broadly defined as meaningful and discernible behaviors, as one basis for classification. Rather than conducting an abstract search for etiologies, it would appear more fruitful to investigate such empirical correlates of symptomatology as reactions to specific forms of treatment, outcome in the disorders, and case history phenomena. Similarly, the relationship of symptomatology to laboratory measures (e.g., pursuit eye movements, Holzman & Levy, 1977) warrants further study.

Descriptive Classification, Theory Construction, and Underlying Process

It has frequently been the case that investigators concerned with describing symptoms have been less interested in underlying processes (e.g., Langfeldt, 1937; Schneider, 1959) while those with a psychodynamic orientation (e.g., Allport, 1955; Freud, 1946; Laing, 1967; Rogers, 1951) have viewed symptoms as peripheral phenomena with limited relevance for the elucidation of underlying processes. However, symptom description in no way mitigates against "dynamic" or process interpretations of psychopathology.

Fundamental in the organismic–developmental view is the distinction between surface appearance or outer form and underlying process or inner meaning (Werner, 1937). This distinction has been conceptualized by Lewin (1946) in terms of genotypes and phenotypes. A single genotype can give rise to different phenotypes (i.e., outward appearances), while the same phenotype can be due to different genotypes. Quite disparate symptoms can, on the basis of developmental principles, be assigned similar meanings. Conversely, certain symptoms that bear surface similarities may in fact reflect quite different underlying processes (Kohlberg et al., 1972; Zigler & Phillips, 1961c). For example, it is open to question whether "withdrawal" in the depressive is qualitatively of the same nature as "withdrawal" in the schizophrenic or whether the suicidal attempt of the depressive is the equivalent of a more histrionic attempt made by a psychopath.

Our work on the developmental approach to psychopathology clearly attests to the efficacy of symptom classification based on underlying processes. In this chapter we review studies that demonstrate relationships between various modes of symptom classification derived from developmental principles and premorbid social competence. In addition to supporting the view that symptoms, when ordered through reference to underlying processes, can contribute to the understanding of psychopathology, the research to be reviewed directly addresses the argument raised by Cromwell. Premorbid social competence and the process–reactive distinction in schizophrenia are overlapping constructs. Thus Cromwell's argument for the value of laboratory measures based on their relation to the process–reactive distinction can be applied equally to the symptom orderings employed in our research, since these orderings also relate to premorbid competence or the process–reactive distinction. Further evidence for the efficacy of symptom study will be presented in later chapters, inasmuch as the developmental orderings of symptomatology to be described here have also been found to be related to diagnosis, self-image disparity and defensive style, and psychiatric outcome. Our view concerning the value of developmental thinking for the understanding of symptomatology has received further support from evidence reviewed by Kohlberg et al. (1972) and Santostefano and Baker (1972) concerning the predictive efficacy of symptoms when ordered according to developmental principles.

These findings that symptoms when ordered developmentally can predict to major variables of clinical interest are relevant to the questions raised by Strauss and his colleagues. In differentiating positive symptoms that appear as active processes (e.g., hallucinations, delusions, catatonic motor behavior) from negative symptoms that primarily reflect an absence of certain modes of functioning (e.g., blunting of affect), Strauss, Carpenter, and Bartko (1974) observed that the former had little prognostic significance, a finding that has been replicated in other studies (Harrow, Bromet, & Quinlan, 1974; Hawk, Carpenter, & Strauss, 1974; Knight et al., 1979; Strauss & Carpenter, 1974a, 1977). As we indicated, the developmental approach has led to quite different findings. The critical issue appears to be the manner in which discrete symptoms are grouped and interpreted. Whereas frequently symptoms are classified additively, with patients having more symptoms (e.g., hallucinations and delusions, or feelings of self-reproach and psychomotor agitation/retardation) being seen as more severely disturbed (Brown & Harris, 1978; Harder et al., 1980), the developmental formulation would emphasize that variations in the form of symptom expression are related to variations in developmental level. As will be indicated in this chapter, such ordering based on developmental principles has given rise not only to symptom clusters with predictive validity but also to the discovery of relations between discrete symptoms that would be classified as positive (i.e., hallucinations and delusions) and premorbid competence (Zigler & Levine, 1983b).

Neither does the empirical study of symptomatology require, as Sarbin and Mancuso (1980) suggest, an isolated and exclusive focus on the maladaptive aspects of an individual's behavior. A central thesis in the developmental approach to psychopathology is that there is a continuity between adaptive and maladaptive functioning. As a reflection of maturity level, the individual's behavioral style is not presumed to be altered after the person has been designated "pathological." Within the person's particular level of functioning, some inappropriate responses may have been substituted for more effective coping mechanisms, but, as was indicated earlier in this volume, it is essential to recognize the range of adaptive behaviors an individual displays, even in the midst of disordered episodes.

Summary: The Place of Symptom Analysis in Research on Psychopathology

The longstanding controversies over the place of symptom study in psychopathology have provided the field with a broader perspective on pathological phenomena and necessitated the closer theoretical scrutiny of the relation of symptom expression to fundamental processes in psychopathology and thus to such important variables as etiology, outcome, and, ultimately, the treatment of disorder. Our position regarding the major objections to symptom analysis is that research failures in symptom study seem to derive from an empiricism that has been lacking in theoretical elaboration. As the research results to be presented in the next section indicate, when symptoms are conceptually organized and interpreted as reflections of major underlying dimensions, they can elucidate much about the nature of people.

The place of symptoms in psychopathology is far from contrived. It is the symptoms of disorder that are particularly distressing to patients and their relatives (Freeman & Simmons, 1963) and that are noted by psychiatrists in case history records as primary reasons for hospitalization. What seems needed is not a scrapping of the descriptive approach, but an accelerated program of empirical research. The naturally occurring symptom that has been the focus of impressively detailed descriptive study by psychiatrists over the past 80 years would seem to be an appropriate cornerstone for such renewed efforts. However, given the complexities encountered thus far in the attempt to unravel the mysteries of psychopathology, a multidirectional research approach seems warranted. The predictions of treatment response and outcome are central aims for the understanding of psychopathology. In addition to focusing on these variables, however, the broader examination of relationships among various other measures (e.g., symptoms, premorbid competence, performance on appropriate laboratory tests and other cognitive measures, personality variables) can serve to expand our nomological networks with respect to developmental constructs and constructs deriving from other formulations. In other studies, symptoms and laboratory measures can be incorporated as converging operations (Garner, Hake, & Eriksen, 1956) permitting the evaluation of alternative hypotheses.

SYMPTOM PATTERNS, BEHAVIORAL STYLE, AND DEVELOPMENTAL LEVEL

The developmental approach to psychopathology does not view symptoms solely as indexes of some pathological state. Rather, specific symptom patterns are presumed to reflect a continuity in behavior or life-style with the pre- and postmorbid periods. A central dimension influencing these patterns of behavior is presumed to be that ubiquitous construct, the individual's developmental level. Based on this position, a number of aspects of patients' symptom pictures have been examined in a series of studies. Predominant are (a) the interpretation of symptom clusters as indicative of role orientations; (b) the categorization of symptoms along an action–thought continuum; and (c) recent inquiries into developmental differences associated with symptom pictures involving hallucinations versus delusions. A review of this work will constitute the remainder of the chapter.

Symptoms as Indicative of Role Orientation

The Empirical Isolation of Symptom Clusters

The key historical effort that gave rise to this theoretical approach was a study by Phillips and Rabinovitch (1958) in which three symptom clusters were empirically isolated and conceptualized as indicative of three general role orientations that appeared to reflect the individual's implicit assumptions about the self and relations to others.

The case history records of 604 patients admitted to Worcester State Hospital between 1948 and 1952 were examined for the presenting symptoms noted. A symptom referred to the description of a patient's behavior by a psychiatrist at the time of initial institutional contact or the description of behavior presented by referring physicians as the primary reason for hospitalization. The symptoms included specific behaviors (e.g., suicidal attempt), general behavior patterns (e.g., irresponsible behavior), thoughts (e.g., suicidal ideation), somatic reactions (e.g., headaches), and general affect states (e.g., tense). The sample included only patients for whom at least two presenting symptoms were recorded. The sample was randomly divided into two groups of 302 cases each, with the first group serving as the pilot subsample and the second allowing for replication of the initial findings.

Utilizing the procedure with the pilot sample, three groups of symptoms were isolated such that the symptoms within each group tended to co-occur with each other but not to co-occur with the symptoms in the other two groups. The first group included the following symptoms: withdrawn, feels perverted, suspiciousness, hallucinations, bizarre ideas, sexual preoccupations, apathetic, perplexed; these symptoms were conceptualized as reflecting a withdrawal from others. The following symptoms were included in the second group: threatens assault, drinking, rape (and incest), emotional outbursts, irresponsible behavior, robbery, lying, disturbed–destructive, perversions, assaultive; these symptoms appeared to reflect turning against others or self-indulgence. The symptoms in the third group were suicidal attempt, compulsions, doesn't eat, bodily complaints, insomnia, headaches; these appeared indicative of turning against the self. With these clusters empirically isolated and conceptualized, their applicability was then tested employing the second subsample (N = 302). The groupings statistically obtained in these analyses conformed to the ones discovered with the pilot sample.

These empirically isolated symptom clusters were conceptualized as representing three patterns of role taking indicative of the individual's implicit assumptions about the self and relations to others. Phillips and Rabinovitch further proposed a developmental ordering of the three symptom clusters. Avoidance of others was conceptualized as reflecting a lack of differentiation in self–world relationships and thus as representing the lowest developmental form. At an intermediate level, the orientation of self-indulgence and turning against others was viewed as indicating the differentiation of self and others without the internalization of social mores. Finally, inasmuch as it implies the introjection of social values and the ability to take the role of internalized others, turning against the self was conceptualized as the more socially mature role orientation.

Social Competence and Role Orientation

The developmental formulation concerning the three role orientation symptom clusters were examined in two subsequent studies (Zigler & Phillips, 1960, 1962).

The symptoms comprising the three role orientation categories are presented in Table 4.1. Over the course of 25 years of research, a few symptoms employed in this early work have been deleted because they occurred too infrequently to permit statistical analysis. Thus, Table 4.1 presents those symptoms that have continued to be employed in our work. Throughout the research, a presenting symptom refers to the description of a patient's behavior by a psychiatrist at the time of initial institutional contact or the description of behavior presented by referring physicians as the primary reason for hospitalization. Utilizing this definition of a presenting symptom, high levels of interjudge agreement have been obtained in rating each of the symptoms in Table 4.1 for their presence or absence in case history records. Glick et al. (1985) reported kappa values ranging from .77 to 1.00 for each of these symptoms. According to guidelines proposed by Cicchetti and Sparrow (1981), the chance-corrected interjudge agreement was thus "excellent" for all symptoms employed to construct role orientation categories.

Other investigators have similarly reported high levels of interjudge agreement in scoring symptoms from case records (Phillips, 1968b; Ullmann & Gurel, 1962) and in formulating diagnoses based on the application of recent research criteria to case records (McGlashan, 1984). Ullmann and Gurel (1962) further compared ratings of symptoms based on case record examination with ratings independently obtained through interviews with the patients. The agreement between these two methods of symptom rating was highly significant. As Strauss and Harder (1981) noted, if adequate reliability can be demonstrated, case record analysis represents a valuable tool for clinical research. Since this method provides access to large amounts of information, it is particularly well suited to the initial formulation and testing of hypotheses.

TABLE 4.1. Categorization of Symptoms by Role Orientation

Self-Deprivation and Turning Against the Self	Self-Indulgence and Turning Against Others	Avoidance of Others
Suicidal attempt	Maniacal outbursts	Suspiciousness
Suicidal ideas	Drinking	Perplexed
Euphoria	Robbery	Delusions
Doesn't eat	Irresponsible	Hallucinations
Bodily complaints	behavior	Sexual preoccupation
Tense	Assaultive	Apathetic
Self-depreciatory	Threatens assault	Withdrawn
Depressed	Emotional outbursts	Depersonalization
Mood swings	Fire setting	
Insomnia	Disturbed–destructive	
Compulsions		
Obsessions		

Zigler and Phillips (1960) categorized presenting symptoms recorded in the case history records of 1053 (652 male and 401 female) state hospital patients on the basis of role orientation and related this categorization to patients' scores on each of the six component indexes of premorbid social competence.

The major hypothesis in this investigation—that higher social competence scores would be associated with symptoms indicative of self-deprivation and turning against the self—was clearly borne out. In contrast to patients displaying this symptom picture, individuals manifesting symptoms indicative of either self-indulgence and turning against others or avoidance of others obtained lower social competence scores.

Previous findings that female patients obtained higher social competence scores than their male counterparts led to the further expectation that symptoms indicative of turning against the self would be more frequently manifested in women than in men. This expectation was likewise confirmed. Whereas females were more likely to display symptoms reflecting a turning against the self, symptoms in the turning-against-others category were more frequently displayed by males. The interpretation of gender differences remains highly problematic for developmental thinking. Yet gender consistently emerges as a robust variable in the research on psychopathology. The issue of gender will thus be broadly considered in Chapter 11.

A final expectation in this study was that symptoms indicative of turning against others would be associated with higher social competence scores than would symptoms indicative of avoidance of others. This expectation was based on Phillips and Rabinovitch's (1958) conceptualization of the three role orientations as reflecting three developmental levels, with the turning-against-others category occupying the intermediate position. This expectation was not borne out. In fact, there was some tendency for symptoms in the avoidance-of-others category to be associated with higher levels of social competence than symptoms indicative of turning against others although the differences between these two symptom categories were not significant. Subsequent research has similarly yielded no differences between the turning-against-others and avoidance-of-others symptom categories on developmental measures (Zigler & Phillips, 1962) or higher scores for individuals in the avoidance-of-others category (Quinlan et al., 1980). In contradistinction to the formulation of Phillips and Rabinovitch (1958), the data thus support a two- rather than three-level conceptualization of developmental differences between role orientations, with turning against the self representing a higher level of psychological functioning than the alternative lower modes of either turning against others or avoidance of others.

The finding that avoidance of others is associated with similar or higher levels of social competence than turning against others presents certain conceptual difficulties. In regard to diagnosis, as will be indicated in Chapter 5 the role orientation of avoidance of others predominates in schizophrenic patients, whereas turning against others characterizes personality disorder groups. Thus, based on role orientation categories, the results of Zigler and Phillips (1960) would seem to imply that schizophrenia is characterized by developmentally higher functioning than are the personality disorders. Yet such a view runs counter to the widely held assumption that schizophrenia represents a dominance of primitive operations compared with the somewhat higher level of functioning presumed to characterize personality disorder patients (Fenichel, 1945; Goldman, 1962). In addition, symptoms in the avoidance-of-others category are predominately thought oriented, whereas those in the turning-against-others category are mainly action oriented (Phillips, Broverman, & Zigler, 1968). As will be indicated in the next section, representation in thought is presumed to reflect a developmentally higher mode of functioning than unmodulated expression in direct action. The overlap between the avoidance-of-others role orientation and the thought end of the action–thought continuum underscores the need for more fine-grained distinctions within the avoidance-of-others category. The work of Zigler and Levine (1983b) concerning developmental differences associated with symptom pictures involving hallucinations versus delusions represents just such an effort and will be reviewed later in this chapter.

One explanation for the general absence of differences in social competence scores between patients displaying the role orientations of turning against others versus avoidance of others rests with the social competence measure. As indicated in Chapter 3, this measure gives greater emphasis to variables related to instrumental role functioning and deemphasizes social participation. If, as was recommended in Chapter 3, the scale were modified to include more items reflecting social participation, higher social competence scores might be obtained by patients displaying the role orientation of turning against others as compared with those displaying symptoms indicative of an avoidance of others. Some data to be presented in Chapter 5 concerning the social competence scores of schizophrenic and personality disorder patients are consistent with this possibility.

Alternatively, and especially in light of the association between action-oriented symptoms and the turning-against-others role orientation (and conversely between thought symptoms and avoidance of others), the possibility must be entertained that turning against others and avoidance of others represent alternative but equally immature styles of responding. In this sense, lower developmental level could be conceptualized as a genotype giving rise to the alternative phenotypes of (a) symptomatology reflecting turning against others most frequently manifested by personality disorder patients, and (b) symptomatology indicative of avoidance of others typically displayed by schizophrenic patients. Further research is needed in support of these explanations, which are not mutually exclusive.

With regard then to the question of whether role orientation is best conceptualized as reflecting two (turning against the self higher than both turning against others and avoidance of others) or three (each role orientation representing a step along a developmental continuum) levels, our research to date has been more consistent with a two-level model. However, additional work is needed, first to determine the degree to which the deemphasis of social participation on the social competence scale may have influenced previous findings, and second to evaluate the two-level model more broadly using various types of developmental measures. Such measures could include real–ideal self-image disparity and extreme response style (see Chapter 10) and Loevinger's (Loevinger & Wessler, 1970) sentence completion test.

The developmental interpretation of symptom expression was further explicated by Zigler and Phillips (1962). In contrast to traditional formulations that have viewed symptoms as discrete entities, Zigler and Phillips argued that surface disparities in symptom expression have an underlying developmental continuum. In regard to the process–reactive distinction in schizophrenia, the developmental position suggests that rather than representing dichotomous conditions these two forms represent different points along a single developmental continuum. As such, they would be expected to be distinguished by developmental differences in symptom expression. More specifically, the role orientation of turning against the self would be expected to be more characteristic of reactive patients, whereas the symptom patterns of process individuals would be expected to be more indicative of either avoidance of others or turning against others. The developmental formulation further generates the hypothesis that differences in symptom expression between process (less mature) and reactive (more mature) individuals would not be limited to schizophrenia but would be manifested across a broad range of diagnoses.

The Zigler-Phillips Premorbid Social Competence Index was employed as an indicator of maturity level, and the case histories of 806 state hospital patients in four diagnostic groups—schizophrenia ($N = 298$), manic-depressive ($N = 74$), psychoneurotic ($N = 159$), and character disorder ($N = 275$)—were examined for presenting symptoms. Symptoms were categorized according to the three role orientations presented in Table. 4.1. A symptom score was devised that would reflect the relative dominance within an individual's symptom picture of symptoms within the turning-against-the-self category as opposed to the dominance of symptoms falling within the other two categories.

Consistent with the view that the process–reactive distinction represents a single dimension related to maturity level, developmentally orderable differences appeared in the gross symptomatic pictures presented by process and reactive patients. In both the schizophrenic sample and the nonschizophrenic group individuals having high social competence scores also tended to have high turning-against-the-self symptom scores, while individuals having low social competence scores more frequently displayed symptoms involving avoidance of others or self-indulgence and turning against others.

Whereas the traditional bifurcation of the schizophrenic syndrome into process and reactive types emphasizes the factors of premorbid social adequacy, nature of onset, and outcome and gives little attention to symptomatology, the results of Zigler and Phillips (1962) suggest that symptomatology can be meaningfully related to this distinction. Such an approach makes of psychopathology a unitary phenomenon rather than a collection of discrete entities. Not only can various diagnostic groups and subgroups be interrelated, but the major variables of interest in psychopathology (e.g., premorbid competence, symptomatology, prognosis) can be conceptualized as interrelated expressions of an underlying maturity dimension rather than as unique, unrelated parameters.

The recurrent relationship noted by Zigler and Phillips between role orientation and premorbid social competence has been reaffirmed in other studies (Mylet et al., 1979; Raskin & Golob, 1966; Sanes & Zigler, 1971) and also confirmed cross-culturally (Draguns et al., 1970; Phillips, 1968a; Seifert, Draguns, & Caudill, 1971). The developmentally higher status of symptoms indicative of turning against the self as compared with turning against others has received additional support from findings that suicidal patients (both those who threatened and those who attempted suicide) obtained higher Rorschach developmental scores than assaultive patients, including individuals who only threatened assault (Phillips, 1966, cited in Phillips, 1968a). Inasmuch as the developmental differences appeared between harm to the self and harm to others irrespective of whether symptom expression was symbolic (threatened) or occurred in action, these findings represent a clear instance where role orientation has predictive significance independent of the action–thought continuum. (Further evidence of the partial independence of these two modes of symptom classification will be presented in Chapter 5.)

Symptom Classification Based on the Action–Thought Continuum

Symptom Expression in Action versus Thought and the Concept of Vicariousness

Whereas the role orientation formulation emphasizes the internalization of societal standards concomitant with development, classification along the action–thought continuum derives from the fundamental assumption in developmental thought that expression in action is ontogenetically prior to representation in thought. As was indicated in Chapter 2, the transformation from immediate, direct, and unmodulated response patterns to indirect, ideational, conceptual, and symbolic or verbal modes of knowing and responding is viewed as a basic process underlying discontinuity in development. The consequences of this transformation for coping effectiveness have been elucidated by Werner (1957) and Werner and Kaplan (1963). When the self and the object world are responded to as immediate "things-of-action," the individual's ability to structure actively and thus to respond purposively to and control internal and external circumstances is severely limited. By contrast, when at higher levels the self and the object world are regarded as objects of contemplation, active structuring becomes possible and far wider options become available for planning, for purposive selection among response alternatives, and, thus, for mastery and control.

In accordance with this formulation, Phillips and Zigler (1961) classified symptoms along an action–thought dimension and hypothesized that this classification would be related to maturity level as assessed by premorbid competence scores. An examination of the case history records of 793 (480 male, 313 female) state hospital patients resulted in the tabulation of presenting symptoms that could be clearly placed in action or thought categories. As was the case with role orientation, certain symptoms employed in this initial research were subsequently deleted because they were found to occur too infrequently to permit statistical analysis. Table 4.2 presents those symptoms in the action and thought categories that continue to be employed in our research. Inasmuch as all of the symptoms retained to define the action and thought categories are ones also included in the categorization of role orientation, the "excellent" levels of chance-corrected interjudge agreement previously reported apply to the scoring of these symptoms.

TABLE 4.2. Categorization of Symptoms Along an
Action–Thought Continuum

Action Category	Thought Category
Accused of murder	Suspiciousness
Assaultive	Phobias
Compulsions	Delusions
Robbery	Obsessions
Fire setting	Suicidal ideas
Emotional outbursts	Sexual preoccupation
Irresponsible behavior	Threatens assault
Maniacal outbursts	Depreciatory ideas against self
Drinking	Perplexed
Suicidal attempt	Depresonalization

The patients were then classified into pure action, pure thought, or mixed symptom groups. All individuals who manifested only symptoms of the action variety were placed in the action group. Those who manifested only symptoms of the thought variety were placed in the thought group, while patients whose symptoms were equally divided in number between the action and thought categories were placed in the mixed group. This procedure results in 182, 247, and 136 individuals being assigned to the action, thought, and mixed groups, respectively. Of the original sample of 793 patients, therefore, 429 or 54 percent displayed either only action symptoms or only symptoms of the thought variety, providing some indication that these two main classes of symptoms do cluster and are far from randomly distributed across individuals. Recent unreported data have provided further evidence for the nonrandom distribution of symptoms with respect to both categorization along the action thought continuum and regarding role orientation. In a sample of 146 affective disorder, 145 neurotic, and 157 personality disorder inpatients, 45 percent of the patients displayed "pure" symptom configurations comprising either *only* thought symptoms or *only* symptoms of the action variety. Likewise, with respect to role orientation, 63 percent of that sample displayed "pure" configurations comprising symptoms in *only* one role orientation category. For both types of symptom categorization, these proportions significantly exceeded chance expectancy.

Consistent with the developmental formulation, Phillips and Zigler (1961) obtained a highly significant relationship between overall premorbid social competence scores and the categorization of symptoms along the action–thought dimension ($p < .001$). The symptoms of the more socially competent individuals tended to occur in the sphere of verbalization and ideation rather than in the sphere of action. By contrast, the less socially competent patients were more likely to display symptoms in the sphere of direct or gross action rather than ones of the ideational or verbal variety. The social competence scores of patients in the mixed group (equal number of thought and action symptoms) fell between those of patients in the thought and action categories. In addition to its relationship to overall social competence scores, the tendency to display thought rather than action symptoms was found to be associated with higher scores on each of the six component premorbid social competence indexes.

Considerable other evidence also substantiates the relatively low developmental status of action symptoms. Patients whose symptoms involve action have been found to obtain lower Rorschach developmental-level scores than patients with thought symptoms (Kruger, 1954; Misch, 1954). Action symptoms have been found to decrease with age during childhood (Prugh et al., 1953; Santostefano, 1970). In our own work (Glick et al., 1985), action, as compared with thought, symptoms were found much more frequently in younger than in older first-admission psychiatric patients ($p < .0001$). Moreover, action-oriented or externalizing symptoms in childhood have been associated with lower levels of academic and interpersonal competence (Garmezy et al., 1979; Rolf, 1972) and have been interpreted as reflecting distortions in ego development (Kohlberg et al., 1972).

The relationship between developmental level and behavioral style is not presumed to be altered by adjustment status. The developmental position assumes that at both higher and lower maturity levels there exist effective patterns of coping as well as pathological deviations from these patterns. Thus, rather than representing a regression in the usual sense, pathology is presumed to involve the substitution of inappropriate for appropriate methods of coping within that level of maturity that characterizes the individual.

A second study reported by Phillips and Zigler (1961) focused on the concept of vicariousness, originally employed in the sensory-tonic theory of perception (Werner & Wapner, 1952). This study more directly addressed the issue of the continuity between premorbid and pathological functioning. The concept of vicariousness suggests that a functional equivalence exists between action and thought such that if behavior in either of these modes is blocked for whatever reason it will be rechanneled into the alternative form of expression. In viewing action and thought as behavioral equivalents, the concept of vicariousness appears to contradict the developmental position that maintains that increasing maturation is accompanied by a corresponding increase in the dominance of ideational and verbal forms of expression over overt action. In an effort to reconcile the principle of vicariousness with the developmental position regarding action versus thought, Phillips and Zigler (1961) in a second study predicted that the action behaviors of developmentally advanced individuals who display an atypical action-dominated orientation would be developmentally higher in character than the action behaviors of developmentally less advanced individuals. Analogously, it was expected that the thought behaviors of developmentally less advanced individuals who employ an atypical thought-dominated orientation would be developmentally lower in character than the thought behaviors of maturationally higher individuals.

Required to test this proposition were: (a) a measure of the individual's maturity level (social competence scores were employed); (b) a criterion whose presence indicates that the individual is employing an atypical behavioral orientation; and (c) a set of broad behavioral referents that not only mirror the individual's orientation but can also be rationally ordered to a developmental continuum. Developmental theory, as well as empirical findings in the psychology of occupations (Roe, 1956), was employed to derive a criterion of atypicality. Since high social competence individuals would more frequently be expected to have occupations that emphasize conceptualization or the manipulation of symbols (professional and managerial, sales, and clerical), individuals of relatively high social competence who had labor (i.e., action-oriented) occupations were classified as atypical. Antithetically, individuals of low social competence with occupations that emphasize conceptualization or the manipulation of symbols and are in this sense thought oriented were likewise classified as atypical. Within each broad (thought-oriented vs. action-oriented) occupational category, the requirements of job performance permit some ordering to a developmental continuum. This can be more clearly seen in the labor categories of unskilled, semiskilled, and skilled. Nevertheless, an analogous ordering from low to high of clerical, sales, and professional/managerial occupations was also proposed. The study utilized only male patients, since males more typically had occupational histories. The specific predictions of the study were (a) that individuals who had exhibited a relatively high level of premorbid competence but whose occupations were in the labor categories would more frequently have jobs falling at the upper end of the unskilled–skilled continuum than would low social competence individuals in the labor categories and (b) that individuals who had exhibited relatively low levels of premorbid competence but who held jobs in the categories of professional and managerial, sales, and clerical would more frequently have jobs falling at the lower end of the clerical–professional continuum in comparison with their higher competence counterparts.

Concerning the continuity between premorbid and pathological functioning, it was further hypothesized that individuals who display atypical orientations in normal (occupational) functioning would likewise manifest atypical orientations in symptom manifestation. Specifically, therefore, it was predicted that high competence individuals with occupations in the labor category would more frequently manifest action symptoms than would individuals of equally high premorbid competence with occupations in the professional and managerial, sales, and clerical categories. Similarly, low competence individuals with occupations in these latter categories were expected to manifest symptoms of the thought variety more frequently than individuals of similarly low competence with occupations in the labor categories.

The case histories of 464 male patients whose occupations could be classified according to the criteria specified were examined. Social competence scores for this study were based on the variables of age, intelligence, education, employment history, and marital status. All predictions were confirmed. The majority of high social competence individuals who had occupations in the labor categories were found to have been employed in skilled or semiskilled occupations, whereas the majority of their low competence counterparts had occupations in the unskilled category ($p < .001$). Analogously, low social competence individuals whose occupations fell in the clerical, sales and managerial, and professional categories were more likely to have been employed in clerical jobs, whereas their high competence counterparts more frequently held jobs in the sales and managerial and professional categories ($p < .005$). Finally, the patients' atypical orientations in occupational functioning were found to be mirrored in patterns of symptom expression. Within the high competence groups, therefore, individuals in the labor category were found to manifest more action symptoms than their counterparts with more conceptual, symbolically oriented occupations ($p < .01$). Similarly, within lower competence groups, individuals with more conceptually oriented occupations evidenced more thought symptoms than their counterparts with occupations in the labor categories ($p < .01$).

In regard to the relationship between developmental level and vicarious functioning, these findings were interpreted as indicating that vicarious functioning does occur within developmental levels, but that the formal characteristics of that functioning mirror the develomental level of the individual manifesting it. For example, it has been found that artificially immobilizing normal adult subjects can lead to increased production of human movement responses on the Rorschach (Korchin, Meltzoff, & Singer, 1951). In applying their conceptualization to these findings, Phillips and Zigler (1961) suggested that this particular substitution of thought for action is only possible for subjects of a high developmental level who have the potential to produce a relatively high proportion of human movement responses. By contrast, if ideation is substituted for action in individuals at lower developmental levels, the formal quality of the ideation would be expected to mirror the individual's lower level of functioning.

The finding that even atypical behavioral orientations persist across both the normal and the pathological phases of individuals' functioning provides additional support for a continuity view of premorbid and pathological behavioral styles. Symptom manifestation appears to be neither arbitrary nor merely an outgrowth of specific disease processes. Instead, the symptoms an individual displays appear to mirror a specialization or life-style that extends to adaptive as well as disordered functioning and that is intimately related to the maturational level attained. In regard to the action–thought dimension as well as role orientation in symptomatology, individuals who display greater maturity in their premorbid functioning continue to manifest developmentally higher forms of functioning even in symptomatic behavior. Characteristic behavioral styles remain congruent between premorbid and symptomatic periods in the individual's life and across adaptive (occupation) and maladaptive (symptomatic) areas of functioning.

Symptom Expression in the Spheres of Action, Thought, and Affect

Symptom classification along the action–thought continuum was later modified by Zigler and his colleagues (Phillips et al., 1966, 1968) to encompass three spheres of preferred mode of symptom expression: expression in action, in thought, or in affect. As is the case with all symptom classifications deriving from the developmental perspective, symptoms are not viewed solely as indexes of some pathological state. Rather, specific symptom patterns, in this case the particular patient's dominant or preferred sphere of symptom expression, are presumed to reflect a continuity in behavior with the premorbid and postmorbid periods. On rational grounds, Phillips et al. (1966) classified the presenting symptoms recorded in the case histories of 504 (287 male and 217 female) state hospital patients of varying diagnoses into three categories of sphere dominance. The symptoms comprising the thought and action categories are presented in Table 4.2, and seven additional symptoms defined the affect category: apathetic, depressed, euphoria, maniacal outbursts, mood swings, temper outbursts, and tense.

The major concern in the Phillips et al. (1966, 1968) studies was with the relationship of sphere dominance to psychiatric diagnosis, and this aspect of the work will be reviewed in Chapter 5. Nevertheless, two facets of the research are pertinent here. The first involves a developmental classification, based upon premorbid competence scores, of symptoms within each sphere of symptom dominance (Phillips et al., 1966). Given the concept of specialized horizontal development discussed in Chapter 2, a considerable range of maturity levels would be expected within each sphere of preferred expression style. Just as not all action symptoms would be expected to reflect equally low forms of functioning, neither would all thought symptoms be expected to indicate uniformly higher forms. Social competence values were obtained for each symptom and combination of symptoms within a symptom (thought, action, or affect) category, free from the presence of other symptoms within that category. On this basis, thought, action, and affect scales were constructed. Each final scale included only those symptoms and symptom combinations that (a) based on t-tests represented significantly different points along the social competence continuum, and (b) occurred in a sufficient number of cases to make them suitable for statistical

TABLE 4.3.   Social Competence Level and Symptom Scales

Scale	Level	Symptoms	Mean Competence Scores
Thought	High	Suicidal ideas; self-depreciatory	50.75
	Intermediate	Suspicious; suspicious and threatens assault; perplexed	44.17
	Low	Hallucinations; hallucinations and suspicious[a]	41.56
Affect	High	Depressed; depressed and tense	48.30
	Intermediate	tense; apathetic; apathetic and depressed	42.98
	Low	Temper outbursts; temper outbursts and tense	33.84
Action	High	Suicidal attempt; suicidal attempt and drinking	50.62
	Low[b]	Robbery; drinking; sexual deviation, except homosexuality; assaultive; assaultive and drinking	43.71

[a]It will be noted that "suspicious" appears at more than one level. If it is found as the only thought symptom or appears in combination with "threatens assault" it is at the second level of competence. If it occurs in combination with hallucinations it is at the third level. Further, in contrast to the intermediate or low position of the symptom "suspicious" in this study, subsequent research has indicated an association between "suspiciousness" and high social competence or developmental level (Zigler & Levine, 1983a). This disparity across studies may be due to sample differences inasmuch as Zigler and Levine examined only schizophrenic patients.

[b]Only two levels of competence could be distinguished for symptoms used in the construction of the action scale.

treatment. The three scales, with symptoms ordered from high to low on the basis of social competence values, are presented in Table 4.3.

Also pertinent to this chapter are the relationships discovered between sphere dominance and role orientation in symptomatology (Phillips et al., 1968). These relationships are schematized in Table 4.4. Patients classified as thought dominant primarily exhibited the role orientation of avoidance of others and tended to lack the role orientations of turning against the self and turning against others. Patients characterized as action dominant tended to be classified as turning against others and as turning against the self, but not as avoiding others, while patients who were affect dominant tended to be characterized as exhibiting the role orientation of turning against the self and to show a lack of the role orientation of avoiding others. Here it is important to note that despite the overlap of symptoms between the two classification systems each categorization system was found to retain a considerable amount of independent variance (67 percent).

As was indicated earlier, the positive relationship discovered between dominance in the sphere of thought and the role orientation of avoidance of others underscores the ambiguity regarding the develomental status of the avoidance-of-others category and the need for more refined symptom classi-

TABLE 4.4.   Relation Between Sphere Dominance and Role Orientation

Sphere-dominance Categories	Turning Against Self	Turning Against Others	Avoidance of Others
Thought	−	−	+
Action	+	+	−
Affect	+		−

Note: + = positive relationship; − = negative relationship.

fication within this category. Further, the finding that action symptoms are associated with both turning against the self and turning against others points to the possibility of employing the action–thought dimension to differentiate more finely symptoms within the turning-against-the-self category.

In light of the predictive significance of affect symptoms (Huber, Gross, & Schüttler, 1975; Knight et al., 1979; McCabe, 1976b; McCabe et al., 1972; Roff, 1975; Taylor & Abrams, 1975b; Vaillant, 1962), the inclusion of affect as a third sphere of symptom dominance considerably broadens the measure. However, unlike the action–thought continuum, which represents a basic transformation during development, expression in affect cannot be seen as characteristic of certain developmental stages rather than others. A more complex relationship between affective expression and developmental level must be envisioned. It may be that certain affects (e.g., depression vs. anger) may more typically be dominant at different developmental levels, but the evidence is ample that the major emotions can be experienced at almost any point in development (e.g., Werner, 1948). We concur, therefore, with the position of Arieti and Bemporad (1978) that the fruitful question is not whether certain emotions are experienced by individuals at different developmental levels, but how differences in developmental status influence the manner in which the affects are experienced and expressed. As a result of this type of thinking, we have not employed the affect category in subsequent research. By contrast, the action–thought distinction and the role orientation formulation, which are both directly derived from developmental presuppositions, continue to form major dimensions in our analyses of symptom expression.

A Developmental Interpretation of Hallucinations and Delusions

Whereas in earlier investigations Zigler and his colleagues examined a broad spectrum of symptoms, recent work (Zigler & Levine, 1983b) has demonstrated the usefulness of the developmental approach for making more fine-tuned distinctions between specific symptoms (hallucinations and delusions). These two symptoms, among the most noted phenomena in the field of psychopathology, are defining criteria for the diagnosis of schizophrenia (American Psychiatric Association, 1980; Schneider, 1959; Spitzer & Endicott, 1978). It has been traditional in psychiatric practice either to treat hallucinations and delusions as discrete phenomena with emphasis placed on differentiating between them (e.g., Kazdin, Bellack, & Hersen, 1980) or, more commonly, to regard them as psychologically equivalent manifestations of a more basic psychopathological entity; namely, thought disorder (Prentky et al., 1979, 1980; Lewine, 1980; Tsuang et al., 1974; Taylor, 1972). Thus a frequently encountered phrase in the psychiatric literature is "hallucinations or delusions." Hallucinations and delusions have both been characterized as positive symptoms, and the point has been made that such symptoms (e.g., delusions, hallucinations, distractibility, catatonic motor disorders) are of little value as prognostic indicators (Strauss & Carpenter, 1974a, 1977; Strauss et al., 1974).

The developmental interpretation, however, suggests a different relationship between hallucinations and delusions. Being neither unrelated nor psychologically equivalent, hallucinations and delusions are presumed to represent contiguous areas on an underlying continuum that is itself defined by a collection of frequently noted developmental processes, for example, decentering, egocentricity, differentiation, and hierarchic integration (Feffer, 1967; Lidz, 1978; Piaget, 1954; Santostefano & Baker, 1972; Werner, 1948). Employing such dimensions as amount and quality of ideation and self–nonself differentiation, developmental analyses would generate the hypothesis that delusions represent a higher form of function than do hallucinations. Such a hypothesis is consistent with the many expositions in which hallucinations are viewed as sharing a commonality with other such developmentally immature phenomena as dreams, eidetic imagery, and imaginary playmates (Feffer, 1967; Hartmann, 1975; Horowitz, 1975; Lidz, 1978; Lucas, Sainsbury, & Collins, 1962; Savage, 1975; Siegel & West, 1975; West, 1975).

This theoretical ordering of hallucinations and delusions was examined by Zigler and Levine (1983b). The case histories of three samples of schizophrenic patients were examined: 217 (138 paranoid, 79 nonparanoid) male patients in a VA hospital; 215 (126 paranoid, 89 nonparanoid) state hospital male patients; and 207 (122 paranoid, 85 nonparanoid) state hospital female patients. Within each sample, patients were assigned to one of three symptom subgroups: (a) patients for whom hallucinations, but not delusions (i.e., bizarre ideas), were noted; (b) patients for whom delusions, but not hallucinations, were noted; and (c) patients for whom both hallucinations and delusions were noted.

The major hypothesis was that individuals at a lower developmental level, as evidenced by premorbid competence scores, would manifest hallucinations, whereas patients at a higher developmental level would more frequently manifest delusions. In addition, Zigler and Levine predicted that the developmental level of patients having both symptoms would fall between the levels of the patients having a single symptom. In view of the developmental formulation, patients who manifest *both* hallucinations and delusions constitute a particularly interesting group. In standard psychiatric practice and research, patients having both symptoms are viewed as being more severely disordered than patients having but one of the two symptoms (Brown & Harris, 1978; Harder et al., 1980). Thus this approach would lead one to expect that patients having both symptoms would be at a lower developmental level (i.e., "more regressed," Lidz, 1978), displaying poorer premorbid adjustment, than schizophrenics having but one of the two symptoms. However, the developmental position generates a different prediction. Viewed developmentally, the symptom configuration presented by the patient having the two symptoms would be seen as having both the lower-level coloration represented by the hallucinations and the higher-level coloration represented by the delusions. Thus the social competence scores of this group would be expected to fall between those of the other two groups.

The findings confirmed the predicted relationships between developmental level and symptoms manifested. Schizophrenic patients who displayed hallucinations were found to be at a lower developmental level as assessed by the premorbid social competence index, while those who manifested delusions were at a higher developmental level ($p < .002$). The social competence scores of patients manifesting both symptoms tended to fall between those of the single-symptom groups, although this linear trend was not robust ($p < .04$) and only became apparent when sample and diagnosis (paranoid vs. nonparanoid) were ignored and the social competence scores of the total and heterogeneous group of schizophrenics were examined.

As was the case in earlier investigations, these findings point to the heuristic and predictive value of symptom study when descriptive classification is integrated with theoretical analysis (Neale & Oltmanns,1980). Symptoms as well as signs can be related to premorbid social competence and, given the prognostic significance of this latter variable (Cromwell, 1975), a promising line of future investigation would be the relationship between the specific symptoms of hallucinations and delusions and psychiatric outcome. Given the occurrence of hallucinations and delusions in disorders other than schizophrenia, one may also wonder whether they would be similarly related to premorbid competence in other diagnostic groups.

Inasmuch as developmental thinking presupposes a continuity between adaptive and maladaptive forms of functioning as well as across diagnostic categories, a general model of normalcy, schizophrenia, delusions, hallucinations, and the interrelationship of these phenomena to developmental level can be advanced (see Figure 4.1). While there is some overlap in developmental levels, schizophrenic patients as a group are at a lower developmental level than are nonpathological individuals. Again, while there is some overlap between schizophrenic patients showing either hallucinations or delusions, those who show only hallucinations are at a lower developmental level than those who manifest only delusions.

Just as depressive delusions shade into normal guilt and concern (Strauss, 1969), certain hallucinatory experiences are not far removed from a variety

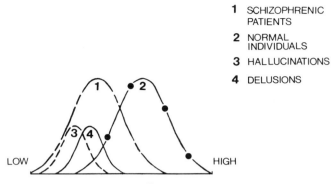

Figure 4.1. Developmental level and hallucinatory and delusional phenomena in schizophrenia and normal functioning.

of normal sensory and perceptual phenomena (Martin & Chapman, 1982; Mintz & Alpert, 1972; Siegel & West, 1975). Thus normal individuals at lower developmental levels might also be expected to experience perceptual phenomena analogous to hallucinations more frequently than their higher developmental level counterparts, whose modes of organizing experience would be more likely to share characteristics of delusional thought. In the case of both phenomena, a critical factor may well be the certainty with which the individual asserts that the hallucination-producing stimuli or the contents of the delusion are external to the self. In a comparison of schizophrenic and normal subjects predisposed to vivid imagery, Mintz and Alpert (1972) concluded, "It is success in performing the task of differentiating the source as inside or out that determines whether the experience is vivid imagery or an hallucination" (p. 316). Similarly, the hallucinations of nonschizophrenic patients have been found to carry less conviction of objective reality than those of schizophrenics (Lowe, 1973; Mayer-Gross, Slater, & Roth, 1969; Sedman, 1966), and this characteristic has furthermore been associated with favorable prognosis (Hill, 1936; Jansson, 1968; Lowe, 1973). A reemergence of reality testing has also been noted concomitant with improvement in delusional patients (Sacks, Carpenter, & Strauss, 1974).

Finally, we are in essential agreement with the views and evidence presented by Strauss (1969) that symptoms should be treated not as discrete all-on-none phenomena but rather as continuous phenomena. However, while Strauss emphasizes the more-or-less nature of a symptom (present, absent, or questionable), the developmental formulation would emphasize that variations in the form of a symptom are related to variations in the underlying developmental level. Thus Zigler et al. (1976) pointed to the need for more fine-grained structural analyses of particular symptoms. In regard to delusions, while the symptom may appear in both high competence and low competence individuals, developmental thinking suggests that the delusions of the less mature individual would be global, disorganized, and unmodulated whereas in the high social competence patient they would be more organized, articulated, and hierarchical. Such structural differences in the delusions of process and reactive schizophrenic patients have been reported by Heilbrun and Heilbrun (1977). While the evidence for a distribution of hallucinations that reflects an underlying developmental continuum is not as compelling as in the case of delusions, it is our feeling that a parallel exists. Two promising directions for further investigation can be suggested. The first involves an examination of the correlates of the particular sense modalities in which the hallucination arises, for example, auditory, visual, tactile, and so on. Alternatively, hallucinations can be classified on the basis of (a) degree of insight versus conviction of objective reality (Jansson, 1968; Mayer-Gross et al., 1969; Sedman, 1966); (b) duration (Hill, 1936; Lowe, 1973); and (c) relation to actual experiences and interpersonal relationships (Freeman, Cameron, & McGhie, 1966). The combined use of these criteria was proposed by Strauss (1969), and inasmuch as all have been related to boundary articulation in self–world relationships (Blatt & Wild, 1976), each criterion can be conceptualized developmentally.

CONCLUSIONS

A number of workers have questioned the value of symptom study for the understanding of psychopathology. In opposition to that view, the research reviewed in this chapter points to the usefulness of symptom analysis. As we indicated previously, symptoms have considerable importance to clinical practitioners as well as to patients and their families. The work reviewed here suggests that they may have no less value for researchers concerned with prediction. What seems crucial is the elucidation of principles whereby discrete symptoms can be meaningfully ordered.

The early developmental work (Phillips & Zigler, 1961; Zigler & Phillips, 1960, 1962) concerning symptom classification based on role orientation and expression in action versus thought demonstrates the potential of the developmental approach for bringing order to the confusing diversity of symptom pictures patients present. Ordered developmentally, disparate symptoms have been found to cluster and to be related to premorbid social competence. (Additional evidence regarding the relationships of these symptom categories to outcome and to such personality variables as the self-image will be reviewed in subsequent chapters dealing with these topics.) More recent work (Zigler & Levine, 1983b) has concentrated on making more fine-grained developmental distinctions between symptoms (e.g., hallucinations and delusions) that have traditionally been regarded as equivalent. Fundamental in all these efforts has been the distinction between underlying process and surface appearance (Lewin, 1946; Werner, 1937). The developmental approach has provided fruitful bases for ordering and differentiating symptom pictures. Equally important, this approach allows for a continuity to be envisioned between adaptive and maladaptive (symptomatic) functioning.

Rather than being outmoded, then, descriptive efforts to understand and classify patients on the basis of presenting symptoms seem to have a potential that is far from realized. What is required is an expanded program of empirical research. In addition to conducting the careful examination of the correlates of various theoretically ordered symptom combinations, workers should follow a neglected avenue of research, namely, off-quadrant cases, for example, developmentally low individuals displaying thought symptoms or turning against the self and depression, and developmentally high individuals displaying an action orientation. The need to distinguish more finely developmental differences within such symptom categories as delusions and depression has already been discussed. The principle of horizontal development, articulated in Chapter 2, further dictates the finer discrimination of higher and lower developmental forms within the action symptom category. Broad life-style characteristics, such as a predilection for expression in thought or action, are determined by more than the individual's developmental level (Phillips & Zigler, 1961). Specialization within either domain is possible for individuals of both high and low developmental levels. Whichever domain becomes accentuated, however, the formal quality of the responses of more and less mature individuals would be expected to differ, necessitating the more fine-grained differentiation of developmental level within action and thought categories.

CHAPTER 5

Psychiatric Diagnosis: Issues in Classification and Contributions of a Developmental Approach

Symptoms have traditionally been the primary criteria for psychiatric diagnosis. Although alternative bases for classification have been suggested (Carpenter, 1976; Cromwell, 1975, 1984), it seems likely that the notation and analysis of circumscribed symptoms and/or symptom clusters will remain integral to classification in psychopathology. The question that continues to face us is how to interpret and organize the myriad forms of symptom expression so that patients can be placed into homogeneous categories that are informative with regard to such major variables of clinical interest as treatment and outcome.

ISSUES IN DIAGNOSIS

Diagnostic efforts have been a focal point of controversy for decades. The difficulty in reliably assigning individuals to diagnostic groups has recently led to major research efforts to increase the precision of diagnosis. At the same time, a variety of arguments have been advanced for the abolition of diagnostic classification. Opponents view such classification as a sterile and meaningless enterprise that at best may be irrelevant to clinical practice and at worst may actually harm patients. Pleas for the abandonment of psychiatric classification have come from such diverse positions as existentialism, behavior therapy, and the community mental health movement (Phillips & Draguns, 1971). Some have even questioned the existence of mental disorders and have argued that the phenomena are produced through the process of labeling individuals and then reifying the labels employed (Braginsky, Braginsky, & Ring, 1969; Laing, 1967; Rosenhan, 1973, 1975; Sarbin & Mancuso, 1980; Szasz, 1961).

With Meehl (noted in Kimble, Garmezy, & Zigler, 1974) and Strauss and Carpenter (1981), we reject the view that mental disorders are created through a process of labeling; we instead adopt the position that mental disorders are a collection of real, circumscribable phenomena that must be ordered if they are to be examined. This latter position is compelling in light of several observations: (a) the dramatic and strikingly deviant behaviors encountered in the mental disorders; (b) the variety of reliably observable forms in which psychopathology is expressed; (c) the fact that historical recordings of mental disorders predate the relatively recent diagnostic and treatment efforts by many centuries (Zilboorg & Henry, 1941); (d) the comparable incidence of certain disorders across widely varying cultures (Sartorius et al., 1978; Strauss, 1979; Wing & Nixon, 1975); (e) the fact that most mental disorders entail a considerable amount of phenomenologically experienced pain and/or unhappiness (while there may be secondary gains, these gains do not appear to offset their negative concomitants); (f) evidence for genetic factors in the transmission of many disorders (Cancro, 1979; Gottesman & Shields, 1972, 1982; Kety et al., 1975; Klerman, 1978); and (g) the discovery of a physiological screening method for depressive psychosis (Carroll et al., 1981; Kalin et al., 1981) and the successful treatment of this disorder with psychopharmaceutical agents.

On Classification

Reduced to its essentials, diagnostic classification involves the establishment of categories by which phenomena can be ordered. The number of class systems that potentially may be constructed is limited only by our ability to abstract from our experience. The principles employed to construct such classes may be inductive, deductive, or a combination of both and may vary on a continuum from the closely descriptive to the highly abstract.

Class membership may involve nothing more than descriptive compartmentalization, with its only utility being greater ease in the handling of data. Alternatively, the attributes or correlates of class membership may be widespread and far-reaching in their consequences. The originators of a classificatory schema may assert that specified behavioral correlates accompany class membership. This assertion is open to test. If the hypothesized correlates represent the full heuristic value of the diagnostic schema and class membership is found to be unrelated to these correlates, then the schema should be revised or discarded. Without some method for ordering phenomena, the possibility of prediction does not exist, and prediction represents the cornerstone in scientific effort. As we indicated in Chapter 1 and as Popper (1972) has strongly affirmed, the essential aspect of a scientific theory is that it must allow for the derivation of hypotheses that are as open to disproof as to proof. Operating within the context of a predictive psychology, one argues for the necessity of a classificatory system even though particular diagnostic schemata may be rejected as irrelevant, futile, or obscure.

Another aspect of taxonomy is in need of clarification. When a phenomenon is assigned to a class, certain individual characteristics of that phenomenon are lost forever. No two class members are identical. In fact, a single class member may be viewed as continually differing from itself over time. Classification thus necessarily involves the loss of uniqueness although it provides a more than compensatory gain. This gain is represented in the significance of the class attributes and correlates. A conceptual system minimizes the loss inherent in classification to the extent that only irrelevant aspects of a phenomenon are forfeited in the classificatory process.

Reliability and Validity

It is mandatory for a classificatory system to be reliable since reliability refers to the definiteness with which phenomena can be ordered by classes. If a system does not allow for such a division of phenomena, it can make no pretense of being a classificatory schema. While certain extraclassificatory factors (proficiency of the clinicians, biases of the particular clinical settings, etc.) may influence it, reliability is primarily related to the precision with which classes of a schema are defined. Since the defining characteristic of most classes in psychiatric diagnosis is the occurrence of symptoms in particular combinations, the reliability of the system mirrors the specificity with which the various combinations of symptoms (syndromes) have been spelled out.

Reliability in diagnostic classification has until recently been problematic. Earlier diagnostic systems (DSM-I and DSM-II) were characterized by vague definitions of disorders and a failure to specify the boundaries of diagnostic class categories. The diagnostic categories frequently encompassed overlapping criteria, and exclusion criteria were not formulated. Much in diagnostic judgment was left to the discretion of the clinician, and wide variations in diagnosis often resulted, particularly across nations (Cooper et al., 1972) and decades (Blum, 1978). The bulk of research focused on the levels of interclinician agreement attained. The problems in reliably assigning patients to diagnostic categories bolstered arguments against the entire diagnostic enterprise.

However, as Meehl (1973) indicated, the deficits even in the earlier diagnostic systems may have been overstated:

> There are, of course, good reasons for being skeptical about diagnostic rubrics and even more skeptical about their current application in a psychiatric tradition that de-emphasizes training in diagnostic skills. But it is regrettable to find that the majority of beginning graduate students in clinical psychology "know" that "mere diagnostic labels" have no reliability or validity, no theoretical significance, no prognostic importance and no relevance to treatment choice. (p. 272)

Often cited in support of this widespread impression that psychiatric diagnosis is so unreliable as to be useless is Rosenhan's (1973) report. Yet, as

Farber (1975) made clear, Rosenhan's data actually revealed high interdiagnostician reliability. In all but 1 of the 12 instances in which a pseudopatient, falsely reporting auditory hallucinations, was admitted, the individual was diagnosed schizophrenic. The Rosenhan report does underscore the very poor treatment provided in many psychiatric hospitals. And it does indicate that clinicians are not on guard to the possibility that patients may be fabricating major symptoms. Yet, in the absence of some physiological measure quite outside of the patient's control that can unequivocally indicate whether a symptom is present, the clinician, as Farber (1975) noted, has little choice but to accept the patient's report and rely on presenting behavior. Further, it is heartening that diagnosticians are not unduly mistrustful of patients both from the standpoint of treatment and in light of the unlikelihood that patients would frequently fabricate such socially devalued and diagnostically meaningful symptoms as auditory hallucinations.

Diagnostic judgments based on DSM-I and DSM-II appear not to have been as unreliable as many statements suggest. So long as diagnosis was confined to broad diagnostic categories and carried out by well-trained clinicians with adequate exposure to the patient, reasonable levels of interclinician agreement were possible (Meehl, 1973; Spitzer & Fleiss, 1974; Zigler & Phillips, 1961b), as was stability of diagnosis over subsequent admissions (Babigian et al., 1965). The question of how modest reliability could be achieved despite imprecision in definition is a major focus of the research to be described later in this chapter.

Major research efforts in the last decade have been directed toward correcting nosological imprecision. These efforts have eventuated in a variety of research diagnostic systems, which include the Schedule of Affective Disorders and Schizophrenia (Spitzer & Endicott, 1978), the New Haven Schizophrenia Index (Astrachan et al., 1972), the St. Louis Criteria of Feighner and associates (Feighner et al., 1972), the "Flexible Diagnostic System" (Carpenter, Strauss, & Bartko, 1973), the Present State Examination (PSE) (Wing et al., 1977), and the Research Diagnostic Criteria (RDC) of Spitzer and associates (Spitzer, Endicott, & Robins, 1975). That this research renaissance occurred at a time when many clinicians were repudiating the entire diagnostic enterprise again underscores the central importance of classification for a predictive psychology. Formal aspects and specific contents of these research diagnostic systems have now been incorporated in DSM-III (American Psychiatric Associations, 1980).

The major aim of the research diagnostic systems was to enhance reliability through precise definitions of diagnostic criteria. All adopt an atheoretical approach toward defining and classifying disorders. The diagnostic categories are operationally defined on the basis of presenting symptoms, and criteria for exclusion as well as inclusion are specified. Frequently data collection is standardized through structured interviews. As was not the case with DSM-I and DSM-II, very little is left to the discretion of the clinician. In effect, for both the research systems and DSM-III, once presenting symptoms have been decided upon, diagnosis is automatic. That such increased precision and standardization would enhance reliability is axiomatic, and considerable data have now been presented to indicate satisfactory levels of interjudge reliability for both the research diagnostic systems (Haier, 1980; Neale & Oltmanns, 1980; Zubin et al., 1975) and most categories of DSM-III (Spitzer, Forman, & Nee, 1979). Moreover, Tsuang et al. (1981) have presented data indicating high levels of stability over time in patients' diagnoses when research criteria are employed.

However, the strategy that permitted increased reliability may have created new definitional problems and reduced not only the coverage of certain diagnostic concepts but possibly also their validity (Carey & Gottesman, 1978; Romano, 1977). Inasmuch as schizophrenic diagnosis has been the focus in research, most of the issues have been raised with regard to that diagnostic category. Morey and Blashfield (1981b) pointed to the danger of "the illusion of precision" (p. 267) in DSM-III. For example, the options allowed in DSM-III permit an individual to be diagnosed as schizophrenic "on the basis of relatively uninformative symptoms" (Morey & Blashfield, 1981b, p. 267). Another problem is the surprisingly low agreement across the various research diagnostic systems and DSM-III in regard to which patients are classified as schizophrenic (Gift et al., 1980; Kendell, Brockington, & Leff, 1979; Strauss & Gift, 1977).

Reliability in diagnosing schizophrenia has been enhanced by substantially narrowing the diagnostic concept. Fewer patients are now included in this category (Chapman & Chapman, 1980; Eysenck, Wakefield, & Friedman, 1983; Haier, 1980; Spitzer, Williams, & Skodol, 1980). Although DSM-III is designed to be applicable to all patients, this full coverage is achieved through the use of a number of vaguely defined "wastebasket" categories (e.g., "atypical psychosis"). Whether such a narrowing of the diagnostic concept will prove to be informative is an empirical question requiring extensive investigation. However, the increased precision and reliability of diagnosis will greatly facilitate such research.

When attention is shifted from characteristics that define a class to the correlates of class membership, this implies a shift in concern from the reliability of a system to its validity. Diagnostic efforts to date have almost totally revolved about the issue of reliability and its close corollary, the achievement in classification of acceptable rates of false positives and false negatives. Understanding a disorder has much more to do with the validity of a classification system than with its reliability. We may be able to place individuals into classes with great reliability without beginning to understand why they are manifesting those symptoms that lead to class inclusion. Compounding the problem is our current awareness that patients displaying the same surface features (i.e., symptoms) may be doing so in spite of differing causative factors.

In part the almost exclusive focus of research on the issue of reliability may reflect some conceptual confusion concerning the distinction between the reliability and validity of a classificatory system. Whereas reliability concerns the principles upon which classes are formed, validity is concerned with the predictions or valid statements that can be made about phenomena once they are classified. A conceptual difficulty lies in the overlap between the classifying principles and the class correlates. If a classificatory system is reliable, it is also valid to the extent that we can predict that the individuals within a class will exhibit certain characteristics, namely, those behaviors or attributes that serve to define the class. Moving beyond these defining characteristics, other predictions associated with class membership can vary from simple extensions of the classifactory principles to correlates that would appear to have little connection with these principles. One may for example predict that individuals displaying certain symptoms (e.g., the presence of delusions or self-depreciation) will have histories involving more favorable premorbid adjustment or will respond differently to drug treatment regimens. These correlations have little direct connection with the symptoms themselves. The predictions are open to test, and evidence may or may not be found to support them.

While some degree of reliability in the original classification is necessary if groups are to be formed, these examples represent instances where there is considerable independence between reliability and validity. Rather than having intrinsic merit, reliability can be seen as "a 'service concept' used to assess the extent that measurement error limits validity" (Carey & Gottesman, 1978, p. 1458). When one is choosing a diagnostic system, consideration of reliability should be subordinate to validity, inasmuch as the most reliable system may not be the most valid.

Instructive here are the variety of correlates of DSM-I and DSM-II categories. In view of the extensive criticism of these diagnostic systems, the surprising fact is that so many valid predictions could be derived from class memberships. Within these systems, the broad diagnostic categories were able to differentiate patients with better and worse psychiatric outcomes (Farber, 1975; Gunderson et al., 1974; Lewine, Watt, Prentky, & Fryer, 1978; Marsh, Glick, & Zigler, 1981; Ostow, 1973) and with respect to a variety of other variables including family history of mental disorder, communication styles in families, biological variables, and pharmacologic responsivity (Carpenter, 1976). The relationships discovered in our work between diagnosis and a number of different indicators of maturity level will be reviewed later in this chapter. One example of the predictive efficacy of narrower diagnostic groupings, is paranoid–nonparanoid status in schizophrenia. The many variables associated with this distinction will be described in Chapter 6.

As we indicated, the issue of validity has been underemphasized both in earlier research concerned with DSM-I and DSM-II and with regard to the recently developed diagnostic systems. Now that reliability in diagnosis has been much improved, indications are that the question of validity will become a major focus of research (Blashfield & Draguns, 1976; Haier, 1980). However, some preliminary findings raise the question of whether the improved reliability of the newer systems will, in fact, yield greater predictive validity.

Carey and Gottesman (1978) describe a number of situations where increased reliability in diagnosis can actually result in decreased validity. Greater precision in diagnosis has been achieved through an almost exclusive focus on "positive symptoms," which as identified by Strauss et al. (1974) involve the presence of disordered forms of functioning (e.g., hallucinations) rather than a diminution of "normal" functions as is the case with "negative symptoms" (e.g., withdrawal and blunted affect). Yet, as Carey and Gottesman indicated, such negative symptoms may be of sufficient theoretical importance that they are valid despite moderate to low levels of reliability. Schneiderian (1959) first-rank symptoms are positive symptoms that have been featured in the criteria of Feighner et al. (1972) and the PSE (Wing et al., 1977) and that are thus also prominent in RDC (Spitzer et al., 1975) and DSM-III (American Psychiatric Association, 1980) diagnoses of schizophrenia. Yet in a number of studies these symptoms have not been found to be significantly related either to outcome (Bland & Orn, 1979; Carpenter, Strauss, & Muleh, 1973; Hawk, Carpenter, & Strauss, 1975; Kendell et al., 1979; Silverstein & Harrow, 1978) or to such prognostic indicators as premorbid social competence and chronicity (Carpenter, Strauss, & Muleh, 1973; Silverstein & Harrow, 1978). Preliminary findings employing other research systems for diagnosing schizophrenia have also been inconclusive, frequently yielding nonsignificant relationships to outcome criteria (Bland & Orn, 1979; Hawk et al., 1975). Although Kendell et al. (1979) reported that some research definitions of schizophrenia were more effective than others in predicting outcome, these authors noted that all definitions "were more successful at predicting a poor symptomatic outcome than a poor social outcome" (Kendell et al., 1979, p. 25).

Further, in narrowing the definition of schizophrenia, DSM-III and the research diagnostic systems have excluded the schizophrenia spectrum concept. Yet data on family histories of mental disorder suggest that there may be important genetic associations between the various spectrum manifestations of the disorder and the more circumscribed schizophrenic syndrome (Cancro, 1979; Kety et al., 1975). Moreover, Tamminga and Carpenter (1982) reported that schizophrenics as defined by the narrower criteria of DSM-III were not distinct from patients with schizophrenia-like psychoses (e.g., schizophreniform psychosis, atypical psychosis) in their responsiveness to pharmacological treatment. All of these instances where greater reliability may not enhance validity point to the importance of a continuum view of mental disorder. In short, reliability has been improved by emphasizing what is unique to disordered functioning. In contrast to this emphasis, the research on the developmental approach to psychopathology to be presented later in this chapter provides convincing demonstration of the importance of taking into account nonpathological aspects of functioning even when forming symptom-based groupings of patients.

The Homogeneity–Heterogeneity Parameter

Heterogeneity Within Diagnostic Categories

Each of the broad categories of disorder (e.g., schizophrenia, affective disorder) encompass individuals who are heterogeneous in symptom expression as well as with regard to a variety of other measures. As Zigler and Phillips (1961b) pointed out, homogeneity within diagnostic classes is not required for reliability. *Reliability* refers to the agreement in assigning individuals to different diagnostic categories, whereas *homogeneity* refers to the diversity of behavior subsumed within categories. The distinction between these two classificatory requirements is explicitly acknowledged in the "Chinese menu" lists of diagnostic criteria that characterize DSM-III and the various research diagnostic systems. The categories, while quite reliable, subsume diverse phenomena. For example, different individuals can be diagnosed as schizophrenic on the basis of widely varying symptom pictures.

Contrary to the views of some (Bannister, 1968; Rotter, 1954), heterogeneity at the level of broad class categories does not appear to be a substantive criticism of classificatory schemata. A common feature of classificatory systems is that they utilize classes that contain subclasses. An example drawn from biology would be a genus embracing a number of species. If for example schizophrenia is conceptualized as a genus, it cannot be criticized on the grounds that all its members do not share a particular attribute. Such a criticism would involve a confusion between the more specific attributes of the species and the more general attributes of the genus. This is not to assert that schizophrenia does in fact possess the characteristics of a genus. Considerable evidence suggests that the class "schizophrenia" comprises such divergent forms that this category will have to be replaced by an aggregate of entities that does constitute a legitimate genus. However, when a genus is formulated, it cannot be attacked because of its heterogeneous nature since genera are characterized by such heterogeneity.

To criticize a classificatory system because its categories subsume heterogeneous phenomena is to make the error of assuming that homogeneity is a quality that inheres in phenomena when in actuality it is a construction of the observer or classifier. One can, for example, eschew symptom-based classificatory criteria in favor of alternative dimensions, for example, premorbid social competence, and argue that groups formed on this alternative basis are more homogeneous. But is this in fact the case? If premorbid social competence is conceptualized as a general dimension in psychopathology rather than as a subcategory dimension within schizophrenia (Klorman et al., 1977; Zigler et al., 1979), the high premorbid competence category would include many individuals with depressive psychoses, a substantial number of paranoid schizophrenic patients, and many neurotic individuals. Conversely, the low premorbid competence category would include many disorganized and undifferentiated schizophrenic patients and many personality disorder patients. While the groups formed on this basis would be more homogeneous with regard to premorbid competence, they would probably display greater heterogeneity with regard to certain symptoms (e.g., the presence of hallucinations) and even with respect to outcome [1] than the traditional diagnostic groupings of schizophrenia, affective disorder, and personality disorder.

Homogeneity is ultimately determined by the resultant correlates or attributes of class membership. As such, a criticism of heterogeneity leveled against a classificatory schema is frequently nothing more than a plea for the utilization of a new classificatory principle so that attention may be focused on particular class correlates or attributes not considered in the original schema. While this plea may be a justifiable one depending on the significance of the new attributes, it has little to do with the homogeneity, in an absolute sense, of phenomena. Indeed, following the formulation of a new classificatory schema, the heterogeneity criticism could be directed against it by the adherents of the old system, since the phenomena encompassed by the new categories would probably not be considered homogeneous when evaluated by the old classificatory principle.

It has recently been argued that the traditional approach to psychiatric diagnosis, which emphasizes the homogeneity of individuals included within a class, should be replaced with a prototypic approach in which individuals are viewed as being more or less like the class prototype, thereby permitting considerable heterogeneity among individuals grouped together within a class (Cantor et al., 1980). It should be noted that, whether discrete categories or prototypes are employed, the homogeneity of individuals grouped within a class or category is relative, being defined by the classificatory principle underlying the diagnostic schema. Substituting the prototypic for more traditional approaches earns us little unless we possess a metadiagnostic principle to determine how heterogeneous the cases included in the category can be before the categorization loses its usefulness. Any prototype or hypothetical construct would certainly be meaningless if there was no method by which to identify exemplars of the construct. What must be recognized is that workers in the area of psychopathology, be they clinicians or researchers, do not ultimately examine heuristic fictions that we label prototypes or hypothetical constructs. Prediction requires that concepts be specified through public operations that designate the observable referents of the construct.

Heterogeneity Across Diagnostic Categories

Reliability of psychiatric diagnosis is not determined by the number or diversity of symptoms that any diagnostic category encompasses; it is however determined by the extent to which the same symptoms appear in more than one category of the system. The substantial symptom overlap across diagnostic categories that was apparent in the earlier diagnostic systems appears not to have been appreciably altered in the newer systems despite their more stringent criteria. Evidence of thought disorder including hallucinations, delusions, and Schneiderian first-rank symptoms of schizophrenia has for example been found in substantial numbers of affective disorder patients (Carlson & Goodwin, 1973; Carpenter, Strauss, & Muleh, 1973; Clayton, Pitts, & Winokur, 1965; Goodwin, Alderson, & Rosenthal, 1971; Harrow & Quinlan, 1977; Ianzito, Cadoret, & Pugh, 1974; Lowe, 1973; Pope & Lipinski, 1978). Similarly, moderate to severe levels of depression appear to characterize a majority of hospitalized psychiatric patients, whatever the specific diagnosis (Knights & Hirsch, 1981; Lewine et al., 1980; Noyes et al., 1980; Strauss et al., 1978; Wadeson & Carpenter, 1976; Wittenborn, 1977).

These high frequencies of depression reported for all patients point to an aspect of diagnosis that has received little attention. Diagnosis is further complicated by the situation of the patient at the time the diagnosis is made. Particularly with respect to depression, it is difficult to determine how much the presenting symptomatology reflects the condition that precipitated hospitalization and how much it represents a reaction to hospitalization or its possibility. The duration criterion of a 2-week period put forth in DSM-III provides little assistance in making this determination.

In DSM-III and many of the research diagnostic systems, differential diagnosis in the face of overlapping symptoms is accomplished through the specification of exclusion criteria and decision trees. Reliability is thus maintained despite symptom diversity. These newer systems have explicated the decision-making process whereby individuals are assigned to diagnostic classes but do not appear to have altered the process substantially. Clinical diagnosis has always depended upon the empirical observation of the variety of symptoms a patient displays. Once the symptoms have been noted, diagnosis depends upon a weighting of (a) the frequency with which a patient displays symptoms indicative of one diagnostic class as compared with others; (b) the relative importance of various symptoms for determining diagnosis; and (c) such other factors as the duration of disturbance, the nature of onset, and possible etiology.

What must be recognized is that the clinician has always functioned as a diagnostic system. The contribution of the research diagnostic systems has not been to alter the basic judgments required for diagnosis or even in many instances the criteria utilized. For example, the first-rank symptoms identified on the basis of clinical observation by Schneider (1959) as pathognomonic for schizophrenia are prominently featured in most research diagnostic systems. The value of these systems is that they objectify and thus make uniform across clinicians the criteria and the chain of decisions necessary for diagnosis.[2]

Another approach for reducing heterogeneity across diagnostic classes involves the application of multivariate statistical techniques directed toward the discovery of statistically circumscribable clusters of symptoms. Although sometimes employed to differentiate the broad class categories (i.e., schizophrenia, anxiety, and affective disorder [Kendell & Gourley, 1970; Roth et al., 1972], "numerical taxonomy" (Skinner, 1981; Sneath & Sokal, 1973) has been more frequently applied for the construction of subcategories within schizophrenia (Carpenter et al., 1976; Lorr, Klett, & McNair, 1963) and the affective disorders (for reviews of this research see Blashfield & Morey, 1979; MacFayden, 1975). As with the research diagnostic systems, the contribution of this approach has been to reduce subjectivity through the use of uniform analytic methods (Garside & Roth, 1978), which as Paykel (1981) noted enables us "to lift the debate . . . on . . . classification . . . from personal bias and polemic to empirical research" (p. 360). However, the variety of statistical models that can be applied in deriving symptom clusters and the nature of clustering procedures present problems in interpretation and necessitate careful strategies for validation. Morey, Skinner, and Blashfield (in press) provide a clear and thoughtful discussion of these issues. As these authors illustrate, differing clustering methods applied to the same data may yield markedly different solutions. Further, these various statistical procedures maximize chance findings. Thus, clusters statistically discovered should be replicated in a variety of ways (Morey et al., in press). Little effort to date has been directed toward the validation of the symptom clusters disclosed (Carpenter et al., 1976; Garside & Roth, 1978; Skinner, 1981), although an important exception here is the relationship discovered by Overall et al. (1966) between statistically identified depressive subtypes and response to drug treatment. Therefore, while informative, the statistical approach to the construction of diagnostic classes is not a standard of homogeneity against which other classifications can be evaluated.

Neither have these methods resulted in any substantial conceptual advance in our understanding of the major syndromes in psychopathology. As Paykel (1981) noted, "the great syndromes in psychiatry were identified by penetrating clinical observers, not applied statisticians" (p. 360). Further, as Garside and Roth (1978) commented, "It is a chastening thought that virtually all the diagnostic concepts in current use have resulted from the observations of clinical observers who were professionally active more than half a century ago" (p. 53).

Diagnosis and Theoretical Formulation

Following the tradition of descriptive psychiatry, the recent statistical and research approaches to diagnosis focus on manifest symptoms and are essentially theory free. In this approach, there is the danger that these psychiatric classifications may describe only superficial phenotypes. As Zubin and Steinhauer (1981) noted:

> There is a tendency for these [semistructured interview] techniques to generate
> the kinds of data for which they originally were calibrated. . . . surprise and

unexpected findings are ruled out by the limitations of the instrument, and new and unpredicted possibilities are unlikely to arise. Diagnostic success is built on 34 centuries of careful phenomenological observation of mental patients by astute clinicians. (p. 478)

The central importance of theory in diagnostic classification has been emphasized by Bannister (1968), Hempel (1961), and Skinner (1981).

In the work to be reviewed below, the developmental formulation was applied in an examination of the processes underlying diagnostic judgment. While the research was conducted with patients diagnosed on the basis of DSM-I, the focus of this work on the implicit assumptions made by clinicians in assigning patients to diagnostic groups remains relevant. As the work suggests, theoretical assumptions may always have played a more central role in symptom-based diagnosis than has been recognized. It has been asserted that diagnosis is based on the "feel of the case" and/or the clinician's phenomenological state when interacting with the patient (Thorne, 1953). In regard to schizophrenia, Pao (1979) described this state at some length as a sense of lack of rapport, a "special atmosphere" or barrier created by the patient. Clearly such an aura approach would demand much further systematization before either the reliability or the validity of the clinician's classification could be assessed. The work presented below suggests that clinicians in arriving at a diagnosis may not rely on the simple summation of symptoms but rather may employ symptoms as indicators whereby they infer broader life-style characteristics of the patient. This activity of the clinician itself constitutes a diagnostic system that must be explicated if it is to be informative.

SYMPTOMATOLOGY, MATURITY LEVEL, AND DIAGNOSIS: EMPIRICAL WORK

The traditional psychiatric syndromes are defined primarily by patterns or constellations of symptoms. The assumption is that individuals whose symptoms differ are suffering from different disorders and therefore different patterns of symptoms should be differentially related to major variables of clinical interest (e.g., treatment and outcome). The symptom clusters employed to define the various syndromes are not theoretically derived but empirically based. They are dependent either upon the accumulated observations of clinicians that certain symptoms co-occur whereas others do not or, more recently, upon statistical methods that more precisely and objectively indicate co-occurrence and disjunction. Alternative symptom clusters derived from developmental theory were described in the previous chapter. The question then arises as to how these conceptually derived clusters or symptom categories (reflecting role orientation and placement along an action–thought continuum) compare with the symptom-based categories (syndromes) of traditional psychiatric diagnosis. Do these two modes of symptom classification in fact differ or might the developmental clusters reflect no more than the assigning of new names to the traditional categories of psychiatric diagnosis? The evidence to be presented in this section suggests that the two methods of symptom classification are not identical, although some overlap exists. The implications of this overlap are considered as they relate both to the understanding of traditional diagnosis and to directions for further refinement in the classification of psychiatric disorders.

Symptom Expression, Role Orientation, and Diagnosis

Zigler and Phillips (1961c) examined the relationship between symptom manifestation and inclusion in a particular category within traditional psychiatric diagnosis. A second objective of the study was to compare traditional diagnosis with the system of psychiatric classification based on role orientation (Phillips & Rabinovitch, 1958; Zigler & Phillips, 1960, 1962).

Despite the many criticisms of traditional psychiatric diagnosis, relatively few studies had previously examined the relationship of symptom manifestation to the diagnosis assigned. The nature of this relationship pertains to the issues of both heterogeneity and reliability in psychiatric diagnosis. As indicated earlier in this chapter, broad diagnostic groupings (corresponding to genera) can subsume heterogeneous phenomena and still allow for the reliable assignment of individuals to diagnostic categories. Although a decrease in the reliability of a category is invariably accompanied by an increase in its heterogeneity, categories that subsume quite heterogeneous phenomena are not necessarily unreliable. More problematic is the overlap of symptoms across diagnostic groups. The reliability of psychiatric diagnosis is not determined by the number or diversity of symptoms that any diagnostic class encompasses but by the extent to which the same symptoms appear in more than one category of the system. Based on previous work (e.g., King, 1954; Wittenborn & Weiss, 1952; Zigler & Phillips, 1961b), Zigler and Phillips (1961c) began with the assumption that each of the broad categories of traditional psychiatric diagnosis was both heterogeneous (subsumed a large number of diverse symptoms) and reasonably reliable (any particular symptom would tend to occur in only one category). A first objective of the study was to evaluate this position empirically. A second aim was to determine the degree of overlap between conventional psychiatric diagnosis and role orientation symptom categories.

The study was based on an examination of the case records of 793 patients admitted to Worcester State Hospital between 1945 and 1957. Four broad DSM-I diagnostic categories were represented: 75 (37 male and 38 female) manic-depressive patients; 152 (81 male and 71 female) psychoneurotic patients; 287 (165 male and 122 female) schizophrenic patients; and 279 (197 male and 82 female) character disorder patients. The group categorized as manic-depressive included a variety of forms of psychotic depression as well as manic-depressive psychosis and thus can be considered roughly equivalent to the affective disorder groups in later diagnostic systems (DSM-II and DSM-III). In regard to DSM-III, the one obvious exception is that all patients in the Zigler-Phillips (1961c) manic-depressive group were psychotic. (The changed diagnostic status of neurotic forms of depression in DSM-III will present some problems in comparing future studies to research conducted before 1980.)

Table 5.1 presents the percentage of patients in the entire sample and in each diagnostic group who manifested each of the presenting symptoms we continue to employ in our work. The symptoms are listed in the order of their frequency of occurrence in the total sample. As can be seen from Table 5.1, each diagnostic category encompassed individuals who were extremely heterogeneous in symptom expression. Also evident is the substantial overlap of symptoms across diagnostic categories. The high frequency of depression and anxiety (tense) that appeared regardless of diagnostic category has continued to be a prominent finding (Lewine et al., 1980; Strauss, Kokes, Ritzler, Harder, & Van Ord, 1978; Wittenborn, 1977).

In order to assess the degree of relationship between specific symptoms and diagnostic categories, chi-square analyses were performed to evaluate the tendency of each of the symptoms either to occur or not to occur in each of the four diagnostic categories. Contingency coefficients were then computed for each of the contingency tables that resulted in a significant chi-square. Table 5.2 presents all significant ($p < .05$) contingency coefficients. The contingency coefficient can only be positive in value. Nevertheless they are tabled here as negative in the instances where the relationship between symptom and diagnosis was such that the symptom tended not to occur with that diagnosis.

In the total of 140 comparisons originally made between the presence or absence of a symptom and diagnosis, 67 significant relationships appeared. However, as Table 5.2 indicates, the degree of relationship as estimated by the contingency coefficient tended to be small.

A certain degree of relationship, therefore, appeared between symptom manifestation and diagnosis. However, the most striking finding of the study was that the magnitude of these relationships was generally so small that membership in a particular diagnostic group could be seen as conveying only minimal information about the symptomatology of the patient. A wide variety of symptoms were found to be related to more than one major diagnostic category. Since the basis for diagnostic classification is ostensibly symptom manifestation, the question arises as to why such classification has been found to be reasonably reliable across broad diagnostic groups in spite of the fact that particular symptoms tend to occur with surprisingly comparable frequency across diagnostic classes.

One possible answer is that, although single symptoms may not grossly differentiate diagnoses, configurations of symptoms do so discriminate. In opposition to this view are some findings (Freudenberg & Robertson, 1956)

TABLE 5.1. Percentage of Individuals in Total Sample and in Each Diagnostic Category Manifesting Each Symptom

Symptom	All Patients (N = 793)	Manic-Depressive (N = 75)	Psychoneurotic (N = 152)	Character Disorder (N = 279)	Schizophrenia (N = 287)
Depressed	38	64	58	31	28
Tense	37	32	46	33	36
Suspiciousness	35	25	16	17	65
Drinking	19	17	14	32	8
Hallucinations	19	11	4	12	35
Suicidal attempt	16	24	19	15	12
Suicidal ideas	15	29	23	15	8
Bodily complaints	15	21	21	5	19
Emotional outbursts	14	17	12	18	9
Withdrawn	14	4	12	7	25
Perplexed	14	9	9	8	24
Assaultive	12	5	6	18	5
Self-depreciatory	12	16	16	8	13
Threatens assault	10	4	11	14	7
Sexual preoccupation	10	9	9	6	14
Maniacal outbursts	9	11	6	7	12
Bizarre ideas (delusions)	9	11	1	2	20
Robbery	8	0	3	18	3
Apathetic	8	8	8	4	11
Irresponsible behavior	7	3	7	9	7
Euphoria	5	17	2	2	5
Mood swings	5	9	5	4	4
Insomnia	5	11	7	3	5
Doesn't eat	4	9	4	2	4
Obsessions	3	8	3	1	4
Depersonalization	3	4	1	0	6
Phobias	2	4	5	0	2

TABLE 5.2.   Magnitude of the Relationship Between Symptoms and Diagnoses

Symptom	Manic-Depressive	Psychoneurotic	Character Disorder	Schizophrenia
Category 1				
Self-deprivation				
and turning against the self				
Suicidal attempt	.07			−.07
Suicidal ideas	.13	.10		−.16
Euphoria	.19		−.08	
Bodily complaints		.09	−.20	.10
Tense		.09		
Self-depreciatory			−.09	
Depressed	.17	.19	−.11	−.16
Mood swings				
Insomnia	.08			
Phobias		.10	−.09	
Obsessions	.09		−.10	
Doesn't eat	.09			
Category 2				
Self-indulgence and				
turning against others				
Maniacal outbursts				.08
Drinking			.24	−.20
Robbery	−.08	−.09	.27	
Irresponsible				
behavior				
Assaultive		−.09	.12	
Threatens assault			.11	−.08
Emotional outbursts			.10	−.10
Category 3				
Avoidance of others				
Suspiciousness		−.19	−.27	.42
Perplexed		−.07	−.13	.21
Bizarre ideas (delusions)		−.13	−.18	.27
Hallucinations		−.18	−.13	.30
Sexual preoccupation			.09	.11
Apathetic			−.09	.09
Withdrawn	−.09		−.15	.24
Depersonalization			−.11	.15

that complex combinations of symptoms do not lead to greater differentiation between diagnoses. Another possiblity is that symptoms are not sufficiently unitary indexes. As we noted in Chapter 4, "withdrawal" in the depressive may be of a qualitatively different nature than "withdrawal" in the schizophrenic. Borrowing an analogy from physics, if diagnostic categories represent the molecules and symptoms the atoms in the analysis of psychiatric disorders, more fine-grained levels of analysis will be required if the understanding of psychopathology is to advance. Certainly physics would not have proceeded far if analysis had remained at the level of the atom.

We mentioned earlier the view of some (Pao, 1979; Thorne, 1956) that the experienced clinician uses an internal reference system in diagnosis. If such is the case, the explication and closer analysis of these implicit operations could suggest valuable directions for further refinements in our diagnostic system. In addition, the clinician may be responding to some global configuration that transcends symptomatology or to criteria that lie beyond the domain of psychiatry proper. The findings of Zigler and Phillips (1961c) concerning the relationship of role orientation to diagnosis, as well as other evidence to be presented in this chapter regarding the relationship of diagnosis to developmental indexes, are consistent with this interpretation of the diagnostic process.

Table 5.2 also groups the presenting symptoms according to the three role orientation categories, and inspection of this table points to some overlap between role orientation and diagnosis. The self-deprivation and turning-against the-self category was positively related to both the manic-depressive and psychoneurotic categories but negatively related to the other two. The self-indulgence and turning-against-others category was positively related to a diagnosis of character disorder but negatively related to schizophrenic diagnosis. Avoidance of others was positively related to the schizophrenic diagnostic category but negatively related to character disorder and psychoneurotic diagnosis.

While some correspondence appears to exist between these alternative modes of symptom categorization, the findings make it clear that the two are not identical systems differing only in name. One might neverthless ask why the two systems correspond at all since one derives from a theoretical formulation not generally employed in common psychiatric practice whereas the other is atheoretical in nature and based upon empirical observations regarding the co-occurrence of symptoms. A possibility is that clinicians implicitly incorporate an evaluation of the overall maturity level of the patient in assigning diagnoses. If such an evaluation implicitly enters the diagnostic process, its influence may proceed in a number of possible directions. One possibility is that upon encountering a depressed and self-disparaging individual the diagnostician infers a higher developmental level leading to the assignment of neurotic or affective reaction diagnoses. Alternatively, when confronted with a patient who displays evidence of greater maturity (e.g., one who has met such basic societal expectancies as being married and steadily employed in a responsible position), the clinician may more frequently look for and focus upon depressive symptomatology leading to the diagnosis of depression. Finally, the symptoms noted and evidence of higher competence may be part of a larger and more general network of implicit assumptions that are related to maturity level. In regard to all these possibilities, it is important to note that depressive symptomatology does not automatically or inevitably lead to a diagnosis of affective reaction or depressive neurosis (DSM-II) or affective disorder (DSM-III). Depression at moderate or severe levels has been found to characterize the majority of psychiatric inpatients (Glick et al., 1985; Knights & Hirsch, 1981; Roy, 1980; Wadeson & Carpenter, 1976; Wittenborn, 1977). As an example, Lewine et al. (1980) found the symptom of depression was manifested by 74 percent of schizophrenic, 75 percent of personality disorder, 86 percent of neurotic, and 86 percent of affective reaction patients. And Strauss, Kokes, Ritzler, Harder, & Van Ord, (1978) reported moderate or severe depression in 92 percent of a large sample of first-admission psychiatric patients falling into many diagnostic groups. Even the duration criterion specified in DSM-III ("nearly every day for a period of at least two weeks") would scarcely be sufficient to exclude many patients in the other diagnostic groups (e.g., personality disorder individuals) from the affective disorder category. Depression, then, is clearly a nondistinctive symptom that is found in other disorders almost to the same degree that it is found in the depressive syndromes. Corresponding to the findings of Zigler and Phillips (1961c), this recent evidence suggests that symptoms alone do not determine diagnosis.

The finding of a relationship between role orientation symptom clusters and conventional psychiatric diagnosis is also relevant to the heterogeneity issue. If heretogeneity is defined simply as the number of symptoms that appear in any diagnostic category, the results of Zigler and Phillips (1961c) support the view that conventional diagnostic categories are heterogeneous in basic phenomena. However, an alternative solution to the heterogeneity–homogeneity problem can be offered. Homeogeneity may be defined in terms of the imposition of some organizing principle on otherwise discrete and apparently random pathological events. Homogeneity is thus a construction of the classifier rather than a quality that inheres in symptomatic behaviors. The Phillips and Rabinovitch symptom clusters represent just such an attempt at conceptual classification. Thus they provide a means for viewing diverse pathological behaviors as fundamentally homogeneous in nature.

Developmental Differences Between Diagnostic Groups

Social Competence and Diagnosis

Consistent relationships have been obtained between premorbid social competence scores and diagnosis. Employing a sample of 793 (480 male and 313 female) psychiatric inpatients, Zigler and Phillips (1961a) found that significantly higher social competence scores characterized affective reaction (manic-depressive) and psychoneurotic patients as compared with schizophrenic and personality disorder (character disorder) groups. This finding has been subsequently replicated (Zigler et al., 1979; Lewine et al., 1980). In both these later studies, affective disorder patients obtained significantly higher premorbid competence scores than neurotics, and the scores of the neurotic groups were significantly higher than those of schizophrenic and personality disorder patients. As in the Zigler and Phillips (1961a) study, the schizophrenic and personality disorder groups did not differ significantly in social competence scores.

The higher developmental status of patients with affective disorder and neurotic diagnoses is not surprising inasmuch as patients in both these (DSM-II) diagnostic groups frequently display depression, a symptom presumed to reflect the greater internalization of societal standards and consequent social guilt. However, the absence of differences between schizophrenic and personality disorder patients is counterintuitive. Given the behaviors exhibited by schizophrenics, one is tempted to view schizophrenia as a developmentally lower form than the personality disorders (Goldman, 1962; Werner, 1948).

A number of explanations for the low scores of personality disorder patients can be advanced. In part, the explanation may be with the nature of the premorbid social competence measure. If the social competence index penalized social withdrawal more than it presently does, schizophrenics might prove to be lower than personality disorder patients. (As indicated in Chapter 3, the authors feel that the social competence index does not adequately reflect differences in everyday social participation, e.g., friendships, social activities, organizational participation.) Because the Zigler-Phillips index reflects typical accomplishments of adulthood, it has also been suggested (Zigler et al., 1979) that the young age of many personality disorder patients may result in attenuated scores for this group.

Some preliminary data suggest that young age is insufficient to account for the low social competence scores of personality disorder patients but that the lack of emphasis on everyday social participation may be a contributing factor in the low social competence scores of this group. We have compared the social competence scores of younger (under 25 years) and older (25 years and older) personality disorder and schizophrenic patients. If the young age of personality disorder patients were a primary factor contributing to their low scores, one would expect an absence of significant differences in social competence between groups of young personality disorder and schizophrenic patients but significantly higher scores for older personality disorder patients in comparison to their schizophrenic counterparts. In neither the younger nor the older age group did personality disorder and schizophrenic patients differ significantly in overall social competence or on the component indexes of education, occupation, and employment history. However, at both age levels, the personality disorder patients obtained higher scores than the schizophrenics on the marital status variable, suggesting that if more measures of social participation were included personality disorder patients would obtain higher social competence scores.

Yet the possibility must be entertained that personality disorder diagnosis does reflect a developmentally low pattern of functioning, albeit one that is different from the pattern typically displayed by schizophrenic patients. Developmentally low action-oriented symptoms are predominant in personality disorder diagnosis. As noted in Chapter 4, evidence has not been forthcoming that symptoms indicative of turning against others (associated with personality disorder diagnosis) are related to more advanced functioning than are symptoms reflecting avoidance of others and associated with schizophrenic diagnosis. In fact Quinlan et al. (1980) have presented some evidence to suggest that avoidance of others may be associated with higher developmental status than turning against others.

Social Competence, Symptom Expression, and Diagnosis

The relationship between maturity level and psychiatric diagnosis was further examined by Phillips, Broverman, and Zigler (1966). One aspect of this investigation involved categorization within each of three spheres of symptom dominance (thought, action, and affect) of symptoms indicative of developmentally higher, intermediate, and lower levels of functioning. These categorizations, based on empirical relations discovered between the specific symptoms and social competence, were presented in Table 4.4 of the preceding chapter. The relationship between these more fine-grained symptom categories and social competence was examined, and the relationship of these levels of symptom expression to diagnosis was investigated as well.

The case history records of 504 patients (287 males and 217 females) admitted to Worcester State Hospital between 1945 and 1957 were examined. Four broad disgnostic categories were represented: manic-depressive (N = 47); schizophrenia (N = 182); psychoneurotic disorder (N = 98); and character disorder (N = 177). The number of patients in each diagnostic category manifesting symptoms or symptom combinations at each of the three developmental levels (defined by social competence scores) for each sphere-dominance symptom scale is presented in Table 5.3. (It should be noted that a single patient could be included in more than one scale.)

Chi-square analyses revealed significant relationships between scores on each scale and diagnosis. On the thought scale, psychoneurotic and to a lesser extent character disorder patients were characterized by relatively high-level thought symptoms while the reverse was true for schizophrenic patients. On the action scale, psychoneurotic patients manifested high-level symptoms while character disorder patients had low-level symptoms. Findings with the affect scale indicated high-level symptoms for manic-depressive and psychoneurotic patients, while the schizophrenic and character disorder groups were characterized by lower-level affect symptoms. In general, then, the psychoneurotic and manic-depressive patients displayed symptoms indicative of higher levels of social maturity than did schizophrenic and character disorder patients. Further, the particular pattern of symptoms differentiated within pairs of developmentally higher or lower diagnostic groups. The manic-depressive's higher level of social maturity was evidenced most clearly in affect whereas the psychoneurotic tended to manifest high-level symptoms in all three areas. Schizophrenic patients expressed their immaturity primarily in the sphere of thought and character disorder patients in the sphere of affect.

TABLE 5.3.   Relationships Between Symptom Scales and Diagnosis

Symptom Scale	Manic-Depressive	Schizophrenia	Psychoneurotic	Character Disorder
Thought				
Level 1	5 (4.4)	5 (20.1)	19 (9.9)	19 (13.4)
Level 2	7 (5.6)	31 (25.6)	9 (12.6)	14 (17.0)
Level 3	2 (3.8)	27 (17.2)	3 (8.4)	9 (11.4)
	$\chi^2 = 35.58, p < .001$			
Affect				
Level 1	21 (14.0)	39 (51.1)	45 (35.9)	46 (49.9)
Level 2	0 (6.5)	37 (23.3)	12 (16.4)	20 (22.8)
Level 3	2 (2.5)	8 (9.4)	2 (6.6)	16 (9.2)
	$\chi^2 = 33.49, p < .001$			
Action				
Level 1	11 (8.4)	16 (17.3)	24 (15.1)	22 (32.0)
Level 2	9 (11.5)	25 (23.6)	12 (20.8)	54 (43.9)
	$\chi^2 = 15.94, p < .005$			

Source: "Social Competence and Psychiatric Diagnosis" by L. Phillips, I.K. Broverman, and E. Zigler, 1966, Journal of Abnormal Psychology, 71. Copyright 1966 by American Psychological Association. Reprinted by permission of the publisher.

Note: Frequencies expected by chance alone are presented in parentheses.

For those patients (a minority of the total sample) who appeared on more than one of the symptom scales, chi-square analyses revealed significant positive relationships between level of symptom expression across all three scales. The maturity dimension examined in this study thus appears to be a pervasive one. The symptoms of a patient across spheres of functioning were not idiosyncratic but appeared to be a consistent expression of the patient's maturity level.

Phillips et al. (1966) thus identified another dimension of symptom expression on which developmental level was found to be related to diagnosis. Although clinicians show some consistency in placing patients into the major nosological categories, the process underlying this reliability remains a mystery. As suggested by Zigler and Phillips (1961c), one possibility is that, although clinicians orient themselves toward presenting symptoms, the actual process of diagnosis is mediated by the clinician's implicit ordering of these symptoms along certain dimensions. One of these dimensions appears to be that of maturity level. In this sense then, the experienced diagnostician can be seen as an analogue of a multiaxial diagnostic system, forming judgments along a variety of implicit dimensions. To the extent that the developmental orderings described here are employed by clinicians, the reliablity of diagnosis despite the heterogeneity of specific symptoms can be understood as mediated by such implicit developmental orderings. While such a concept is much too ephemeral to be of value in an understanding of the diagnostic process, it does suggest that the diagnostician employs the patient's total behavioral picture in order to arrive at a diagnosis.

Sphere Dominance, Role Orientation, and Diagnosis

Although the experienced clinician may take a broader view of the patient and diagnose on the basis of "the feel of the case" rather than purely by textbook symptom criteria, it is unreasonable to assume that the diagnostician ignores the specific symptoms of a patient in deciding on a diagnosis. Rather, it would appear that the symptom picture is employed as one among a number of possible indicators of the patient's general behavioral style.

A central assumption in the developmental approach to psychopathology is that there is a continuity between adaptive and maladaptive forms of functioning. Symptoms are not viewed solely as indexes of some pathological state but are seen as reflections of the patient's general behavioral style, which characterizes premorbid as well as postmorbid functioning. Sphere dominance or the tendency to use thought, action, or affect as the primary vehicle for self-expression represents one aspect of general behavioral style. A second aspect of life-style involves the patient's role orientation or social role as expressed in symptomatology. The social role construct refers to the individual's general orientation or attitude toward both the self and others. In an attempt to articulate further the implicit developmental dimensions that may underlie reliability in diagnosis, Phillips, Broverman, and Zigler (1968) investigated the relative contributions of both sphere dominance and role orientation to the diagnostic placement of patients. A central thesis of this study was that it would be not the presence or absence of specific symptoms within sphere-dominance or role orientation categories that would determine diagnosis, but rather the patient's predominant pattern of symptom expression. Thus for both sphere dominance and role orientation symptom scores were constructed to reflect the patient's predominant mode of expression in one sphere or orientation rather than the other two. These symptom scores were then expected to be related to diagnosis.

The case history records of 762 patients, 455 males and 307 females, admitted to Worcester State Hospital between 1945 and 1957 were examined. The patients were placed into four major diagnostic categories, manic-depressive, schizophrenic, psychoneurotic, and character disorder, using the same criteria as were employed by Zigler and Phillips (1961a).

The role orientation categories, previously presented in Table 5.1 of Chapter 4, were modified in this study in an effort to make them more representative of social role and to have thought, action, and affect symptoms fairly evenly represented in each of the three role categories. This necessitated a reduction of the symptoms defining each role category. The 13 symptoms retained were those that occurred most frequently in the hospital population. The four symptoms retained in the turning-against-the-self category were suicidal ideas, self-depreciatory, suicidal attempt, and depressed.

In the turning-against-others category, the symptoms were threatens assault, assault, robbery and temper outbursts, while for the avoidance of others category, the symptoms were suspicious, perplexed, hallucinated, withdrawn, and apathetic. Each patient was classified according to the predominant role orientation he or she displayed.

A highly significant relationship appeared between sphere-dominance categories and diagnosis ($\chi^2 = 147.06$, $df = 6$, $p < .001$). The distribution of the three sphere-dominance categories across the four diagnostic groups is presented in Table 5.4. As can be seen from Table 5.4, schizophrenics tended to be thought dominant, while psychoneurotic and character disorder patients tended not to display thought dominance. Character disorder patients tended to be action dominated, whereas schizophrenic patients tended to display a lack of action dominance. Psychoneurotic and manic-depressive patients tended to be affect dominant, while character disorders tended to lack affect dominance.

TABLE 5.4.   Relationship Between Sphere-Dominance Categories and Diagnosis

Diagnosis	Sphere-Dominance Categories		
	Thought	Action	Affect
Psychoneurotic	20 (34.25)	24 (30.37)	48 (27.37)
Manic-depressive	13 (19.36)	15 (17.16)	24 (15.47)
Character disorder	32 (61.81)	102 (54.80)	32 (49.38)
Schizophrenia	129 (78.56)	31 (69.65)	51 (62.77)

Source: "Sphere Dominance, Role Orientation, and Diagnosis" by L. Phillips, I.K. Broverman, and E. Zigler, 1968, *Journal of Abnormal Psychology, 73.* Copyright 1968 by American Psychological Association. Reprinted by permission of the publisher.

Note: Frequencies expected by chance alone are shown in parentheses. $\chi^2 = 147.06$; $df = 6$; $p < .001$, $C = .469$.

A highly significant relationship likewise appeared between role orientation and diagnosis ($\chi^2 = 237.29$, $df = 6$, $p < .001$). The distribution of the three role orientation groups across the four diagnostic categories is presented in Table 5.5. This table indicates that, while manic-depressive and psychoneurotic patients were characterized by the role orientation of turning against the self, schizophrenics tended not to employ this role. Character disorders tended to employ the turning-against-others role orientation, while schizophrenic patients tended to lack this role orientation. The schizophrenics were predominantly characterized by the role orientation of avoidance of others, whereas the three other diagnostic groups lacked this orientation.

The magnitude of the relationships of sphere dominance and role orientation to diagnosis was further assessed by means of contingency coefficients, corrected for number of categories. The resulting contingency coefficients of .596 for the sphere-dominance–diagnosis relation and of .711 for the role orientation–diagnosis relation suggest that each style variable is an important component underlying the known reliability of psychiatric diagnosis. However, partial regression analyses pointed to the greater contribution of role orientation than sphere dominance to diagnostic variance.

As was indicated in Chapter 4, role orientation and sphere dominance are interrelated categorizations that nevertheless each retain a considerable amount of independent variance. In light of this degree of independence, an effort was made to assess the combined relation of sphere dominance and role orientation to diagnosis. Chi-square and contingency coefficient analyses yielded highly significant findings ($\chi^2 = 553.38$, df $= 28$, $p < .001$; $C =$

TABLE 5.5.   Relationship Between Role Orientation and Diagnosis

Diagnosis	Turning Against Self	Turning Against Others	Avoidance of Others
Psychoneurotic	59 (31.43)	13 (16.95)	20 (43.61)
Manic-depressive	36 (17.76)	5 (9.58)	11 (24.65)
Character disorder	57 (56.71)	68 (30.58)	41 (78.69)
Schizophrenia	26 (72.08)	10 (38.87)	175 (100.03)

Source: "Sphere Dominance, Role Orientation, and Diagnosis" by L. Phillips, I.K. Broverman, and E. Zigler, 1968, *Journal of Abnormal Psychology, 73.* Copyright 1968 by American Psychological Association. Reprinted by permission of the publisher.

Note: Frequencies expected by chance alone are shown in parentheses. $\chi^2 = 237.29$; $df = 6$; $p < .001$, $C = .559$.

.717). The combination of role orientation and sphere dominance appeared, therefore, to account for virtually all that is reliable in psychiatric diagnosis; the remaining variance in conventional diagnosis may well represent random error inherent in assigning diagnoses on an intuitive and subjective basis.

The results lend considerable credence to the view that the psychiatric diagnosis assigned by the clinician corresponds in substantial degree to the patient's general behavior patterns or life-styles rather than to the individual symptoms or discrete symptom combinations that the patient presents. The findings of this study and the ones previously reviewed suggest that a symptom should not be regarded as a simple actuarial phenomenon that unerringly leads to a diagnosis. Rather the symptom appears to be a complex indicator that allows the clinician to derive inferences about the patient's general style of behavior.

The complexity of such indicators can be seen in such symptoms as "threatening assault," "suicidal thoughts," "attempted suicide," and "assaultive behavior." While traditional diagnostic systems (DSM-I through

DSM-III) and the various research approaches derived from the same fundamental assumption about symptom expression are based upon the simple notation of the presence or absence of individual symptoms, quite different classifying principles have been proposed and examined in this research emanating from the developmental approach to psychopathology. In this work, individual symptoms are related in quite different ways to various life-styles. Thus suicidal attempt and suicidal ideas both indicate a role orientation of turning against the self, but suicidal attempt is categorized as an action symptom whereas suicidal ideas represent symptom expression in thought. It is not, then, any simple summation of individual symptoms that corresponds to diagnosis; rather, particular life-styles as inferred from specific constellations of symptoms are related to the psychiatric diagnosis assigned by the clinician.

Seifert, Draguns, and Caudill (1971) replicated the Phillips et al. (1968) study employing a sample of 412 patients admitted to four psychiatric hospitals in Tokyo, Japan, during 1958. As with the work at Worcester State Hospital, the case records of patients in four diagnostic categories were examined: manic-depressive, schizophrenic, neurotic, and character disorder. Social competence, sphere dominance, and role orientation were scored in accordance with the procedures employed by Phillips et al. (1966, 1968).

Chi-square analyses revealed significant relationships between diagnosis and each of the variables of role orientation, social competence, and sphere dominance (all $ps < .001$). As with the finding obtained in the United States, role orientation and sphere dominance were found to be partially independent, with role orientation making a somewhat greater contribution than sphere dominance to the variance in diagnosis. Partial regression analyses that included social competence levels as well as sphere-dominance and role orientation scores indicated that the predictors of diagnosis in decreasing order of efficacy were role orientation, social competence, and sphere dominance. The partial regression coefficients for these three variables were .273, .221, and .212, respectively. Although some differences did appear in the symptom pictures of the Japanese as compared with U.S. patients, the findings of Seifert et al. (1971) parallel those of Phillips et al. (1966, 1968) and provide documentation across cultures of the contribution of developmentally interpreted life-style variables to the assignment of diagnosis.

Summary of the Research and Implications

Some method of classifying disordered behavior is required for the predictive study of psychopathology. Traditional psychiatric diagnosis represents an atheoretical mode of classification based on symptom manifestation. Developmental thinking has generated alternative categories for organizing symptoms. While the two modes of symptom classification are not identical, substantial relationships have appeared between the major categories of conventional diagnosis and the patient's developmental level as assessed by dominant role orientation, symptom expression in action versus thought, and premorbid social competence. These relationships found in our research have implications for the understanding of traditional diagnosis, and they suggest certain directions for further work.

Despite the overlapping and nonspecific symptom criteria employed in DSM-I and DSM-II, reasonable levels of reliability could be achieved for the major nosological categories using these systems. Such reliability in the assignment of diagnosis appears to follow from the consistency with which diagnosticians independently infer styles of life from individual symptom manifestations. The research that we have just reviewed indicates that psychiatric diagnosis is a complex indicator of at least three general dimensions of human behavior, namely, dominant mode of expression, social role, and general competence level. Each is conceptualized as a partially independent indicator of the broad underlying dimension, the patient's developmental level. The issue of heterogeneity in symptom expression is understood within this framework. Homogeneity is a construction of the classifier, not a quality that inheres in phenomena themselves. The modes of symptom classification (sphere dominance and role orientation) examined in this research provide a means for viewing diverse pathological behaviors as fundamentally homogeneous in nature. The classification of symptoms employing these parameters was found to account for a very substantial proportion of the variance in diagnosis and thus apparently for almost all that is reliable in psychiatric diagnosis.

The research diagnostic systems, the major components of which have now been incorporated in DSM-III, represent a major effort to increase reliability in diagnosis through the precise definition of symptom criteria. While these efforts represent an important advance for psychiatric classification and research on pathological syndromes, they have not resulted in any major breakthrough in the understanding of psychopathology. Research has only begun to examine the validity of these new classificatory systems. Nevertheless the question has been raised as to whether reliability may have been achieved at some cost to validity. Greater attention to principles seems necessary in the elaboration of diagnostic distinctions. As Garside and Roth (1978) cautioned, "No new description is likely to make its mark unless there is in the observer's head a new concept that corresponds to how things are in the world" (p. 53).

The value of developmental thinking for such conceptual elaboration is illustrated by the research reviewed in this chapter. Further, this work suggests that developmental constructs may, in fact, have been implicitly employed by clinicians in assigning diagnoses described as based on "the feel of the case." The individual diagnostician can thus be seen as comprising a diagnostic system wherein individual symptoms are employed to infer broader life-style characteristics of the patient with an important implicit dimension being that of the patient's developmental level. Clearly such implicit assumptions require explication and systematization if their reliability and validity are to be assessed. The work reviewed in this chapter represents an effort in this direction.

As the research indicates, the approach to symptom classification of traditional diagnosis and that generated by developmental thinking are not mutually exclusive. Developmental thinking may even be implicitly employed in formulating diagnoses using the traditional system. Given that these are alternative modes of symptom classification, questions nevertheless arise as to the relative value of each. At an empirical level, the two methods of symptom classification can be compared and determinations made as to which correlates more strongly with other major variables of clinical interest. As will be reported in later chapters, the symptom categories derived from developmental principles have been found to be related to outcome, certain personality variables, and defensive style, in addition to diagnosis and premorbid competence. Evidence presented in Chapter 4 also indicated that this method of symptom classification as well as other methods based on case record information is satisfactorily reliable and correlates with symptom notation based on face-to-face interviews with the client. The validity of the traditional diagnostic categories has been underinvestigated although it appears that this deemphasis will soon be remedied. It is nevertheless noteworthy that despite less than optimal reliabilities the major categories in DSM-I and DSM-II were found to be related to many variables of central importance in psychopathology. The underinvestigation of the correlates of the major categories in traditional diagnosis may reflect an implicit confidence, based on clinical experience, in the predictive efficacy of these categories. For example, the fact that schizophrenic patients have poorer outcomes than other and especially nonpsychotic groups has occasionally been demonstrated in research. Primarily, however, this relationship seems so self-evident that its research demonstration seems almost superfluous.

An amalgamation of the two approaches is also possible. Our theoretically derived approach to symptom classification has elucidated basic processes underlying diagnosis. A fundamental construct in our work, premorbid social competence, is now represented in DSM-III as Axis V. Developmental principles may also serve as a fruitful basis for delineating subclasses within the major nosological categories. Establishing reliable and valid subclasses of patients within diagnostic groups has remained extremely problematic (Carpenter & Stephens, 1979; Haier 1980; Skinner, 1981). The potential of the developmental approach for illuminating issues in subclassification will be illustrated in the following chapter, which deals with the paranoid–nonparanoid distinction in schizophrenia.

REFERENCE NOTES

1. Although as a group personality disorder patients are characterized by low social competence scores, they display relatively favorable outcomes. By contrast, al-

though affective reaction and paranoid schizophrenic patients display better outcomes than other psychotic groups, their outcomes are nonetheless poorer than those of personality disorder patients. Research regarding outcome will be reviewed in Chapter 9.

2. The degree to which the operations that eventuate in a diagnosis have now been explicated is evidenced by the computer programs (Spitzer & Endicott, 1968; Wing, 1970) that, once the patient's symptoms have been identified, can carry out diagnostic decision making.

CHAPTER 6

The Paranoid–Nonparanoid Distinction in Schizophrenia

Workers since the time of Kraepelin have sought a more differentiated taxonomy of schizophrenia. Symptom and nonsymptom criteria have been proposed as bases for establishing more homogeneous subclasses of schizophrenic patients. On the one hand, the symptom-based subclassificatory schema proposed by Kraepelin has persisted almost unchanged into DSM-III. Thus our official nomenclature continues to categorize schizophrenic patients into disorganized, catatonic, paranoid, and undifferentiated subtypes. (Relabeling hebephrenic schizophrenics as disorganized in DSM-III is more of a semantic than a substantive endeavor.) A longstanding and widely investigated alternative to symptom-based classification involves the use of case history data to bifurcate the schizophrenia syndrome into process or poor premorbid and reactive or good premorbid subtypes. More recently, as was discussed in Chapter 4, performance on a variety of laboratory measures, including perceptual tasks, has also been advocated as a more meaningful basis than symptomatology for schizophrenia subclassification and for linking clinical manifestations of the disorder to underlying biochemical processes and genetic mechanisms (Cromwell, 1975, 1984). That no satisfactory method of subclassification has yet been agreed upon is underscored by Haier's (1980) assertion that the delineation of schizophrenia subtypes remains a primary task for the 1980s.

While an adequate subclassificatory system appropriate to all schizophrenic patients has yet to be devised, the paranoid–nonparanoid distinction represents one subdivision that has been found to correlate with a variety of other aspects of patients' behavior, including premorbid adjustment and performance on many perceptual and cognitive tasks. The paranoid–nonparanoid distinction thus represents a clear instance where symptom- and non–symptom-based methods of classification are not mutually exclusive. A question that remains is why these classificatory schemata are related while based on such diverse criteria.

The present chapter will first consider symptom-based efforts at subclassification in schizophrenia. We will turn then to the paranoid–nonparanoid distinction, and the relation of this dimension to premorbid social competence will be examined closely. Inasmuch as not all studies have confirmed a paranoid status–premorbid competence relationship, reasons for the non-confirmatory instances will be considered. Of even greater importance is the need to explain why paranoid schizophrenics frequently display higher pre-morbid competence than nonparanoid schizophrenics. One possibility is that both these (symptom- and non–symptom-based) characteristics of patients reflect an underlying developmental dimension. Other behavioral differences between paranoid and nonparanoid schizophrenic patients will then be reviewed and related to the developmental-level construct.

SUBCLASSIFICATION IN SCHIZOPHRENIA

The search for more homogeneous symptom pictures has been prominent in the century-old effort to discover meaningful subclasses (or subtypes) of schizophrenia. Taking a lead from the natural sciences, workers have viewed schizophrenia as something akin to a genus (a class containing individuals with diverse symptoms) that can be further divided into subclasses of individuals who display more homogeneous symptom pictures.

Two somewhat overlapping symptom-based approaches to the subclassification of schizophrenia can be identified. Both approaches are essentially empirical and differ only in the extent to which statistical methodology is employed. The first approach, which can be labeled clinical–observational and traced from Kraepelin through DSM-III (Carpenter & Stephens, 1979; Neale & Oltmanns, 1980), resulted in the classic subdivision of schizophrenia into simple, hebephrenic, catatonic, and paranoid subtypes. These classical subtypes of schizophrenia have been criticized as unreliable and lacking in validity (Carpenter et al., 1976; Carpenter & Stephens, 1979; Strauss & Carpenter, 1981). Relatively few patients nowadays display classic simple, hebephrenic, or catatonic symptom pictures. Thus the majority of these classic categories account for a very small proportion of individuals diagnosed schizophrenic. Moreover, a single patient frequently displays symptoms characteristic of a number of these subtypes. Hence undifferentiated schizophrenia is a frequently employed subtype diagnosis. In light of these diagnostic problems, Carpenter and Stephens (1979) concluded that "subtypes classified along course or prognostic lines may be more clinically useful" (p. 490). Concurring with Cromwell (1975), these authors also pointed to the value of premorbid competence as a classificatory dimension. While we agree with the view of Carpenter, Strauss, and their colleagues in regard to most of the classic schizophrenia subtypes, our view of the utility of the paranoid category diverges from the position of these authors. As the data presented in this chapter will indicate, paranoid and nonparanoid schizophrenic patients appear to differ in regard to many behavioral characteristics.

The second approach, discussed in Chapter 5, involves the construction of subcategories of schizophrenia through the empirical discovery of statistically circumscribable clusters of symptoms among patients all labeled schizophrenic (Carpenter et al., 1976; Lorr et al., 1963). While informative, the statistical approach has not yet resulted in any conceptual advances in our understanding of schizophrenia. To illustrate, Lorr et al. (1963) identified six subtypes through their statistical procedures: excited–hostile; hostile paranoid; intropunitive; retarded; disorganized; and excited–grandiose. However, these authors were not able to place most schizophrenic cases into the subtypes with accuracy. Carpenter et al. (1976) examined the symptoms of 600 schizophrenic patients and identified four subgroups: typical, flagrant, insightful, and hypochondriacal. The large majority of cases ($N = 439$) were classified as typical. With so many of the patients having been placed into one category, the usefulness of the system is called into question. Carpenter et al. themselves questioned the value of their discovered subtypes on the grounds that the validity of the sub-types (relationships to traits other than the defining symptoms) was as yet unknown.

TABLE 6.1. The Process–Reactive Distinction

Criterion	Process	Reactive
Premorbid adjustment	Poor; marked sexual, social, and occupational inadequacy	Relatively adequate prepsychotic social, sexual, and occupational adjustment
Onset of disorder	Gradual, with no identifiable precipitating stress	Sudden, with clear-cut precipitating stress
Age of onset	Frequently in late adolescence	Generally later in life
Course and outcome	Deteriorating course, poor prognosis	Good prognosis

Over the past three or four decades, there has been a growing awareness of the potential value of constructing subclassifications of schizophrenia based on more than symptomatology. Thus we currently subdivide schizophrenic patients into the overlapping bifurcations of (a) process versus reactive; (b) poor versus good premorbid; and (c) early versus late onset (Carpenter & Stephens, 1979; Garmezy, 1970; Kokes et al., 1977). In presenting the criteria defining the process-reactive distinction, Table 6.1 indicates the relationship among these three methods of categorization. These classification systems utilize information from the premorbid phase of the life history and the course of illness, focusing on such variables as the type and age of onset. Unlike symptom-based subclassification systems, which emphasize reliability of diagnosis, the non–symptom-based groupings explicitly attend to both the reliability (of classifying schizophrenics on the basis of premorbid history) and the validity (the prediction of outcome of the disorder) of the classification system. Thus the expected class correlate of being classified as a good premorbid or reactive schizophrenic is a more favorable outcome than being classified as a poor premorbid or process schizophrenic. While a clear distinction can be drawn between symptom-based and non–symptom-based classification systems, the two taxonomies are not necessarily orthogonal. For example, good premorbid schizophrenic patients who have late onset are typically found in the paranoid rather than the nonparanoid subtypes.

PREMORBID SOCIAL COMPETENCE AND PARANOID–NONPARANOID STATUS IN SCHIZOPHRENIA

Research with Male Schizophrenic Patients

A relation between premorbid social competence and paranoid–nonparanoid status in schizophrenia was first reported by Goldstein, Held, and Cromwell (1968). Utilizing three samples of male state hospital schizophrenics, these authors found that patients with good premorbid adjustment were more likely to be diagnosed paranoid than were patients whose premorbid adjustment had been poor. Although Goldstein et al. (1968) did not explicitly interpret their findings within a developmental framework, they did offer cognitive superiority as one of a number of alternative explanations for the higher premorbid competence scores of the paranoid patients. Cognitive superiority was required, they suggested, for the formation of delusions and hence a diagnosis of paranoid type. In contrast to the results obtained by Goldstein et al., Johannsen et al. (1963) found no relation between paranoid–nonparanoid status and premorbid adjustment in a Veterans Administration (VA) hospital sample.

The paranoid status–premorbid competence relation was first examined within the developmental approach to psychopathology by Sanes and Zigler (1971). A frequent clinical assumption has been that paranoid schizophrenic patients are characterized by a higher developmental level than nonparanoid schizophrenic patients (Blatt & Wild, 1976; Eysenck, 1961; Swanson et al., 1970). A similar view of paranoid–nonparanoid differences has been advanced within the organismic-developmental perspective (Siegel, 1953).

Utilizing the case records of 37 male state hospital schizophrenic patients, Sanes and Zigler (1971) examined the relationship between paranoid–nonparanoid status and the developmental variables of premorbid social competence and symptom expression reflecting the role orientation of turning against the self. A modification of the Zigler-Phillips (1960) social competence and symptom expression reflecting the role orientation of turning against the self. A modification of the Zigler-Phillips (1960) social competence scale was employed (see Chapter 3 for a presentation of the scale). Primarily, the modification involved the inclusion of income as a sixth social competence index. As has been the case in many studies, IQ was not employed as an index in this investigation. The symptoms comprising the three role orientation categories of turning against the self, turning against others, and avoidance of others were described in Chapter 4 and are listed in Table 4.1. A symptom score was devised that would reflect the relative dominance within an individual's symptom picture of symptoms within the turning-against-the-self category as opposed to the dominance of symptoms falling within the other two role orientation categories.

Consistent with the research described in Chapter 4 (Zigler & Phillips, 1960, 1962), patients of higher social competence more frequently displayed the role orientation of turning against the self. Furthermore, the individual indexes of age, marital status, occupation, and employment history were found to be significantly related to this role orientation, whereas educational level and income were not.

However, consistant with the findings of Johannsen et al. (1963) and in contrast to those reported by Goldstein et al. (1968), no relationship was found between premorbid social competence and paranoid–nonparanoid diagnosis.

In an effort to reconcile this discrepancy in findings, Cromwell (personal communication reported in Sanes & Zigler, 1971) noted two variables: type of population and number of hospitalizations. Cromwell hypothesized that, for the Goldstein et al. findings to hold, studies must include patients of very low cognitive and conceptual development, patients more likely to be found in state rather than in VA hospitals. This factor is important in view of the fact that the Goldstein et al. samples were obtained in state hospitals and the Johannsen et al. sample in a VA hospital. The Sanes and Zigler study was conducted in a state hospital but employed a relatively small number of subjects. The number of admissions was not controlled in any of the three investigations, although both Goldstein et al. and Sanes and Zigler reported that the number of admissions was unrelated to their findings. Nevertheless, Cromwell was of the opinion that the relationship between premorbid social competence and paranoid–nonparanoid status discovered by Goldstein et al. is more likely to be found at first admission than at later admissions.

In order to test these propositions, Zigler and Levine (1973) examined the paranoid status–social competence relationship in state and VA hospital schizophrenic patients who varied also in number of previous admissions. The case histories of two samples of male schizophrenic patients were examined. The VA hospital sample consisted of 295 male patients admitted to the West Haven, Connecticut, VA hospital between 1960 and 1970. Of these, 173 were diagnosed as paranoid schizophrenic (39 first admissions, 34 second admissions, 22 third admissions, 23 fourth admissions, and 55 patients with five or more psychiatric admissions). There were 122 patients diagnosed as nonparanoid schizophrenic (25 first admissions, 36 second admissions, 17 third admissions, 10 fourth admissions, and 34 patients with five or more admissions). The state hospital sample consisted of 300 male schizophrenic patients admitted to Fairfield Hills Hospital in Connecticut between 1964 and 1972. There were 150 patients diagnosed as paranoid schizophrenic and 150 diagnosed as nonparanoid schizophrenic. Each diagnostic group included an equal number ($N = 30$) of patients of each admission status (one, two, three, four, and five or more admissions).

The Zigler-Phillips social competence index was employed and scored in the traditional way, described in Chapter 3. The five variables of age, education, marital status, occupation, and employment history were used as social competence indexes, and each variable was divided into three categories with each category conceptualized as representing a step along a social competence continuum.

The relationship of role orientation to paranoid–nonparanoid status, social competence, and type of hospital was also examined. The scoring of role orientation was based upon the categorization of symptoms described in Chapter 4 and utilized by Sanes and Zigler (1971). For each of the three role orientations (turning against the self, turning against others, and avoidance of others), a symptom score was computed that reflected the relative dominance of symptoms within that category as opposed to symptoms falling within the other two role orientation categories.

Clear support was found for the view that a relationship between paranoid–nonparanoid status and premorbid social competence would be discovered in a state hospital but not in a VA hospital population. The mean premorbid social competence scores for paranoid and nonparanoid patients in both hospitals are presented in Table 6.2. Consistent with the findings of Goldstein et al. (1968) but inconsistent with those of Sanes and Zigler (1971), state hospital schizophrenic patients with a diagnosis of paranoid type had significantly higher social competence scores than those with the diagnosis of nonparanoid type. Consistent, however, with the findings of Johannsen et al. (1963), no relationship appeared between paranoid–nonparanoid status and social competence scores within the VA sample. The findings thus support Cromwell's view that for the paranoid status–social competence relation to hold a population must be employed in which a considerable number of patients are of very poor premorbid social competence. The postulated lower competence of state as compared with VA hospital patients was confirmed.

Whereas the developmental formulation posits that premorbid competence and paranoid status are positively related because both reflect higher developmental levels of functioning, an alternative explanation, discussed at some length in the previous chapter, is that this connection may already exist in the clinician's mind. In assuming that paranoid schizophrenia reflects developmentally higher functioning, the clinician, when confronted

TABLE 6.2. Mean Social Competence Scores of Male Schizophrenic Patients

Diagnosis	State Hospital			VA Hospital		
	N	M	SD	N	M	SD
Paranoid	150	.97	.42	173	.91	.40
Nonparanoid	150	.65	.36	122	.86	.42

with a high social competence individual, may be more prone to assign a paranoid than nonparanoid schizophrenic diagnosis. In order to explore this alternative explanation for the premorbid competence–paranoid status relationship, the symptoms of the paranoid and nonparanoid schizophrenic patients were compared. Within each of the two samples (VA patients for whom no relationship was found between premorbid competence and diagnosis and state hospital patients for whom such a relationship did appear), paranoids more frequently displayed delusions and suspiciousness whereas nonparanoids more frequently exhibited depression. In at least one of the two hospitals, nonparanoids more frequently displayed the symptoms withdrawn, apathetic, and obsessions.

Corresponding to the developmental differences reflected in social competence scores, the patients in the VA hospital more frequently displayed symptoms in the category of the turning-against-the-self role orientation whereas patients in the state hospital were more likely to display symptoms predominantly in the symptom categories found to be associated with lower premorbid adequacy (turning against others and avoidance of others). With respect to specific symptoms, VA patients more frequently displayed the symptoms tense, drinking, suicidal ideas, insomnia, suicidal attempt, psychosomatic disorders, and fears own hostile impulses, whereas state hospital patients were more likely to display the symptoms emotional outbursts, perplexed, apathetic, irresponsible behavior, and euphoria.

Within each diagnostic category, changes in symptom picture with increasing admissions were found to be more marked in the VA than in the state hospital population. Especially interesting were the findings that with an increasing number of admissions VA paranoids were less likely to display the symptoms of suspicious or bizarre ideas (the two symptoms found to be most closely associated with the paranoid–nonparanoid distinction). This finding lends support to the hypothesis advanced by Strauss (1973) that paranoid symptomatology disappears with repeated hospitalizations. It is not clear whether with added admissions the paranoids no longer are suspicious or delusional or whether over the course of admissions they have learned not to evidence such symptoms. In any case, even with this change in symptom manifestation, these patients were still labeled paranoid, which may reflect little more than that if a patient is diagnosed as a paranoid this diagnosis tends to be employed in future admissions.

With respect to paranoid–nonparanoid differences in role orientation, in the VA sample paranoid as compared with nonparanoid schizophrenic patients had lower turning-against-the-self scores, although this difference was not significant for state hospital patients. Across both hospitals, good social competence nonparanoids had higher turning-against-the-self scores than poor social competence nonparanoids, but no such difference was found for paranoids.

In regard to the avoidance-of-others role orientation category, the paranoid schizophrenics in both hospitals were found to have higher scores than the nonparanoid schizophrenic patients. Reminiscent of the findings with the turning-against-the self orientation, good social competence nonparanoids were found to have lower avoidance-of-others scores than poor social competence nonparanoids but no difference in this score related to the social competence level of the paranoid patients. As with the turning-against-the-self scores, confirmation of earlier findings (Zigler & Phillips, 1960, 1962) regarding the relationship of social competence to role orientation was obtained for nonparanoids but not for paranoids. However, in this earlier work (Zigler & Phillips, 1960), one symptom for men did not fit the general pattern of findings. Suspiciousness, though in the avoidance-of-others category, was clearly related to higher rather than lower levels of premorbid competence. Similarly, the earlier work suggested and later research (Zigler & Levine, 1983b) confirmed that the symptom of delusions, while in the avoidance-of-others category, is associated with higher rather than lower levels of premorbid competence. As would be expected given the diagnostic criteria for paranoid schizophrenia, these two symptoms alone more frequently characterized the paranoid patients in both samples examined by Zigler and Levine (1973). Accordingly, Zigler and Levine (1973) suggested that the "role orientation formulation is not on sound grounds when dealing with patients whose symptomatology is particularly characterized by suspiciousness and bizarre ideas, that is, paranoid schizophrenics" (p. 198).

The absence of a relationship between higher premorbid competence and the role orientation of turning against the self for paranoid patients foreshadows the formulation to be presented in the next chapter. That is, if paranoia is a mechanism employed by individuals to ward off a breakthrough into consciousness of depressive thought and its accompanying painful affective components, to the degree that this mechanism is successful paranoid patients would be expected to display fewer symptoms of the turning-against-the-self or depressive variety.

Once this shortcoming of the role orientation formulation with respect to paranoid patients is noted, the developmental approach to psychopathology does appear capable of providing an explanation for the positive relationship between paranoid status and premorbid competence discovered in this and previous studies. Within this formulation, paranoid schizophrenics could be viewed as having obtained a higher developmental level in their premorbid period and as manifesting symptoms, as for example, suspiciousness and delusions, indicative of this higher level. While a general picture emerges of the paranoid schizophrenic as a developmentally higher individual than the nonparanoid schizophrenic, a word of caution is in order. Although a relationship was found between paranoid–nonparanoid status and premorbid social competence in the state hospital sample, a fairly sizable number of paranoids had a poor premorbid history. An even higher percentage of nonparanoids had a good premorbid history. Paranoid–nonparanoid status thus far from exhausts the variance on the premorbid social competence measure. If the main determinant of behaviors of clinical interest (e.g., performance on psychological tests, response to treatment, prognosis) is the individual's general level of maturity in cognitive, emotional, and social functioning, of which premorbid competence is itself a far from perfect measure, then knowledge of the individual's diagnosis will be of some but not great predictive value.

The diagnosis is a reflection of the symptoms, and individual symptoms represent behaviors that are much too gross to provide precise information about the individual's developmental level. As discussed previously in Chapter 4, while suspiciousness or delusions may be grossly related to developmental level, what must be remembered is that such symptoms will be found in individuals at every developmental level. What is needed is some more direct index of the developmental level of the symptom in question. Such an index could be obtained through a more fine-grained structural analysis of the symptoms manifested by the paranoid patients being investigated. Thus, while both good and poor premorbid paranoids might exhibit suspiciousness and delusions, the developmental formulation would suggest that the suspiciousness and delusions of the poor premorbid paranoid would be global, disorganized, and unmodulated whereas such symptoms in the good premorbid paranoid would be more organized, articulated, and hierarchical.

Premorbid Competence and Paranoid–Nonparanoid Status in Female Schizophrenic Patients

The relationship of premorbid social competence to paranoid–nonparanoid status in female schizophrenic patients was examined by Zigler, Levine, and Zigler (1977). As Wahl (1977) noted, the issue of gender differences has been largely ignored in schizophrenia research. Consistent with Wahl's observation, no previous studies had examined the social competence–paranoid status relationship in female patients.

The case histories of 300 female schizophrenic patients admitted to Fairfield Hills Hospital in Connecticut between 1966 and 1972 were examined. Paralleling Zigler and Levine's (1973) study, this sample comprised 30 patients of each diagnosis (paranoid and nonparanoid) for each of five categories of admission status (one, two, three, four, and five or more admissions). Social competence was assessed employing the Zigler-Phillips social competence index. The five variables of age, education, marital status, occupation, and employment history were examined and scored in the traditional manner. The presenting symptoms appearing in each patient's case history were also recorded.

The mean social competence scores for each Diagnosis × Admission Status subgroup and for the total sample are reported in Table 6.3. As was the case with the male state hospital schizophrenics examined by Zigler and Levine (1973), the female paranoid schizophrenics were found to have higher social competence scores than nonparanoids, F (1, 290) = 28.31, p < .001).

Chi-square analyses were performed to examine the relationship between each of the five component social competence indexes and diagnosis. Two of the five analyses proved to be significant, indicating that paranoid patients were older (χ^2 = 47.57, p < .001) and obtained higher marital status scores (χ^2 = 16.84, p < .001) than nonparanoid patients. This first study employing females thus takes its place alongside those conducted with males that have found that paranoid schizophrenics have higher premorbid competence scores than nonparanoid schizophrenics (Goldstein et al., 1968; Neale, Kopfstein, & Levine, 1972; Zigler & Levine, 1973). Inasmuch as the females examined were state hospital patients, the findings are consistent with the view that the premorbid competence–paranoid status relationship is more likely to be observed in state hospital samples.

With respect to admission status, an interaction effect of borderline significance (p < .06) indicated a tendency for premorbid competence and paranoid–nonparanoid status to be more strongly related in first- and second-admission patients than in patients having three or more admissions. This result is consistent with the findings of Neale et al. (1972). However, other investigators have not found the acute–chronic dimension to be operative in the premorbid competence–diagnosis relation (Eisenthal, Harford, & Solomon, 1972; Zigler & Levine, 1973). Further study and additional theoretical direction (Strauss, 1973) seem needed to uncover the role of the acute–chronic variable in determining whether the premorbid competence–paranoid status relationship will be found.

Goldstein et al. (1968) raised the possibility that the relation discovered between premorbid competence and diagnosis is due to a tendency of diagnosticians to classify individuals with good premorbid histories as paranoid. Although Goldstein's group rejected this interpretation, it is important to demonstrate empirically that the diagnoses under investigation were made on the basis of symptomatology rather than on other factors such as the patient's premorbid competence. This demonstration is especially necessary given the findings reported in Chapter 5, which strongly suggest that clinicians' implicit assumptions about a patient's developmental level can influence the diagnosis assigned. The findings of Zigler and Levine (1973) that two symptoms, suspiciousness and the presence of delusions, were significantly more frequent in the paranoid samples provides some evidence that diagnosis was based on symptom manifestation. Similarly for the female pa-

TABLE 6.3. Mean Social Competence Scores for Female State Hospital Schizophrenic Patients

| | Admission Status | | | | | | | | | | | | |
| | 1 | | 2 | | 3 | | 4 | | 5 + | | Total | |
Diagnosis	M	SD	M	SD	M	SD	M	SD	M	SD	M	SD
Paranoid	1.20	.44	1.21	.36	1.21	.31	1.18	.34	1.15	.40	1.19	.37
Nonparanoid	.83	.46	.90	.43	1.04	.37	1.01	.39	.95	.45	.95	.42

Note: $N = 30$ for each subgroup or a total of 150 paranoid and 150 nonparanoid subjects.

tients in this study, suspiciousness and delusions were found to be more prevalent in paranoids than nonparanoids, again suggesting that differential diagnosis was based on presenting symptoms.

Finally, the premorbid social competence scores of the female patients were compared with those of the males employed by Zigler and Levine (1973). Compared to the males, the females in both paranoid and nonparanoid groups obtained significantly higher overall social competence scores and significantly higher scores on the three component indexes of age, marital status, and occupation. As discussed in Chapter 3, the higher premorbid social competence scores of female patients has been a highly consistent finding. Given the variety of gender differences that have been discovered in psychopathology research and the consequent importance of this variable both for the understanding of psychopathology and as a phenomenon that has not been adequately incorporated in developmental thought, the entire issue of gender differences will be closely examined in Chapter 11.

Other Research, Methodological Considerations, and Theoretical Significance

In the majority of studies discussed thus far, paranoid–nonparanoid status in schizophrenia and premorbid social competence have been found to be related. However, in our own work and that of other investigators, evidence regarding the magnitude of this relation has been somewhat inconsistent. Along with a brief review of the findings already discussed, this section will consider additional data concerning the paranoid status–premorbid competence relation and factors that may influence it. This effort will include an attempt to illuminate methodological problems and to suggest how apparent inconsistencies in the literature might be resolved. Finally, the theoretical significance of the relation of paranoid diagnosis to premorbid competence will be addressed. This central issue has received relatively little attention.

Review of Studies and Determinants of Positive Versus Negative Findings

Let us review briefly the studies already discussed. Goldstein et al. (1968) first observed that state hospital schizophrenic patients with good premorbid adjustment were more likely to be diagnosed as paranoid than those with poor premorbid adjustment. In contrast to this finding, Johannsen et al. (1963) employed the same measure of premorbid adjustment but found no relation between paranoid status and premorbid adjustment in a VA hospital sample. Utilizing a small sample of public hospital patients, Sanes and Zigler (1971) also reported no relation between social competence and paranoid diagnosis. The small size of the sample in this study does not make it a particularly sensitive test. The influence of type of hospital and the acute–chronic dimension on the premorbid competence–paranoid status relation was examined by Zigler and Levine (1973). In line with Cromwell's (cited by Zigler & Levine, 1973) suggestion, premorbid adjustment and diagnosis were found to be related for state hospital but not for VA hospital patients.

Number of previous admissions (presumed to reflect chronicity) was not found to be a factor influencing this relation. Zigler et al. (1977) likewise found a premorbid competence–paranoid status relation for female state hospital patients. In addition, tentative evidence suggested that this relation might be more marked in acute than chronic patients.

Inasmuch as their sample comprised primarily state hospital patients, the relation obtained by Neale et al. (1972) between premorbid competence and paranoid status is likewise consistent with the view that type of hospital moderates this relationship. Further, in the Neale et al. (1972) study, the premorbid competence–diagnosis relation appeared to be influenced by the acute-chronic status of the patients.

A particularly critical test of the premorbid competence—diagnosis relation was conducted by Eisenthal et al. (1972). This study involved a large number of patients, both acute and chronic, in three hospitals (one state and two private). Furthermore, summing across the three hospitals, the percentage of poor premorbid patients found in the sample was higher than that in the Goldstein et al. (1968) sample. Given Cromwell's views concerning the importance of the range of social competence represented in the patient sample and the chronicity factor, the Eisenthal et al. investigation was a sensitive test of the premorbid adjustment–diagnosis relation. Nevertheless, this relation was not found in the combined sample, in any single hospital sample, or in the acute or chronic subgroups.

A final piece of conflicting evidence was presented by McCreary (1974), who found that VA hospital patients with relatively good premorbid histories were more likely to be diagnosed as paranoid, whereas patients with poor premorbid histories were more likely to be classified as chronic undifferentiated. While this finding is consistent with those earlier studies discovering a relation between premorbid competence and diagnostic status, it is disparate to the extent that the finding was obtained in a VA as opposed to a state hospital sample.

The presupposition that premorbid competence and paranoid status would be related primarily in patient samples that include a substantial number of low competence individuals was directly examined by Goldstein (1978). One hundred and twelve (62 male and 50 female) acute schizophrenic patients were categorized into five levels (ordered from low to high) on the basis of premorbid competence scores. With respect to the first four levels of premorbid adjustment, highly significant relationships appeared between premorbid competence and paranoid–nonparanoid status. With each increasing level of premorbid adequacy, a higher proportion of patients was diagnosed as paranoid. In contrast to this clear linear trend at the first four levels of social competence, patients at the highest social competence level were not found to be more frequently diagnosed as paranoid rather than nonparanoid schizophrenic. A similar trend was found for both male and female patients even though as a group the females obtained significantly higher premorbid competence scores. The less frequent paranoid symptomatology at the highest competence level did not appear to be an artifact of the patients' willingness to report paranoid symptoms. Given other findings concerning the high premorbid adjustment of schizoaffective patients (cf. below) Goldstein suggested that the highest adjustment group may have included many individuals of this subtype.

Why the social competence–paranoid status relation is found in some investigations and not in others is an issue that remains open to conjecture. The simplest explanation for the somewhat divergent findings is that the social competence–diagnosis relation is not a particularly robust one and will only be found in certain circumscribed populations of schizophrenic patients. The relative weakness of this relation can be seen from examining the subject samples of Zigler and Levine (1973) and Zigler et al. (1977). Although these studies obtained positive results, both samples contained a relatively high proportion of poor premorbid paranoids and good premorbid nonparanoids. Thus knowledge of patients' status on either the social competence dimension or the paranoid–nonparanoid typology does not predict with great accuracy their position on the other dimension.

The social competence–paranoid status relation does seem more likely to be found in samples that include substantial numbers of low competence patients. In addition to presenting suggestive evidence concerning the influence of type of hospital on the social competence–paranoid diagnosis relationship, Goldstein's (1978) findings more directly demonstrate that this relationship may not hold for very high social competence schizophrenic patients, quite possibly of the schizoaffective type. The classification of schizoaffective patients has been problematic. Their inclusion within the schizophrenia category is open to question, as is the homogeneity of individuals within the schizoaffective diagnostic class (Pope et al., 1980; Scharfetter & Nusperli, 1980; Tsuang, 1979). A schizoaffective diagnosis or the presence of diagnosable mania or depression in schizophrenic patients has been associated with more favorable prognosis (McCabe, 1976a; Vaillant, 1962; Wittenborn, McDonald, & Maurer, 1977), and in comparison to other schizophrenic groups schizoaffective individuals have been found more frequently to display family histories positive for affective disorder (Procci, 1976; Scharfetter & Nusperli, 1980; Tsuang, Dempsey, & Rauscher, 1976). As a consequence of their apparent distinctiveness, schizoaffective individuals have in DSM-III been removed from the schizophrenia category. Utilizing DSM-III criteria, then, one might expect a more consistent relationship to appear between premorbid competence and paranoid status.

Evidence concerning the importance of the acute–chronic variable in determining whether the premorbid competence–diagnosis relation will be found has to date been only marginal. Finally, the variability of findings across hospitals and particularly the absence of a premorbid competence–paranoid diagnosis relation in the Eisenthal et al. (1972) data raise the possibility (Cromwell, 1975) that differing diagnostic practices may also contribute to the variability in results. Cromwell argued that in better-staffed private or training hospitals clinicians spend a longer time examining and listening to patients upon admission and that the longer a patient is listened to the greater the possibility that he or she may emit a false idea that can lead to the diagnosis of paranoid. The failure of Zigler and Levine (1973) to discover a difference in the prevalence of delusions between their VA and state hospital samples weakens Cromwell's argument somewhat. Certainly the Zigler and Levine study cannot be considered a definitive test of Cromwell's hypothesis that the more time a clinician examines and attends to a patient the more likely it is that he or she will receive a diagnosis of paranoid. A test of this hypothesis would demand the close investigation of the relation between particular diagnostic procedures employed with patients and the diagnosis these patients ultimately receive.

Methodological Considerations

Although some patterns can be extrapolated from findings concerning the premorbid competence–paranoid status relationship, further research must be conducted before the exact nature of this relation can be fully illuminated. Zigler, Levine, and Zigler (1976) enumerated a number of methodological problems that make comparisons of findings across studies difficult and that could be alleviated in future work. The first has been the use of a number of different measures of premorbid competence, and in one case marital status alone (Neale et al., 1972). Although this problem is vitiated somewhat by the repeated findings of significant interrelations between the various measures (Garfield & Sundland, 1966; Gittelman-Klein & Klein, 1968; Held & Cromwell, 1968; Levinson & Campus, 1978; McCreary, 1974; Rosen et al., 1971), these relations are not of the magnitude that allows one to conclude that any premorbid adjustment measure is the equivalent of any other. Of particular relevance is the evidence reviewed in Chapter 3 that premorbid competence is a multidimensional construct (e.g., Kokes et al., 1977; Salokangas, 1978; Strauss & Carpenter, 1974, 1977; Zigler & Levine, 1981b). The different scales appear to give different emphasis to different facets of the construct. For example, while some measures (e.g, Phillips, 1953; Wittman, 1941) emphasize social and sexual adjustment, others give considerable weight also to work functioning (e.g., Evans et al., 1973; Zigler & Phillips, 1960). Evidence for the differential predictive significance of the separate factors discovered in premorbid competence (Strauss & Carpenter, 1974b, 1977; Glick et al., 1983) argues against any broad assumption of equivalency between the various scales.

Given the now-demonstrated importance of the range of premorbid competence scores, another difficulty in comparing findings across studies is the practice of many investigators of bifurcating their populations of schizophrenics into good and poor premorbid subjects on the basis of a median split or by employing relatively arbitrary cutoff points on whatever premorbid social competence scale they choose. Besides the fact that the median splits on different scales have been found to divide the same sample differently (Garfield & Sundland, 1966), this practice makes it all but impossible to compare the absolute values of social competence found across studies. Goldstein's (1978) findings further underscore the necessity of using finer gradations in social competence scores inasmuch as he found that it was at the highest of five levels of social competence that the relation to paranoid status ceased to hold. Numerical scores that can be obtained on a number of premorbid social competence measures in addition to the Zigler-Phillips index would not only be most helpful when comparing findings across studies but would also permit the use of more sensitive parametric statistics as opposed to the nonparametric analyses that have predominated in research in this area.

Another problem with the research done in this area to date is the relatively cavalier manner in which the issue of reliability of measurement has been treated. While workers typically report the reliability of the premorbid competence measure used, they often do not report the reliability of measurement involved in assigning patients to the paranoid and nonparanoid groups. If we are ever to discover the true relation between measures of premorbid competence and diagnostic status, we must know the reliability of both measures so that we might correct for the attenuation in the relationship between the two measures produced by the lack of perfect reliability present in both measures.

An especially significant methodological issue concerns the heterogeneity–homogeneity of individuals placed within the diagnostic categories under investigation. The failure of researchers to demonstrate consistently that paranoid schizophrenics are characterized by a relatively good premorbid history may be due to nothing more than the fact that the categories of paranoid and nonparanoid schizophrenia contain patients who are extremely heterogeneous in regard to their basic psychological makeups. Therefore one could not expect to discover a simple relation of great magnitude between paranoid status and premorbid social competence unless one first reduced the heterogeneity of individuals included in these diagnostic categories. What appears to be required is a more fine-grained diagnostic grouping that reduces the number of off-quadrant cases, that is, poor premorbid paranoids and good premorbid nonparanoids, obtained even in those studies that have resulted in positive findings.

As indicated both in Chapter 4 and previously in this chapter, the developmental approach to psychopathology provides some theoretical direction for the construction of more fine-grained diagnostic distinctions within the paranoid schizophrenia category. While the paranoid symptoms of suspiciousness and delusions appear to be grossly indicative of developmentally higher levels of functioning, these two symptoms can be found at every maturity level. Thus Zigler and Levine (1973) suggested that a clearer relation between premorbid competence and diagnostic status would be obtained if the paranoid schizophrenia category were differentiated further through the application of developmental principles to the structural analysis of the symptoms (e.g., delusions and suspiciousness) of the paranoids under investigation.

Support for the proposition that the category of paranoid schizophrenia embraces a heterogeneous mix of individuals and for the view that this diagnostic category can be profitably differentiated further by employing developmental criteria is contained in the findings of Freedman and his colleagues (Freedman et al., 1967, 1970). These investigators distinguished between two subclasses of paranoid schizophrenic patients: A negative propensity to change group was characterized by more differentiated cognitive functioning, social participation, and belligerence, whereas a positive propensity to change group was characterized by less complex cognitive functioning, social withdrawal, and lack of belligerence. As has been variously documented in this volume, such phenomena as degree of differentiation in cognitive functioning and social participation are intimately related to level of development attained. Consistent with the argument of Zigler and Levine (1973), Freedman and his colleagues found that their subgroups of paranoids were discriminable in the expression of their paranoid symptomatology. The positive-propensity paranoids (low premorbid subjects?) had significantly higher-intensity ratings of ideas of persecution and ideas of reference and lower-intensity ratings of anticipated unfair treatment than did the negative-propensity paranoids (high premorbid subjects?).

Just as the heterogeneity of patients included in the paranoid schizophrenia category may reduce the magnitude of the empirical relation discovered between premorbid competence and diagnostic status, this relation may be attenuated further by the heterogeneity of those patients grouped together in the category of nonparanoid schizophrenia. It should be remembered that the majority of work on the premorbid competence–paranoid status relation utilized patients diagnosed according to DSM-II, a system that includes schizoaffective disorder within the schizophrenia category. The comparison groups for the paranoid schizophrenics, while largely composed of schizophrenics diagnosed as chronic undifferentiated, also included patients diagnosed as schizoaffective, simple, catatonic, and hebephrenic. Schizoaffective patients in particular are distinguishable from these other groups on the basis of higher premorbid competence scores (Lewine, Watt, & Fryer, 1978). As the reader will recall, Goldstein's (1978) findings suggest that the more frequent relations discovered between paranoid status and premorbid competence in state as compared with VA hospital samples may in part be due to a larger number of schizoaffective patients in VA hospital nonparanoid schizophrenic samples. If such is the case, one might expect more consistent relations between paranoid status and social competence in samples diagnosed according to DSM-III criteria since schizoaffective patients are now excluded from the schizophrenia category. At the same time, however, the narrowing of the schizophrenia category with DSM-III may also exclude a number of low competence individuals previously diagnosed as schizophrenic on the basis of negative (e.g., apathetic, withdrawn) rather than positive (e.g., auditory hallucinations, delusions) symptoms. How the changes in the diagnosis of schizophrenia brought about by DSM-III affect the paranoid status–social competence relation is an empirical question deserving research attention. Beyond this, however, the question of how to form more homogeneous subgroups of nonparanoid schizophrenic patients remains unresolved. DSM-III has done little to alter the traditional subdivision of schizophrenia into paranoid, catatonic, undifferentiated, and disorganized (or hebephrenic) subtypes, and, as was indicated previously, with the exception of the paranoid group, there is little support for either the reliability or the validity of the other schizophrenia subtypes. Some slight reduction in heterogeneity might be achieved by using undifferentiated schizophrenics alone to serve as a comparison group for paranoid schizophrenics. The finer diagnostic subdivision of nonparanoid schizophrenic disorder requires extensive theoretical and empirical effort. One direction for such efforts involves more fine-grained analyses of the types and structural characteristics of nonparanoid schizophrenic symptoms.

Theoretical Significance

One must finally ask two questions: (a) Why should anyone care whether premorbid competence is related to paranoid–nonparanoid status in schizophrenia? And the corollary to this question (b) What might the magnitude of this relation be? In dealing with these questions, one could take refuge in the old and metatheoretically viable position that the discovery of a well-substantiated empirical relation between two variables is worthwhile in its own right, and any complete theory of psychopathology would have to be capable of incorporating the discovered relation. The actual magnitude of the relation becomes important since it would influence the theory constructor's incentive to encompass the relation theoretically.

The research in this area suggests, however, that something more is involved than the simple effort to confirm or disconfirm the existence of an empirical relation that would have to be encompassed by a theory whose initial construction lies somewhere in the future. Since the time of Kraepelin, a distinction has been made between paranoid and nonparanoid schizophrenia, and the general view has been that paranoid schizophrenia represents a less disorganized and less pathological form than other types of schizophrenic disorder.

Likewise, as discussed in Chapter 3, the concept of premorbid social competence has been employed by workers in the area of psychopathology for several decades. One can think of few hypothetical constructs that have generated more empirical research over the past 25 years than that of premorbid social adequacy. It s interesting to note that, viewed historically, the paranoid–nonparanoid distinction and the premorbid social competence construct were both generated to aid psychopathologists in dealing with a problem that became more apparent over the years—the sheer heterogeneity of phenomena included in the psychiatric classification of schizo-phrenia.

Unfortunately, the premorbid competence concept became a victim of its own success in the prediction of outcome in schizophrenia, with the work over the years confined primarily to the repeated demonstration that pre-morbid competence is related to outcome, the development of a plethora of measures of premorbid competence, and repeated investigations of how the various measures of premorbid competence are related to one another. As indicated in Chapter 3, what has been lacking is sufficient theoretic elabora-tion of the underlying conceptual dimensions assessed by premorbid adjust-ment scales. The primitive theoretical usage of the premorbid concept in the field of psychopathology is highlighted by the fact that some 45 years after its introduction (Wittman, 1941) psychopathologists have yet to reach a consen-sus as to why premorbid social competence is related to prognosis in schizo-phrenia. This appears to be another instance in which workers have not mastered the principle that one can have prediction without having under-standing.

This is not to suggest that hypotheses have not been advanced and exist-ing theoretical frameworks employed in efforts to explain why premorbid competence should be related to prognosis as well as to other clinical phe-nomena. Two general interpretive approaches have been advanced. The first, a psychological approach, is the developmental view that the predictive efficacy of the premorbid competence construct derives from the relation of premorbid competence with a very basic feature of the individual's function-ing, namely, the person's developmental level. Within this framework, therefore, paranoid status is likewise viewed as a developmentally higher form than most nonparanoid types of schizophrenic disorder.

The second major approach to why measures of premorbid competence have predictive efficacy is that this construct and the measures of it reflect not so much the psychological makeup of individuals as the social–cultural nexus that the individual experienced and that heavily influenced his or her socialization, roles, and value systems. This social–cultural nexus would also be an important determinant of the specific stresses to which the indi-vidual was subjected, which in turn might be critical to whether the individ-ual ever became pathological. Within this social–cultural approach (see Turner and Zabo, 1968, for a relatively clear statement of this position), the preponderance of action-type symptoms in poor premorbid patients would be explained in terms of these patients' membership in a lower socio-economic class. In the socialization practices of the lower socioeconomic group, acting out is much more permissible than in the middle-class so-cialization practices experienced by patients designated as good premorbids. Since the defining symptoms of paranoid schizophrenia (delusions and suspi-ciousness) are both of the thought variety, an alternative explanation is that both the higher premorbid competence scores and the symptoms displayed by paranoid schizophrenics reflect the higher socioeconomic status of these patients.

These issues that have been raised concerning the paranoid–nonparanoid distinction and premorbid social competence suggest that the many empirical studies of the relation between these two variables are not directed essentially toward the confirmation or disconfirmation of the existence of an isolated empirical relation. Rather the effort would appear to approach the theoretical explication of these two constructs, which, though widely used in the area of psychopathology, have nonetheless remained ambiguous. Some theoretical order could be brought to these two constructs if workers employing them would deal with two pressing problems: (a) the definitional problem in which the operational measures of these constructs have a clear and convincing relation to the underlying conceptual dimensions represented by these two constructs; and (b) the clear designation by the theorist who employs these constructs of exactly how they are related to the other constructs in the nomothetic network that the theorist is employing when attempting to make understandable that plethora of phenomena placed under the rubric *psychopathology*.

PARANOID–NONPARANOID DIFFERENCES IN COGNITIVE–PERCEPTUAL FUNCTIONING

The validity of the symptom-based distinction between paranoid and other schizophrenic forms is further documented by a broad body of evidence that paranoids perform quite differently from nonparanoid schizophrenics on a variety of cognitive–perceptual tasks. This evidence, summarized in Table 6.4, generally indicates that the paranoid schizophrenic patient is more intact and less disturbed than the nonparanoid schizophrenic. Further, many of the differences discovered between paranoid and nonparanoid schizophrenics have been interpreted developmentally as reflecting more mature responses on the part of paranoid patients. Blatt and Wild (1976) in particular emphasized the more mature cognition and perception of the paranoid schizophrenic patient and cited a number of the findings summarized in Table 6.4 in support of their formulation. Drawing upon the work of Piaget and findings regarding ontogenetic change, Silverman (1964) interpreted the overinclusive thinking and the size underestimation of paranoid schizophrenics as indicative of a more mature level of functioning than typically displayed by nonparanoid schizophrenics. Differences in Rorschach developmental-level scores and in frequencies of immature word associations relate to measures that are explicitly developmental and that have been employed also in ontogenetic research (Friedman, 1953; Hemmendinger, 1953; Hemmendinger & Schultz, 1977; Siegel, 1953; Youkilis & DeWolfe, 1975).

TABLE 6.4.   Paranoid-Nonparanoid Differences in Behavior

Less distractibility in paranoid than nonparanoid schizophrenics (confirmatory: McGhie, 1970)

Greater rigidity and resistance in shifting concepts for paranoid than nonparanoid schizophrenics (confirmatory: McCormick & Broekema, 1978; Asarnow & MacCrimmon, cited by Cromwell & Pithers, 1981)

Greater boundary articulation in paranoid than nonparanoid schizophrenics (confirmatory: Fisher, 1964, 1966; Johnson, 1980)

More overinclusive thinking in paranoid than nonparanoid schizophrenics (confirmatory: Payne, Matussek & George, 1959; Silverman, 1964; Payne & Caird, 1967; no difference: Hawks, 1964; Goldstein & Salzman, 1965)

Greater ability to process complex information in paranoid than nonparanoid schizophrenics (confirmatory: Hirt, Cuttler, & Genshaft, 1977)

Higher Rorschach developmental-level scores for paranoid than nonparanoid schizophrenics (confirmatory: Siegel, 1953; no difference: Harder & Ritzler, 1979)

Fewer immature word association responses for paranoid than nonparanoid schizophrenics (confirmatory: Youkilis & DeWolfe, 1975)

Higher IQ scores for paranoid than nonparanoid schizophrenics (confirmatory: Trapp & James, 1937; Mason, 1956; Watson & Baugh, 1966)

Superior performance on a variety of cognitive tasks for paranoid than for nonparanoid schizophrenics (confirmatory: Eliseo, 1964; Shakow, 1963; Hamlin & Lorr, 1971)

Greater sensitivity in signal detection for paranoid than nonparanoid schizophrenics (confirmatory: Price & Eriksen, 1966; Rappaport & Hopkins, 1969; Rappaport, et al., 1971; McDowell, Reynolds, & Magaro, 1975)[a]

Faster reaction time for paranoid than nonparanoid schizophrenics (confirmatory: Cromwell & Pithers, 1981)

Greater size underestimation (presumably due to more extensive scanning) in paranoid than nonparanoid schizophrenics (confirmatory: Rausch, 1952; Weckowitz, 1957; Hartman, 1962; Silverman, 1964; Venables, 1964; Davis, Cromwell, & Held, 1967; Neale & Cromwell, 1968; Vojtisek, 1976; no difference: Lovinger, 1956; Weckowitz & Blewett, 1959; Price & Eriksen, 1966; Kopfstein & Neale, 1971; Neale, Davis, & Cromwell, 1971; Strauss, Foureman, & Parwatikar, 1974)

Greater perceptual closure in paranoid than nonparanoid schizophrenics (confirmatory: Snyder, 1961; Johannsen, Friedman, & Liccione, 1964)

More minimal perception of autokinetic motion in paranoid than nonparanoid schizophrenics (confirmatory: Sexton, 1945; Schlossberg & Rattok, 1974)

Greater susceptibility to Muller-Lyer illusion effects for paranoid than nonparanoid schizophrenics (confirmatory: Kar, cited by Cromwell & Pithers, 1981)

Source: ''Paranoid Schizophrenia: An Unorthodox View'' by E. Zigler and M. Glick, 1984, *American Journal of Orthopsychiatry, 54*. Reprinted, with permission, from the American Journal of Orthopsychiatry; copyright 1984 by the American Orthopsychiatric Association, Inc.
[a]Rappaport, Hopkins, and Hall (1972) reported the *opposite* finding of lesser sensitivity for paranoid patients.

SUMMARY AND CONCLUSIONS

A variety of symptom- and non–symptom-based modes of subclassification have been proposed and investigated in an effort to reduce the heterogeneity of the schizophrenia diagnostic class. The paranoid–nonparanoid distinction in schizophrenia has been extensively researched and appears to be a particularly promising avenue for bringing some order to the current complex state of affairs surrounding this diagnostic class. A major non–symptom-based bifurcation of the schizophrenia category has involved the overlapping constructs of process versus reactive and high versus low premorbid social competence. The preponderance of evidence indicates that paranoid schizophrenic patients typically obtain higher social competence scores than nonparanoid schizophrenics. This finding argues for the higher developmental status of the paranoid subtype. Despite this general direction of the research findings, nonsignificant relations between premorbid competence and paranoid status have appeared. The premorbid competence–paranoid status relation thus does not appear to be especially robust; apparently it is influenced by the range of social competence scores of the patients examined. Paranoid status and premorbid competence are more likely to be related in samples containing substantial numbers of low competence individuals, as is typically the case in state as compared with VA hospitals. Some marginal evidence suggests that the premorbid competence—paranoid diagnosis relation may appear more frequently during acute rather than chronic phases of disorder. Unfortunately, a number of methodological problems have made it difficult to compare findings across studies. In regard to the developmental formulation, the paranoid–nonparanoid subdivision is based upon very gross symptomatic differences (the presence or absence of delusions and/or suspiciousness). More fine-grained developmental distinctions would require a close structural analysis of the symptoms, an examination, for example, of the degree of articulation and organization manifested in the delusion or suspicion.

The relationship of paranoid status to a variety of indexes of cognitive and perceptual functioning has been examined in many studies. In general, this evidence suggests that the paranoid schizophrenic is more intact and less disorganized than the nonparanoid. Moreover, the majority of the cognitive and perceptual differences found between paranoid and nonparanoid schizophrenic patients are consistent with the view that paranoid schizophrenia represents a higher developmental form. As in the work concerning premorbid competence, nonsignificant findings have sometimes appeared. Characteristic in both these bodies of work, however, is an absence of findings that are opposite to expectation. That is, while nonparanoid samples are not always significantly different from paranoid ones, nonparanoid schizophrenics almost never obtain scores indicating more effective functioning than their paranoid counterparts. The more fine-grained structural analysis of the quality of organization evident in the patient's delusions or suspicions might permit a more precise demarcation of high versus low developmental individuals within the paranoid category. Such a subdivision might result in a more clearly confirmatory pattern of findings.

The large number of behavioral differences that have been discovered between paranoid and nonparanoid schizophrenic patients argue for the viability of at least some traditional symptom-based diagnostic distinctions.[1] Moreover, the research reviewed in this chapter clearly indicates that symptom- and non–symptom-based modes of classification are not mutually exclusive. While they represent divergent aspects of patients' behavior, symptomatology (e.g., the presence or absence of delusions and/or suspiciousness), premorbid competence, and cognitive and perceptual performance on a variety of measures and laboratory tasks have been found to be intercorrelated. One explanation for these empirically discovered relationships is that each of these characteristics represents a behavioral manifestation of a broad underlying dimension, the patient's developmental level. With respect to the other class subdivisions of schizophrenia (e.g., hebephrenic, undifferentiated), no particular developmental ordering can be suggested. As is reminiscent of the position espoused in Chapter 4, symptom-based diagnostic distinctions appear to be meaningful and to provide considerable knowledge about individuals only if the symptom patterns can be analyzed and interpreted as reflections of major underlying dimensions (e.g., developmental level).

These many differences noted between paranoid and nonparanoid schizophrenic patients in conjunction with other findings to be reviewed in the next chapter have led us to question the inclusion of paranoid patients within the schizophrenia category. An alternative diagnostic formulation concerning paranoid schizophrenia will be presented in the next chapter.

REFERENCE NOTE

1. In addition to the differences reviewed in the chapter, paranoid schizophrenic patients have typically been found to be older on first psychiatric admission than nonparanoid patients (Gift et al., 1981; Winokur et al., 1974; Zigler & Levine, 1981a). These findings will be discussed in Chapter 9.

CHAPTER 7

Paranoid Schizophrenia: An Unorthodox View

From the time of Kraepelin, descriptive psychiatry has given rise to a cornerstone view in the area of psychopathology, namely, that there are two and only two major functional psychoses: schizophrenia and the affective disorders. While some workers have argued that these pathologies represent the extremes of some underlying continuum (Kendell & Gourley, 1970), the almost universal view in the field is that they represent two distinctly different disorders. Table 7.1 lists the symptoms—both empirically discovered and as viewed by clinicians (Cantor et al., 1980)—that maximally differentiate the two disorders, as well as the defining symptoms found in DSM-III. The strongest support to date for the two-disorder view is the fact that patients differing in the symptoms thought to define the two illnesses react differently to psychopharmaceutical agents.

Although workers have frequently expressed some unease with the classification (see Kendler & Tsuang, 1981, for a review of positions taken on the issue), paranoid schizophrenia has continued to be conceptualized as a subtype within the schizophrenia category. In the previous chapter, we reviewed the many behavioral differences that have been found between paranoid and nonparanoid schizophrenic patients. The implications of these differences are considered in the present chapter, namely, that the dissimilarities discovered between paranoid and nonparanoid schizophrenic patients and the various similarities that have been noted between paranoid and depressed patients suggest an unorthodox formulation: Rather than representing a true schizophrenia, paranoid schizophrenia, or at least some forms of this disorder, might more fruitfully be conceptualized as a phenotypic expression of an underlying depressive mode.

PARANOID SCHIZOPHRENIA AND SCHIZOPHRENIA

In comparison with nonparanoid subtypes, paranoid schizophrenic patients typically obtain higher social competence scores, are older on first psychiatric admission, and demonstrate less disorganization and a greater reliance on conceptual or developmentally higher modes of information processing

TABLE 7.1. Symptom Criteria for Schizophrenia and the Affective Disorders

Reference	Schizophrenia	Affective Disorder
Cantor et al. (1980)[a]	Associative disturbance (12) Hallucinations (11) Inappropriate affect (9) Delusions (8) Autism (7) Flat affect (7) Affective disturbance (extreme) (6) Ambivalence (6) Ideas of reference (5) Bizarre content (4) Difficulty with interpersonal relations (4) Thoughts being controlled (through insertion) (4) Bizarre behavior (3) Difficulty with anger (3) Onset under age 40 (3) Poor reality testing (3) Poor social skills (3)	Depression (sad) (10) Mania (9) Disorder of mood (elation, euphoria) (8) Decreased sleep (5) Hyperactivity (5) Disturbances in appetite and other somatic functions (4) Family history of affective disorders (4) Grandiosity (4) Impairment of functional capacity (4) Irritability (4) Absence of precipitating event (3) Despair and hopelessness (3) Flight of ideas (3) Inappropriate affect (3) Low self-esteem (3) Psychomotor retardation (3)
Fowler et al. (1980)	Suspicious about people's intentions for at least 6 months, ever Objects have special meaning, currently Heard voices, ever Preoccupied, inattentive, fails to answer questions Interviewer doubts credibility of information Specified speech abnormality	Much energy for at least 2 weeks, currently Very cheerful for at least 2 weeks, currently Depressed for at least 1 month, ever

147

TABLE 7.1. (continued)

Reference	Schizophrenia	Affective Disorder
Kendell and Gourley (1970)[b]	Delusions of organized persecution Hears voices nearly every day Delusions of bodily control Impaired interpersonal relation-ships Subjective experience of disor-dered thought Auditory hallucinations Blunting of affect Admitted because of violence or risk of violence	More outgoing and gregarious recently "Manic" speech Loss of appetite Always prone to mood swings Behavioral concomitants of depression Recent increase in activity Always nervous or highly strung Depression worse in mornings Previous episodes with full recovery Major psychological stress in last year
DSM-III (1980)	Bizarre delusions (e.g., of being controlled thought insertion, etc.) Somatic, grandiose, religious, ni-hilistic, or other delusions Delusions with persecutory or jeal-ous content if accompanied by hallucinations Auditory hallucinations Incoherence, marked loosening of associations, markedly illogical thinking, or marked poverty of con-tent of speech if associated with at least one of the following: (a)	Either a major manic or a major depressive episode A. Symptom criteria for a manic episode at least three of the following: Increase in activity or physical restlessness More talkative than usual or pressure to keep talking Flight of ideas or subjective experience that thoughts are racing Inflated self-esteem (grandiosity, which may be delusional) Decreased need for sleep Distractibility Excessive involvement in activities that have a high potential for painful consequences that is not recognized (e.g., buying sprees)

blunted, flat, or inappropriate affect; (b) delusions or hallucinations; (c) catatonic or other grossly disorganized behavior

B. Symptom criteria for a major depressive episode at least four of the following:
Poor appetite or significant weight loss (when not dieting) or increased appetite or significant weight gain
Insomnia or hypersomnia
Psychomotor agitation or retardation
Loss of interest or pleasure in usual activities, or decrease in sexual drive
Loss of energy; fatigue
Feelings of worthlessness, self-reproach, or excessive or inappropriate guilt (either maybe delusional)
Complaints or evidence of diminished ability to think or concentrate, such as slowed thinking or indecisiveness not associated with marked loosening of associations or incoherence
Recurrent thought of death, suicidal ideation, wishes to be dead, or suicide attempt

[a]Following Cantor et al. (1980), the numbers in parentheses are the numbers of clinicians who listed that feature as descriptive of patients in the respective diagnostic categories.

[b]The 10 symptoms found in discriminant function analysis to characterize most clearly each diagnostic group. Within each group, the order of symptoms listed is from most to least discriminating.

on a variety of cognitive–perceptual tasks (see Chapter 6). Most striking are instances where the cognitive–perceptual performance of nondisturbed individuals has been found to fall between that of paranoid and nonparanoid schizophrenic patients. Such extreme differences have been found in visual size estimation, susceptibility to Muller-Lyer illusion effects, and incidental recall (Cromwell & Pithers, 1981). On each of these tasks, the functioning of the paranoid patients was characterized by a degree of overconstancy and low redundancy, that is, a hypersensitivity and vigilance to stimuli that exceeded even that of normal control subjects. In the same vein, Hirt, Cuttler, and Genshaft (1977) found that paranoid schizophrenics were able to process information at even higher levels of complexity than were nonpsychiatric subjects. The distinction formulated by Magaro and his associates (Magaro, 1980; McDowell, Reynolds, & Magaro, 1975) between the information processing of the paranoid schizophrenic, which involves an overreliance on conceptual operations, and that of the nonparanoid schizophrenic, which is characterized by an overdependence on perceptual information, similarly polarizes paranoid and nonparanoid functioning (Cromwell & Pithers, 1981). The information processing of normal individuals is presumed to be based upon an integration of the two polar modes of thought.

Evidence for so many differences in the behavior of paranoid and nonparanoid schizophrenic patients generates an intriguing hypothesis: that paranoid schizophrenia is not a true schizophrenia and should not be included in this diagnostic category. While radical, this hypothesis has been suggested by a number of workers. As early as 1944 Henderson and Gillespie asserted that all paranoid psychotic disorders, including paranoid schizophrenia, should be separated from the nonparanoid schizophrenic disorders (noted by Kendler & Tsuang, 1981). Several more recent reviews have contained arguments consistent with this theme. Meissner (1981) argued that the schizophrenic and paranoid processes are "two separate and discriminable processes . . . that . . . operate relatively independently in the formation and deformation of human personality" (p. 611). Magaro (1981b) concluded that "considering the paranoid as independent of schizophrenia is more consistent with the research literature" (p. 632) and that "there is enough description of the underlying cognitive process unique to the paranoid and distinct from the schizophrenic to warrant a separate inclusive category" (p. 632). Cromwell and Pithers (1981) also raised the distinct possibility that paranoid schizophrenia is not a true form of schizophrenia. A corollary to the hypothesis under discussion is that there are three, rather than two, major psychoses: the affective disorders, schizophrenia, and a group of paranoid disorders that includes paranoid schizophrenia. This tripartite approach to the psychoses is consistent with Meissner's (1981) conclusion that in factor-analytic work on symptomatology discriminable factors have been found for paranoid, nonparanoid, and affective conditions. Also consistent with our hypothesis is the longstanding diagnostic practice of European psychiatrists. European diagnostic schemata follow more directly from Kraepelin's formulation than is the case in the United States, where Bleuler's influence is more strongly felt. Many patients diagnosed as paranoid schizophrenic in the United States would receive other diagnoses in Europe, for instance, delusional disorder, paraphrenia, and reactive psychosis (Hay & Forrest, 1972; Kendler & Tsuang, 1981; Kringlen, 1980; Leonhard, 1975).

DEPRESSION, PARANOIA, AND PARANOID SCHIZOPHRENIA

Traditionally, the second major class of psychosis has been the affective disorders, defined symptomatically in Table 7.1. Although this general class includes a number of more circumscribed conditions (e.g., unipolar vs. bipolar depression), the basic symptom common to all these disorders appears to be an underlying depression (a mood disorder characterized by dysphoria). In the area of psychopathology, the word *depression* is confusing since it refers both to a circumscribed symptom and to a disorder that has a number of symptomatic characteristics in addition to the feeling called depression.

A number of similarities can be noted between paranoid conditions and depression. Both depression and paranoia have been viewed as ubiquitous modes. Both can be ordered along a continuum of severity, and, in terms of surface features, both involve a preoccupation with the self.

Depression

The ubiquitousness of depression either as a symptom or as a psychotic disorder has received ever greater recognition. Taylor and Abrams (1981b) cited a broad body of evidence indicating that affective disorder is the most prevalent major mental disorder in western society. These investigators noted that when modern research criteria are employed 25 to 30 percent of patients admitted for acute psychiatric illness have affective disorders. Many workers have also called attention to the widespread occurrence of depression as a full-blown psychotic disorder (Klerman, 1978; Silverman, 1968; Weissman, Myers, & Harding, 1978). Estimates indicate that anywhere from 18 to 23 percent of women and 8 to 11 percent of men will have a significant depressive episode at some point in their lives (American Psychiatric Association, 1980). Approximately 4 to 8 million Americans are treated for depression each year (Hackett & Adams, 1974), although the number who actually suffer from the disorder has been reported to be as high as 20 million (Gibson, 1978). The high prevalence of depression has led some to conclude that our era is an "age of depression" (Arieti & Bemporad, 1978; Messer, 1979).

Formulations about the processes underlying depression include psychoanalytic models (e.g., Abraham, 1960; Freud, 1957); models that focus on ego functioning (Bibring, 1953); the cognitive model advanced by Beck

(Beck, 1967; Kovacs & Beck, 1978), which emphasizes the negative expectations of depressed persons; and Seligman's (1975) formulation regarding learned helplessness and beliefs about the uncontrollability of outcomes. Reviews of these positions have been cogently presented by Akiskel and McKinney (1973, 1975) and Arieti and Bemporad (1978).

Despite differences in the underlying processes specified by the various models, considerable agreement exists about the conscious experience of depression. Characteristic of depression are low self-esteem, self-devaluation, and a view of the self as insufficient to live up to one's aspirations or to effect outcomes, particularly positive ones (Beck, 1967; Bibring, 1953; Seligman, 1975). The conviction of inadequacy is accompanied by a sense of personal responsibility for outcomes, especially failures, and a consequent self-castigation and self-denigration colored by feelings of sadness, guilt, and hopelessness (Abramson & Sackeim, 1977; Beck, 1967; Freud, 1957; Lichtenberg, 1957; Seligman, 1975). The negative expectations of depressed individuals can also be seen in their tendency to exaggerate external problems, interpret "trivial impediments as substantial," and read "disparagement into innocuous statements by others" (Kovacs & Beck, 1978, p. 526).

A hallmark of the psychodynamics of depression is the great salience given to the self, which becomes a focal point of concern and assessment. Depressive individuals continually ask whether they are measuring up to internalized demands and typically conclude that they are not. Hoch (Strahl & Lewis, 1972) described the depressive as overwhelmed by superego demands. Noting the self-referential quality in depression, Kovacs and Beck (1978) also viewed the depressive as placing too great demands on the self. The self-depreciation and self-preoccupation of the depressive were further described by Funabiki et al.(1980). The depressive's sense of inadequacy results in a need for self-punishment. This need is manifested in the pained and dysphoric depressive who often feels he or she does not deserve to live (Abramson & Sackeim, 1977; Kovacs & Beck, 1978). Indeed, the great unhappiness experienced by the depressive (Knauth, 1975) is often painful enough to result in suicide.

Unsurprisingly, the need to escape the psychic pain of the dysphoric mood leads the depressive to employ coping mechanisms, which themselves may be maladaptive. If no ameliorative mechanism is employed, the patient is seen upon hospitalization as a unipolar depressive. Depressives often attempt to escape their pain and/or medicate themselves with alcohol. Arieti and Bemporad (1978) noted that a common form of masked depression is alcoholism, with patients often revealing their depression during alcohol-free intervals. Two separate studies found that 44 percent of alcoholic patients had secondary diagnoses of depression (Robins et al., 1977; Weissman & Myers, 1978). Further, most depressive alcoholics have been found to respond satisfactorily to antidepressants such as imipramine (Arieti & Bemporad, 1978).

Alcohol may not only make the pain of depression tolerable but may further provide a psychodynamic escape hatch for the depressive. Alcohol use has been conceptualized as a "self-handicapping strategy," protecting self-esteem by allowing failure to be attributed to the disruptive effects of the liquor rather than to a lack of personal competence (Jones & Berglas, 1978; Tucker, Vuchinich, & Sobell, 1981).

A rather transparent mechanism employed by depressives is mania in which the person denies inadequacies and unhappiness. In mania the depression is turned upside-down and the sufferer in effect states, "I am not inadequate and unhappy. I am great, and I am very happy." As Arieti and Bemporad (1978) noted, the flight of ideas encountered in mania frequently has as its goal the maintenance of a superficial euphoria and an escape from intruding thoughts that may bring about depression.

The central importance of depressive dynamics appears in disorders in addition to alcoholism and mania. Very high frequencies of moderately severe or severe depression, as a circumscribed symptom, have been reported in psychiatric patients with primary diagnoses such as schizophrenia, neurotic reaction, and personality disorder (Knights & Hirsch, 1981; Lewine et al., 1978, 1980; Noyes et al., 1980; Roy, 1980; Strauss, Kokes, Ritzler, Harder, & Van Ord, 1978; Wadeson & Carpenter, 1976; Wittenborn, 1977). As an example, Lewine et al. (1980) found the symptom of depression was manifested by 74 percent of schizophrenic, 75 percent of personality disorder, 86 percent of neurotic, and 86 percent of affective disorder patients. Depression is clearly a nondistinctive symptom that is found in other disorders almost to the same degree that it appears in the syndrome of psychotic depression.

In order to separate the almost omnipresent symptom of depression in psychopathology from the presence of a full-blown depressive psychotic disorder, severity and duration criteria are employed. Dysphoric mood accompanying such other indications as poor appetite, insomnia, loss of energy, and so on, must be experienced "nearly every day for a period of at least two weeks" before a psychotic depressive disorder can be diagnosed (American Psychiatric Association, 1980). Complicating the matter further is the growing acceptance of the continuity view of depression in which common depressive feelings are seen as less severe but similar to clinical states (Arieti & Bemporad, 1978; Blatt, D'Afflitti, & Quinlan, 1976; Brown & Bunney, 1978; Funabiki et al., 1980; Strahl & Lewis, 1972). Thus depression might be conceptualized as a continuum that ranges from a brief blue mood through neurotic depressive illness to psychotic depressive illness (Brown & Bunney, 1978).

In view of this continuity concept and the fact that everyone must at some time experience periods of unhappiness, workers must entertain the hypothesis that depression is inherent in the human condition. In reviewing a number of psychoanalytically derived models of depression, Arieti and Bemporad (1978) point to a common underlying assumption that depression is "an almost basic state which has to be defended against in either an abnormal or a healthy fashion" (p. 35).

Paranoia

Our major argument is that paranoia is a mechanism employed by individuals to ward off a breakthrough into consciousness of depressive thought and its accompanying painful affective concomitants. This view is fully consistent with Meissner's (1978) treatment of the paranoid process in which depression, feelings of personal inadequacy, and diminished self-esteem are seen as central psychodynamic issues in paranoid disorders. As Meissner (1978) stated, "paranoid patients can only relinquish their paranoid stance at the risk of encountering a severe depression" (p. 125). The view that paranoia is a defense against a sense of inferiority and accompanying feelings of guilt has been advanced by many other workers (Dollard & Miller, 1950; Lewis, 1979a, 1979b; Nydas, 1963; Salzman, 1960; Schwartz, 1963, 1964; Sullivan, 1956). Paranoia might then be viewed as a restitutive mechanism much like other ego defense mechanisms (Freud, 1967). Perhaps paranoia might be considered a broader "style" variable that includes such well-known defense mechanisms as denial, projection, and introjection (Meissner, 1978).

If paranoia is a means of protection against depression, a number of parallels should exist between the two phenomena. An obvious feature shared by depression and the paranoid mechanism is that each can be either a circumscribed symptom or a full-blown disorder.

The ubiquitous presence of paranoid mechanisms has been widely noted (Freedman & Schwab, 1978; Magaro, 1981a; Meissner, 1978, 1981; Torrey, 1981; Wurmser, 1980.) Meissner (1978) has termed the paranoid process "endemic to human psychological functioning" (p. 817) inasmuch as paranoid mechanisms serve the essential function of maintaining "the integrity and sense of inner cohesion of the self" (Meissner, 1981, p. 628).

As is the case with depression, paranoid symptomatology is encountered frequently in a number of nosological groups. Freedman and Schwab (1978), for example, noted paranoid symptoms in 70 percent of patients with psychotic depressive reactions, in 50 percent of affective disorder patients examined, and in 63 percent of patients with psychotic organic brain syndrome (see Davison & Bagley, 1969, for additional data regarding this latter group). Paranoid mechanisms have also been observed in nonpsychotic psychiatric patients (Freedman & Schwab, 1978) and among (nonpathological) college students (Chapman & Chapman, 1980; Heilbrun, 1972; Heilbrun & Bronson, 1975).

In terms of surface features, paranoia and depression both involve a preoccupation with self. The general dynamics of the paranoid process appear directed at assuaging the individual's sense of inadequacy. This view is consistent with Colby's (1975, 1976, 1977) formulation of paranoid processes as a defense against shame and humiliation. Triggered by feelings of inadequacy, paranoid mechanisms forestall humiliation by "blaming others for wronging the self" (1977, p. 55). Heilbrun's model of paranoid thinking

(Heilbrun, 1971, 1972; Heilbrun & Bronson, 1975) also emphasizes low self-esteem, sensitivity to social evaluation, and concern with rejection. In this framework, paranoid delusions can be viewed as "defensive assertions of superiority [and] attempts at restitution after severe impairment of self-esteem" (Heilbrun & Madison, 1978, p. 326). Given the thrust of our argument, the effectiveness of the paranoid process in assuaging a sense of personal inadequacy is derived from (a) projection of the inadequacy onto the outside world and (b) the self-enhancement or sense of importance that accompanies persecutory delusions including ideas of reference. The paranoid can essentially reassure the self that "far from being inadequate, I must be very important and valuable if everyone is so interested in me."

As in the case of depression, many workers have suggested that the paranoid processes can be placed along a continuum of severity extending from florid delusions of persecution or grandiosity all the way to the mild and more reality-based interpersonal sensitivities, cautiousness, and rationalizations of normal individuals (Chapman & Chapman, 1980; Freedman & Schwab, 1978; Kendler & Tsuang, 1981; Meissner, 1978, 1981; Strauss, 1969; Zigler & Levine, 1983b).

Paranoid Schizophrenia

A second relevant continuum frequently encountered in the psychopathology literature involves only disturbed or disordered individuals and is best labeled a schizophrenia–nonschizophrenia continuum of paranoia. Such a concept is certainly supported by the research on the diagnostic stability of paranoid psychotic disorders reviewed by Kendler and Tsuang (1981). Results from this research argue for a subdivision of paranoid disorders into a number of types with some, but not all, eventuating in schizophrenia.

Whether a paranoid disorder is thought to reflect schizophrenia is typically determined by how disorganized or incomprehensible the paranoid delusion is. In addition to the intactness of thought, the probability of the delusion's being true must be considered. A patient who reports that voices on the radio are talking about him is expressing a belief that is possible but improbable. A patient who advances the belief that she has been pregnant for 14 years is holding a belief that is impossible. Although diagnosticians are reluctant to admit it, it is extremely difficult to determine when a delusion is so strange, incomprehensible, or implausible that it must be reflective of schizophrenia. If an individual reports that he is Jesus Christ returned to earth to save humanity, this assertion would be taken by most clinicians as prima facie evidence of a delusion of grandiosity indicative of paranoid schizophrenia. Yet there is nothing particularly incoherent in such an assertion. Furthermore, if one is willing to entertain the possibility of the Second Coming, then this individual cannot be labeled schizophrenic on the grounds that the belief is totally impossible.

Given such difficulties, the paranoid spectrum extending from true paranoia through paranoid schizophrenia must be called into question. The paranoid spectrum, though a widely accepted concept, has posed difficulties to diagnosticians from the time of Kraepelin to the present day. As Meissner (1981) noted, "Kraepelin was troubled by and unable to resolve the question . . . [of] the degree of conjunction or distinction diagnostically between paranoia and schizophrenia" (p. 614). Such confusion is mirrored in the fact that the distribution of patients across the paranoid spectrum is extremely skewed in the direction of many diagnoses of paranoid schizophrenia and almost no diagnoses of nonschizophrenic paranoia. (As noted earlier, this state of affairs has been truer for American diagnosticians than for those in Europe.)

Venables and O'Connor (1959) determined that the distinguishing items in their paranoid schizophrenia scale were delusions of control, reference, persecution, and grandeur. In their methodological review, Ritzler and Smith (1976) found: "Delusions of persecution and grandeur head the list, but are not ubiquitous. In some cases, *any* delusion is sufficient to qualify a patient as paranoid" (p. 213). It would appear that false beliefs (delusions) are encountered too frequently to be used as indicative of schizophrenia. As argued above, the essence of such beliefs (and the paranoid process in general) is the protection they afford the individual when confronted with a sense of personal inadequacy. This can be seen clearly in some odd beliefs of the aged. An older man whose memory is such that he cannot remember where he put his glasses achieves considerable ego protection by asserting that "someone has been hiding my glasses." By the same token, it is not surprising that the paranoid process is encountered so frequently in the blind (Meissner, 1978) and is associated with the experience of deafness (Houston & Royse, 1954; Zimbardo, Andersen, & Kabat, 1981). '

Meissner (1981) argued that the schizophrenic and paranoid dynamics are two separate and discriminable processes that operate relatively independently. Meissner felt that these two processes may intermingle and that this contributes to the schizophrenic spectrum of psychopathology. Our central argument is that the diagnosis of paranoid schizophrenia reflects the paranoid process (the patient asserts some delusional belief) but has little to do with schizophrenia. This suggests that workers should abandon the paranoid schizophrenia spectrum and in its place adopt a notation of whether the patient does or does not display the paranoid process. Support for the view that paranoid schizophrenics should be included within the general class of "paranoia" comes from the similar perceptual styles encountered in paranoids and paranoid schizophrenics (Meissner, 1981).

It may be helpful to think in terms of genotypes and phenotypes. A single genotype can give rise to different phenotypes (i.e., outward appearances), while the same phenotype can be due to different genotypes (Lewin, 1946). Our view is that paranoid disorder is essentially a phenotype that can be found in conjunction with a number of differing genotypes. Schizophrenia and depression, on the other hand, are like genotypes each of which gives rise to a number of phenotypes. The model for this conceptualization is presented in Figure 7.1.

RELATION OF PARANOIA TO DEPRESSION AND MANIA: TESTS OF THE FORMULATION

If the phenotypes presented in Figure 7.1 are associated with the common genotype of depression, then these phenotypes should share certain features and demonstrate a certain overlap. One test then of our formulation is whether or not there are similarities between paranoia and other phenotypes of depression and/or whether there are systematic relations between these various phenotypes stemming from the depressive genotype.

The presence of paranoid symptoms in depressive disorders has frequently been noted (Freedman & Schwab, 1978; Hamilton, 1969; Kantor & Glassman, 1977; Retterstol, 1975; Swanson, Bohnert, & Smith, 1970; Toone & Ron, 1977). Delusions of persecution have been reported in one-fifth of patients with affective disorders (Bowman & Raymond, 1931), even when rigorously diagnosed (Winokur, Clayton, & Reich, 1969). Allen (1967) pointed out how depression and paranoia may substitute for one another, with the depression being the primary underlying feature in paranoid patients. Meissner (1978) noted that Melanie Klein also viewed paranoid and

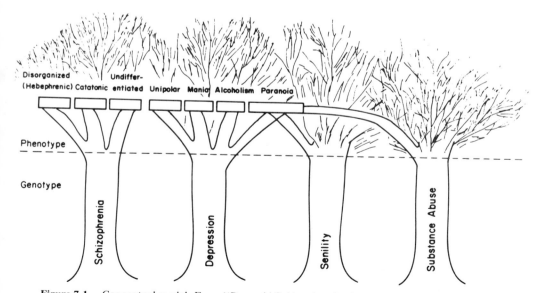

Figure 7.1. Conceptual model. From "Paranoid Schizophrenia: An Unorthodox View" by E. Zigler and M. Glick, 1984, *American Journal of Orthopsychiatry, 54.* Copyright 1984 by the *American Journal of Orthopsychiatry.*

depressive states as closely related. The overlap between depressive and paranoid features has certainly been emphasized by Arieti and Bemporad (1978), who described paranoid features in various forms of severe depression. In regard to mild depression, they noted "an almost paranoid feeling that others are overly conscious of their behavior" (p. 167) and "that others watch their every move" (p. 161). This overlap in paranoid and depressive symptomatology was also discerned by Kraepelin (1921), who described both delusional mania and paranoid melancholia. As Kendler and Tsuang (1981) recorded, at one point Kraepelin felt that many acute forms of delusional psychoses were types of manic-depressive disorder.

While considerable evidence points to the operation of paranoid mechanisms in depression, the reverse appears less frequently. Paranoid patients often do not evidence depression. Zigler and Levine (1983a) found more depressive coloration in the symptoms of nonparanoid than in those of paranoid schizophrenics. On the surface, this might seem surprising. If paranoid schizophrenics are typically found to have better premorbid adjustment than nonparanoid schizophrenics and depressive features are typically found to be associated with higher premorbid adjustment, why don't paranoid schizophrenics evidence more depression than their nonparanoid counterparts? This apparent contradiction can be resolved if we assume that paranoia frequently constitutes an effective defense against depression. The high-level individual may thus express the underlying depression in depressive symptomatology or may invert the depressive process and express the depression in paranoia. Depression, then, should appear in paranoia to the extent that the paranoid defenses crumble. As will be discussed later in this section, depression should be discovered in paranoid schizophrenics to the extent that their delusions are not particularly fixed or become weakened.

The phenotype that paranoia most resembles is not that of unipolar depression but rather that of mania. Mania and paranoia have much in common. In both instances, the disordered individual turns the depression upside-down and asserts his or her worth and well-being. The similarity of symptoms in manic conditions and paranoia was emphasized in the comprehensive review by Pope and Lipinski (1978). For example, delusions have been recorded for 73 percent of manic patients (Clayton, Pitts, & Winokur, 1965); in separate samples, persecutory delusions were found in 42 percent, 53 percent (Taylor & Abrams, 1973, 1975a), and 65 percent of manic patients (Carlson & Goodwin, 1973). The difficulty in distinguishing paranoid and manic patients on the basis of symptomatology has likewise been stressed by Breakey and Goodell (1972), Lipkin, Dyrud, and Meyer (1970), Slater and Roth (1969), and Swanson et al. (1970). Meissner (1978) put the authors' position succinctly when he stated:

> The paranoid defenses take their place alongside the manic defenses as major strategies to avoid and diminish the pain of depression and lowered self-

esteem. . . . At their pathological extremes, the paranoid psychoses and the manic depressive psychoses are often difficult to differentiate. (p. 26)

A study by Abrams, Taylor, and Gaztanaga (1974) lends support to our central view that paranoid schizophrenics are much more likely to be depressed individuals who show the symptoms of mania than to be true schizophrenics. In this study only 2 of 41 paranoid schizophrenics satisfied research criteria for schizophrenia, whereas one-half of them satisfied research criteria for mania. Analogously Lipkin et al. (1970) reported that manics are often misdiagnosed as paranoid schizophrenics. Arrayed against such evidence are the findings of Kay et al. (1976), that paranoid patients could be reliably differentiated from those with affective psychoses. As was not the case with the other investigations cited, the patients in the Kay et al. study were over 50 years of age. However, other investigators have reported paranoid ideation as a predominant symptom in elderly depressed patients (Gerner, 1979; Ward, Strauss, & Ries, 1982; Young, 1972).

Swanson et al. (1970) and Kovacs and Beck (1978) charted the course of the giving way of depressive mechanisms to paranoid defenses. Depressive mechanisms are usually employed first, with paranoid defenses being resorted to when these are not successful. Most relevant to our view that paranoia most resembles mania is the formulation of Carlson and Goodwin (1973). These workers delineated three stages in the course of mania. In the third and most severe stage, the patients showed paranoia, ideas of reference, and hallucinations. Seventy-five percent of the patients in their sample displayed delusions, and 65 percent displayed delusions of persecution.

Thus far we have discussed the commonality in the psychodynamics of the paranoid and affective disorders as well as the overlap in their symptomatologies. A final question to be raised is whether there are other similarities (e.g., in the course of the disorder, response to treatment) between paranoid and affective illnesses. As noted earlier, paranoid schizophrenics (as compared to other subtypes) tend to have a later age of onset, and their premorbid functioning tends to be relatively good. The same statements are true of individuals suffering from the affective disorders (Zigler et al., 1979; Zigler & Phillips, 1961a). At the level of cognitive functioning, manics and paranoids have both been found to manifest a high degree of over-inclusiveness (Meissner, 1981).

Such evidence shows not only that paranoid schizophrenia is similar to affective disorders but also that it is dissimilar to nonparanoid schizophrenia. Many additional differences between these schizophrenic groups were reviewed in Chapter 6. Particularly relevant to the discussion here are findings suggesting genetic differences. Kendler and Davis (1981) provided some evidence that there is a lower genetic loading for schizophrenia in paranoid versus nonparanoid patients. Paranoid schizophrenics have been found to have fewer first-degree relatives afflicted with schizophrenia than hebephrenics (Tsuang & Winokur, 1974; Winokur et al., 1974), while hebe-phrenic–catatonic patients have been found to have almost twice as many schizophrenic family members as paranoid schizophrenics (Larson & Nyman, 1970; Winokur et al., 1974). Watt et al. (1980) found no increased risk of schizophrenia in the siblings of paranoid psychotic probands over what would be expected in the general population. Arana (1978) concluded, "The classical subtypes [hebephrenic, paranoid, simple, catatonic] do not seem genetically bundled, although more cases of schizophrenia appear to be present in the families of nonparanoid patients" (p. 125).

Family studies suggest that there is a genetic link between paranoid schizophrenia and the affective disorders. Pope and Lipinski (1978) stated:

> "Schizophrenics" of the good-prognostic categories [which include paranoid schizophrenics] show typically two to three times as much familial affective illness as schizophrenia; poor-prognosis groups show a twofold to threefold difference in the opposite direction. The virtual unanimity of this literature spanning three continents and 60 years is persuasive; it is difficult to explain these data other than by the hypothesis that many or most cases of "good-prognosis schizophrenia" are in fact cases of MDI [manic-depressive illness]. (p. 817)

Abrams et al. (1974) found that in comparison with nonparanoid schizo-phrenic patients paranoid patients who satisfied research criteria for mania displayed more family history of affective illness and alcoholism and a better treatment response. By contrast, this paranoid group did not differ from manic patients on any demographic, treatment–response, or family history variables.

Our central position is that paranoid schizophrenics are not true schiz-ophrenics but are rather depressed patients who, like manics, employ mech-anisms to deny their sense of inadequacy and unhappiness. Ultimate validation for such a view would rest in the finding that paranoid schizo-phrenics respond favorably to a drug known to be effective for manics (i.e., lithium carbonate). Evidence in this direction exists, although it comes from relatively small patient samples and weak controls (Freedman & Schwab, 1978; Lipkin et al., 1970; Pope & Lipinski, 1978). Larger-scale studies of the effectiveness of lithium carbonate with patients currently diagnosed as para-noid schizophrenic would be a promising avenue of future research. A report of endocrinological evidence for depression (nonsuppression on a dexameth-asone suppression test) in a patient with paranoid symptoms (Ward et al., 1982) suggests another direction for more systematic investigation.

Supplementing the research concerned with biochemical indicators of de-pression and psychopharmacological responsiveness, a close examination of the course of paranoid symptom manifestation could provide a means for testing the formulation advanced here. Inasmuch as the paranoid delusion is construed as a defense against depression, one would expect depressive symptomatology to be manifested either in early stages in the formation of delusions or at the time when paranoid symptomatology is abating. By contrast, when the delusion is solidified and well organized, evidence of depression should be minimal. The degree of the patient's conviction of the delusion should thus be negatively related to depressive symptomatology. Postpsychotic depression (the emergence of marked depression at the point when schizophrenic symptomatology is abating) has been noted by a number of investigators (e.g., Bowers & Astrachan, 1967; Siris, Harmon, & Endicott, 1981; Steinberg, Green, & Durell, 1967), although the frequency of the phenomenon has varied across studies, with some authors (e.g., Shanfield et al., 1970) reporting little evidence of postpsychotic depression. This research has been thoughtfully reviewed by McGlashan and Carpenter (1976). In none of these studies were the schizophrenic patients differentiated by subtype. Our formulation generates the expectation that postpsychotic depression would be found primarily in paranoid schizophrenic patients (or a subgroup of such patients). The investigation of postpsychotic depression in paranoid versus nonparanoid schizophrenic patients would thus provide a further test of our formulation and might also serve to explain the different frequencies of the phenomenon reported across studies.

The strong form of the hypothesis advanced in this paper is that paranoid schizophrenia is not a true schizophrenia but is best conceptualized as one of several possible responses to an underlying depressive mode. A weaker form of the hypothesis (Cromwell & Pithers, 1981; Meissner, 1981) is that the category of paranoid schizophrenia includes individuals of two types: (a) depressives and (b) true schizophrenics who respond to the basic schizophrenic process with a paranoid overlay. What would be common to both groups is the presence in the symptom picture of delusions. Perhaps it is time to forgo concentrating on the gross characteristics of the delusion (persecution, grandiosity, ideas of reference, somatic) and look instead at its more fine-grained formal characteristics (Zigler et al., 1976). Perhaps the two hypothesized subgroups of paranoid schizophrenia will differ in their delusions in regard to degree of differentiation, reality orientation, degree of commitment, and, finally, how much the delusion suggests guilt and self-depreciation, which would indicate the breakthrough into consciousness of depressive ideation.

SUMMARY

Paranoid and nonparanoid schizophrenic patients have found to differ on many behavioral indexes. In some instances, the performance of non-disturbed individuals fails between that of paranoid and nonparanoid schizophrenics. The distinctiveness of the paranoid group generates the hypothesis that paranoid schizophrenia is not a true schizophrenia and should not be included in this diagnostic category.

By contrast paranoia shares many features with the affective disorders, defined in terms of the presence of underlying depression. As either a symptom or a psychotic disorder, depression is widespread. A hallmark of the psychodynamics of depression is the great salience given to the self, which becomes a focal point of concern and negative evaluation. Alcoholism and mania are common mechanisms employed to prevent the breakthrough into consciousness of depressive thought and affect. Inasmuch as depression can be conceptualized as a continuum that ranges from brief feelings of melancholy through the affective disorders, the experiences of depression may be inherent in the human condition. A high frequency of paranoid symptoms has been noted in patients with various nonparanoid disorders. In terms of surface features, paranoia and depression both involve a preoccupation with self. The general dynamics of the paranoid process appear directed at assuaging the individual's sense of inadequacy.

Paranoid schizophrenia appears to reflect the paranoid process but to have little to do with schizophrenia. Like mania and alcoholism, paranoid disorder (including paranoia and paranoid schizophrenia) can be conceptualized as a phenotype associated with the underlying genotype of depression. By contrast, schizophrenia and depression can be viewed as genotypes each of which gives rise to a number of phenotypes. Paranoia may therefore represent one of a number of mechanisms for coping with an underlying depression. While unorthodox, this formulation is consistent with a number of findings concerning similarities between paranoid, depressed, and manic patients. Paranoid symptoms have frequently been observed in depressive disorders, and it is difficult to distinguish paranoid and manic patients on the basis of symptomatology. Similarities between paranoid and affective disorder patients can likewise be found in regard to the course of the disorder, family history of psychopathology, and treatment response.

CHAPTER 8

A Developmental Approach
to Alcoholism

Alcohol abuse has been described since ancient times (Morey, 1984). The traditional view has been that excessive drinking signifies a unitary disorder. However, little evidence supports this view (Morey, 1984; Skinner, Glaser, & Annis, 1982). Few personality characteristics have been found to be unique to alcoholics. Particularly telling are findings that alcoholics at different age and intelligence levels are more dissimilar from each other than they are from their nonalcoholic counterparts (Hoffman & Nelson, 1971). The consensus has thus developed that alcoholism is a label applied to a heterogeneous group of individuals whose ingestion of alcohol brings them to the attention of such social institutions as hospitals, courts, or self-help groups like Alcoholics Anonymous. Beyond this tautology, there is, as Miller (1976) clearly documented, no agreed-upon definition of alcoholism. How, then, can understanding and treatment proceed?

Historically, three approaches can be identified. Driven by an understandable desire for conceptual parsimony and/or simplicity, many theorists continue to argue that the diversity encountered in the behavior of any large group of alcoholics masks a common underlying set of psychodynamics such as dependency and its expression (Gomberg, 1968; Jones, 1968; Sanford, 1968). Evidence regarding such common underlying characteristics has to date been equivocal (for extensive reviews of research efforts to isolate personality characteristics distinctive to alcoholics see Barnes, 1979; Miller, 1976). In regard to dependency, for example, Vaillant (1980) presented data to suggest that, rather than being an antecedent characteristic, oral dependency may be a consequence of alcoholism. In his long-term follow-up of Harvard sophomores, different antecedent variables were found to be associated with oral dependency than with alcoholism. However, after the individual began to abuse alcohol, oral themes emerged. In a number of studies (see especially Barnes, 1979, for a review of this research), alcoholics have been found to obtain higher psychopathic deviate (*Pd*) scores on the MMPI than normal control subjects and psychiatric patients, suggesting another dimension that might underlie alcoholic disorders. However, as MacAndrew and Geertsma (1964) and Morey (1984) pointed out, the commonality found for alcoholic individuals may reflect little more than the inclusion in the *Pd* scale of a number of specific items concerning drinking. Further, rather than representing an antecedent and thus a possible predisposing characteristic, the high Pd scores might represent a consequence of alcohol abuse and its attendant social problems. A second approach involves emphasizing the diversity of behavior encountered in alcoholics and moving on to the construction of a more differentiated diagnostic system. In such classification schemata a variety of subtypes are defined by different test profiles on such instruments as the MMPI or by complex behavioral profiles involving both psychological test and nontest behaviors. Careful reviews of this research have been provided by Barnes (1979), Miller (1976), Morey (1984), and Morey and Blashfield (1981a). Inasmuch as the studies commonly employ multivariate clustering techniques, a number of the issues raised in Chapter 5 concerning numerical taxonomy apply here. As Morey (1984) and Morey and Blashfield (1981a) indicated, different clustering methods yield different solutions, and careful consideration must be given to decisions concerning the number of clusters to be generated. Further, as Morey and Blashfield noted, the majority of studies on alcoholism have failed to provide adequate validation of the clusters discovered. Exceptions here are studies by Finney and Moos (1979) and Whitelock, Overall, and Patrick (1971).

It should be noted that these two approaches—the effort to uncover a common underlying dynamic and attempts to define discrete alcoholism subtypes—are not mutually exclusive. It is also possible to combine them, conceptualizing alcoholism as a diagnostic category like schizophrenia where in addition to certain core characteristics (e.g., auditory hallucinations) identifiable subtypes can be delineated (e.g., disorganized, catatonic). An interesting example of this combined approach can be found in the efforts of Knight (1937), who developed a typology differentiating the essential from the reactive alcoholic. While Knight viewed all adult alcoholics as generally passive, dependent, and emotionally immature (the core of the disorder?), as operationally defined by Rudie and McGaughran (1961), essentials differed dramatically from reactives in a variety of ways, including psychological defenses utilized, everyday life-style, and actual drinking behaviors. A central thrust of the research to be reviewed in this chapter is that this essential–reactive typology reflects an underlying maturity dimension.

A third approach involves (a) accepting the great psychological diversity of alcoholics as a basic given; (b) treating alcohol ingestion as a phenotypic symptom that provides little information about underlying psychological processes; and (c) employing an empirically grounded theoretical frame of reference to establish a typology of alcoholism, a typology that would be as applicable to nonalcoholics as to alcoholics. Our developmental formulation is not presumed to be limited to any particular diagnostic group nor even to pathological forms of functioning. Yet, as previous chapters have indicated, measures presumed to reflect differences in underlying developmental level have been found to distinguish major diagnostic groups (e.g., affective disorder, personality disorder, schizophrenia) and to differentiate subgroups within a particular diagnostic category (e.g., paranoid and nonparanoid schizophrenia). This same conceptualization has been applied to alcoholism. As has been the case with other diagnostic groups, the developmental approach does not view alcoholism as a unitary disease entity possessing correlates of interest unique to the particular diagnostic category. Across a variety of diagnoses, the individual's developmental level is expected to be associated with phenomena of clinical and practical interest, for example, premorbid history, age of onset, nature of precipitating factors, specific symptom picture, and outcome.

Primarily, the research to be reviewed here concerns the application of the premorbid competence construct to alcoholism. In addition to this research, the symptom drinking has from the outset of the developmental work been included in the self-indulgence and turning-against-others role orientation category (e.g., Phillips & Rabinovitch, 1958; Zigler & Phillips, 1960). While not synonymous with alcoholism, this symptom is certainly central to the disorder. Both the inclusion of drinking in the self-indulgence and turning-against-others category and the fact that this symptom involves expression in action rather than thought suggest that drinking (and by extension alcoholism) reflects a developmentally lower form of functioning. However, such a categorization may well overlook the heterogeneity of individuals diagnosed as alcoholic. For example, while sociopathy and impulsivity (associated with developmentally lower forms of functioning) have been found to characterize some alcoholics, depression and anxiety (associated with higher levels of functioning) have been found to be dominant in other alcoholic individuals (Goldstein & Linden, 1969; Schuckit et al., 1969; Winokur, Rimmer, & Reich, 1971). Likewise, Vaillant's 1980 sample comprised individuals who not only displayed high potential (Harvard sophomores selected as displaying superior adjustment) but by conventional standards evidenced considerable accomplishment in adult life. Although the question of the developmental status of the symptom drinking has never been directly addressed in our own work, a number of findings suggest that the developmental status of this symptom is at best equivocal. Most germane is the finding of Zigler and Phillips (1960) that drinking, unlike most other symptoms in the turning-against-others category, tended to be associated with intermediate or high levels of social effectiveness. In more recent studies, no associations have appeared between drinking and social competence (Zigler & Levine, 1983a) or between drinking and other developmental indicators (Glick et al., 1985). Some implications of the role orientation formulation for the study of alcoholism will be discussed later in the chapter. At this point, we merely want to indicate that the inclusion of drinking in the turning-against-others category may not adequately reflect the developmental status of this particular symptom and that alcoholism as a diagnostic entity appears to encompass individuals who may vary widely in developmental level.

SOCIAL COMPETENCE AND THE ESSENTIAL–REACTIVE DISTINCTION IN ALCOHOLISM

A typology differentiating between essential and reactive alcoholics was proposed by Knight (1937) almost 50 years ago. Clinically, Knight viewed the essential alcoholic as presenting the more severe alcoholism problem and being characterized by immaturity, economic and emotional dependence, irresponsibility, pleasure seeking, and an inability to establish or maintain deep relationships or long-term goals. Also included in the picture of the essential alcoholic was an early onset of drinking, without any precipitating events, and a basic orality manifested by a willingness to consume any beverage or drug in order to achieve the desired pharmacological effect. This pattern of indiscriminate ingestion as well as easily upset eating habits was viewed as resulting in gastrointestinal symptoms.

Knight described the reactive alcoholic as presenting a less severe problem with a better prognosis than the essential alcoholic. The reactive alcoholic, whose drinking started at a later age and often after a precipitating event, was seen to have greater psychosexual maturity, a higher level of education and occupation, and less erratic drinking and eating habits, and to be more responsible. It should be noted that, while Knight viewed the reactive alcoholic as being more mature than the essential alcoholic, in keeping with psychoanalytic thought, he viewed all adult alcoholics as generally passive, dependent, and emotionally immature.

Rudie and McGaughran (1961) employed Knight's clinical descriptions in constructing the essential–reactive alcoholism scale. With this scale, these investigators confirmed the hypothesis that alcoholics could indeed be differentiated into two subtypes on the basis of the behavioral indicators emphasized by Knight. Rudie and McGaughran found that compared to essential alcoholics reactive alcoholics manifested a more complex defense system with greater emphasis on intellectualization and generally showed a higher degree of overall defensiveness. Essential alcoholics obtained higher scores on marital difficulty, psychopathic adjustment, conflict with parents, unstable home, hedonism, marital irresponsibility, and unmonitored feeling and emotion. Reactive alcoholics, on the other hand, scored higher on educational achievement, occupational accomplishment, overall achievement, and socioeconomic level of the conjugal family. There were no significant group differences between the two groups in age, intelligence, or parental socioeconomic status.

In interpreting Rudie and McGaughran's (1961) findings, Sugerman, Reilly, and Albahary (1965) noted many parallels between the essential–reactive dimension in alcoholism and the process–reactive dimension in schizophrenia. Employing the developmental thinking of Zigler and Phillips (1962), these investigators suggested that, just as Zigler and Phillips found a general maturity dimension underlying the process–reactive distinction in schizophrenia, so might the essential–reactive distinction in alcoholism be related to general maturity. Sugerman et al. confirmed this possibility by discovering a positive relationship between the essential–reactive scale scores and maturity as measured by the Zigler-Phillips social competence index.

It is not surprising to discover that an alcoholism scale constructed to assess selected aspects of a general life-style is related to a social competence measure that has been found to be related to style of functioning, as reflected in role orientation. Thus the description of the reactive alcoholic as one who has attained a higher level of psychosexual development, has assimilated cultural values and is constrained by anxiety and guilt, employs intellectualizing defenses, and shows considerable responsibility and social competence despite the drinking is most reminiscent of the higher developmental individual (described in Chapter 4) whose life-style is characterized by a turning against the self. The description of the essential alcoholic as an individual fixated at a lower level of psychosexual development, emotionally and economically dependent and culture combative, who evidences unmonitored expressions of feeling or emotion and avoids social responsibility and who has a hedonistic orientation that leads to direct immediate pleasure seeking without the constraints of anxiety, guilt, or intellectualizing defenses greatly resembles the lower developmental individual whose life-style is characterized by self-indulgence and turning against others.

However, the positive relationship discovered by Sugerman et al. between placement on the essential–reactive dimension and social competence was somewhat at odds with the findings of Rudie and McGaughran, who found no significant differences between their extreme groups of essential and reactive alcoholics on the variables of age and intelligence. (In regard to the education variable, Rudie and McGaughran found no differences between their small sample of essentials and reactives on this variable, but in their enlarged sample they did find that reactives attained higher educational levels than did essentials.)

Levine and Zigler (1973) further examined the relationship between essential–reactive scale scores and maturity level as assessed by the social competence index. This investigation compared all subscale and total scores on both measures.

The Levine and Zigler study also examined whether the dimension assessed by the essential–reactive scale is unique to alcoholism. Does the essential–reactive scale assess a dimension independent of the general maturity dimension that, as previous chapters indicated, has been found to apply across a variety of diagnostic groups and for nonpathological individuals as well? Further, since all previous research employed the essential–reactive scale only with alcoholics, no evidence was available to indicate how helpful the scale might be in discriminating between alcoholic and other disorders.

Levine and Zigler (1973), therefore, examined the relationship of essential–reactive scores to social competence in three samples of male patients:

20 psychiatric patients with a primary diagnosis of alcoholism; 20 psychiatric patients without psychosis (primarily depressive reaction patients); and 20 medical and/or surgical patients without psychiatric symptomatology who were suffering from relatively minor physical problems (e.g., hernia, appendectomy). The social histories of the two nonalcoholic samples were examined and interviews were conducted to ensure that none of these subjects was an undiagnosed alcoholic.

The Rudie-McGaughran Essential–Reactive Alcoholism Scale is a 69-item scale with 55 scorable items and 14 filler items. There are eight subscales:

1. Economic dependence (7 items): Dependence upon others for economic support (e.g., work status of wife and reasons for her working)
2. Emotional dependency (12 items): Willingness to make decisions and to assume jobs with responsibility
3. Persistent application to reality tasks (12 items): Schooling, number of jobs held, and management and saving of money
4. Age of patient at onset of drinking and possible causes of drinking (2 items)
5. Relationship to friends (6 items): Dependency on friends and preference for acquaintances as opposed to intimate friends
6. Character traits (7 items): The alcoholic's dependency while drinking and how the drinking affects relationships
7. Presence of gastrointestinal symptoms and multiform oral gratifications (6 items): Physical symptoms, eating habits, and how often the individual craves a drink
8. Will imbibe anything that has the desired pharmacological effect (3 items): Use of drugs and nonbeverage alcoholic products

The variables of intelligence, education, occupation, employment history, and marital status, scored as described in Chapter 3, were employed to form high and low social competence subgroups. High social competence was determined by a score of 2 on at least three of the indexes. Low social competence was defined as a mean score not exceeding .80. Whereas with earlier studies, including that of Sugerman et al. (1965), age was employed as a component of social competence, this was not the case with the Levine and Zigler study. Given the population examined and the criteria employed to define high and low competence groups, the inclusion of the age variable would have placed too great constraints on subject selection. Therefore, the relationship of age to the essential–reactive dimension was analyzed separately.

The social competence and alcoholic scale scores of the groups are presented in Table 8.1. Consistent with the findings of Sugerman et al. (1965), a

Diagnosis × Social Competence Level analysis of variance computed on the alcoholism scale scores revealed a highly significant relationship between overall social competence and total scores on the essential–reactive scale. The Diagnosis × Social Competence interaction did not approach significance, although as will be discussed below the diagnostic groups did differ in alcoholism scores.

TABLE 8.1.   Social Competence and Essential–Reactive Scale Scores

Group	N	Age		Social Competence		Essential–Reactive Scale	
		M	SD	M	SD	M	SD
Alcoholic	20	44.1	7.18	1.16	.50	15.55	3.96
High social competence	10	46.5	6.70	1.62	.19	13.70	3.80
Low social competence	10	41.7	6.83	.70	.20	17.40	3.17
Psychiatric	20	39.6	12.83	1.23	.60	11.30	4.23
High social competence	10	46.8	7.86	1.80	.18	8.90	4.28
Low social competence	10	32.4	12.80	.66	.18	13.70	2.45
Medical	20	45.6	9.42	1.09	.50	7.75	3.14
High social competence	10	47.6	8.53	1.56	.15	6.00	2.14
Low social competence	10	43.6	9.85	.62	.17	9.50	3.01

Source: "The Essential–Reactive Distinction in Alcoholism: A Developmental Approach" by J. Levine and E. Zigler, 1973, Journal of Abnormal Psychology, 81. Copyright 1973 by American Psychological Association. Reprinted by permission of the publisher.

   Parallel analyses employing each of the five social competence components were likewise significant. With respect to each of the components of intelligence, education, occupation, employment history, and marital status, higher competence was associated with lower (less essential) alcoholism scores. Additional analyses revealed that these relationships were not due merely to the overlap of a small number of items on the social competence and alcoholism measures. As hypothesized, older age was also found to be associated with less essential scores for the entire patient group and for the alcoholic sample analyzed separately.

   That the essential–reactive dimension in alcoholism may be reducible to a general developmental or maturity dimension in the same manner as the process–reactive distinction in schizophrenia was supported by the findings that the relationship between the essential–reactive alcoholism scores and social competence was not unique to alcoholics but could be found in non-alcoholic neurotic patients and in individuals of nonpathological functioning as well. Such a formulation highlights the universality of a general developmental dimension in behavior and makes of psychopathology a more unitary phenomenon rather than a collection of discrete entities, each conceptualized in terms of unique dimensions and parameters.

While the essential–reactive scale was constructed primarily to differentiate types of alcoholic patients, the inclusion in the study of nonalcoholics permitted the examination of the scale's ability to discriminate alcoholics from other groups. As indicated previously, highly significant differences appeared between the three patient groups in overall essential–reactive alcoholism scores. The alcoholic patients obtained higher (more essential) scores than did the psychiatric patients who in turn obtained more essential scores than did the medical patients. Significant differences also appeared between the three patient groups on six of the eight subscales of the essential–reactive measure: economic dependence; persistent application to reality tasks; age at onset of drinking and possible causes; relationship to friends; character traits; and presence of gastrointestinal symptoms. As would be expected from the total scale score analysis, for each of the subscales where a main effect for group was found, alcoholics obtained higher (more essential) scores than did the other two groups, with the difference between the alcoholic and the medical patients being most pronounced.

The simplest explanation for these group differences lies in the content of the scale items. Thirteen of the 55 scorable items are alcohol related and produced, as would be expected, higher scores in alcoholics than in nonalcoholics. However, the overall findings indicated that a factor other than item content also contributed to the highly significant groups effect discovered. Thus, it was found that subscales having none (economic dependence and relationship to friends) or only 1 of 11 items relevant to alcohol ingestion (persistent application to reality tasks) were also associated with group differences. Furthermore, the alcohol-content factor cannot explain the difference in scale scores discovered between the neurotic and nonpsychiatric patients, unless one assumes that the neurotics have a much greater drinking problem than nonpsychiatric individuals.

A second explanation should be entertained to explain at least a portion of the group differences discovered. It appears that the essential–reactive scale is in large part assessing a general developmental dimension, and it is possible that the three groups, although equated on the social competence index, are nevertheless not equated on this underlying dimension for which the social competence index served as the measure. Given the pervasive nature of the developmental-level construct, as well as the obvious limitations of the social competence index, it is not farfetched to argue that an individual's developmental level is far from perfectly assessed by the social competence index. Indeed, we have already pointed out that the social competence index is too narrow a measure of maturity and does not give sufficient weight to interpersonal relations, a factor heavily weighted in the essential–reactive scale. This explanation generates the view that, although they were equated on the social competence index, the normals were at a higher maturity level than the neurotics, who in turn were at a higher level than the alcoholics.

Such a view is consistent with the finding of Zigler and Phillips (1961a) that, regardless of diagnosis, hospitalized mental patients obtain lower social competence scores than the general population. As we mentioned earlier in this chapter, it may be simplistic to assume that alcoholic individuals are homogeneous in regard to developmental level. Nevertheless, the neurotic patients examined in this study primarily displayed depressive symptomatology, which has repeatedly been found to be associated with higher developmental functioning than the self-indulgent symptomatology, which at least in part characterizes alcoholism. The view that alcoholics are in general characterized by a relatively low developmental level is consistent with the emphasis of Knight and other clinicians. It does not, however, negate the need for a more differentiated taxonomy of alcoholic disorder. The implication of the argument being advanced here is that (if the items relevant to alcohol ingestion are ignored) Rudie and McGaughran may have inadvertently constructed a better measure of maturity level than the social competence index of Zigler and Phillips, or at least a measure that can be used to augment this rather limited indicator.

Finally, correlational analyses utilizing only the alcoholic sample revealed that, in contradistinction to all other subscales on the essential–reactive measure, Subscale 7, "Presence of gastrointestinal symptoms," was (a) positively related to social competence, and (b) negatively related both to total essential–reactive scores and to the six remaining subscales on this measure. The intercorrelations of essential–reactive scores are presented in Table 8.2. That more essential scores on Subscale 7 would be obtained by high competence individuals is consistent both with developmental theorizing and with empirical findings, reviewed in Chapter 4, that somatization as characterized by gastrointestinal symptoms is more characteristic of the higher than of the lower developmental individual. Further research to examine the correlates and the utility of Subscale 7 seems warranted.

In summary then, the results of Levine and Zigler augment the findings of Sugerman et al. and provide firm support for the view that the essential–reactive distinction in alcoholism reflects an underlying maturity dimension. Not only did a relationship appear between overall social competence and essential–reactive scale scores, but each of the component indexes of social competence and age was found to be significantly related to the essential–reactive measure. Alcohol abuse can thus be added to the list of psychopathological disorders for which developmental differences have been found to be related to major variables of interest. Moreover, as would be expected given the evident developmental nature of the measure, essential–reactive scores were found to differentiate high and low developmental individuals in nonalcoholic and nonpsychiatric samples as well as within the alcoholic group.

Some further evidence of the applicability of the developmental-level construct to alcoholic and nonalcoholic samples was provided by Levine and Zigler (1976). This study utilized the same sample as was employed in the

TABLE 8.2. **Intercorrelations Between Total Essential–Reactive Scale and Subscale Scores for Alcoholics**

Subscale	1	2	3	4	5	6	7	8	Total Score
1. Economic dependence		-.17	.00	-.13	.45**	.35	-.19	.08	.47**
2. Emotional dependency			.13	.59***	.10	-.06	-.52**	-.30	.29
3. Persistent application to reality tasks				.53**	.02	.38*	-.24	.17	.73****
4. Age at onset of drinking and possible causes					.13	.16	-.31	.08	.61***
5. Relationship to friends						.13	-.55**	.23	.38*
6. Character traits							-.12	-.27	.66***
7. Presence of gastrointestinal symptoms and multiform oral gratifications								.08	-.31
8. Will imbibe anything for the desired pharmacological effect									.12

Source: "The Essential–Reactive Distinction in Alcoholism: A Developmental Approach, by J. Levine and E. Zigler, 1973, Journal of Abnormal Psychology, 81. Copyright 1973 by American Psychological Association. Reprinted by permission of the publisher.

* $p < .10$
** $p < .05$
*** $p < .01$
**** $p < .001$

1973 investigation and examined the influence of developmental level and psychodynamic themes on the humor responses of the three patient groups: alcoholic patients, nonpsychotic psychiatric patients, and nonpsychiatric (medical) patients. Developmental research unrelated to issues in psychopathology has demonstrated a high correlation between humor comprehension and IQ (Levine & Redlich, 1960; Zigler, Levine, & Gould, 1966). Some evidence that individuals at higher developmental levels enjoy humor more than individuals at lower developmental levels was found in a study by Maslow (1970). In surveying 3000 college students to discover the critical attributes that characterize those students who are most likely to mature into self-actualizers, Maslow found that a sense of humor became even more characteristic of individuals as they approached the self-actualizing ideal. The finding that a well-developed sense of humor is a characteristic of increased maturity is not at all surprising in view of the growing evidence that the healthy expression of humor is associated with a broad array of socially adaptive behaviors and positive functioning (Flugel, 1954; Kris, 1952; Levine, 1963, 1969; McGhee, 1974; White, 1959; Zigler, Levine, & Gould, 1967).

The developmental position emphasizes a continuity across various psychopathological conditions and between pathological and nonpathological individuals at the same developmental level. In contrast to this position, the various psychodynamic approaches to alcoholism share the view that alcoholics suffer from some circumscribed conflicts or intrapsychic difficulties that differentiate alcoholics from nonalcoholics who are assumed to suffer from these intrapsychic difficulties to a much lesser degree. With respect to intrapsychic conflicts, a large body of evidence has indicated that individual variation in psychodynamics manifests itself in the individual's reactions to humor stimuli having particular content themes (Grziwok & Scodel, 1956; Hetherington, 1964; Hetherington & Wray, 1964; Levine, 1968; Levine & Abelson, 1959; Levine & Redlich, 1955; Redlich, Levine, & Sohler, 1951). (For instance, the individual conflicted about sexuality will have a different reaction in regard to comprehension, mirth response, and judgment of funniness of cartoons or jokes with a sexual content than would individuals not conflicted in this way.) The examination of the humor responses of alcoholic and nonalcoholic patients at higher and lower developmental levels thus permitted a test of the developmental position in comparison to frequently employed psychodynamic approaches to alcoholism. However, in view of the wide array of conflicts that have been attributed to alcoholics, selection of the humor content themes to be employed represented a difficult and ultimately arbitrary decision. The themes finally selected were those that have appeared with some frequency in discussions of conflicts particularly characteristic of alcoholic patients, that is, marital relations, dependency, and self-indulgence. If alcoholics do suffer from any or all of the conflict themes chosen, the psychodynamic orientation would generate the expectation of a Diagnosis × Humor Content theme interaction, with the alcoholics displaying different reactions than the other two groups to some or all of the humor content themes. The developmental position, which asserts that alcoholic–nonalcoholic differences are attenuated if one controls for the level of maturity attained, generates the expectation of no difference between alcoholics and nonalcoholics in their humor responses. Furthermore, since even among adults the individual's level of maturity has proven to be such a pervasive determinant of so many psychologically important behaviors (e.g., Achenbach & Zigler, 1963; Phillips & Zigler, 1961; Zigler & Phillips, 1960, 1961d), it would be surprising if the individual's level of maturity did not influence responses to humor stimuli. The developmental position thus generates the expectation that, while diagnostic status would not be related to reactions to humor stimuli, the person's position on the social maturity dimension would be so related.

The 60 male patients, 10 high competence and 10 low competence individuals in each of three diagnostic groups (alcoholic patients, nonpsychotic psychiatric patients, and nonpsychiatric medical patients), were thus administered a modification of the mirth response test of Redlich et al. (1951). Each subject was presented with 27 cartoons, 9 representing each of the three psychodynamic content themes (marital relations, dependency, self-indulgence). Upon initial presentation, each subject was asked to judge each cartoon as to whether it was funny or not (funniness rating). The subject's spontaneous mirth responses (e.g., no mirth, half smile, laugh) were also recorded. The cartoons were then presented a second time and the subject was asked to explain each cartoon (comprehension measure).

The major thrust of the findings was that the patient's social competence or maturity level was a much more important determinant of the three humor measures than was the individual's diagnostic group membership. High competence individuals obtained higher scores on each of the three humor measures (comprehension, mirth, and rating of funniness) than did their low competence counterparts. By contrast, the only significant effect involving diagnostic status was a three-way interaction among diagnosis, social competence, and cartoon theme with respect to the funniness rating. This interaction reflected an atypical pattern of funniness scores obtained by the alcoholic patients with respect to marital relations cartoons. Specifically, this was the one instance out of nine comparisons where high competence patients displayed lower funniness ratings than did low social competence individuals.

FURTHER WORK ON THE DEVELOPMENTAL APPROACH TO ALCOHOLISM

While few investigators have uncovered evidence for a unitary behavioral dynamic underlying alcoholism, a study conducted by Overall and Patrick (1972) provided some support for a unitary view of alcoholic disorder. In this methodologically sophisticated factor-analytic study, Overall and Patrick found a single large alcoholism factor. They also isolated 10 much smaller specific factors that were not thought to be fundamental features of alcoholism. In investigating the psychological correlates of their unitary alcoholism factor, Overall and Patrick concluded that high scores on this major factor are associated with subjective states of discomfort, anxiety, and depression. An association between alcoholism and depression has frequently been suggested in the literature on alcoholism. Secondary depression is often noted in alcoholic patients (Donovan et al., 1977; Robins et al., 1977; Weissman & Myers, 1978; Winokur, Rimmer, & Reich, 1971), and such individuals have been found to respond satisfactorily to antidepressants (Arieti & Bemporad, 1978). Unfortunately, inspection of the 42 questions most heavily loaded on the Overall and Patrick unitary factor reveals that this factor could not possibly be a broad factor gauging an underlying dynamic characteristic of all alcoholics. (Overall and Patrick make no claim that their factor has such features.) Actually, the Overall and Patrick unitary factor appears to be a narrow one (in the conceptual if not the statistical sense) in that it reflects little more than the patient's characteristic drinking behavior and the close concomitants of the patient's drinking pattern. The words *drinking, drunk, alcoholic, and/or drinker* appear in each of the 42 questions (e.g., "Do you almost always drink too much if you drink at all?" "Are you now an alcoholic?" "Do you frequently have the shakes after drinking?").

Levine and Zigler (1981) thus advanced the hypothesis that the Overall and Patrick unitary factor essentially assesses the severity of the patient's drinking problem but does not illuminate the psychodynamics of the alcoholic. It should be recognized that, while every alcoholic can be placed somewhere on the severity continuum, this continuum may be essentially independent of alcoholics' psychodynamics and/or other continua such as level of maturity. Thus, individuals with quite different psychodynamics could fall at exactly the same point on the severity continuum. Analogously, individuals suffering from quite different degrees of severity of alcoholism could have the same underlying dynamics.

In order to test this hypothesis, Levine and Zigler (1981) examined the relation between the Overall-Patrick scale and an independent measure of severity of alcoholism, the number of alcoholism programs the patients had previously experienced. Further, the findings of Overall and Patrick generated the expectation that patients scoring high on the unitary scale score should also score high on depression. The Beck Depression Scale was utilized in order to test this expectation. Since certain items on the Overall-Patrick are similar to the drinking behavior items found on the Rudie-McGaughran scale, Levine and Zigler also examined the degree of relation between these two important scales. A final concern was with the relationship between each of the alcoholism scales and maturity level reflected in social competence scores.

These relations were examined in a sample of 20 male patients in an alcoholic treatment program at the West Haven Veterans Administration Hospital in Connecticut. All were identified as chronic alcoholics who had no history of psychiatric problems other than alcoholism. The sample thus represented a constricted range of alcoholics, primarily older individuals thought to be suffering from a debilitating degree of alcoholism. Given the constricted range of the sample, any relations discovered would be expected to be conservative estimates of the true relations between the variables of interest.

The correlations among the variables examined are presented in Table 8.3. Consistent with the hypothesis that the Overall-Patrick scale assesses the severity of alcoholism, a significant correlation was found between this scale and the number of previous programs in which the patients participated. The Rudie-McGaughran scale was also found to be significantly related to the number of previous programs measure. The two alcoholism scales were found to be significantly related to each other, a not particularly surprising finding in view of the overlap of drinking behavior items on the two scales, although it should be noted that the common variance assessed by the two scales is only about 30 percent of the overall variance. In large part, therefore, the two scales appear to be independent measures. This conclusion is further supported by the different relations discovered between these two scales and the social competence measure. The Rudie-McGaughran scale was found to be significantly related to the social competence measure while the Overall-Patrick scale was not found to be so related. The relation between the Rudie-McGaughran scale and the social competence index found in this study is consistent with the previous findings reported in this chapter (Levine & Zigler, 1973; Sugerman et al., 1965). Contrary to the expectation derived from the Overall and Patrick (1972) findings, no significant relation between the Overall-Patrick and Beck scale scores was found by Levine and Zigler. Given the frequently reported relation between alcoholism and depression, this is somewhat surprising; it may be due to the selective sampling procedure employed in this particular study. The older alcoholic willing to admit his alcoholism may have come to accept his alcoholism and therefore not display the depression and/or anxiety noted by Overall and Patrick. Indeed, if these patients had clinically observable degrees of depression they would be more likely to be placed on the psychiatric as opposed to the medical hospital ward.

The Overall-Patrick scale appeared to assess the severity of the patient's alcoholism while the Rudie-McGaughran measure appeared to assess both severity *and* an underlying maturity dimension of the sort assessed directly by the social competence index. While the severity dimension can conceptually be differentiated from the dimension of high versus low maturity, the developmental formulation would suggest that these two aspects of functioning would be interrelated. As we indicated in Chapter 2 and will elaborate in Chapter 9, the greater coping resources available to high developmental individuals might mitigate against some severely debilitating consequences of

TABLE 8.3. Correlations of Measures

	Social Competence Index	Rudie-McGaughran Scale	Overall-Patrick	Beck Depression
Number of previous alcoholism programs	.21	.51*	.53*	.03
Social competence index		−.48*	−.25	−.06
Rudie-McGaughran scale			.55*	.01
Overall-Patrick				−.20

*$p < .05$

alcoholism and contribute to more favorable prognoses. A promising avenue of future research would appear to be the investigation of the relations among the Overall-Patrick scale, the Rudie-McGaughran scale, the social competence index, and outcome of alcoholic disorder. We would then be in a position to assess how well the severity factor isolated by Overall and Patrick and the typologies of Rudie and McGaughran and Zigler and Levine predict outcome, a variable of considerable practical and theoretical interest.

The premorbid competence–outcome relationship in alcoholism was investigated in a methodologically sophisticated study by Finney and Moos (1979). Briefly, a modification of the Zigler-Phillips scale was employed to assess premorbid competence. A sample of 387 alcoholic individuals receiving treatment in five different types of residential settings was examined. Based on cluster analyses that took into account personality and environmental variables as well as premorbid competence, four low competence and four high competence alcoholic subtypes were isolated. Overall, premorbid competence was found to be significantly related to more favorable outcome on each of five variables: alcohol consumption; abstinence; physical impairments related to drinking; rehospitalization for alcoholism; and occupational functioning. Despite these findings that high competence patients showed more positive outcomes across all measures, Finney and Moos noted that slightly less than 13 percent of all outcome variance was accounted for by membership in the eight subgroups isolated.

Additional evidence that individuals at lower developmental levels may display more debilitating forms of alcoholism was provided by Morey, Skinner, and Blashfield (1984). Utilizing a sophisticated cluster-analytic methodology with a large sample (725 male and female alcoholic individuals), these authors empirically isolated three alcoholic subtypes differing along a severity dimension. Whereas individuals in the Type A group displayed the least severe drinking practices and associated unfavorable consequences, those in the Type C category evidenced the most severe drinking problems. Type B individuals occupied an intermediate position on the severity dimension. These subtypes, isolated in the derivation phase of the research, were then validated with respect to a variety of external variables, including sociodemographic characteristics, personality variables, degree of psychopathology, and intellectual functioning. It is pertinent to developmental level as reflected in social competence scores that individuals in the Type C (schizoid, severe alcohol dependence) category were more likely than individuals in the other two groups to be unemployed, on welfare, and either divorced or separated. Further, the Type C alcoholics were less educated, obtained lower scores on WAIS subtests, and had fewer dependents than individuals in the other two groups. By contrast, alcoholics in the Type A category were highest of the three groups in socioeconomic status (SES), displayed the greatest social stability, and had lost the fewest jobs. These differences discovered by Morey et al. between alcoholic subgroups differing in severity of drinking can thus be related to the social competence components of intelligence, education, occupation (SES), employment history, and marital status. With respect to almost all psychopathology variables examined, Type C individuals were the most disturbed and Type A the least disturbed. Finally, in regard to personality characteristics, Type A alcoholics showed more internal locus of control and less impulsivity than individuals in the other two categories. By contrast Type C individuals were the most aggressive of the three groups.

Another direction for further developmental research concerns the symptomatology displayed by alcoholic individuals. As indicated at the beginning of this chapter, alcoholics have been found to obtain elevated scores on the psychopathic deviate (PD) scale of the MMPI. Heightened impulsivity and hostility have also been noted in alcoholic samples (Cisin & Cahalan, 1968; Ritson, 1971; Williams, McCourt, & Schneider, 1971). Barnes (1979) reviewed a number of studies in which higher depression (D) scores on the MMPI were found for alcoholics as compared with normal control subjects. Other research mentioned previously (e.g., Donovan et al., 1977; Overall & Patrick, 1972; Robins et al., 1977; Weissman & Myers, 1978; Winokur et al., 1971) also indicated substantial levels of depression in alcoholic individuals. Evidence from cluster analyses suggests that heightened psychopathic deviancy versus depression may designate distinct alcoholic subtypes. The first two alcoholism clusters isolated by Goldstein and Linden (1969) involved a psychopathic personality pattern with emotional instability and a neurotic personality pattern involving depression and anxiety. As Morey and Blashfield (1981a) carefully documented, these two clusters have now been replicated in many studies of alcoholic individuals. Some evidence for a distinction between alcoholism involving sociopathy and that involving depression has likewise emerged from research concerned with family history of mental disorders. Based on structured interviews, Winokur et al. (1971) isolated three subgroups of alcoholics: primary alcoholics; depression alcoholics; and sociopathy alcoholics. Whereas depression was found to be more frequent in the first-degree relatives of depression alcoholics, sociopathy was found more frequently in the first-degree relatives of sociopathy alcoholics. By contrast, alcoholism appeared more frequently in first-degree family members of primary alcoholics. Substantial gender differences also appeared among the three alcoholism groups. Whereas primary and sociopathy alcoholics were predominantly male, depression alcoholics were predominately female. A similar relationship between depression alcoholism and affective disorder in first-degree family members was observed in a female sample by Schuckit et al. (1969).

The symptom clusters involving depression and anxiety versus sociopathy, poor impulse control, and aggressiveness would seem to mirror the role orientation clusters of symptoms indicative of turning against the self versus self-indulgence and turning against others. Furthermore, the role orientation formulation, discussed in Chapter 4, would seem to provide a means for applying developmental principles in the formation of more homogeneous subgroups of alcoholic individuals. The expectation would be that alcoholics displaying depression or turning against the self would show higher developmental functioning as indicated by premorbid competence than would alcoholics whose symptom pictures reflected turning against others. This application of the role orientation formulation could be further extended to the consideration of outcome. As will be discussed in the next chapter, some evidence has been presented to indicate an association between the role orientation of turning against the self and more favorable outcome (Phillips & Zigler, 1964).

Finally, a shortcoming in many studies on alcoholism has been the narrowness of the samples utilized (Finney & Moos, 1979; Morey, 1984). Primarily male, blue-collar, VA or state hospital patients have been examined. Research concerned with developmental differences in the functioning of alcoholic individuals and other studies concerned with alcoholic personality types or subtypes require the examination of a broad range of individuals including women and white-collar and professional workers.

SUMMARY

Rather than indicating a unitary disorder, the label *alcoholism* appears to encompass a heterogeneous group of individuals with a wide range of behavioral characteristics. In attempting to come to terms with the heterogeneity, some investigators have continued to search for common psychodynamic principles underlying the diversity of alcoholics' behavior. Others have worked to delineate discrete alcoholism subtypes. Developmental thinking provides a third approach. Alcohol ingestion is treated as a phenotypic symptom, and the broad developmental-level construct is employed to order the diversity of behaviors manifested by alcoholics just as this construct has been applied to many other maladaptive and adaptive forms of behavior.

The many parallels between the essential–reactive distinction in alcoholism (Knight, 1937; Rudie & McGaughran, 1961) and the social competence dimension defined by Zigler and Phillips (1960, 1962) were first noted and empirically demonstrated by Sugerman et al. (1965). Levine and Zigler (1973) provided further evidence not only that overall social competence and essential–reactive scale scores were significantly intercorrelated but that each of the component indexes of social competence was significantly related to essential–reactive scores. The interpretation of the essential–reactive distinction as a reflection of general maturity level was further supported by findings that premorbid competence and essential–reactive scores were found not only for alcoholic individuals but for other psychiatric and nonpsychiatric patients as well. Some additional evidence of the applicability of the developmental-level construct to alcoholism was provided by findings that maturity level, as reflected in premorbid competence scores, was a much more important determinant of humor responses to different psychodynamic content themes than was the individual's diagnostic status (alcoholic inpatients vs. nonalcoholic psychiatric and medical patients) (Levine & Zigler, 1976). The developmental approach to alcoholism was further investigated by Levine and Zigler (1981). A unitary alcoholism dimension discovered by Overall and Patrick (1972) was interpreted by Levine and Zigler as reflecting severity of drinking problems. In order to explore this interpretation, Levine and Zigler examined relationships among Overall-Patrick alcoholism scale scores, severity of alcoholism as indicated by participation in previous alcoholism treatment programs, essential–reactive alcoholism scale scores (Rudie & McGaughran, 1961), and premorbid social competence. The intercorrelations among these measures suggested that Overall-Patrick scale scores primarily reflect severity of alcoholism whereas scores on the essential–reactive measure reflect both severity of the drinking problem and an underlying maturity dimension. One issue requiring continued investigation concerns the relationship between developmental level and both severity of and outcome in alcoholic disorder. A further direction for developmental analysis involves the application of the role orientation formulation to the symptoms manifested by alcoholic individuals.

CHAPTER 9

Developmental Level
and the Course and Outcome
of Psychiatric Disorders

The understanding of and the ability to predict the course and outcome of psychiatric disorders are of central concern in all considerations of psychopathology. What current dysfunctions presage in terms of future life adjustment is certainly an overriding concern for patients, their families, the clinicians who must counsel them, and those who are responsible for practical administrative decisions. Thus, as Cromwell and Pithers (1981) emphasized, the prediction of outcome and also increased understanding about treatment effectiveness stand as primary aims for research in psychopathology.

Developmental thought generates the broad expectation that individuals at higher developmental levels should display a less debilitating course of disorder and a more favorable psychiatric outcome than persons with similar disorders who function at lower developmental levels. The finding of Zigler and Phillips (1961a) that as a group state hospital psychiatric patients obtain lower premorbid competence scores than the population at large is consistent with this developmental expectation in that it suggests a greater prevalence of debilitating disorder in individuals at lower developmental levels. However, the developmental view does not imply that vulnerability to disorder is reducible to developmental level. As indicated in Chapter 3, higher developmental levels of functioning may, in fact, create certain kinds of problems that developmentally less mature individuals would be less likely to experience. Such problems associated with higher developmental status include internal dilemmas resulting from the greater internalization of societal standards and consequently heightened guilt. The greater frequencies of symptoms indicative of turning against the self and of affective disorder diagnoses in high competence individuals (see Chapters 4 and 5) point to this downside aspect of higher developmental status as does the repeated finding, to be discussed in the next chapter, that higher developmental individuals evince greater disparity between their view of themselves and their image of what they would like to be. However, despite these problems that may particularly accrue to higher developmental levels of functioning, the increased differentiation and hierarchical integration that accompany development inherently allow for greater adaptability and coping effectiveness. This inseparability of organizational changes in development from their functional concomitants was discussed in Chapter 2. As indicated there, the structural changes that define development necessarily give rise to increased capacities for planning, for understanding self–world relationships, for exerting active control over both the environment and internal need states, for flexibility in problem solving, and simultaneously for stability in functioning. With such greater adaptive resources at their disposal, high developmental individuals should less frequently succumb to life's stresses, and, if they break down, such individuals should cope more actively and determinedly with the problems related to the disorder. The greater resources of such persons would likewise be expected to buffer the influence of internal factors including genetic predisposition to disorder. Again, this would suggest that such individuals should less frequently become psychologically disordered, might manifest the disorder later in life, and should display more favorable psychiatric outcomes than individuals who function at developmentally lower levels.

Given the intrinsic interconnection between developmental level and coping effectiveness, the developmental formulation takes a broader view of prognosis than the more typical concern with outcome following the appearance of definable and debilitating forms of psychopathology. As will be discussed in more detail later in the chapter, within the developmental approach to psychopathology, prognosis is defined by three related measures, each of which retains a considerable degree of independence: (a) whether or not the individual becomes mentally ill; (b) the age at which this illness becomes manifest; and (c) the outcome of the illness after initial treatment and/or institutionalization. In accordance with this definition of prognosis, the research to be reviewed in this chapter considers not only the course and outcome of disorder after psychiatric disturbance has become manifested but also the age of onset of disorder.

While prognosis should generally be more favorable for individuals of high developmental level, this variable is presumed to interact with a variety of other factors to influence the onset and course of psychiatric disorder. These other factors include such broad classes of variables as genetic predisposition and environmental determinants of behavior. Further, as will be discussed in the next section, outcome following the appearance of disorder appears to be a multidimensional variable comprising a number of partially independent functions, each with somewhat specific predictors (Keniston, Boltax, & Almond, 1971; Lewinsohn & Nichols, 1967; Schwartz, Myers, & Astrachan, 1975; Strauss & Carpenter, 1974b, 1977). These partially independent aspects of outcome include social adjustment, work adjustment, symptomatology, and hospitalization. Such a model might also apply to the other aspects of prognosis considered within the developmental formulation. For example, it would not be surprising if the age of symptom onset differed from the time at which social or instrumental (academic or work) role dysfunctions first became evident. Inasmuch as the age of onset variable has been less frequently investigated, the applicability of a multidimensional model to this aspect of prognosis remains speculative. Nevertheless, the complexity of the variables influencing outcome as well as the complexity of outcome variables themselves makes it unlikely that relationships between discrete variables (e.g., the person's developmental level) and outcome will be robust. Thus, while some relationships between developmental level and outcome might be expected, the relationship would not be expected to be especially robust.

DEVELOPMENTAL LEVEL AND THE OUTCOME OF MANIFEST PSYCHIATRIC DISORDER

Our research has concentrated on the relationship between developmental level as reflected in premorbid competence scores and hospitalization measures of psychiatric outcome. Corroborating the work to be discussed that emphasizes hospitalization is some evidence provided by other investigators (Garmezy et al., 1979; Strauss & Carpenter, 1977; Strauss, Kokes, Carpenter, & Ritzler, 1978) that premorbid competence may be related to other outcome dimensions (e.g., social and work adjustment). Finally, in addition to the premorbid competence variable, relationships between other developmental indicators (e.g., role orientation in symptomatology) and psychiatric outcome will be considered.

Premorbid Social Competence and Psychiatric Outcome in Schizophrenic and Nonschizophrenic Patients

Central to the developmental position is the assumption that premorbid social competence will be related to psychiatric outcome not only for schizophrenic patients but for other diagnostic groups as well. The premorbid adjustment/premorbid social competence construct had its origin in efforts to bifurcate the schizophrenic syndrome into process (poor premorbid history) and reactive (good premorbid history) subtypes, presumed to be dichotomous with regard to etiology, the course of the disorder, and outcome. The classic definitions of process and reactive schizophrenia have frequently been summarized (e.g., Chapman, Day, & Burstein, 1961; Garmezy & Rodnick, 1959; Herron, 1962; Higgins, 1964; Zigler & Phillips, 1962). The process schizophrenic was described as displaying poor premorbid adjustment, an early and insidious onset of psychosis with no indication of clear precipitating stress, and a course of illness characterized by gradual deterioration and poor prognosis. The basis for the disorder was generally assumed to be organic. By contrast, reactive schizophrenia was conceptualized as psychogenic in origin, with the onset precipitated by severe stress in an individual with relatively good premorbid adjustment, and characterized by favorable prognosis. Considerable evidence suggests that rather than representing two discrete conditions (as in process vs. reactive schizophrenia) premorbid competence is best conceptualized as a unitary dimension (Becker, 1959; Garmezy, 1970; Higgins, 1964; Kantor & Herron, 1966; Zigler & Phillips, 1962). The construction of premorbid competence measures has for the most part been atheoretical, based primarily upon empirical relations discovered between a variety of factors in a patient's premorbid history (or a patient's responses to questions concerning the premorbid period) and psychiatric outcome. Not surprisingly given the origin of the measures, positive relations between premorbid social competence and outcome have typically been found for schizophrenic patients (e.g., Garmezy, 1970; Strauss & Carpenter, 1977). Although some recent reports (Bromet, Harrow, & Kasl, 1974; Harrow & Grossman, 1984) have suggested that the premorbid competence–outcome relationship in schizophrenia may not be as robust as previously thought, other recent studies have underscored the substantial contribution of premorbid social competence to outcome variance for schizophrenic patients (Knight et al., 1979; Möller et al., 1982; Roff & Knight, 1978; Stoffelmayr, Dillavou, & Hunter, 1983). While informative, these findings with schizophrenic patients alone cannot compare the efficacy of the developmental formulation to the more traditional view that good versus poor premorbid adjustment represents a dimension (or categorization) specific to the schizophrenic syndrome.

An Initial Investigation

If premorbid competence represents a broad though imperfect benchmark of maturity level, the relation of this variable to outcome should not be specific to schizophrenia but should be found for patients with nonschizophrenic diagnoses as well. This developmental interpretation of the premorbid competence–outcome relationship was first examined by Zigler and Phillips (1961d). The case histories of 251 first-admission psychiatric patients diagnosed as suffering from various (schizophrenic and nonschizophrenic) functional disorders were examined. All patients had been admitted to Worcester State Hospital between 1945 and 1954. Premorbid social competence scores were based upon the six indexes of age, intelligence, education, occupation, employment history, and marital status, scored in the manner described in Chapter 3. As in previous studies, the overall competence score for each patient was the mean of the scores obtained on the six component indexes. The outcome measures employed were (a) length of initial hospitalization; (b) following discharge from the hospital, the patient's readmission to any psychiatric hospital in Massachusetts; and (c) for those patients readmitted, the time interval from discharge from the first admission to the second admission. In addition, those patients who were never discharged from the hospital were compared with those who had been released. The median of the distribution of social competence scores was employed to form high and low competence subgroups. Chi-square analyses revealed that, in comparison with the low competence group, high competence patients were more likely to have been released from the hospital, had shorter initial hospitalizations, and were less likely to be rehospitalized. No significant relationship appeared between premorbid competence and the length of time between release and readmission for patients readmitted to a hospital.

Additional analyses were performed utilizing a different procedure to establish high and low competence subgroups. In regard to the initial analyses, Zigler and Phillips noted that the averaging procedure employed and the distribution of competence scores were such that a patient high on only one or two competence indexes could be included in the high competence group. In order to circumvent this problem, all patients who fell above the median of the distribution on at least four of the six social competence indexes were included in the high competence group. Conversely those who fell below the median on at least four of the six indexes comprised the low competence group. Utilizing this procedure, 30 patients (16 schizophrenic, 7 manic-depressive, and 7 psychoneurotic) were included in the high competence group while 36 (25 schizophrenic, 4 manic-depressive, 3 psychoneurotic, and 4 character disorder) patients comprised the low competence group. The outcome measures previously employed were utilized, and the high competence patients were again found to have shorter initial hospitalizations and to be less likely to be rehospitalized. As in the earlier analyses, premorbid competence was not found to be related to the length of time between release and readmission for patients readmitted to a hospital.

The findings of Zigler and Phillips (1961d) are thus consistent with the developmental formulation. In samples comprising nonschizophrenic as well as schizophrenic psychiatric patients, premorbid competence was found to be related to length of initial hospitalization and to whether or not the patient was readmitted following release. Further, low competence patients were more likely to remain continuously hospitalized.

Premorbid Competence and Outcome Among Male Schizophrenic and Nonschizophrenic Patients

The developmental interpretation of the premorbid competence–outcome relationship was called into question by the findings of Rosen, Klein, Levenstein, & Shahinian, (1969). These investigators found the typical premorbid competence–outcome relation for a heterogeneous group of patients and for a schizophrenic subgroup, but no such relation was found for nonschizophrenic patients examinedseparately. In fact, some slight evidence was found indicating a negative relation between premorbid social competence and outcome for nonschizophrenic patients. However, the number of nonschizophrenics examined by Rosen et al. was relatively small. The nonschizophrenic group also had a disproportionate number of female patients. This is significant because gender has been found to be a moderator variable in premorbid competence relationships (Farina, et al., 1963: Rosen, Klein, &

Gittelman-Klein, 1969). In addition, although some of the findings reported by Rosen et al. are at variance with the developmental formulation, others are consistent with the Zigler-Phillips argument. On three of the four outcome measures employed by Rosen et al., poor premorbid nonschizophrenics displayed poorer outcomes than did good premorbid nonschizophrenics. Only on the fourth outcome measure was a reversal found in which good premorbid nonschizophrenics displayed poorer outcome than did poor premorbid nonschizophrenics.

Other research findings are at variance with the position of Rosen and his colleagues and consistent with the Zigler-Phillips formulation. A widely used premorbid competence scale, the Elgin, was found to be positively related to outcome with manic-depressive patients (Wittman & Steinberg, 1944). Strauss and his colleagues (Strauss, Kokes, Carpenter, & Ritzler, 1978) observed parallel relations between premorbid competence and outcome in nonschizophrenic and schizophrenic patient samples. Other investigators have also noted that the premorbid competence–outcome relation appears to be independent of diagnosis or severity of pathology (Mendel, 1976; Orr et al., 1955; Turner & Zabo, 1968). In addition, favorable outcome for nonpsychotic patients has been associated with various components of the Zigler-Phillips social competence index. This research was surveyed by Phillips (1968a) and by Garmezy et al. (1979).

In light of this conflicting evidence and the shortcomings noted regarding the findings of Rosen, Klein, Levenstein, & Shahinian (1969), Zigler, Glick, and Marsh (1979) further examined the premorbid competence–outcome relationship in schizophrenic and nonschizophrenic patient samples. This study was based upon an examination of the case histories of 381 male state hospital patients with the following diagnoses: schizophrenic reaction $(N = 92)$; affective disorder $(N = 89)$; neurotic $(N = 98)$; and personality disorder $(N = 102)$. Included in the schizophrenic group were 40 paranoid, 22 chronic undifferentiated, 23 simple, and 7 hebephrenic schizophrenic patients. These patients were first admitted to Fairfield Hills Hospital in Connecticut between 1966 and 1970. In order to avoid confounding effects of changing hospital administrative policies regarding admission and discharge, the attempt was made to have the number of patients in each of the diagnostic categories comparable for each of the years of first admission.

As was the case in both the Zigler and Phillips (1961d) and Rosen, Klein, Levenstein, & Shahinian (1969) studies, the Zigler-Phillips index was employed to assess premorbid competence. The variables of age, education, occupation, employment history, and marital status were examined and scored in the traditional manner. Three outcome measures were employed, representing a composite of the measures utilized by Rosen, Klein, Levenstein, & Shahinian (1969) and Zigler and Phillips (1961d). The measures were (a) the length of initial hospitalization; (b) the total length of rehospitalizations during the follow-up period; and (c) number of readmissions. The follow-up period was 3 years after discharge from the first admission.

For the measures of length of initial hospitalization and total length of rehospitalization, the overall median of the distribution of scores on each outcome measure was employed to establish favorable and unfavorable outcome subgroups. In order to examine the relationship of premorbid competence to number of readmissions, patients exhibiting none versus one or more readmissions were compared. Table 9.1 presents the mean premorbid competence scores of patients displaying favorable versus unfavorable outcomes on each of these measures.

With respect to the length of initial hospitalization and total length of rehospitalization measures, two separate 2 (Favorable vs. Unfavorable Outcome) × 4 (Diagnosis) analyses of variance performed on premorbid competence scores revealed significant relations between premorbid competence and each outcome measure. As was described in Chapter 5, social competence was also significantly related to diagnosis, with affective reaction patients displaying the highest scores and schizophrenic and personality disorder patients obtaining the lowest premorbid competence scores. However no Diagnosis × Outcome subgroup interactions appeared in either analysis (each $p > .50$).

In order to investigate the possibility that a Subgroup × Diagnosis interaction did in fact exist, separate t-tests were performed for each diagnostic group on premorbid social competence, parallel to the analyses described for length of initial hospitalization and total length of rehospitalization. (Because of the clear directionality of the hypotheses, one-tailed tests of significance were employed in the t-tests.) In each of the eight t-tests (four diagnostic groups on two outcome measures), the favorable-outcome subgroup scored higher on social competence than the unfavorable-outcome subgroup. With regard to the length of initial hospitalization measure, the relation was significant for psychoneurotic patients ($p < .05$), approached significance for affective reaction and personality disorder groups (each $p < .10$), and did not approach significance for schizophrenic patients. On the total length of rehospitalization measure, higher social competence scores were significantly related to more favorable outcome for schizophrenic patients ($p < .05$), tended to be related to better outcomes for affective reaction patients ($p = .07$), and were not significantly related to outcome in psychoneurotic or personality disorder groups.

In regard to whether or not the patient was rehospitalized, a chi-square analysis computed utilizing the total sample indicated that high competence patients were less likely to be rehospitalized. As was the case with the other outcome measures, no evidence was found indicating that the patient's diagnosis influenced the relation between premorbid competence and outcome.

Higher premorbid competence scores were thus found to be related to better outcomes in all diagnostic groups examined, and no interactions involving diagnosis were discovered. Moreover, in separate analyses performed within each diagnostic group, the premorbid competence–outcome relations obtained with the schizophrenic patients were not appreciably dif-

TABLE 9.1. Mean Premorbid Competence Scores for Patients in Favorable- and Unfavorable-Outcome Subgroups

	Diagnosis									
	Schizophrenia		Affective Disorder		Neurotic		Personality Disorder		Total	
Outcome Subgroups	N	M	N	M	N	M	N	M	N	M
Length of initial hospitalization[a]										
Favorable	27	.84	34	1.43	53	1.22	75	.78	189	1.06
Unfavorable	65	.79	55	1.29	45	1.05	27	.64	192	.94
Total length of rehospitalization[a]										
Favorable	11	.97	12	1.42	10	1.16	13	.66	46	1.05
Unfavorable	22	.64	12	1.11	9	1.02	6	.47	49	.81
Number of readmissions										
None	52	.80	60	1.38	77	1.16	81	.78	270	1.03
One or more[b]	40	.80	29	1.28	21	1.07	21	.59	111	.94

[a] In days.

[b] For some patients who were rehospitalized, information was not available regarding the total length of rehospitalization. Thus the N's for these two measures vary slightly.

ferent from those obtained with other diagnostic groups. These overall findings are consistent with the developmental formulation and augment results reported by other investigators who observed significant relations between premorbid adjustment and outcome criteria, other than measures of hospitalization, in nonschizophrenic as well as schizophrenic patients (Garmezy et al., 1979; Strauss, Kokes, Carpenter, & Ritzler, 1978).

Within the schizophrenic group, patients with higher competence scores displayed better outcomes on all three hospitalization measures. However, the relation was significant only for the total length of rehospitalization measure. The absence of a significant relation between premorbid competence and length of initial hospitalization in the schizophrenic group is at variance with the results of some other studies (Bromet et al., 1974; Turner & Zabo, 1968; Zigler & Phillips, 1961d). However, other investigators (Lewine, Watt, & Fryer, 1978; Strauss & Carpenter, 1974b, 1977) failed to obtain significant relations between premorbid competence and hospitalization measures of outcome with schizophrenic patients. The lack of uniformly significant results in this and other studies is consistent with a conceptualization of outcome as multidimensional and multidetermined (Möller et al., 1982; Salokangas, 1978; Schwartz et al., 1975; Strauss & Carpenter, 1974b, 1977). Inasmuch as social adjustment, work adjustment, and hospitalization have been found to represent partially independent outcome functions, each with somewhat specific predictors, the relation between social and work attainment as predictor variables and hospitalization measures of outcome would not be expected to be especially robust. Particularly with schizophrenic patients, the diagnostic label might override other considerations (e.g., evidence of competence) in determining length of hospital stay on a first admission.

Overall, the results obtained with the nonschizophrenic patients were similar to those observed with the schizophrenic group. Within each nonschizophrenic diagnostic category, higher social competence was associated with a more favorable outcome on each of the hospitalization measures. Most consistent were findings obtained on the length of initial hospitalization measure. On this measure, the premorbid competence–outcome relation attained or approached significance within each nonschizophrenic diagnostic group. On the rehospitalization measures, results did not attain significance. However, relatively small numbers of nonschizophrenic and particularly nonpsychotic (psychoneurotic and personality disorder) patients were rehospitalized, rendering statistically significant differences less likely. The consistent pattern of premorbid competence–outcome relations obtained with nonschizophrenic as well as schizophrenic patients supports the argument that premorbid competence and outcome will be related over a variety of diagnoses. Nevertheless, the lack of uniformly significant findings in this investigation, as well as results reported by Strauss, Kokes, Carpenter, & Ritzler (1978), suggests that this relationship, occurring as it does between noncorresponding predictor and outcome variables, is not a particularly robust one for either patient group.

The finding that higher competence scores characterized patients in both psychotic (affective disorder) and nonpsychotic (neurotic) diagnostic categories just as low competence scores typified both schizophrenic and personality disorder groups supports the argument that social competence is not reducible to vulnerability to psychosis or severity of pathology (Turner & Zabo, 1968; Zubin & Spring, 1977).

The relationship of premorbid competence to outcome has relevance also to what has been termed the "revolving door" sequence of psychiatric hospitalization. The treatment of mental patients has changed dramatically over the past two decades. Single admission to mental health facilities with a relatively long duration of stay has given way to a pattern characterized by an early, brief period of initial stay, often followed by readmission to the hospital at a later time (Blum, 1978; Connecticut State Department of Mental Health, 1972; Sheehan, 1982).

All patients do not display this revolving door pattern of brief initial institutionalization followed by later readmission. The work of Braginsky et al. (1969) suggests that the revolving door patient is the inadequate individual who has difficulty in meeting societal expectations. Such an individual is viewed as using the mental hospital as a refuge. This line of thought generates the hypothesis that patients characterized by poor premorbid social competence would have initial hospitalizations of brief duration. Standing in opposition to this formulation is the evidence just reviewed, which suggests that higher premorbid competence scores would characterize patients with brief rather than long initial hospitalizations.

Current thinking concerning the nature of the revolving door phenomenon embraces the view that patients with very brief initial hospitalizations are the ones who are most likely to be rehospitalized. The rationale underlying this view is that patients are hospitalized for periods that are too brief to provide effective therapeutic interventions, with the result then being a later readmission. In contrast to this view is the position that there is a general prognostic factor associated with premorbid social competence that should result in both a shortened period of initial hospitalization and a decreased possibility of readmission. Finally, diagnosis should differentiate those patients who display a very brief initial hospitalization from patients having a longer initial hospital stay. One would expect, for example, that patients with a diagnosis indicative of greater disorganization (e.g., schizophrenia) would be less likely to be rehospitalized for a very brief period than patients who had received a more benign diagnosis (e.g., personality disorder).

Marsh, Glick, and Zigler (1981) further analysed the Zigler et al. (1979) data in reference to these issues. The 381 male first-admission patients in the four diagnostic categories (schizophrenia, affective reaction, psychoneurotic, and personality disorder) were divided into three subgroups on the measure of length of initial hospitalization: short (under 15 days), medium

(15 through 90 days), and long (over 90 days). Fifteen days was dictated by the hospital's practice of holding a diagnostic staff conference by the end of 15 days of hospital stay. Ninety days was chosen as a convenient breaking point in the frequency distribution. Dividing the patients into subgroups was a means of focusing attention on patients who were widely disparate on this measure. A 3 (Length of Initial Hospitalization subgroup) × 4 (Diagnosis) analysis of variance performed on the patients' premorbid competence scores revealed a significant main effect for diagnosis $(p < .001)$ and a main effect of borderline significance for length of initial hospitalization $(p = .06)$. Patients with shorter initial hospitalizations had higher premorbid competence scores. As in previous studies, the schizophrenic and personality disorder patients obtained significantly lower social competence scores than neurotic patients whose scores in turn were significantly lower than those of the affective reaction group. In regard to rehospitalization, a chi-square analysis revealed that patients with higher premorbid competence scores were less likely to be rehospitalized. In further chi-square analyses, length of initial hospitalization and incidence of readmission were each found to be related to diagnosis (both p's $< .005$). With respect to both variables, schizophrenic patients displayed poorer outcomes than the other diagnostic groups while the most favorable outcomes were evidenced by the personality disorder group.

Higher competence patients were less likely to have long initial hospitalizations or to be rehospitalized. Thus both outcome measures appear to be influenced by the phenomenon of general coping adequacy that is reflected in the patient's premorbid competence scores.

The finding that length of initial hospitalization and incidence of readmission were related to diagnosis is both consistent with earlier findings (Hawk, Carpenter, & Strauss, 1975) and reassuring to theorists and the patients and their families. This finding represents some evidence that stands in refutation to the view now widely held that psychiatric hospitals are staffed by mental health workers who are so unaware of the psychodynamics of the patients in their care that they are willing to admit patients who have no need for psychiatric care (Crown, 1975; Millon, 1975; Rosenhan, 1973) and are willing to discharge indiscriminately patients badly in need of further treatment. To the extent that psychiatric diagnosis represents some indicators of the patient's psychodynamics and adequacy of functioning (as it certainly must), the finding that diagnosis is related to length of hospitalization and incidence of rehospitalization represents evidence contradictory to this widely held negative view of psychiatric hospitals.

The differences discovered between diagnostic groups in both premorbid competence and outcome scores are also reassuring given the use of DSM-II hospital diagnosis for patient classification in this and the Zigler et al. (1979) study. The reliability of such criteria for patient classification has been questioned, although Meehl (1973) and Zigler and Phillips (1961b) have reported that reasonable reliability can be obtained using DSM-II criteria when only broad diagnostic distinctions (e.g., schizophrenia, affective disorder, neurosis) are involved. Evidence has also been presented that groups formed on the basis of DSM-II hospital diagnosis differ in the symptom pictures they present (Lewine et al., 1978; Glick et al., 1985). The highly significant differences in premorbid competence and outcome scores found for the various diagnostic groups examined by Marsh et al. (1981) and Zigler et al. (1979) conform with clinical wisdom and thus provide some indication that the patients in the four diagnostic groups examined did differ in expected ways in regard to two major variables of clinical interest.

Premorbid Competence and Outcome Among Male and Female Nonschizophrenic Patients

Because the relation between premorbid competence and outcome has been found to vary as a function of gender (Farina et al., 1963; Held & Cromwell, 1968; Rosen, Klein, & Gittelman-Klein, 1969), Zigler et al. (1979) examined only male patients in order to test hypotheses concerning this relation uncomplicated by sex. Whether premorbid competence and outcome are related for female patients thus remains undetermined. Especially in regard to social competence, findings obtained with males cannot be presumed to hold for females. Further, the applicability of the premorbid competence construct even to male nonschizophrenic patients continues to be controversial (for cogent reviews concerning this issue see Garmezy et al., 1979; Klorman et al., 1977; Strauss, Kokes, Carpenter, & Ritzler, 1978). Glick and Zigler (in press) thus examined the premorbid competence–outcome relationship in male and female first-admission patients with the following nonschizophrenic diagnoses: affective disorder (71 males, 75 females); neurotic (75 males, 70 females); and personality disorder (82 males, 75 females). These patients were admitted to Fairfield Hills Hospital in Connecticut between 1971 and 1976. In order to control for effects of changing administrative policies regarding admission and discharge, the attempt was made to have the number of patients in each Gender × Diagnosis subgroup comparable for each year of first admission. Because the diagnostic groups were formed on the basis of DSM-II hospital diagnoses, the presenting symptoms of the patients in the three groups were compared. Overall, the presenting symptom pictures corresponded to clinical expectations for the diagnostic groups examined. The outcome measures employed were identical to those in the Zigler et al. (1979) study: (a) length of initial hospitalization; and (b) total length of rehospitalizations during a follow-up period of 3 years after discharge from the first admission. The variables of age, education, marital status, occupation, and employment history were used as social competence indexes. However, this study employed the revised scaling of the education and occupation variables recommended by Zigler and Levine (1981b) and described in Chapter 3.

In order to examine the relationship between premorbid competence and each outcome measure, the overall median of the distribution of premorbid competence scores was employed to form high and low subgroups. For both the length of initial hospitalization and the total length of rehospitalization measures, square root transformations were employed to stabilize the variance, and analyses of variance were performed on the transformed outcome scores. In regard to the length of initial hospitalization, a 2 (High vs. Low Competence) × 3 (Diagnosis) × 2 (Gender) analysis of variance revealed significant main effects for premorbid competence and diagnosis. High competence individuals had shorter initial hospitalizations. A Newman-Keuls comparison indicated that the affective disorder patients had significantly longer initial hospitalizations than the other two diagnostic groups. Two significant interaction effects (between social competence and diagnosis and between diagnosis and gender) appeared primarily to reflect the very long initial hospitalizations of low competence female affective disorder patients.[1] The mean lengths of initial hospitalization for all subgroups are presented in Table 9.2. Further analyses of variance examined the premorbid competence–outcome relationship separately for each gender. These analyses revealed a significant relationship between premorbid competence and length of initial hospitalization for the female subsample, and a relationship of borderline significance ($p < .08$) for the males examined separately. For both genders, a highly significant relationship appeared between diagnosis and outcome, reflecting the significantly longer hospitalizations of affective reaction patients.

TABLE 9.2.   Mean Days of Initial Hospitalization

Group	Low Competence			High Competence		
	N	M	SD	N	M	SD
Affective disorder						
Male	22	40.32	35.07	49	28.49	29.89
Female	19	161.58	393.90	56	35.96	42.35
Neurotic						
Male	32	20.34	40.80	43	17.49	28.76
Female	40	16.60	22.08	30	12.83	13.52
Personality disorder						
Male	65	27.49	47.92	17	16.18	21.85
Female	55	12.73	12.26	20	13.05	15.77

In this nonschizophrenic sample, only 62 of the 448 patients examined were rehospitalized. Because of this smaller N, two two-way analyses of variance (Social Competence × Gender; Social Competence × Diagnosis) were required to examine relationships to total length of rehospitalization. Taken together, these analyses indicated that high competence patients were rehospitalized for shorter periods than their low competence counterparts and that nonpsychotic (neurotic and personality disorder) patients had shorter rehospitalizations than the affective disorder group. To analyze the premorbid competence–outcome relation separately for each gender, t-tests were performed. This relation was found to be significant for males and of borderline significance for females.

Premorbid Competence and Outcome: Other Evidence and Further Research Questions

Taken together, the developmental studies reported here (Glick & Zigler, in press; Marsh et al., 1981; Zigler et al., 1979; Zigler & Phillips, 1961b) provide consistent evidence that premorbid competence is related to outcome for nonschizophrenic patients of both genders just as it has been found to relate to outcome with schizophrenic samples. Findings of other investigators provide further evidence that premorbid competence is related to outcome in a variety of nonschizophrenic groups. This research supplements our own in that it encompasses outcome criteria other than hospitalization measures and includes studies with prospective as well as retrospective designs. In one such prospective study, Strauss, Kokes, Carpenter, & Ritzler (1978) examined schizophrenic and nonschizophrenic samples with respect to each of the following outcome criteria: duration of hospitalization; social relations; employment; symptom severity; and total outcome. For both samples, the variables of premorbid employment and social relations (the major dimensions of social competence) were found to provide the best prediction of all outcome criteria. However, duration of hospitalization was least strongly related to the predictor variables examined. In contrast to this finding but consistent with our own work, Prentky et al. (1980) found that of the many predictor variables they examined, premorbid competence (as assessed by the Zigler-Phillips index) was the most potent predictor of length of hospitalization $(r = .38, p < .001)$. Their sample comprised patients with diagnoses of schizophrenia, personality disorder, neurotic disorder, and depressive psychosis. The majority of the patients examined were nonschizophrenic, and almost half were nonpsychotic. A relationship between social competence as assessed by a modified version of the Zigler-Phillips scale and outcome was likewise noted by Finney and Moos (1979) for alcoholic patients participating in a variety of inpatient and outpatient treatment programs. Other investigators also obtained significant relations between premorbid competence variables and outcome in groups of patients with varying diagnoses but containing a sizable number of nonschizophrenic patients (Bookbinder & Gusman, 1964; Jacobs et al., 1972, 1973; Orr et al., 1955; Slater, 1943). Moreover, variables associated with social competence have been related to improvement in outpatient psychotherapy (Luborsky et al., 1971) and for patients suffering from certain physical disorders (Garmezy et al., 1979; Holmes, et al., 1961; Luborsky, Todd, & Katcher, 1973; Phillips, 1968a). Despite the few nonsupportive findings already discussed, the preponderance of evidence points to the applicability of the premorbid competence construct for the prediction of outcome in a wide variety of patient groups and with respect to multiple outcome criteria. The view that the prognostic importance of premorbid competence variables extends beyond specific manifestations of schizophrenic disorder was also emphasized by Mendel (1976):

> It is not the illness that predicts the prognosis; it is the total human being who predicts the prognosis. If someone is bright, beautiful, talented, rich, part of a society that appreciates him, and comes from a family and an environment that offers much support, then he has a good prognosis for life. If the same individual also has schizophrenia, then he has a good prognosis for living with his schizophrenia. . . . We must not ask what the difference between good prognosis and poor prognosis in schizophrenia is, but rather we must ask what the difference between good prognosis and poor prognosis for life is. The prognosis for schizophrenia is the same as the prognosis for life. (p. 68)

The relation of social competence variables to favorable life outcome may even pertain to nonpatient groups and extend to individuals at the opposite end of the adjustment spectrum from schizophrenic patients. In his 35-year prospective study of Harvard sophomores originally selected on the basis of superior adjustment, Vaillant (1974, 1975, 1978) found that marital stability and satisfaction and career adjustment were highly related to broad indexes of adult life adjustment. Conversely, those individuals with evidence of psychopathological problems were significantly less likely to display good marital or work adjustment. As Vaillant (1974) concluded, it was the "men's successes . . . not their symptoms or their failures [that] predicted subsequent mental health" (p. 20). These findings, he noted, accord with the conclusion of Kohlberg, LaCrosse, and Ricks (1972) that "the best predictors of absence of adult mental illness and maladjustment are the presence of various forms of competence and ego maturity rather than the *absence* of problems and symptoms as such" (p. 1274). These conclusions underscore both the positive emphasis of the developmental approach, discussed in Chapter 1, and the efficacy of such an emphasis. Across a very broad spectrum of psychological adjustment and success in life outcome, positive coping capabilities related to developmental level have been found to be associated with favorable outcome. In this regard, Vaillant (1971, 1975) also emphasized maturity in ego functioning as the dimension underlying the competencies of the effective individuals in his sample. Further, he provided evidence that indexes of marital and work adjustment were related to other indicators of ego development including maturity of defenses.

Turning from the broad view of competence that encompasses all individuals to the circumstances of those whose adjustment is sufficiently impaired to require psychiatric hospitalization, the question remains: What mediates the discovered relationship between premorbid competence and/or the construct that the authors feel is reflected in this measure, that is, developmental level, and more favorable outcome? Several explanations may be advanced, and they are not mutually exclusive. First, high competence patients may be more likely to enter and/or profit from psychiatric treatment (Bookbinder & Gusman, 1964; Rubinstein & Lorr, 1956; Sullivan, Miller, & Smelser, 1958). Alternatively, considerable evidence has now been presented (Achenbach & Zigler, 1963; Phillips & Zigler, 1964; Zigler & Phillips, 1962) that high, as compared to low, developmental patients are more likely to have incorporated the values of society and to display more guilt and anxiety. Thus a pathological solution to life's problems and the institutionalization to which such a solution leads are probably less acceptable to the developmentally high than to the developmentally low individual. This unacceptability of a pathological solution should result in an improved prognosis. Finally, Zigler & Phillips (1961b) have suggested that the problems that precipitate the mental disorder in high competence patients are more circumscribed and solvable than those that precipitate the mental disorder in low competence patients.

Analyses of the contribution of the various components of premorbid competence to psychiatric outcome should help to elucidate mediating processes in this relationship. Analyses undertaken by Strauss, Carpenter, and their colleagues with schizophrenic (Strauss & Carpenter, 1974b, 1977) and nonschizophrenic samples (Strauss, Kokes, Carpenter, & Ritzler, 1978) have suggested that the different aspects of social competence (e.g., social vs. work adjustment) may each relate most strongly to its corresponding outcome function. However, these authors found few relationships between social competence variables and the outcome function of length of hospitalization. Yet, as indicated previously, Prentky et al. (1980), in stepwise regression analyses, isolated social competence as an especially potent predictor of length of hospitalization. Their analyses compared overall social competence with other predictor variables including symptomatology, early experience, and personality characteristics. They did not consider the differential contributions of the various components of social competence.

Stepwise regression analyses were performed by Glick, Marsh, and Zigler (1984) utilizing the premorbid competence and outcome data of Zigler et al. (1979). As described previously, the data were derived from an examination of the case history records of 381 male patients with diagnoses of schizophrenia, affective reaction, psychoneurotic disorder, or personality disorder. As discussed in Chapter 3, factor analyses of the Zigler-Phillips social competence index with both schizophrenic (Zigler & Levine, 1981b) and nonschizophrenic samples (Glick et al., 1984) have yielded three orthogonal factors. Typically age and marital status load together, education and occupation comprise a second factor, and employment history loads separately on a third factor. Glick et al. (1984) examined the relative contribution of each of these factors to the overall variance of the outcome measures of length of initial hospitalization and total length of rehospitalization. Utilizing the social competence factor scores as predictor variables, stepwise regression analyses were performed on each outcome measure for the entire sample and each diagnostic group examined separately. While previous analyses (Zigler et al., 1979) revealed significant relations between premorbid competence and both outcome measures, the stepwise regression analyses performed on the entire sample yielded only two very modest relationships between factor scores and either outcome measure. Employment history (Factor 3) was the only factor found to be significantly associated with the length of initial hospitalization, although it accounted for a very small proportion of the total variance $(R^2 = .015)$. In regard to the total length of rehospitalization, only the education–occupation factor was significantly related to this variable. Within the schizophrenic, neurotic, and personality disorder subgroups, no single factor was found to account for a significant proportion of the variance on either outcome measure. By contrast, however, substantial relationships appeared between factor scores and both outcome measures for the affective reaction subsample. For these patients, the education–occupation factor accounted for 5 percent $(R^2 = .052)$ of the total variance in length of initial hospitalization and for 24 percent $(R^2 = .241)$ of the total variance in length of rehospitalization. Moreover, employment history accounted for an additional 12.5 percent of the variance in length of rehospitalization. For this group of patients, then, 37 percent of the total variance in length of rehospitalization could be accounted for by two factors of the social competence measures.

These studies represent beginning efforts to identify the aspects of social competence that contribute most strongly to variance in outcome. However, the various studies are not directly comparable. They employ different social competence measures and consider different aspects of outcome functioning. These differences across studies may account for the discrepancies in relationships observed. Further, it should be noted that in the Glick et al. study the strongest relationship appeared with respect to a very small subset of patients, affective reaction individuals who were rehospitalized $(N = 24)$. Further research to delineate those aspects of social competence that contribute most strongly to the relationship of this variable to outcome should first of all encompass a number of social competence indexes. As was indicated in Chapter 3, the various measures of social competence, while they have been found to be intercorrelated, include quite different types of items. For example, as we noted earlier, the Zigler-Phillips measure emphasizes instrumental role functioning and the striving for advancement to the relative exclusion of items reflecting social participation. One explanation for the absence of any significant relationships between the age/marital status factor and outcome in the Glick et al. (1984) study may be that this factor imprecisely reflects level of social participation and involvement. As exemplified in the work of Strauss and Carpenter, the use of multiple outcome criteria continues to be preferable. Particularly in regard to rehospitalization measures for nonschizophrenic patients, sizable samples are needed, as many of these individuals are not rehospitalized. The Glick et al. data suggest at least the possibility that different relationships between aspects of premorbid competence and outcome may appear as a function of diagnosis. The relations discovered with the affective reaction subgroup were quite different from those obtained for patients with other diagnoses. It is also possible that for individuals at different social competence levels different factors in social competence may most strongly influence outcome variance. The different findings obtained for affective reaction patients as compared to other groups in the Glick et al. study, rather than reflecting a difference due to diagnosis, might be attributable to the higher overall premorbid competence of this diagnostic subgroup. Of the factors discovered in premorbid competence, the education–occupation factor most strongly reflects the influence of variables external to the individual (i.e., SES). By contrast, the age–marital status factor may be conceptualized as less determined by environmental variables, whereas the third factor, employment history, can be interpreted as reflecting an interaction between the individual's motivation and coping skills and the opportunities provided by the environment that are reflected in SES (see Chapter 3). For higher competence individuals with more adequate coping effectiveness and a greater incorporation of societal expectations and consequent social guilt, the ability to stay out of the hospital may be primarily determined by factors external to the individual, namely, SES and employment opportunity. By contrast, for lower competence individuals (the other diagnostic groups in the Glick et al. study), factors more internal to the individual (adequacy in personal and social functioning and motivation) may assume greater importance in determining whether or not the individual is rehospitalized. For such individuals, personal competencies, motivation, and environmental opportunity may all contribute to prognosis with no one factor assuming overriding importance. Garmezy (1970) stressed the need to separate differences due to diagnosis from those related to overall social competence level. In samples of sufficient size, separate stepwise regression analyses for subgroups of high versus low competence patients in various diagnostic categories could help to disentangle social competence level from diagnosis. Finally, inasmuch as our formulation centers upon the broad developmental-level construct for which premorbid competence serves as one approximate gauge, a broader research strategy would be to investigate the contribution to overall outcome variance of a variety of developmental indicators in addition to premorbid competence. Included in such a multiple regression analysis could be scores reflecting self-image disparity and extreme response style (Achenbach & Zigler, 1963; Mylet et al., 1979) and role orientation and symptom expression in thought versus action (Phillips & Zigler, 1964).

Developmental Level, Symptom Expression, and Psychiatric Outcome

If greater maturity tends to be associated with more favorable outcomes, this relationship ought to be evident across a variety of indicators of developmental level. Levine (1959) reported a significant positive relationship between Rorschach developmental level and likelihood of hospital discharge in a sample of psychiatric patients with various functional disorders. In a nonpsychiatric sample, Lane (1955) found that higher Rorschach developmental-level scores were associated with greater social effectiveness in everyday functioning. The developmental categorizations of symptomatology based on role orientation and symptom expression in thought versus action were described in Chapter 4. Based on these categorizations, developmental thinking would generate the hypotheses that: (a) patients whose symptom pictures indicate a turning against the self would display better outcomes than patients whose symptom pictures reflect the role orientation of either turning against others or avoidance of others; and (b) symptom pictures involving expression in thought rather than in action would be associated with more favorable outcomes.

Phillips and Zigler (1964) tested these hypotheses through the examination of the case history records of 251 (129 male and 122 female) first-admission state hospital patients diagnosed as suffering from a variety of functional disorders. All patients were admitted between 1945 and 1954. Based on the role orientation symptom criteria described in Chapter 4, individuals whose number of turning-against-the-self symptoms were at least equal to the total number of symptoms in the other two categories were classified as demonstrating a predominant role orientation of turning against the self. Thirty-nine men and 49 women met this criterion. Analogous criteria were employed to place patients into the turning-against-others (3 men and 3 women) and avoidance-of-others (46 men and 32 women) categories. Because only 6 cases fell into the turning-against-others category, these were dropped from consideration in analyses of the relationship between role orientation and prognosis. The symptom criteria defining expression in thought rather than action were described in Chapter 4. Utilizing these criteria, all patients who manifested only symptoms of the thought type and all patients who manifested only symptoms of the action type were placed in the thought and action groups, respectively. Patients who had approximately the same number of symptoms in each category were placed in a mixed symptom group. This procedure resulted in 82 (39 men and 43 women), 21 (13 men and 8 women), and 86 (43 men and 43 women) patients being assigned to the thought, action, and mixed groups, respectively. The remaining patients were dropped from further consideration in analyses involving the thought–action dimension.

The two outcome measures employed were the length of initial hospitalization and whether following discharge from the hospital the patient was or was not readmitted to any mental hospital in Massachusetts. The median length of hospitalization was employed to divide the patients in the sample into short- (17 months or less) and long-hospitalized (18 months or more) groups. Although the length of hospitalization measure is vulnerable to contamination because of its sensitivity to changes in hospital administrative policies, additional analyses indicated a relative stability in length of hospital stay during the years covered by the study. The Zigler-Phillips index was employed to assess premorbid social competence utilizing all six component variables.

The relationship between the occurrence of each of the individual symptoms and each outcome measure was examined in chi-square analyses. Only seven of the symptoms examined were found to be significantly related to outcome. For men, hallucinations, sexual preoccupation, and being withdrawn were all found to be associated with longer hospitalization. For women, being tense or depressed was associated with shorter hospitalization, and being suspicious with longer hospitalization, while being withdrawn was associated with a greater likelihood of rehospitalization following discharge. However, the total number of relationships discovered did not exceed what might be expected due to chance alone.

The analyses of the relationship between role orientation and the two outcome measures were done separately for men and women and are presented in Table 9.3. As can be seen in Table 9.3, role orientation was found to be related to length of hospitalization in the predicted manner for women ($p <$ .001), with a trend in the same direction being found for men ($p <$ .20). No significant relationship was found between role orientation and rehospitalization in either the male or female samples. Because role orientation has been found to be related to premorbid competence, which in turn has been found to be related to length of hospitalization, a further $2 \times 2 \times 2$ (Role Orientation $\times$ High vs. Low Premorbid Competence $\times$ Gender) analysis of variance was performed on length of hospitalization scores in order to assess whether the relationship between role orientation and length of hospitalization was due solely to the higher premorbid competence scores of turning-against-the-self patients. In this analysis, role orientation was found to be significantly related to length of hospitalization. The relationship between social competence and length of hospitalization, though in the expected direction, did not reach the .05 level of significance. Neither the main effect of sex nor any of the interactions between variables was significant. It appears, therefore, that a relationship exists between role orientation and outcome, independent of the social competence effect.

With respect to the relationship between the thought–action dimension and outcome, the relatively small number of patients in the action group ($N = 21$) necessitated comparisons between patients in the thought group and those in the mixed and action groups combined. In these analyses no significant relationships were found between thought–action orientation and length of hospitalization. Contrary to expectation, men in the thought group were more likely to be rehospitalized than men in the mixed/action group, with this trend also being found for women. These findings are incongruent with the combined findings that thought patients obtain higher premorbid competence scores than mixed or action patients (see Chapter 4) and that premorbid competence tends to be positively related to outcome. In order to examine this apparent contradiction in findings, a $2 \times 2 \times 2$ (Thought–

TABLE 9.3. Relationship of Role Orientation to Outcome Measures

	Length of Hospitalization			Rehospitalized Following Discharge		
	17 Months or Less	18 Months or More	Total	No	Yes	Total
Men						
Turning against the self	24	15	39	23	14	37
Avoidance of others	20	26	46	30	10	40
	44	41	85	53	24	77
	$\chi^2 = 2.07^*$			$\chi^2 < 1$		
Women						
Turning against the self	36	13	49	38	10	48
Avoidance of others	8	24	32	20	7	27
	44	37	81	58	17	75
	$\chi^2 = 16.49^{**}$			$\chi^2 < 1$		

Source: "Role Orientation, the Action–Thought Dimension, and Outcome in Psychiatric Disorder" by L. Phillips and E. Zigler, 1964, *Journal of Abnormal and Social Psychology, 68.* Copyright 1964 by American Psychological Association. Reprinted by permission of the publisher.

$^*p<.20$
$^{**}p<.001$

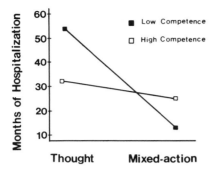

Figure 9.1. Mean length of hospitalization for high and low social competence thought and mixed action groups. From "Role Orientation, the Action–Thought Dimension, and Outcome in Psychiatric Disorder" by L. Phillips and E. Zigler, 1964, *Journal of Abnormal and Social Psychology, 68.* Copyright 1964 by the American Psychological Association. Reprinted by permission of the publisher.

Action Orientation × High vs. Low Premorbid Competence × Gender) analysis of variance was performed on the length of hospitalization measures. A significant social competence effect was found, and the interaction between thought–action orientation and premorbid competence was likewise significant. However, this interaction, which is depicted in Figure 9.1 held only for the thought patients. As can be seen in Figure 9.1, high competence thought patients had a shorter period of hospitalization than did low competence thought patients, whereas mixed/action patients in the two competence groups had hospitalizations of approximately the same duration. In order to test the possibility that a similar interaction might in fact characterize the relationship to rehospitalization, a Wilson's (1956) distribution-free analysis of variance based on the chi-square technique was performed to assess the relationship of premorbid competence and thought–action orientation to whether the patient was rehospitalized or not. Thought patients were more likely than action patients to return to the hospital. Although no significant social competence effects were found, a significant interaction was found between social competence and the thought–action dimension. This interaction, shown in Figure 9.2 primarily reflected the greater tendency of low than of high competence thought patients to be rehospitalized.

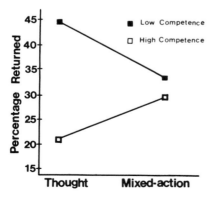

Figure 9.2. Percentage of high and low social competence thought and mixed action groups returned to the hospital. From "Role Orientation, the Action–Thought Dimension, and Outcome in Psychiatric Disorder" by L. Phillips and E. Zigler, 1964, *Journal of Abnormal and Social Psychology, 68.* Copyright 1964 by the American Psychological Association. Reprinted by permission of the publisher.

The findings thus supported the hypothesis that prognosis, defined by length of hospitalization, would be more favorable for patients manifesting symptoms of the turning-against-the-self variety than for those displaying the role orientation of avoidance of others. The very nature of the two role orientations makes this relationship between symptomatology and prognosis understandable. As indicated in Chapter 4, the person who assumes a role orientation of turning against the self has incorporated the values of society and experiences guilt and anxiety when he or she does not successfully meet these values. A pathological solution to life's demands and subsequent hospitalization would be unacceptable to such a person. Antithetically, the avoidance-of-others role orientation is characterized by a state of withdrawal and isolation in which the person neither is concerned with societal demands nor feels compelled to cope with such demands. It would appear to be this withdrawal from society and turning inward that makes for poorer prognosis.

Inasmuch as Phillips and Zigler examined the diagnostically heterogeneous sample as a unit, their data do not indicate the degree to which role orientation and outcome might be related within specific diagnostic groups (e.g., anxiety disorder, affective disorder, schizophrenia). Other evidence suggests, however, that depressive symptomatology and, by extension, the role orientation of turning against the self[2] may be related to favorable outcome within a variety of diagnostic groups. A highly consistent finding has been that in schizophrenia good prognosis and remission are associated with depressive symptomatology and with a family history of affective reaction rather than schizophrenia (e.g., Huber, Gross, & Schüttler, 1975; McCabe, 1976b; McCabe et al., 1971, 1972; Roff, 1975; Schooler et al., 1967; Stephens, 1978; Stephens, Astrup, & Mangrum, 1966, 1967; Taylor & Abrams, 1975; Vaillant, 1964). While fewer investigators have considered the prognostic significance of depression in nonschizophrenic patients, some findings suggest that depression may be a favorable prognostic sign in nonschizophrenic groups as well. In predominantly nonpsychotic groups, depression is one client characteristic that has been found to be associated with favorable outcome in outpatient psychotherapy (see Luborsky et al., 1971, for a review of this research). Schuckit and Winokur (1972) suggested "a probable association between better prognosis and AD [affective disorder] alcoholism," (p. 677). Finally, within depressive groups, some evidence has suggested that prognosis may be more favorable when the depression is less colored by other symptomatology, as is the case with unipolar as compared with bipolar depressive patients (Depue & Monroe, 1978; Perris, 1966) and with patients who display only depression as compared with a mixture of depression and anxiety (Gurney et al., 1972). These findings buttress the results of Phillips and Zigler (1964) concerning the relation of role orientation to outcome. However, further work is needed to determine the range of disorders to which this symptomatology–outcome relationship may apply.

No simple relationship was found between the thought–action dimension and either outcome measure. In these analyses, premorbid competence was found to be an important mediating variable. One explanation for the absence of clear-cut findings is that the thought–action dimension, while it has been found to be related to developmental level as reflected in premorbid competence scores, is not a particularly fine-grained gauge of developmental differences. It must be recognized that a potential for either action or thought exists at every maturational level. The concept of multilinear or horizontal development was discussed in Chapter 2. With respect to the action–thought dimension, this principle suggests that, in addition to a unilinear trend toward greater expression in thought, a change takes place in the quality or characteristics of behaviors, whether these behaviors be in the spheres of action or thought. With increasing maturity, both these forms of behavior should be characterized by a shift from the global, disorganized, and unmodulated to the more organized, articulated, and hierarchical. Even a cursory examination of the symptoms in the thought category (see Chapter 4, Table 4.2) reveals a heterogeneity in respect to such characteristics. In view of this heterogeneity it is inappropriate to assume that the manifestation of any thought symptom is indicative of high maturity and a consequent favorable prognosis. Some more direct index of developmental level is required to predict a favorable outcome in mental disorder. Such an index could be obtained either through a structural analysis of the particular thought symptoms manifested or through some independent assessment of maturity. Social competence represents one such independent assessment. Thus the finding by Phillips and Zigler that a better prognosis was associated with a thought orientation provided that the patient was at a high competence level is consistent with the argument advanced here.

Finally, the analysis of the relationship of single symptoms to prognosis resulted in nothing more than chance findings. This aspect of the results coincides with findings discussed in Chapter 4. As we indicated there, whereas isolated symptoms may have limited informational value, when these are grouped and ordered according to underlying principles, as for example the individual's developmental level, they have been found to be related to major variables of interest in psychopathology.

Paranoid–Nonparanoid Status in Schizophrenia and Psychiatric Outcome

The position that individuals who function at higher developmental levels will display more favorable psychiatric outcomes is supported by the research using premorbid competence as an indicator of developmental level and by the finding that patients who display the role orientation of turning against the self have shorter initial hospitalizations. The assumption that paranoid schizophrenia may generally reflect higher developmental functioning than nonparanoid schizophrenia generates the expectation that paranoid schizophrenic patients should display more favorable outcomes than nonparanoid schizophrenic patients. However, research findings concerning the relation of paranoid–nonparanoid status to outcome have been contradictory. Kendler, Gruenberg, and Tsuang (1984) and Ritzler (1981) provide reviews of this research. Whereas some studies (e.g., Kendler et al., 1984; Strauss, Sirotkin, & Grisell, 1974; Winokur et al., 1974) have reported better outcomes for paranoid than nonparanoid schizophrenics, other investigators have found no differences between these schizophrenia subtypes (e.g., Hawk et al., 1975) or poorer outcomes for paranoid than nonparanoid schizophrenic patients (e.g., Evans et al., 1973).

We recently analyzed data concerning paranoid–nonparanoid status and psychiatric outcome. The case histories of all patients admitted for the first time with a primary diagnosis of schizophrenia and no secondary diagnosis involving organicity, mental retardation, alcoholism, or drug abuse to four VA hospitals and one state hospital during the years 1966, 1967, and 1968 were examined. A total of 80 (50 paranoid, 30 nonparanoid) VA male, 109 (22 paranoid, 87 nonparanoid) state hospital male, and 160 (57 paranoid, 103 nonparanoid) state hospital female schizophrenic patients were included in the samples. In all samples, the majority of the nonparanoid schizophrenics were diagnosed as chronic or acute undifferentiated. The two outcome measures employed were (a) the length of initial hospitalization and (b) the length of all rehospitalizations during a follow-up period of 3 years after discharge from the first hospitalization. Separate 3 (Group) × 2 (Paranoid–Nonparanoid Status) analyses of variance performed on each outcome measure revealed no significant relationships between paranoid–nonparanoid status and either outcome measure. The only significant finding was that the VA patients had longer initial hospitalizations than the state hospital patients of both genders.

Our preliminary data did not support the developmental view that paranoid schizophrenic patients would display more favorable outcomes than nonparanoid schizophrenic patients, and findings of other investigators have been contradictory on this point. If on so many other measures (see Chapter 6) paranoid schizophrenics appear more effective and less disorganized than nonparanoid schizophrenic patients, why might they not also be consistently found to display better outcomes? A possible explanation lies in the psychodynamics of the paranoid process. In Chapter 7, we advanced the position that paranoia may function as a defense against depression. To give up paranoid ideation would thus entail an emergence of depression. With respect to outcome, therefore, the psychodynamic importance of paranoid symptomatology might outweigh the influence of developmental level. Despite a generally higher developmental level of functioning, paranoia would be maintained as a needed defense against the very painful experience of depression.

DEVELOPMENTAL CORRELATES OF AGE ON FIRST HOSPITALIZATION

In the literature dealing with psychopathology, studies of prognosis are usually confined to the course of a disorder following its onset, typically defined by when the individual comes into contact with a provider of mental health services. An important feature of textbook descriptions of the course of various mental disorders is the age of initial onset. Evidence has now been presented that age of first treatment and outcome are related, with a later first psychiatric treatment associated with a better outcome (Möller et al., 1982; Rosen, Klein, & Gittelman-Klein, 1971). Yet a recognized measurement problem here is that some unspecified time interval elapses between the true onset of the disorder and the time treatment is sought (Lewine, 1980). This situation can be remedied by taking the broader view of prognosis described at the outset of the chapter. As we indicated there, the greater adaptive capabilities of high developmental individuals would be expected not only to contribute to a more favorable outcome of disorder following initial treatment and/or institutionalization but to result in a later age of onset of disorder as well as in a reduced likelihood that the individual would succumb to disorder in the first place.

Age on First Hospitalization in Schizophrenia

In line with the broader view of prognosis, Zigler and Levine (1981a) examined the hypothesis that individuals at higher developmental levels, as gauged by modified premorbid competence scores, would be first hospitalized at an older age. Two other hypotheses were also explored. As discussed in Chapter 6, paranoid schizophrenia can be conceptualized as reflecting a higher developmental status than most nonparanoid forms of the disorder. This view of the paranoid–nonparanoid distinction generates the hypothesis that paranoid schizophrenics would be older on first hospital admission than nonparanoid schizophrenics. Some evidence has been presented that paranoid schizophrenics have a later age of onset and of first hospitalization than those diagnosed as nonparanoid (Gift et al., 1981; Huber et al., 1975; Krupinski & Stoller, 1975; Swanson et al., 1970; Winokur et al., 1974). However, European psychiatrists (see Swanson et al., 1970, p. 28) and others (Kay et al., 1976) have appeared to question whether any difference in age of onset would be found between paranoid and other schizophrenic diagnoses.

To clarify this issue, Zigler and Levine (1981a) compared the ages of first hospitalization in paranoid and nonparanoid schizophrenic subsamples. Gender differences in age upon first hospitalization were also examined. From the standpoint of developmental theorizing, women would be expected to have a later mean age of initial hospitalization. This prediction follows from findings that (a) schizophrenic women compared to men are more frequently diagnosed as paranoid (Hay & Forrest, 1972; Kay et al., 1976; Swanson et al., 1970); (b) women typically attain higher premorbid social competence scores than do men (Raskin & Golob, 1966; Zigler & Levine, 1981b; Zigler et al., 1977); and (c) women are more likely than men to manifest symptoms associated with a higher developmental level, usually of the turning-against-the-self variety. Finally, the ages on first hospitalization of male state hospital versus VA hospital schizophrenic patients were compared because previous work (Zigler & Levine, 1973) has suggested that comparable results are not obtained with VA and state hospital patients.

The case histories of three samples of first-admission schizophrenic patients were examined: a VA hospital sample consisting of 64 male patients; a state hospital sample of 60 male patients; and a corresponding sample of 60 female state hospital patients. The designation of the patients as paranoid or nonparanoid schizophrenic was based upon hospital diagnosis, and this diagnostic distinction was further supported by analyses to symptom differences between patients in the two groups.

For this study, an estimate of premorbid competence was devised based on the marital status and education variables alone. These were scored in the traditional manner. While this is admittedly not as useful an indicator of developmental level as the complete six-item score, these were the only social competence indexes (besides age, which was the independent variable investigated in the study) for which information was available for every patient. As described in Chapter 3, both education and marital status have been found to be highly correlated with overall premorbid competence scores, and in multiple regression analyses each has been found to contribute significantly to the overall score. Inasmuch as education and marital status have consistently been found to load on different factors (Glick et al., 1984; Zigler & Levine, 1981b), these two variables can be viewed as good estimates of the social competence construct. Furthermore, in initial analyses of these data, Zigler and Levine observed similar relationships between the two-item premorbid competence scores and other major variables as have previously been found using the five- or six-item scores. Specifically, utilizing the two-item index, higher premorbid competence scores were obtained by (a) women than men; (b) paranoid as compared with nonparanoid schizophrenics; and (c) VA as compared with state hospital male patients.

Age upon first admission was found to be positively related to the modified premorbid competence scores for most groups examined (see Table 9.4). In brief, the developmental score and admission age were significantly related in the female, state hospital male, combined male, and total-patient-sample groups. The exception was that no such relation was found in the VA sample. In general, then, the first hypothesis of the study was confirmed. The difference in the findings obtained with VA versus state hospital patients is reminiscent of other results concerning premorbid competence and paranoid status discussed in Chapter 6. The absence of significant relations in a VA as compared with a state hospital sample underscores the moderating influence of type of hospital on premorbid competence relationships. It is clear from these data that VA and state hospital residents should not be conceptualized as comparable samples of psychiatric patients. Considerable evidence suggests that VA hospital patients are at a higher developmental level than are state hospital patients (Zigler & Levine, 1973). Just as Wahl (1977) pleaded that greater attention be paid to differences between male and female schizophrenic patients, the differences between state and VA patient groups require close scrutiny. One cannot help wondering how many of the inconsistencies in the literature on psychopathology are due to the fact that some investigations have been limited to VA hospital patients while others have been confined to state hospital patients.

TABLE 9.4.   Correlations Between the Premorbid Social Competence Score and Age upon Admission

Group	N	r
State hospital females		
Paranoid	30	.09
Nonparanoid	30	.59***
Total	60	.36**
State hospital males		
Paranoid	30	.34
Nonparanoid	30	−.07
Total	60	.36**
VA hospital males		
Paranoid	39	.37*
Nonparanoid	25	−.03
Total	64	.22
All males		
Paranoid	69	.35**
Nonparanoid	55	.20
Total	124	.31***
All patients		
Paranoid	99	.29**
Nonparanoid	85	.36***
Total	184	.34***

Source: "Age on First Hospitalization of Schizophrenics: A Developmental Approach" by E. Zigler and J. Levine, 1981, Journal of Abnormal Psychology, 90. Copyright 1981 by American Psychological Association. Reprinted by permission of the publisher.

* $p < .05$
** $p < .01$
*** $p < .001$

The mean ages on admission of the various groups examined are presented in Table 9.5. As can be seen in this table, paranoid schizophrenic patients were found to be approximately 8 years older than nonparanoid schizophrenic patients at their first hospitalization, while women of both diagnoses were found to be approximately 5 years older on first admission than men. With respect to diagnosis, these findings lend further credence to the developmental thesis, discussed at length in Chapters 6 and 7, that paranoid schizophrenia (with its later age of onset) is a higher developmental form than is nonparanoid schizophrenia.

TABLE 9.5. Age on Admission of the Diagnostic Groups

Group	N	M	SD
State hospital females			
Nonparanoid	30	29.37	11.28
Paranoid	30	37.63	12.26
State hospital males			
Nonparanoid	30	24.60	7.10
Paranoid	30	32.37	11.83
VA hospital males			
Nonparanoid	25	31.64	7.06
Paranoid	39	30.74	8.12

Source: "Age on First Hospitalization of Schizophrenics: A Developmental Approach" by E. Zigler & J. Levine, 1981, Journal of Abnormal Psychology, 90. Copyright 1981 by American Psychological Association. Reprinted by permission of the publisher.

The older age of the female first-admission patients was predicted and conforms with other evidence that women obtain higher scores than men on premorbid competence indexes and with respect to developmental categorizations of symptomatology. Other investigators have likewise reported that female schizophrenic patients are older than males at the time of their first hospitalization (Hartman & Meyer, 1969; Hornstra & Udell, 1974; Lewine, 1980, 1981; Lewine, Strauss, & Gift, 1981; Loranger, 1984; McCabe, 1975; Rosenthal, 1971). However, the reasons for the consistently more favorable scores of women remain a mystery. One group of investigators (Lewine et al., 1980), when confronted with the better performance of females, concluded simply and bravely: "That females are more socially competent than males may be a general fact of life" (p. 137). Such an assertion is not too distant from the view that women as compared to men represent a higher life form (DeBeauvoir, 1974; Montagu, 1974). While developmental theorists (e.g., Werner, Piaget, Vygotsky) have tended to ignore the issue of gender difference, there is at present little in developmental theory to suggest that females inherently represent a higher or more advanced developmental form than do males.

One explanation for the gender differences in age of hospitalization is that for women a longer time interval exists between the onset of serious mental disorder and admission to a hospital. While such an explanation is counter to findings by Lewine (1980) and Loranger (1984) that schizophrenic women also display a later age of symptom onset than do men, Hornstra and Udell (1974) advanced the argument that women's social roles provide greater shelter for psychological impairment. This "shelter" hypothesis generates the expectation that women who remain in the refuge of their home, as compared with those who work outside the home, would have a later age of first admission. In order to explore this possibility, Zigler and Levine (1981a) examined the relationship of age on first hospitalization to both work status and diagnosis for the female patients. While the effect of work status was not significant, the employed women were hospitalized an average of more than 5 years later than those not employed outside the home. An interaction effect of borderline significance ($p < .11$) reflected the tendency for paranoid employed women to be hospitalized approximately 10 years later than women in the other three groups. This finding appears consistent with the hypothesis that higher developmental level individuals will have a later age of hospitalization. The reasoning here is that paranoid coloration of the symptom picture and the ability to work outside the home are related indicators (but independent to a considerable degree) of the woman's developmental level. Thus the paranoid women who worked outside the home would be conceptualized as having the highest developmental level of the four groups of women examined and hence the highest age upon first hospitalization.

Alternative explanations for the gender difference in age of hospital admission should be entertained. Men and women are biologically different. It is possible that the general organismic maturation rates of men and women differ, and the gender differences in the age upon hospitalization reflect the same biological factors that underlie the well-documented gender differences in the length of the life span. Another explanation, which has the most appeal to us, involves a combination of (a) sex differences in socialization histories and (b) the time in the life cycle when the two genders encounter particular life stressors capable of precipitating psychological disorder. In our society, late adolescence and early adulthood are critical and demanding periods for both genders. During these times young men and women face strong societal expectancies to form close and meaningful attachments with members of the opposite sex and to obtain employment (or engage in higher-level and thus more demanding educational efforts) in order to become autonomous and contributing members of society. Given the sex role traditions in our society, the pressure to meet these general expectancies may be greater on young men than on young women. Thus a combination of the stress involved in meeting these societal demands and the greater negative reaction by meaningful others if these demands are not met may lead to a greater likelihood that men as compared to women will become seriously disturbed during this period. This hypothesis is related to the view of Forrest and Hay (1971) and Lewine (1980) that men are more likely to be stressed early in life, whereas women are more likely to encounter major stress later in the life cycle.

With respect to premorbid competence, paranoid–nonparanoid status, and the gender differences discovered, the findings of Zigler and Levine (1981a) support the view that higher developmental individuals will be first hospitalized at an older age, just as they have been found to display more favorable outcomes following treatment, than their lower developmental level counterparts.

Age on First Hospitalization in Nonschizophrenic Psychiatric Patients

Within the developmental approach to psychopathology, the usefulness of the premorbid competence dimension is presumed not to be limited to schizophrenia but to be equally applicable to a variety of nonschizophrenic diagnostic groups. Glick, Zigler, and Zigler (1985) extended the formulation of Zigler and Levine (1981a) regarding age upon first hospitalization to nonschizophrenic patients in three diagnostic categories: affective reaction; psychoneurotic disorder; and personality disorder. Within nonschizophrenic as well as schizophrenic patient groups, higher developmental individuals would be expected to display better prognoses, not only in terms of more favorable outcomes following initial treatment, but also with respect to the age at which the disorder becomes sufficiently manifest to require treatment. Paralleling Zigler and Levine's work, a first hypothesis in the Glick et al. (1985) study was that higher competence nonschizophrenic patients would be first hospitalized at an older age than lower competence patients. Another line of inquiry concerned whether developmental differences in symptomatology would also be associated with age on first hospitalization. Utilizing the developmental categorizations based upon role orientation and the action–thought continuum, the prediction was that both the role orientation of turning against the self and a predominance of thought over action in symptom expression would more frequently be found in patients first hospitalized at an older age. Finally, gender differences in age on first hospitalization were again examined. In contrast to the findings with schizophrenic patients, either gender differences in age on first admission have not appeared in nonschizophrenic samples (Lewine et al., 1981; McCabe, 1975) or results have been contradictory (Helgason, 1964; Weissman & Klerman, 1977). The question of whether such differences are unique to schizophrenia or characteristic of a variety of diagnostic groups thus remained unresolved. The further investigation of this issue was dictated by the potential implications of gender differences in hospitalization age, both with regard to developmental thinking about psychopathology (Zigler & Levine, 1981a) and with respect to the delineation of subtypes in schizophrenia.

The case histories of 448 state hospital patients first admitted between 1971 and 1976 were examined. Included in the sample were 146 (71 male and 75 female) affective disorder patients, 145 (75 male and 70 female) neurotic patients, and 157 (82 male and 75 female) personality disorder patients. Premorbid competence was assessed utilizing the variables of education, marital status, occupation, and employment history. Inasmuch as age served as the primary variable being investigated, it was not included in the calculation of premorbid competence. The revised scaling of the education and occupation variables recommended by Zigler and Levine (1981b) and detailed in Chapter 3 was employed for the first time in this study. The overall median of the social competence scores was employed to establish high and low competence subgroups. Role orientation and symptom expression in action versus thought were scored in the manner described in Chapter 4. Not surprisingly, in this nonschizophrenic sample, only 17 of 448 patients displayed avoidance of others as the dominant role orientation. Consequently, this role orientation was excluded from further analyses. Utilizing the symptoms noted for at least 5 percent of the sample, two symptom scores were computed, reflecting the relative dominance of (a) symptoms indicative of self-deprivation and turning against the self versus self-indulgence and turning against others and (b) symptom expression in thought versus action. With respect to the thought–action continuum, patients were categorized into thought, mixed, and action dominant symptom groups. Those with thought–action scores at or above the sixty-seventh percentile were classified as thought dominant. Patients whose scores fell below the thirty-fourth percentile were classified as action dominant, while those with scores between the thirty-fourth and sixty-seventh percentile comprised the mixed symptom group.

The expectation that higher developmental level individuals would be first hospitalized at an older age was confirmed with respect to each of the developmental variables examined. High social competence patients were significantly older on initial hospitalization than low competence patients, $F (1, 436) = 31.57, p < .0001.$[3] Patients with thought dominant symptom configurations were an average of 11 years older when first hospitalized than patients with action dominant symptom pictures, $F (2, 387) = 27.79, p < .0001.$ Older first-admission patients were more likely to show a role orientation of turning against the self, whereas turning against others was more common in the younger patients $(r = .263, p < .0001).$ The mean admission ages of high versus low competence patients are presented in Table 9.6. Table 9.7 presents the ages for patients in the thought, mixed, and action dominant symptom groups. In addition to the examination of composite symptom scores, a Symptom Occurrence (yes vs. no) × Age (younger vs. older) chi-square was computed for each symptom. Of the 21 symptoms displayed by at least 5 percent of the sample, 12 were significantly related to age, and relationships of borderline significance *(p < .10)* appeared for an additional four symptoms. With only one exception (suicidal attempt), symptoms indicative of turning against the self (depressed, tense, insomnia, doesn't eat, mood swings, euphoria, and bodily complaints) and avoidance of others (delusions, suspicious, withdrawn, and perplexed) tended to be associated with older age whereas symptoms indicative of turning against others (irresponsible behavior, disturbed–destructive, threatens assault, robbery) appeared more frequently in younger patients.

TABLE 9.6.   Age on First Hospitalization for Low Versus High Social Competence Patients

Group	Low Competence			High Competence		
	N	*M*	SD	*N*	*M*	SD
Affective disorder						
Male	28	39.18	20.65	43	45.63	14.18
Female	29	51.17	17.12	46	40.65	13.07
Neurotic						
Male	31	34.68	15.16	44	38.27	12.59
Female	40	31.68	10.96	30	33.13	9.51
Personality disorder						
Male	63	21.44	7.41	19	30.21	8.24
Female	49	23.90	7.15	26	27.81	7.24

TABLE 9.7.   Age on First Hospitalization for Patients Displaying Thought, Mixed, and Action Dominated Symptom Pictures

	Thought Dominated			Mixed			Action Dominated		
	N	*M*	SD	*N*	*M*	SD	*N*	*M*	SD
Affective disorder	74	45.49	16.30	44	43.00	17.39	14	40.50	11.28
Neurotic	53	33.55	12.71	21	32.71	9.77	43	31.72	11.84
Personality disorder	20	27.75	9.43	50	24.72	9.52	77	23.23	6.11

In addition to the relationships discovered between age on first hospitalization and the variables of premorbid competence, symptom expression in thought versus action, and role orientation, a highly significant relationship appeared between age and diagnosis. Whereas the mean age for affective disorder patients was 43.9 years, it was 34.6 years for the neurotic group and 24.3 for personality disorder patients. With respect to the relationship between premorbid competence and age, a number of interaction effects appeared. Primarily, these seemed to reflect the substantially older age of low competence female affective reaction patients (see Table 9.6). No interactions appeared with respect to the relationship of age to symptom expression in thought versus action. Finally, no gender differences appeared with respect to either age upon first hospitalization or premorbid competence. With respect to premorbid competence, only the differences between diagnostic groups were significant. A Newman-Keuls comparison of the mean social competence scores of affective reaction *(M = .99)*, neurotic *(M = .87)*, and personality disorder *(M = .60)* patients revealed significant differences between each diagnostic group.

A stepwise regression analysis was performed in order to determine the relative contribution of each of four predictor variables (premorbid competence, role orientation, thought–action scores, and gender) to the overall variance in age on first hospitalization. Each of the developmental measures was found to make a significant independent contribution to the overall variance in age upon first hospitalization. Only gender was unrelated to the criterion variable.

The relationships discovered by Glick et al. between age on first hospitalization and a variety of developmental variables demonstrates the applicability of Zigler and Levine's (1981a) broader view of prognosis to nonschizophrenic patients. However, one notable exception to the general pattern of findings concerns the female affective reaction patients. In contrast to all other groups examined, low premorbid competence was in the female affective reaction subsample associated with substantially older age on first hospitalization (a more favorable prognosis according to our broader view). The same finding was obtained whichever median (for the overall sample or for each Diagnosis × Gender subgroup) was employed to subdivide patients into high and low competence groups. Yet no parallel gender by diagnosis interactions appeared with respect to any symptom measure. Perhaps the revised social competence index resulted in attentuated scores for this substantially older female group. Primarily, however, this unexpected finding points to the need for closer analyses of gender differences within the affective disorder category.

Suicidal attempt was the one symptom in the turning-against-the-self category to appear more frequently in younger patients. This symptom represents one of the few action-oriented manifestations within this role orientation. The independent predictive significance of role orientation and the thought–action dimension was indicated in stepwise regression analyses. Within role orientation categories, therefore, classification along the thought–action continuum may permit the further differentiation of developmentally higher and lower expressions of disorder.

A meaningful question is whether the developmental differences discovered in the symptom pictures of the younger and older patients are specific to first-admission groups. Further research that includes a sample of older patients having a history of psychiatric hospitalization dating from late adolescence or early adulthood might determine whether the symptom differences observed by Glick et al. are a concomitant of age per se or more specifically reflect the limited adaptive resources of patients requiring hospitalization at a relatively young age. The alternatives are not mutually exclusive, and both accord with the developmental formulation.

The absence of gender differences in age upon first hospitalization and premorbid competence for this nonschizophrenic sample contrasts with the consistent findings obtained with schizophrenic patients that females are both older upon initial hospitalization (e.g., Lewine, 1980, 1981; Zigler & Levine, 1981a) and evince higher premorbid competence scores (e.g., De-Wolfe, 1973; Gittelman-Klein & Klein, 1968; Klorman et al., 1977; Zigler & Levine, 1983a) than do their male counterparts. The absence of gender differences in the age upon first hospitalization of nonschizophrenic patients accords with other research results (Lewine, 1981; Lewine et al., 1981). The gender–age difference repeatedly found for schizophrenic patients may thus be specific to that diagnosis. It should be noted, however, that in both the Glick et al. study and the investigations by Lewine and his associates male and female nonschizophrenic patients were only compared within diagnostic categories. Although the patients examined by Glick et al. comprised three diagnostic groups, the groups were formed to include comparable numbers of males and females. It is quite possible that gender differences would be found in a naturalistic sample of first-admission nonschizophrenic patients selected with no gender restrictions. Some basis for this suggestion comes from evidence that personality disorder patients, who tend to be young, also tend to be disproportionately male (Warner, 1978), whereas affective reaction patients, who tend to be considerably older, are also disproportionately female (Dohrenwend & Dohrenwend, 1976; Silverman, 1968; Weissman & Klerman, 1977). The heterogeneity of patients within the schizophrenic diagnostic category can be posited as one explanation of the gender difference in admission age found for this group but not within other diagnostic categories. The higher social competence typically found for female schizophrenic patients might well be reflected in age upon first hospitalization when the range of social competence scores is broad and the sample includes substantial numbers of low competence individuals. One test of this proposition would be to examine gender differences in admission age in subgroups of schizophrenic patients, homogeneous with respect to premorbid competence scores. This proposition also generates the expectation that in a diagnostically heterogeneous, unselected sample of nonschizophrenic patients (where the range of social competence scores would likewise be broad) gender differences would appear in age of initial hospitalization. The consistent findings described previously that affective reaction patients obtain high and personality disorder patients low premorbid competence scores accord with this possibility given the unequal numbers of males and females typically assigned to these diagnostic categories.

Gender differences in psychopathology and the need for far greater attention to this variable will be a major topic of Chapter 11. As we will indicate in that chapter, the closer examination of gender differences within nonschizophrenic diagnostic groups would allow for the clearer demarcation of those relationships that are common across nosological groups from relationships that may pertain only to specific disorders. The work to date on the developmental approach to psychopathology has emphasized commonalities across diagnostic groups. This emphasis was dictated by the fundamental presupposition that there is a continuity between premorbid and pathological functioning such that many characteristics of patients are viewed as representing extensions into the realm of pathological functioning of general behavior patterns associated with different developmental levels. The research already reviewed in this volume attests to the heuristic value of this formulation. Nevertheless, the further refinement of the developmental approach requires that we attend as well to those aspects of pathological functioning that appear to be specific to particular disorders. Consideration of this interaction of pathological with nonpathological determinants of patients' behavior can shed much insight on prognosis, broadly defined.

CONCLUSIONS

Relationships between developmental level and two aspects of prognosis (outcome following initial hospitalization and age upon first psychiatric hospitalization) have been found for both schizophrenic and nonschizophrenic psychiatric patients of both genders. Premorbid competence has been used as a gauge of developmental level, and in addition developmental differences in symptomatology have been found to be associated with age upon first hospitalization. Further, some evidence has suggested that a more favorable outcome following hospitalization is associated with the role orientation of turning against the self. These findings illustrate the import of the developmental-level construct for the understanding of prognosis and outcome and indicate that the usefulness of this construct extends to a variety of patient groups in addition to schizophrenics.

As stated at the outset of this chapter, developmentally higher functioning is not presumed to prevent the occurrence of psychopathology. However, individuals at higher maturity levels should possess greater adaptive resources resulting in improved prognosis. The major exception to this general pattern of findings concerns paranoid as compared to nonparanoid schizophrenic patients. While paranoid patients can be conceptualized as reflecting a higher developmental level than most nonparanoid schizophrenic patients, preliminary work described earlier in this chapter did not indicate a more favorable outcome for the paranoid subtype. The formulation concerning the psychodynamics of paranoia advanced in Chapter 7 provides a possible explanation for the absence of differences in outcome between paranoid and nonparanoid schizophrenic patients. If paranoia does indeed represent a mechanism to ward off the pain of depression, its psychodynamic importance to the individual may outweigh the influence of developmental differences. One line for further work thus concerns the interaction of psychodynamic with developmental variables.

REFERENCE NOTES

1. Because of the strikingly long hospitalizations displayed by this affective reaction subgroup, the question can be raised as to whether these patients were appropriately diagnosed as affective reaction or whether they might in their symptom pictures more closely resemble schizophrenic patients who more typically display long hospitalizations. Utilizing role orientation categories and the action–thought dimension, the symptom pictures of the low competence female affective reaction patients were compared with those displayed by other affective reaction subgroups (e.g., high competence male, high competence female, etc.). No evidence was found to suggest that the low competence female affective reaction patients differed from others in that diagnostic group on any symptom measure examined. (See Chapter 4 for a fuller description of these measures.)

2. As indicated in Chapter 4, the symptoms comprising the role orientation of turning against the self have a depressive coloration, and this role orientation most frequently characterizes depressed patients.

3. In addition to this analysis utilizing the overall median of premorbid competence scores, the median of the distribution of premorbid competence scores within each Diagnosis $\times$ Gender subgroup was employed to form high and low competence groups. A parallel analysis of variance performed for these groups yielded similar findings.

CHAPTER 10

Self-Image:
A Cognitive–Developmental
Approach

The importance of the self-image as a major determinant of human behavior has long been recognized (Allport, 1937; James, 1890; Maslow, 1954; Mead, 1934). Since the seminal work of C.R. Rogers and his colleagues (Rogers & Dymond, 1954), much research in this area has focused on self-image disparity, that is, the disparity between the individual's current view of self (real self) and the ideal person that he or she would like to be (ideal self). Within the Rogerian framework (Rogers, 1951; Rogers & Dymond, 1954) congruence between real and ideal self-images is interpreted as indicating positive self-regard and assumed to be linearly related to personal and social adjustment. As such, a sizable self-image disparity is viewed as being ominous in nature and a sign of maladjustment (Scott, 1958). Based on this interpretation, the reduction of discrepancies between real and ideal self-perceptions has been commonly employed as a measure of improvement in psychotherapy (Raimy, 1948; Rogers & Dymond, 1954; Sheerer, 1949; Stock, 1949).

The cognitive–developmental formulation stands in contrast to the nondevelopmental approach of Rogers and his colleagues. First formulated by Achenbach and Zigler (1963), the cognitive–developmental position interprets an increasing self-image disparity as the natural concomitant of normal growth and development. The twofold rationale for this formulation is as follows:

1. In accord with the developmental principles of Werner (1948, 1957) and Piaget (1951, 1960), higher levels of development imply greater degrees of cognitive differentiation. In any cognition, therefore, the more highly developed person should tend to employ more categories and finer distinctions within each category than should a person of lower development. This greater differentiation should result in a greater likelihood for disparity between an individual's conceptualization of the real self and that of the ideal self. It is important here to

recognize that the self-images are symbolic conceptual constructions and as such are particularly amenable to cognitive analysis.

2. An individual's capacity to experience guilt increases over the course of development with the individual's growing ability for incorporating social demands, mores, and values (Phillips, 1968a; Zigler & Child, 1969; Zigler & Phillips, 1960). The high as compared to the low developmental individual must measure up to many more internalized demands, and these greater self-demands and the guilt that accompanies them should be reflected in a greater disparity between real and ideal self-images than that found for individuals at lower developmental levels.

Our research efforts have provided considerable empirical support for this developmental interpretation of self-image disparity and have led as well to the broadening and to some modifications of the original formulation.

Whereas the research described up to this point has concerned variables important mainly to psychopathology (e.g., premorbid competence, symptomatology, diagnosis, and outcome), self-image is as pertinent to normal personality development as to disordered functioning. The importance of self-image to normal development enabled us to adopt a broad research strategy not possible in the other work on the developmental approach to psychopathology. Specifically, the developmental work on self-image disparity has proceeded in two directions. One direction involves the examination of relationships between magnitude of self-image disparity and other indicators of developmental level (e.g., premorbid competence and developmental categorizations of symptomatology) in adult psychiatric patients. Our second direction involves the examination of self-image disparity in children. Because this issue is applicable to children, traditional developmental indicators can be employed. These indicators, employed in our own work and that of other investigators, include chronological age; IQ as a reflection of mental age; nonegocentricity in role taking; and level of moral reasoning. The developmental formulation regarding self-image disparity has thus been tested using both the more traditional variables of developmental psychology and the measures we employ as indicators of developmental level in adult psychopathology. Although two populations (children and disordered adults) are employed, the underlying developmental issues remain constant. For example, some of the research with children concerns developmental differences in symptom expression. Moreover, the issue of experiential determinants in self-image formation, while more prominently featured in the research with children, pertains also to the interpretation of findings with adult pathological groups. Thus, although two populations are considered, the theoretical formulation proceeds along a single line. Given the focus of this book on adult psychopathology, most of the studies with children will be only briefly summarized. The one exception involves the examination of relations between self-image disparity and symptom pictures displayed by maladjusted children (Katz, Zigler, & Zalk, 1975). A fuller review of these studies with children was provided by Glick and Zigler (1985).

SELF-IMAGE DISPARITY AS A COGNITIVE–DEVELOPMENTAL PHENOMENON: THE ORIGINAL STUDY

The cognitive–developmental interpretation of self-image disparity was first formulated and tested by Achenbach and Zigler (1963) in a study employing 20 (10 male and 10 female) psychiatric patients and 20 (10 male and 10 female) nonpsychiatric (medical) patients as subjects. On the basis of the Zigler-Phillips social competence index, high and low social competence subgroups consisting of equal numbers of males and females were formed within each (psychiatric and nonpsychiatric) sample. Two types of self-image disparity were examined: (a) the disparity between the individual's real and ideal self-image; and (b) the disparity between the real and the social self-image, that is, the self as one believes others see it (Brownfain, 1952). For each (real, ideal, and social) self-image, two instruments differing in the amount of possible response differentiation were employed. One instrument was a questionnaire made up of 30 self-referent statements to which the individual could respond by selecting one of six alternatives for each statement ranging from "very true" to "very untrue." The second instrument was a list of 40 personal traits for which the subject merely circled "yes" or "no" to indicate correspondence to the various (real, ideal, and social) self-images.

The major hypothesis was that within both psychiatric and nonpsychiatric samples the patients of high social competence would show more disparity between their real and ideal self-images than would patients of low social competence, due to the greater differentiation and the greater internalization of societal standards associated with higher maturity levels.

In order to examine further the roles of cognitive differentiation and the internalization of standards as contributors to self-image disparity, two subsidiary hypotheses were formulated. In regard to the disparity between the real and the social self-image, it was again expected that high competence individuals would evidence more disparity than low competence individuals, but that these group differences would be less than for real–ideal disparity. Inasmuch as social guilt should contribute little to real–social self disparity, it would be only the tendency of the high group to differentiate more finely that would increase the amount of disparity manifested. The final prediction concerned differences due to the instrument (questionnaire vs. trait list) employed to gauge the individual's self-concepts. While both instruments would be expected to show greater real–ideal disparity among high as compared with low competence people due to the greater influence of social guilt, the trait list, which permits little response differentiation, was expected to produce smaller differences between the groups, since differences due to finer differentiation in response tendencies would be minimized. Furthermore, the trait list, again because it allows little response differentiation, was expected to produce no differences related to social competence on real–social self disparity inasmuch as this type of disparity in conjunction with the trait list format would remove both the factors of social guilt and cognitive differentiation. The tendencies of patients to give extreme responses ("very true" and "very untrue") on the questionnaire measures were also noted inasmuch as such extreme response tendencies should constitute a further indication of the undifferentiated cognitive style presumed to be associated with developmentally lower forms of functioning. Finally, because differences between psychiatric and nonpsychiatric patients would bear centrally upon the Rogerian formulation, which interprets real–ideal self-image disparity as a sign of maladjustment, differences between these two groups were examined, although no hypothesis was generated.

All hypotheses were confirmed. The pertinent measures of the four groups' performance are presented in Table 10.1. High social competence patients were found to display greater real–ideal self-image disparity than low competence individuals on the questionnaire. The findings also supported the view that both the greater social guilt assumed to be associated with higher social competence and the tendency toward greater cognitive differentiation in high competence subjects contributed to the differences discovered in real–ideal self-image disparity. Where social guilt and response differentiation could both become manifest, as in the real–ideal questionnaire disparity score, the differences between high and low social competence patients were greatest $(p < .001)$. Where only response differentiation but not social guilt was involved (i.e., real–social self disparity as assessed by questionnaire), differences between high and low social competence individuals, while they remained significant, were smaller $(p < .05)$. Similarly, where only social guilt but not response differentiation was involved (i.e., real–ideal disparity assessed by trait list), the effects of social competence while significant were again smaller $(p < .03)$. Finally, where both social guilt and the opportunity for response differentiation were minimal (i.e., real–social self disparity as measured by trait list), no significant differences in disparity appeared between high and low competence groups. In contrast to these predicted relationships obtained between social competence and self-image disparity, psychiatric versus nonpsychiatric status was not found to be related to any of the measures of self-image disparity employed in this study.

Further evidence of the greater cognitive differentiation and finer discrimination of high as compared with low competence subjects was found in the tendency of low competence subjects to use extreme response categories (i.e., "very true," "very untrue") on the questionnaire far more frequently than did high competence individuals $(p < .001)$. While the high competence individuals appeared to make finer discriminations, introducing a number of

TABLE 10.1. Mean Scores for Each Group

Group[a]	Real–Ideal Self Disparity		Real–Social Self Disparity		Extreme Responses on Questionnaire			
	Questionnaire	Checklist	Questionnaire	Checklist	Real Self	Ideal Self	Social Self	Total
High competence								
Psychiatric	21.3	15.0	17.0	5.7	4.1	9.5	3.8	17.4
Nonpsychiatric	21.4	10.9	16.0	6.3	5.3	15.4	5.2	25.9
Low competence								
Psychiatric	12.8	10.3	13.4	7.7	20.3	22.1	20.3	62.7
Nonpsychiatric	17.3	8.8	14.0	7.3	10.5	12.6	8.5	31.6

[a]$N = 10$ for each group.

shades of gray into their judgmental processes, low competence subjects appeared more likely merely to bifurcate their perceptions into extreme categories. While no main effects due to psychiatric status appeared, a significant interaction appeared between social competence and psychiatric status in the number of extreme responses made. This interaction reflected both the tendency for high competence nonpsychiatric patients to use more extreme responses $(M = 25.9)$ than high competence psychiatric patients $(M = 17.4)$ and even more strongly the tendency of low competence psychiatric patients to give many more extreme responses $(M = 62.7)$ than low competence nonpsychiatric patients $(M = 31.6)$. The nature of this interaction suggests that in high competence people who become mentally ill the tendency to discriminate finely either is not affected or is strengthened, while low competence people who become mentally ill tend to discriminate even less finely than prior to their illness. Such a view is consistent with both clinical observations and empirical evidence (Phillips & Zigler, 1964; Zigler et al., 1979; Zigler & Phillips, 1960, 1961b) that high competence patients continue to think about and attempt to cope with the problems that have befallen them and thus evidence a better prognosis than low competence patients, who often lapse into chronicity evidencing inattention, avoidance, and apathy. A significant relationship also appeared between subjects' self-image disparity scores obtained on the questionnaire instrument and those on the trait list. The consistency of the findings of Achenbach and Zigler (1963) provided a strong initial corroboration of the developmental view. Contrary to the Rogerian position, self-image disparity did not appear as a simple function of maladjustment. Indeed those individuals who demonstrated the capacity to achieve in areas most valued in our society (high social competence) were the ones who displayed the greatest self-image disparity. Rather than being ominous in nature, therefore, greater self-image disparity may be a natural concomitant of higher maturity levels.

These developmental findings furthermore pointed to an alternative explanation of other self-image disparity results that previously had been interpreted through a modification of the basic Rogerian position. The findings that neurotic individuals manifest greater real–ideal disparity than either schizophrenics or normals (Hillson & Worchel, 1957) and that sensitizers display greater disparity than repressors (Altrocchi, Parsons, & Dickoff, 1960) led these investigators to advance the position that, although invariably ominous, a large self-image disparity would be found only among individuals employing particular psychological defenses, that is, sensitizers and neurotics. Neurotic patients have consistently been found obtain high social competence scores (Lewine, et al., 1980; Zigler et al., 1979; Zigler & Phillips, 1961a). Moreover, the defining characteristics of repressors as those who use avoidance, denial, and repression as the primary mode of adaptation (Altrocchi et al., 1960) are quite similar to descriptions of individuals who show turning-against-others or turning-away-from-others role orientations (Phillips & Rabinovitch, 1958), which have both been consistently found to be associated with low social competence in psychiatric patients (e.g., Raskin & Golob, 1966; Zigler & Phillips, 1960). Conversely, the description of sensitizers as those who use intellectual and obsessive defenses is similar to the symptomatic picture of individuals manifesting the turning-against-the-self orientation found in high competence patients. In light of these developmental findings, Achenbach and Zigler suggested that the greater self-image disparities of neurotic and sensitizing patients can be subsumed within the developmental framework. That is, different defensive styles are presumed to reflect different levels of underlying maturity and as such the disparity scores of sensitizing patients would be seen as yet another expression of their maturity.

SELF-IMAGE DISPARITY IN CHILDREN

Although the findings of Achenbach and Zigler (1963) represented a convincing beginning demonstration of the efficacy of developmental thinking in the area of self-image disparity, developmental research employing adult subjects is hampered by problems in gauging developmental level in adulthood. These problems were discussed in earlier chapters. While considerable evidence supports the use of premorbid competence as an indicator of maturity level in adulthood, research with children provides a more traditional means for assessing developmental differences, both through the observation of ontogenetic changes and, more importantly, through the use of indexes reflecting developmental differences in cognitive structuring.

Beginning with the work of Katz and Zigler (1967), a series of studies was performed with children (Katz et al., 1975; Leahy, Balla, & Zigler, 1982; Phillips & Zigler, 1980, 1982; Zigler, Balla, & Watson, 1972) in which chronological age, mental age, and other developmental variables were employed as indicators of maturity level. Studies by Leahy (Leahy, 1981; Leahy & Huard, 1976) supplement this work. In addition to considering disparity scores, this research has focused on developmental changes within both the real and ideal self-images. As Wylie (1974) indicated in her comprehensive evaluation of self-image research, a disparity or difference score per se conveys relatively little information. If disparity increases with maturity level, one must also inquire into the qualitative nature of this disparity. Does it reflect a more positive ideal self-image, a more negative real self-image, or both?

Finally, the work with children has been instrumental in broadening the original developmental formulation to include the examination of nondevelopmental experiential factors in self-image disparity and their interaction with developmental determinants.

Children's Self-Image Disparity: Major Research Findings

The studies with children provide substantial support for the cognitive–developmental interpretation that views greater real–ideal self-image disparity as a natural concomitant of development. In the work with children, greater disparity between real and ideal self-images has been associated with a broad array of measures of cognitive maturity, including chronological age (Katz & Zigler, 1967; Katz et al., 1975; Phillips & Zigler, 1980; Zigler et al., 1972), mental age (Katz & Zigler, 1967; Zigler et al., 1972), evidence of non-egocentric thought in a role-taking task (Leahy, 1981; Leahy & Huard, 1976), and developmental level in moral reasoning (Leahy, 1981). Also consistent with the developmental position are findings that greater real–ideal self-image disparity is associated with the presence of thought rather than action symptoms in maladjusted children (Katz et al., 1975). This study will be presented in the next section.

The developmental differences in self-image disparity appear to reflect changes in both the real and the ideal self-images. The findings have been particularly consistent in regard to the ideal self-image. More positive ideal self-images have been found to be associated with higher maturity levels as assessed by all of the measures employed in the various studies, that is, chronological age (Katz & Zigler, 1967; Katz et al., 1975; Phillips & Zigler, 1980; Zigler et al., 1972), mental age (Katz & Zigler, 1967; Leahy et al., 1982; Zigler et al., 1972), the presence of thought rather than action symptoms (Katz et al., 1975), nonegocentric role-taking ability (Leahy, 1981; Leahy et al., 1982), and more mature levels of moral reasoning (Leahy, 1981).

In a number of studies, the real self-images of older children have been found to be less positive than those of younger children (Katz & Zigler, 1967; Phillips & Zigler, 1980; Zigler et al., 1972). Leahy (1981) found that less positive real self-images were associated with higher (postconventional) levels of moral judgment in adolescents. Consistent with these findings obtained with children, Rabinowitz (1966) found that more negative qualities were incorporated into the self-image by 25-year-old subjects in comparison to 18-year-olds. Moreover, Rorschach scores that have been associated with higher maturity levels (i.e., greater M, higher $F + \%$, and a predominance of FC over CF) have been related to lower self-acceptance in college students (Bills, 1953).

Evidence for the reliability and construct validity of self-image disparity for even very young children has been presented by Phillips and Zigler (1982) who, moreover, discovered that different emphases in the real self-image were reflected by different factor structures obtained for younger and older children. In contrast to second graders, fifth graders evidenced a more self-reflective stance. Comparable developmental changes in the content of children's self-images have also been reported by Montemayor and Eisen (1977), Rosenberg (1979), and Harter (1983).

In regard to the idealized self-image, Van den Daele (1968) has reported parallel changes with increasing age in the direction of increased differentiation of societal values. Young children's descriptions of the person they would like to be were found to be hedonistic and conflict avoidant, predicated upon parental actions and admonitions. At intermediate levels, the children's responses reflected cultural and group expectations, while at the highest levels that characterized older adolescents, rigid conformity to social proscription appeared to be replaced by an integrating structure of individualized goals involving personal–social and transcendent values. This developmental trend is obviously reminiscent of the developmental progressions described by Kohlberg (1969) and Loevinger (Loevinger, 1966; Loevinger & Wessler, 1970).

The more positive ideal self-images associated with higher maturity levels can most plausibly be interpreted as a reflection of two developmental processes: (1) the greater incorporation of societal demands and values at higher developmental levels and the consequent increase in social guilt (Achenbach & Zigler, 1963); and (2) the capacity for abstract hypothetical thinking that emerges at higher developmental levels. The ideal self-image, if conceptualized as distinct from the real self, does after all represent an abstraction.

The lowered real self-images that have frequently been found to accompany development may also reflect two aspects of developmental change. In the first place, they may reflect the higher standards incorporated in the ideal self-images. When these standards are applied to the real self-image, this may result in a more negative self-evaluation (Leahy, 1981). In addition, structural changes in the self-concept over the course of development may give different meanings to negative attribution at different developmental levels. At lower developmental levels, the various aspects of the self-concept would be expected to be fused with each other and with the quality of the whole. Thus, self-perception would be expected to have an all-or-none quality such that any perception of negative attributes would negatively color the view of the whole. The admission of negative attribution would, thus, be particularly damaging at this level. At more advanced levels, characterized by greater differentiation and hierarchic integration, it should be possible to consider negative and positive characteristics of the self simultaneously. At higher levels, then, a sense of positive self-regard would not be expected to depend upon a positive evaluation of all aspects of the self or even upon an additive conceptualization whereby the sum of positive qualities exceeds the total number of negative characteristics. (An additive conceptualization presupposes a juxtaposed organization of parts wherein equal value is ascribed to each part.) With increased maturity, the valence of self-regard would be expected to depend upon a more complex organization wherein certain characteristics would assume central importance while other attributes would be of peripheral significance.

A variety of experiential variables that affect how others respond to the individual in everyday social–psychological interactions have been found to have important moderating influences on children's self-images. In comparison to noninstitutionalized children of similar age, institutionalized children have been found to display lower ideal self-images (Zigler et al., 1972) and lower real self-images (Leahy et al., 1982). Ethnicity and low SES were found by Phillips and Zigler (1980) particularly to affect children's ideal self-images. In addition, a variety of other complex and interacting effects of gender, ethnicity, and SES were noted (Phillips & Zigler 1980).

The Effects of Age, Maladjustment, and Symptom Style on Children's Self-Image Disparity

The self-images of children at two age levels (corresponding to the fifth and eighth grades) classified as maladjusted or nonmaladjusted were examined by Katz et al. (1975). In addition, styles of symptom expression displayed by the maladjusted children were classified developmentally along an action–thought continuum and related to their self-images. As described in Chapter 4, symptom expression in action is conceptualized as reflecting a developmentally lower mode, and considerable evidence supports this assumption. A major purpose of the Katz et al. (1975) study was to examine whether the positions of maladjusted children in regard to the action–thought continuum in symptom expression were related to the magnitude of their self-image disparity. Given the presumably developmentally lower status of action symptoms, the prediction was that children exhibiting these symptoms would display less self-image disparity than children exhibiting a thought orientation in symptomatology. In keeping with earlier findings (Katz & Zigler, 1967; Zigler et al., 1972), the expectation in regard to age differences was that older children would display greater self-image disparities than would younger children. Finally, the maladjusted–nonmaladjusted dimension provided an opportunity to test the Rogerian thesis that greater disparity would be associated with maladjusted status per se. This investigation thus provides a direct test of both the Rogerian and developmental formulations.

The children in the study were 80 boys ranging in age from 9 years 6 months to 14 years 6 months, selected from a middle-class school system that had special classes for children designated "emotionally disturbed" that were organized according to chronological age. Placement in these classes constituted the operational definition of psychological maladjustment for the study. Because there were only two girls in these classes, only boys were examined.

Classification along the action–thought continuum was based on a categorization of symptoms as either externalizing (i.e., action) or internalizing (i.e., thought). This categorization was derived from a factor-analytic study of children's symptoms conducted by Achenbach (1966). A finding in this study was that the major proportion of variability in children's symptom expression was accounted for by a bipolar internalizer–externalizer factor. Externalizing symptoms included antisocial, aggressive, and hyperactive behavior, whereas internalizing symptoms included anxiety, depression, withdrawal, and somatic concerns. This factor thus corresponds closely to the action–thought dimension utilized by Phillips and Zigler (1961, 1964) for the classification of adult symptom expression. The classification of children as internalizers or externalizers by Katz et al. (1975) was based upon the total configuration of the symptoms described in the student's record. When the preponderance of symptoms were externalizing, the child was classified as an externalizer. Alternatively, children displaying a preponderance of internalizing symptoms were classified as internalizers. Interrater agreement for this classification was 85 percent, and only children who could be unambiguously classified and who also displayed no signs of organic impairment were included in the study. This yielded a sample of 40 emotionally disturbed boys. The normal sample of 40 boys was then selected from the same school system and matched as closely as possible with the emotionally disturbed group in age, IQ, and racial composition. Thus 20 nonmaladjusted fifth grade boys were matched with 20 maladjusted (10 internalizers and 10 externalizers) boys of equivalent ages and IQs. Similarly, the eighth grade sample comprised 20 nonmaladjusted boys matched with 20 maladjusted (10 internalizers and 10 externalizers) boys. This study employed a six-alternative questionnaire for measuring real and ideal self-images designed to be as similar as possible to the one used by Achenbach and Zigler and yet be relevant for children.

The self-image and self-image disparity scores of all groups are presented in Table 10.2. No support was obtained in this study for the Rogerian position that maladjustment per se is related to self-image disparity. Consistent with the findings for adults by Achenbach and Zigler (1963), emotional maladjustment was found to be unrelated to self-image disparity, whereas both

TABLE 10.2.   Mean Self-Image Scores for Each Group

		Questionnaire Score		
Group	N	Real[a]	Ideal[a]	Real–Ideal Disparity
Fifth grade				
Normal subjects	20	54.25	43.25	11.00
Internalizers	10	66.60	53.60	13.00
Externalizers	10	67.70	62.80	4.90
Eighth grade				
Normal subjects	20	58.65	42.05	16.60
Internalizers	10	57.20	36.20	21.00
Externalizers	10	61.50	52.50	9.00

[a]On both the real and ideal self measures, lower scores reflect a more positive self-concept.

age and symptom style were found to be predictive of the magnitude of self-image disparity.

Regardless of adjustment status, self-image disparity was significantly greater in older children. Moreover, children with externalizing symptoms were found to have smaller self-image disparities than either internalizing or normal children. The disparity scores of the normal and the internalizing children did not differ significantly from each other, although the highest disparity scores were in fact obtained by the internalizing children. The mean disparity scores of the internalizing, normal, and externalizing children were 17.00, 13.80, and 6.95, respectively.

Analyses of the ideal self-image scores once again pointed to the influence of developmental variables (age and symptom orientation) but not to the effects of adjustment status per se. Consistent with the results of Katz and Zigler (1967) and Zigler et al. (1972), older children were found to have higher ideal self-image scores than younger children $(p = .01)$. Similarly, the internalizing and the normal children were found to be quite similar with regard to ideal self-aspirations $(M = 44.90$ and 42.65, respectively), whereas the externalizers had much more negative ideal-self scores $(M = 57.65)$.

In contrast to the findings of Katz and Zigler (1967) and Zigler et al. (1972), the older children in this study were not found to have less favorable real self-images than the younger groups. However, adjustment status was found to influence this aspect of self-perception. Both externalizers and internalizers displayed less favorable real self-images than normal children, although this difference was significant only for the externalizer–normal comparison. Consistent with other findings (Zigler et al., 1972), there was the strong suggestion that, independent of cognitive–developmental variables, the child's life history qualitatively influenced self-image disparity, particularly as regards the real self-image. In the Zigler et al. (1972) study, institutionalized children as a group displayed particularly low real self-images. Just as the life history experiences associated with being placed in an institution may well result in lowered self-regard, it is reasonable to expect that children stigmatized with the label *maladjusted,* removed from the mainstream of their school's activities, and placed in classes for the emotionally disturbed develop an attenuated sense of self-worth. Moreover, the finding that the sense of self-worth was particularly depressed in children with externalizing symptoms is understandable if one remembers that it is just such acting-out children who seem to be least countenanced by peers (Kohlberg et al., 1972), family, school personnel, and community members.

Although the low ideal self-images of the externalizing children may primarily reflect the influence of cognitive–developmental variables (less internalization of societal expectations, and possibly also less ability to think abstractly), the lowered aspirations coupled with the depressed self-regard of this group would seem to raise concern about adaptive consequences. However, rather than being reflected in self-image disparity scores (which were particularly small in this group), the potential source of difficulty would seem to be that these children both think poorly of themselves and show little aspiration for change. As Wylie (1974) has suggested, self-image disparity represents an unanchored difference score. At least as important are the qualitative aspects of the real and the ideal self-images. The same self-image disparity score may have a very different meaning depending upon where along a positive-to-negative continuum the self-images are located. The person with a positive view of self, high aspirations, and a consequently small disparity score would seem to be very different from the individual whose small disparity score reflects an unfavorable view of the self with few aspirations.

SELF-IMAGE DISPARITY IN ADULT PSYCHOPATHOLOGY: FURTHER RESEARCH

Self-Image Disparity, Premorbid Competence, and Defensive Style

Achenbach and Zigler (1963) found that self-image disparity was significantly related to premorbid competence as an indicator of maturity level but not to adjustment status (psychiatric vs. medical patients). Moreover, they suggested that the developmental formulation could encompass the repression–sensitization findings in the self-image disparity literature (Altrocchi et al., 1960; Hillson & Worchel, 1957), inasmuch as sensitizing defenses can be interpreted as reflecting developmentally higher forms of functioning than repressive defenses. A direct examination of the relationship of self-image disparity, adjustment status, defensive style, and premorbid competence in adult psychiatric patients was undertaken by Feder (1968). The only significant relationship uncovered in this study was between self-image disparity and defensive style, with sensitizers showing larger disparity scores than repressors. Neither adjustment–maladjustment (medical vs. psychiatric patients) nor premorbid competence was related to magnitude of self-image disparity. Neither was defensive style found to be associated with maturity level as gauged by the social competence measure. These results, therefore, contradict the developmental thesis on two important points. First, Feder did not replicate Achenbach and Zigler's finding of a positive relation between degree of disparity and developmental level. Secondly, Feder's results did not yield a significant relationship between premorbid competence and defensive style.

A number of procedural aspects of Feder's study may have contributed both to the discrepancy between her results and those of Achenbach and Zigler and to the failure to find any relationship between social competence and the repression–sensitization dimension. The design of Feder's investigation readily suggests one reason why she failed to confirm a relation between defensive style and social competence. Her design required an equal number of repressors and sensitizers at each competence level, thus creating a forced independence between the two variables. Furthermore, in contrast to Achenbach and Zigler's method of scoring premorbid competence on the basis of patients' case history records, Feder classified subjects into high or low social competence groups on the basis of an information sheet that they completed. Yet if low competence individuals are also repressors (who tend to use denial and repression in response to threatening situations) they might tend to falsify information regarding education, occupation, and employment history for an unknown researcher. This, of course, would result in erroneous placement of these subjects into competence groups.

Differences in the self-image measures employed across the two studies may likewise have contributed to the inconsistent findings. Feder's measure was in a Q-sort format, which could be considerably more difficult to complete than the questionnaire and checklist instruments used by Achenbach and Zigler. It is also possible that low competence subjects may have had difficulty rating themselves on some of the Q-sort items, such as "ardent," "candid," or "intuitive." The forced rectilinear distribution of responses on Feder's instrument would also minimize the effects of cognitive differentiation on the task. This might be expected to limit potential differences between subject groups.

Mylet, Styfco, and Zigler (1979) looked into these procedural issues in an attempt to reconcile and/or clarify the conflicting results obtained by Achenbach and Zigler (1963) and Feder (1968). The primary focus of Mylet et al., was on interrelationships between social competence, self-image disparity, and defensive style, although adjustment status was also considered. In addition, the work of Achenbach and Zigler was extended through the examination of the components of self-image disparity (i.e., the real and the ideal self) as well as disparity scores.

Eighty hospitalized male psychiatric and nonpsychiatric patients served as subjects. Based on scores on the Zigler-Phillips social competence index, the groups of 40 psychiatric and 40 medical or surgical patients were subdivided into equal groups ($N = 20$) of high and low competence individuals. All psychiatric subjects were first-admission patients with primary diagnoses of schizophrenia, neurosis, or personality disorder. The medical and surgical patients had no history of psychiatric hospitalization and no illnesses judged to have a major psychiatric component or to be terminal.

Three instruments were employed to measure self-image disparity: the six-alternative questionnaire and the checklist instruments employed by Achenbach and Zigler and the Q-sort measure used by Feder. The repression–sensitization scale used by Altrocchi et al. (1960), as modified by Byrne (1964), was employed to gauge defensive style. To test the possibility that subjects might not have been able to respond knowledgeably to the items in Feder's Q-sort, a multiple-choice vocabulary test containing items from the Q-sort and from the other two self-image measures was devised. To test the hypothesis that defensive style is related to premorbid competence, a correlational procedure was employed in which the repression–sensitization scores of the total sample (differing widely in social competence) were related to competence ratings. A check on biographical information provided by subjects was obtained when possible.

The mean self-image disparity scores on all three measures are presented in Table 10.3. In clear confirmation of developmental expectations, the high competence patients displayed greater real–ideal disparity on the questionnaire, the trait list, and the Q-sort measure.

TABLE 10.3.   Mean Disparity Scores for Each Group

Group[a]	Questionnaire	Trait List	Q-Sort
High competence			
Psychiatric	22.90	12.85	38.70
Nonpsychiatric	22.00	8.60	36.30
Low competence			
Psychiatric	16.00	8.40	29.20
Nonpsychiatric	9.45	7.05	32.25

[a] $N = 20$ for each group.

The tendency of low developmental individuals to give more extreme responses than high developmental groups ($p < .001$) was strongly evident in this study, as it has been in previous work (Achenbach & Zigler, 1963). However, an interesting interaction effect was also noted. A greater difference in extreme responding appeared between the two low competence groups (psychiatric and nonpsychiatric) than between the two high competence groups. This finding lends some support to the suggestion of Achenbach and Zigler that in high competence individuals who become mentally ill the tendency to discriminate finely is little affected, but that low competence people who become mentally ill tend to discriminate even less finely than they did prior to their illness. This phenomenon may underlie the commonly observed and reported pattern in which high competence patients continue to think about and attempt to cope with the problems that have befallen them and thus evidence a better prognosis than low competence patients (Marsh et al., 1981; Zigler et al., 1979; Zigler & Phillips, 1961b).

Contrary to the findings of Achenbach and Zigler, the psychiatric patients were found to have higher self-image disparities than the nonpsychiatric group on the questionnaire ($p < .001$) and trait list ($p < .05$) measures. This finding is consistent with the Rogerian position that maladjusted individuals will have higher self-image disparities than psychologically adjusted individuals. However, in the analysis of the questionnaire measure, the difference in disparity between psychiatric and nonpsychiatric patients was found to hold only for the low competence patients. It thus appears that the high competence individual, even when judged maladjusted, continues to resemble equally high competence individuals considered to be psychologically adjusted.

The difference between the patient groups (high vs. low premorbid competence and psychologically adjusted vs. maladjusted) in self-image disparity appeared to reflect differences in the manner in which these groups assessed both their real and ideal selves. On both the questionnaire and checklist instruments, the high competence patients (in both the psychiatric and nonpsychiatric samples) evidenced lower real self-images than low competence patients $(p < .025)$. In addition, however, the psychiatric patients' assessments of their real selves were lower than those of the nonpsychiatric group $(p < .001)$. The finding that high competence individuals think less well of themselves than low competence individuals, although counterintuitive, is consistent with the developmental theorizing advanced by Zigler and his colleagues. The finding that psychiatric patients have a poorer self-image than nonpsychiatric patient presents a problem of interpretation.

Within the Rogerian framework, a causal chain is suggested whereby the maladjusted individual thinks poorly of himself or herself and as a result experiences dissatisfaction and/or anxiety that leads to the individual's receiving psychological assistance (i.e., going into outpatient treatment or being hospitalized). A quite different interpretation of the low self-image of psychiatric patients can be advanced. Rather than a low self-image resulting in psychiatric status, psychiatric status may result in a low self-image. This latter interpretation is consistent with the view that, in addition to developmental factors, the real and ideal self-images are influenced by gross differences in life histories, especially those differences related to how others react to the individual in everyday social–psychological interactions (Katz et al., 1975; Leahy et al., 1982; Phillips & Zigler, 1980; Zigler et al., 1972). As was the case with institutionalized children and children assigned to special classes for the emotionally disturbed and mentally retarded, it would not be surprising to discover that the stigma associated with being a psychiatric patient, particularly a hospitalized one, would result in a lowered self-image.

However, contrary to the developmental trend observed with children (Katz & Zigler, 1967; Katz et al., 1975; Phillips & Zigler, 1980; Zigler et al., 1972), the low competence patients were found to have higher ideal self-image scores $(p < .05)$ on the questionnaire but not the checklist measure. This finding may have been due to the very strong tendency of the low competence patients to make more extreme responses. Extreme response tendencies have been found to be more marked on ideal self-image ratings (Katz & Zigler, 1967; Phillips & Zigler, 1980), and selecting extreme positive responses would result in higher ideal self scores.

Significant relationships were obtained between the repression–sensitization measure and both social competence and self-image disparity. Consistent with the developmental position, high competence patients, both psychiatric and nonpsychiatric, were found to have higher sensitization scores than low competence patients ($p < .001$). Consistent with the findings of Feder, significant correlations appeared between repression–sensitization scores and each of the three self-image disparity measures ($p < .001$ for the questionnaire and trait list, $p < .01$ for the Q-sort). Psychiatric patients were found to have higher sensitization scores than nonpsychiatric patients, a finding that is not surprising inasmuch as the repression–sensitization measure was based upon MMPI scales that were developed to be sensitive to maladjustment of various types.

Further evidence for the construct validity of self-image disparity (see especially Phillips & Zigler, 1982) was provided by the finding that all three measures (questionnaire, checklist, and Q-sort) were significantly intercorrelated (all p's $< .001$). This does not mean, however, that every measure of self-image disparity is as good as every other measure. Findings from the vocabulary test that low competence patients made more errors than high competence patients ($p < .001$) and that all patients had more difficulty on Q-sort words in comparison with words derived from the other two self-image instruments ($p < .001$) suggest that the Q-sort instrument may be a poor measure of self-image disparity, especially for low competence individuals. Thus the inconsistency between the findings of Achenbach and Zigler and those of Feder appeared in part to be due to the different measures employed in the two studies. In addition, the different procedures employed by Achenbach and Zigler and Feder to assess premorbid competence may have contributed to the divergent results obtained in the two studies. When the information provided by the self-report biographical form from which Feder obtained premorbid competence information was checked against case history records within the psychiatric sample, almost half of the low competence patients were found to have provided inaccurate or misleading information. By contrast, no conflicting information was found for the high competence group.

Self-Image and Psychopathological Disturbance: Other Research Findings

With the exception of work comparing individuals who enter outpatient counseling with those who do not and the self-images of clients at earlier and later points in the course of counseling, there is a relative paucity of information concerning self-image disparity in psychiatric patient groups, particularly inpatients. Nevertheless, certain other findings bear on issues raised by the work of Achenbach and Zigler, Feder, and Mylet et al. In the first place, the relationship between defensive style and self-image disparity noted by Altrocchi et al. (1960), Feder (1968), and Mylet et al. (1979) receives further confirmation from other studies in which lower real–ideal disparity has been found to be associated with denial and repression in normal samples and psychiatric patients (Bauer & Achenbach, 1976; Berger, 1955; Block & Thomas, 1955; Byrne, 1961; Cowen et al., 1957; Zuckerman & Monashkin,

1957). Furthermore, the postulation suggested by Achenbach and Zigler (1963) and tested in children by Katz et al. (1975) that greater self-image disparity would be associated with symptom patterns reflecting more mature forms of functioning is also supported by findings that greater real–ideal disparity and lower real self-images are associated with depression and self-blame and with anxiety in adolescent and adult (psychiatric and nonpsychiatric) subjects (Bills, 1954; Bills, Vance, & McLean, 1951; Cowen et al., 1957; Engel, 1959; Flippo & Lewinsohn, 1971; Guerney & Burton, 1963; Kaplan & Pokorny, 1969; Ohnmacht & Muro, 1967; Rosenberg, 1965; Winkler & Myers, 1963; Zuckerman & Monashkin, 1957). By contrast, paranoid schizophrenics have been found to exhibit less real–ideal disparity than either nonparanoid patients or normal subjects (Havener & Izard, 1962; Rogers, 1958), a finding assumed to reflect characteristic paranoid defenses of denial and projection.

Mirroring the contradictions between the findings of Mylet et al. (1979) and those of Achenbach and Zigler (1963), Feder (1968), and Katz et al. (1975), other research has yielded inconsistent findings concerning the relationship between self-image disparity and adjustment status. Chase (1957) observed greater disparity in psychiatric rather than medical inpatients. In comparison with nonhospitalized normal controls, Zuckerman, Baer, and Monashkin (1956) found greater disparity in psychiatric inpatients. However, no relationship (Zuckerman & Monashkin, 1957) or a relationship opposite to expectation (Zuckerman et al., 1956) was observed between degree of disparity and ratings of patients' adjustment based on the examination of case history summaries. In the Zuckerman et al. study, female patients who were rated as most poorly adjusted displayed less real–ideal disparity. Although their results are not directly comparable to other findings since they employed a nonverbal measure of self-esteem, Ziller and his colleagues (Long, Ziller, & Bankes, 1970; Ziller & Grossman, 1967; Ziller, Megas, & DeCencio, 1964) have repeatedly observed more negative self-evaluations in both hospitalized neuropsychiatric patients and children institutionalized for behavioral problems as compared with noninstitutionalized normal controls. Whether this attenuated self-esteem should be construed as reflecting psychological disturbance or interpreted as resulting from institutionalization, social stigmatization, and other negative experiences associated with psychiatric status is unclear. Certainly the latter interpretation can account for Zuckerman et al.'s (1956) finding that greater real–ideal disparity was associated with psychiatric status but not with degree of disturbance within an inpatient group. At a more general level, it becomes apparent that the effects of institutionalization and other stigmatizing circumstances must be taken into account in research concerned with the relation between psychiatric–nonpsychiatric status and the self-concept. At present, it does not appear possible to determine whether a low self-image results in psychiatric status or conversely whether psychiatric status eventuates in a low self-image (Mylet et al., 1979).

INTERRELATIONSHIPS AMONG FACETS OF SELF-REGARD: A POSSIBLE RECONCILIATION OF DEVELOPMENTAL AND ROGERIAN POSITIONS

The cognitive–developmental formulation stands in contrast to the non-developmental approach of C. R. Rogers and his colleagues. Within the Rogerian framework (Rogers, 1951; Rogers & Dymond, 1954), congruence between real and ideal self-images is interpreted as indicating positive self-regard and assumed to be linearly related to personal and social adjustment. Conceptualized developmentally, such congruence becomes inadequate to gauge feelings of self-worth across maturity levels. While relationships may be obtained between a sense of self-worth and adaptation, the developmental formulation requires a more precise definition of the multifaceted and changing nature of self-regard and a more complex conceptualization of relations between this construct and adjustment.

As facets of self-regard, self-esteem, self-acceptance, the real self-image, and real–ideal self disparity are not equivalent and may reflect different self-evaluating processes. Although these constructs have been distinguished at a theoretical level, they have frequently been treated as overlapping in self-concept research (Harter, 1983; Wylie, 1974). The cognitive–developmental interpretation requires that the various aspects of self-regard be clearly differentiated since relationships between them would be assumed to change over the course of development. Allport (1955, 1961) has differentiated attributive concepts of the real and ideal self (the self-image) from globally organized feelings of self-esteem and self-satisfaction (ego enhancement), presumed to be rooted in earlier experience. If on the basis of structure and origin the self-image is construed as developmentally more advanced, one may question the degree to which the real self-image and disparity between real and ideal self-images reflect or influence self-esteem or self-satisfaction. Is the individual who describes real and ideal self-images differently affectively bothered by the discrepancy, or might the descriptions, particularly at higher maturity levels, be undertaken primarily as cognitive tasks bearing limited relationship to persistent subjective feelings of self-doubt? Extremely negative responses in rating the real self-image and very large real–ideal disparities might conceivably reflect self-doubt more closely than moderate ratings and discrepancies. It is possible that, like basic trust, a global sense of self-esteem derives from early nonverbal experiences and remains somewhat immune to conceptual modification. Like self-esteem, self-acceptance unquestionably implies an emotional component. However, self-acceptance would seem to depend upon developmentally more advanced functioning since it involves an articulated awareness of the self with the ability to recognize and accept negative qualities. A moderately positive rating of the real self and a moderately but not extremely small real–ideal self disparity might most plausibly reflect self-acceptance.

In regard to the capacity of ratings of the real self and of measures of self-image disparity that are subtractive to indicate subjective feelings of self-worth, developmental research findings point to the need for a more complex categorization that can reflect patterns of organization. If magnitude of disparity indicates differentiation and is, therefore, not necessarily an ominous sign, might there be a point beyond which disparity becomes too great and must be interpreted as potentially debilitating? Given the more positive ideal self-image characteristic of higher maturity level, a real–ideal disparity occasioned by a high ideal self-image and occurring at the positive end of the scale must be distinguished from a disparity reflecting a low ideal self-image and an even more negative conceptualization of the real self. Attention must be paid to absolute values of real and ideal self-ratings. However, merely shifting the focus of inquiry from discrepancy scores to absolute values of self-ratings would be insufficient. The real self-image cannot be accepted as an adequate gauge of self-regard, since negative attribution may have different meanings at different developmental levels. Moreover, as Wylie (1974) has suggested, an image of the ideal self may be implied in the rating of the real self-images. Categorization in terms of qualitative change must supplant the measurement of quantitative difference.

The developmental changes that have been observed in the organization of the self-images necessitate a more complex conceptualization of the relationship between the self-images and adjustment. The influence of the ideal self-image on adaptive functioning seems especially to merit wider investigation. Since the ideal self-image has been conceptualized as providing motivation and goal direction, and as facilitating development and permitting the organization and integration of experience (Allport, 1955; Baldwin, 1911; Van den Daele, 1968), a generally positive relationship between a high ideal self-image and adaptation would be expected, but with notable exceptions. Extremely high and unrealistic aspirations could paralyze rather than facilitate adaptive functioning. Such aspirations could also represent denial and the substitution of fantasy solutions for realistic striving. Characteristic in these exceptions is the absence of a perceived relationship between the ideal and the real self-images.

If one applies the orthogenetic principle to these considerations, three levels can be distinguished in the organization of relations between real and ideal self-images. At the earliest level, characterized by global organization, the ideal self-image, being inseparable from the real self-image, could provide no motivation or direction for change. An intermediate level of organization can be conceptualized as involving differentiation with insufficient reintegration of real and ideal self-images. Aware of the discrepancy between the ideal and the actual, an individual at this stage of development might be motivated for change but lack a sense of appropriate directions and means for its accomplishment. Feelings of self-dissatisfaction and helplessness might be especially evident at this stage. At the highest level of organization, the ideal self-image would be expected to be conceptualized in relation to an articulated image of the real self, incorporating personal as well as social values. Rather than desiring to be utterly different or aspiring to unyielding social stereotypes of the ideal person, individuals at this stage might be more likely to envision change as the development and modification of qualities they already perceive in themselves. Thus not only should the reintegration of real and ideal self-images provide motivation for change, but it should also permit conceptualization of appropriate directions and subgoals, thereby facilitating adaptation.

The positions of Kohlberg (1964), Loevinger (1966, 1976), and Van den Daele (1968) are compatible with this formulation in that they posit a curvilinear relationship between developmental level and conformity to external values with the integration of personal and social values characterizing advanced levels. Erikson (1968) has stressed both the cognitive complexity required for an integration of various images of the self and the central importance of this integration in facilitating adult development and adaptation.

Conceptualizing relations between real and ideal self-images on the basis of three levels of organization allows for a reconciliation of findings supportive of the Rogerian position with developmental research evidence and with findings indicating no relation between real–ideal disparity and psychiatric status and/or adjustment. Supportive of the Rogerian position is evidence indicating greater real–ideal disparity in therapy clients than control subjects and a decrease in disparity over the course of successful therapy (Raimy, 1948; Rogers & Dymond, 1954; Sheerer, 1949; Stock, 1949). An intermediate level in the organization of relations between real and ideal self-images may be most characteristic in outpatient therapy clients since their entrance into therapy is frequently self-motivated and accompanied by expressions of self-disparagement, depression, and anxiety. For such individuals, improvement might well entail reintegration of real and ideal self-images with a resulting decrease in real–ideal disparity. In contrast to these clients, a developmentally earlier global level of organization might be more characteristic of certain psychiatric inpatients and of children with action symptoms. For these groups, diminished real–ideal self disparity would not be construed as a favorable sign, and effective treatment might well entail increased disparity.

CHAPTER 11

The Influences of Gender
and Socioeconomic Status
on Psychopathology

Although certain gender differences in psychopathology have been noted repeatedly (e.g., the greater prevalence of depression in women and the higher premorbid competence scores of female as compared with male schizophrenic patients), the issue of gender differences has tended not to be comprehensively treated in the psychopathology literature. As Wahl (1977) noted in a survey of schizophrenia research, very few studies reported analyses of sex differences while a substantial number did not even indicate the sex composition of the sample. Sex differences have been more frequently examined in recent studies, but, as will be apparent from the findings reviewed in this chapter, information about gender differences in psychopathology remains incomplete. Our own work has considered gender differences in (a) premorbid competence, (b) age upon first hospital admission, and (c) symptomatology. The first section of this chapter reviews these findings, examines possible explanations for the gender differences discovered, and notes areas where additional research is needed.

The second half of the chapter examines social class differences in psychopathology. The issue of socioeconomic status takes on particular significance in view of the fact that variables that we have conceptualized as indicators of developmental level (e.g., premorbid competence and symptom configurations involving turning against the self vs. turning against others and expression in action vs. thought) can be interpreted as primarily reflecting social class differences (Nuttall & Solomon, 1965, 1970; Raskin & Golob, 1966; Turner & Zabo, 1968; Zigler & Child, 1973). We are thus confronted with alternative interpretations involving different levels of analysis (sociological vs. psychological). A major issue to be considered in the second section of the chapter is the relative value of the social class interpretation versus the developmental approach for illuminating important processes in psychopathology.

GENDER DIFFERENCES IN PSYCHOPATHOLOGY

Diagnosis and Symptomatology

That women are about twice as likely as men to manifest depression has been amply documented in both clinical studies and community surveys. This evidence has been extensively reviewed by Brown and Harris (1978), Schwab et al. (1968), Silverman (1968), Taylor and Abrams (1981a), and Weissman and Klerman (1977, 1979). This two-to-one female-to-male sex ratio has been observed in most developed countries (Weissman & Klerman, 1979). Within the depressive category, the female-to-male ratio has been found to be higher for unipolar than for bipolar depression (Bland & Orn, 1982; Myers et al., 1984; Taylor & Abrams, 1981a; Weissman & Klerman, 1979; Winokur & Crowe, 1983).

Although women clearly display depression more frequently than men, a further question is whether, when they are depressed, men and women differ in the symptom pictures they display. In samples of nonclinical college students, Funabiki and colleagues (Chino & Funabiki, 1984; Funabiki et al., 1980) found that men reported an increase in smoking when depressed whereas women when they were depressed reported increased food intake, writing to express feelings, and seeking personal support from others. Hammen and Padesky (1977) found that depressed male college students reported inability to cry, loss of social interest, a sense of failure, and somatic complaints whereas the females reported indecisiveness and self-dislike. In contrast to the greater somatization found in males by Hammen and Padesky (1977), Schwab et al. (1968), in an examination of nonpsychiatric medical patients, found more somatic complaints among depressed women and greater personal despair among the men. A limitation in the research to date is that the studies have primarily examined responses on self-report inventories of nonclinical populations, generally college students (Blatt, D'Afflitti, & Quinlan, 1976; Chino & Funabiki, 1984; Funabiki et al., 1980; Hammen & Padesky, 1977). Research examining gender differences in actual symptoms manifested by depressed psychiatric patients is clearly needed.

In contrast to depression, sociopathy, personality disorders, and alcoholism are more frequently diagnosed in males than in females (Carlson, 1981; Dohrenwend & Dohrenwend, 1969; Gomberg, 1974, 1979; Henderson, Krupinski, & Stoller, 1971; Myers et al., 1984; Pitts & Winokur, 1966; Warner, 1978; Weiner & Del Gaudio, 1977). In passing, it should be noted that much of the controversy about whether the prevalence of psychiatric disorder is greater for women than for men or equal for both genders seems attributable to the different diagnoses they receive. When personality disorders have been excluded in defining mental illness, a higher prevalence of disorder has been found for women (Gove, 1979; Gove & Tudor, 1977; von Zerssen & Weyerer, 1982). When personality disorders and alcoholism have been included as categories of mental illness, the genders have not been found to differ in overall rate of psychiatric disorder (Dohrenwend & Dohrenwend, 1969, 1976; Leaf et al., 1984).

The diagnostic pattern whereby women more frequently display depression and men personality disorders and alcoholism is mirrored in findings concerning the symptom pictures of other diagnostic groups. In our developmental categorizations of symptomatology, the role orientation of self-deprivation and turning against the self reflects a depressive orientation and is found most frequently in depressed patients (Zigler & Phillips, 1961c). By contrast, symptoms in the self-indulgence and turning-against-others category are more characteristic of personality disorder patients (Zigler & Phillips, 1961c). This category includes the symptom drinking. A consistent finding in our work has been that within a variety of diagnostic groups women display more symptoms in the turning-against-the-self category than men.

In an examination of the case records of 1053 state hospital patients with various psychiatric diagnoses, Zigler and Phillips (1960) found that women were significantly more likely than men to display 7 of the 12 symptoms examined in the turning-against-the-self category. These symptoms were suicidal attempt, suicidal ideas, euphoria, doesn't eat, self-depreciatory, depressed, and mood swings. By contrast, of the 16 symptoms examined in the turning-against-others category, 6 (assaultive, threatens assault, drinking, accused of robbery, sexual perversions, and accused of rape) were significantly more frequent in men than women, whereas only 2 (maniacal outbursts and irresponsible behavior) were found more frequently in the female patients. Relatively few gender differences appeared with respect to symptoms in the third role orientation category, avoidance of others. Of the 7 symptoms analyzed in this category, women more frequently displayed 2 (perplexed and apathetic).

A similar pattern of greater turning against the self for women and more turning against others for men was found in schizophrenic patients (Zigler & Levine, 1983a). The case histories of 300 male and 300 female state hospital schizophrenic patients were utilized. All patients had a primary diagnosis of schizophrenia and no secondary diagnosis involving organicity, mental retardation, alcoholism, or drug abuse. The male and female samples each consisted of 150 paranoid and 150 nonparanoid patients. The distribution of diagnoses among the nonparanoid men was 99 chronic undifferentiated, 5 acute undifferentiated, 21 simple, 11 schizoaffective, 2 hebephrenic, and 12 catatonic. For the nonparanoid women the distribution was 102 chronic undifferentiated, 10 simple, 25 schizoaffective, 5 hebephrenic, 7 catatonic, and 1 other.

Analyses of variance revealed that female compared to male patients had higher turning-against-the-self symptom scores ($p < .01$) whereas the males obtained higher scores in the turning-against-others symptom category than did the females ($p < .001$). A greater frequency of symptom expression in thought rather than action was also found for female than for male patients

$(p < .001)$. Differences between the genders on each symptom examined were assessed by chi-square analyses. Of the five symptoms noted significantly more frequently for females, two (depressed, insomnia) reflect turning against the self. The other symptoms noted more frequently for women were suspiciousness and perplexed (reflecting expression in thought as well as avoidance of others) and maniacal outbursts (reflecting turning against others). Of the five symptoms found to be more frequent in men, two (irresponsible behavior and emotional outbursts) reflect turning against others while two (withdrawn and apathetic) are among the few symptoms in the avoidance-of-others category that do not also involve expression in thought. The final symptom found more frequently in men, euphoria, as is consistent with most thinking in psychopathology, reflects turning-against-the self. A further finding that among the nonparanoid schizophrenics women were more likely than men to be diagnosed schizoaffective again points to greater depressive overlay in the symptom pictures of female schizophrenic patients.

Other investigators have also reported more depressive symptomatology in female than in male schizophrenic patients (Loranger, 1984; Walker et al., 1985), and, conversely, more frequent alcohol abuse (Walker et al., 1985) and impulsive aggressive behavior (Salokangas, 1978) in male schizophrenic subsamples. Consistent with these differences in the symptom patterns of adult schizophrenics, impulsivity and unsocialized aggressiveness have been found to characterize male but not female preschizophrenic children and adolescents (John, Mednick, & Schulsinger, 1982; Watt & Lubensky, 1976; Watt et al., 1970; Weintraub, Neale, & Liebert, 1975; Weintraub, Prinz, & Neale, 1978). In all these investigations, the female preschizophrenics were more likely to display extreme introversion and anhedonia.

The greater overlay of depressive symptomatology in schizophrenic women renders their symptom pictures more "atypical" than those of schizophrenic men. Gender differences in the frequency of schizophrenia did not appear in earlier research utilizing DSM-I and DSM-II (Dohrenwend & Dohrenwend, 1976). However, the presence of major affective symptomatology constitutes an exclusion criterion for the diagnosis of schizophrenia in a number of recently developed research diagnostic systems, for example, Research Diagnostic Criteria (RDC) (Spitzer, Endicott, & Robins, 1978). Utilizing a number of these newer diagnostic systems, Lewine and his associates (Lewine, Burbach, & Meltzer, 1984; Lewine, Strauss, & Gift, 1981) found significantly more males than females in the schizophrenia category. Inasmuch as it is based upon one of the research systems examined (RDC), Lewine et al. (1984) postulate that DSM-III will also yield "an elevated male to female ratio" (p. 86). As these authors suggest, the very real possibility that with more stringent diagnostic criteria schizophrenia will be found to be more common in males than in females has broad implications for etiological theories about schizophrenia.

A final gender difference related to symptomatology in schizophrenia has been that females are diagnosed paranoid more frequently than males (Freedman, Kaplan, & Sadock, 1972; Hay & Forrest, 1972; Kay et al., 1976; Swanson et al., 1970).

Gender differences in the symptoms displayed by nonschizophrenic male and female patients were analyzed in connection with the Glick et al. (1985) study reviewed in Chapter 9. Examined in this study were the case records of first-admission state hospital patients with the following diagnoses: affective disorder (71 males, 75 females); neuroses (75 males, 70 females); and personality disorder (82 males, 75 females). Although the finding has not been previously reported, the nonschizophrenic women more frequently displayed symptoms indicative of turning against the self whereas the men displayed more symptoms indicative of turning against others ($p < .0005$). In addition, a Gender $\times$ Diagnosis interaction reflected very substantial gender differences within the personality disorder subgroup. Although as a group personality disorder patients displayed symptoms indicative of turning against others, the predominance of symptoms in this category was significantly greater for male than for female personality disorder patients.

In a variety of diagnostic groups, then, women have been found to display more depression and symptoms indicative of turning against the self, whereas men more frequently display action-oriented symptoms involving self-indulgence and turning against others. Possible explanations for the markedly higher rate of depression in women have been evaluated in many reviews (see Brown & Harris, 1978; Hammen & Padesky, 1977; Taylor & Abrams, 1981a; Weissman & Klerman, 1979; Weissman & Paykel, 1974). The higher rate of depression found in women appears to be a real phenomenon and not a reflection of biases in labeling, symptom reporting, or treatment seeking (Amenson & Lewinsohn, 1981; Weissman & Klerman, 1979). The gender differences in depression may in part reflect biological (genetic and neuroendocrinological) variables. In addition a variety of explanations focus on gender differences in social role and in socialization history. The traditional female role has been seen as providing less ego enhancement and more strains than the male role (Bart, 1974; Gove, 1979; Radloff, 1975). Relevant to both the greater depression in women and the presence of more symptoms indicative of turning against others, personality disorders, and alcoholism in men are arguments that women have been more severely socialized than men (Phillips, 1968a; Rosen, Klein, & Gittelman-Klein, 1969; Zigler & Levine, 1981b). In the socialization of females, acting-out behaviors are less countenanced and consideration of others more emphasized than is typical for males.

Within the developmental approach to psychopathology, the symptomatology displayed by women (self-deprivation and turning against the self) and the diagnoses they receive (depression, paranoid schizophrenia) are interpreted as reflecting developmentally higher functioning in comparison with the symptoms (self-indulgence and turning against others) and diagnoses (personality disorder, alcoholism, nonparanoid schizophrenia) observed more frequently in men. Why women should more frequently display symptoms and disorders associated with developmentally higher levels of functioning is unclear. A variety of biological and/or social factors discussed with respect to depression could contribute to this gender difference. However, the pattern of gender differences found with respect to diagnosis and symptomatology is mirrored also in findings that, at least with respect to schizophrenia, women obtain higher premorbid competence scores, are older on first hospitalization, and display better outcomes than men. In light of their consistency with the symptom differences just reported, these findings will be presented before reasons underlying the developmentally higher functioning of female patients are further considered.

Gender Differences in Premorbid Competence and in the Course and Outcome of Disorder

Prognosis can be conceptualized as including the age of onset of disorder or age upon first hospital admission as well as outcome following treatment (see Chapter 9). Premorbid competence scores have been found to be related to each of these prognostic variables. This section will first present gender differences discovered with respect to premorbid competence, age of onset of disorder, and outcome. Following this, possible explanations for the gender differences will be considered.

Findings

PREMORBID COMPETENCE.   A highly consistent finding in schizophrenia research has been that, across a variety of premorbid competence measures, women display a more adequate adjustment than men (DeWolfe, 1973; Farina et al., 1963; Farina et al., 1962; Gittelman-Klein & Klein, 1968; Goldstein, 1978; Klorman et al., 1977; Lane, 1968; Lewine, 1981; Raskin & Golob, 1966; Rosen, Klein, & Gittelman-Klein, 1969; Salokangas, 1983; Zigler & Levine, 1981b, 1983a). In addition, greater premorbid intellectual deficits (Aylward, Walker, & Bettes, 1984) and poorer childhood scholastic competence (Lewine, Watt, & Fryer, 1978) have been found for schizophrenic males compared to females. Some evidence has also been presented that, in naturalistic samples of patients with various diagnoses (schizophrenia, affective disorder, neurotic, personality disorder) selected with no gender restrictions, women obtain higher premorbid competence scores than men (Lewine et al., 1980; Phillips & Zigler, 1964). However, Glick et al. (1985) examined the premorbid competence scores of nonschizophrenic patients in a sample comprising comparable numbers of males and females within each of three diagnostic groups (71 male and 75 female affective disorder, 75 male and 70 female neurotic, and 82 male and 75 female personality disorder patients). In this study, the main effect for gender on premorbid competence scores was not significant.

AGE OF ONSET OF DISORDER AND UPON FIRST HOSPITAL ADMISSION. A highly consistent finding has been that schizophrenic men are considerably younger than schizophrenic women both at onset of disorder and upon first hospital admission. This gender difference in schizophrenia has been observed across cultures and at different historical periods. Lewine (1981) and Seeman (1982) provide extensive reviews of these data. A finding by Zigler and Levine (1981a) that male schizophrenic patients were approximately 5 years younger on first hospitalization than female schizophrenics was replicated by Loranger (1984) with respect to each of three indexes of onset: age at first treatment, age at first hospitalization, and age at which family members first became aware of psychotic symptomatology. The time of onset for males tends to be in the early twenties, whereas onset for females is more likely to occur in the middle or late twenties.

Comparable gender differences in age of onset of disorder or upon first hospitalization have not been found within other specific diagnostic groups, that is, manic-depressive, paranoid psychosis, affective disorder, neurotic, or personality disorder patients (Glick et al., 1985; Lewine, 1980; Lewine et al., 1981; Loranger & Levine, 1978; McCabe, 1975). The possibility does exist, however, that, within a heterogeneous group of nonschizophrenic patients with various diagnoses (e.g., affective disorder, personality disorder) selected with no gender restrictions, women overall would be found to display a later onset of disorder and to be older upon first hospital admission than men. This possibility is supported by findings that personality disorder patients, who tend to be predominantly male, tend also to be young, whereas affective disorder patients, who more frequently are female, tend to be older on first hospital admission than other diagnostic groups (Glick et al., 1985). In a naturalistic sample including patients with both these diagnoses, women overall would be expected to be older on first hospitalization.

OUTCOME OF DISORDER. A considerable body of data now suggests that schizophrenic males display poorer outcomes than schizophrenic females (Affleck, Burns, & Forrest, 1976; Beck, 1978; Hogarty et al., 1974; Huber et al., 1980; Lewine, 1981; Nyman, 1978; Salokangas, 1983; Sartorius et al., 1978; Seeman, 1982). These studies have employed prospective as well as retrospective designs, and gender differences have been reported with respect to each of the following outcome criteria: length of hospitalization and rehospitalizations; rate of relapse; social adjustment; work adjustment; and response to neuroleptics. Little research has examined gender differences in outcome for nonschizophrenic patients. Kirshner and Johnston (1983) reported that in a sample of patients with various diagnoses including neuroses, personality disorder and psychotic disorders (schizophrenia, psychotic depression) women showed greater improvement during hospitalization than men. However, it was particularly in the psychotic category that women showed greater improvement than men. Since this category included schizophrenics, it is possible that the greater improvement found for women across diagnostic groups may have primarily reflected a better outcome of schizophrenic women than men.

Interpretation of the Gender Differences

The findings are certainly consistent with the view that a higher developmental level of functioning more frequently characterizes female than male patients, at least within the schizophrenia category. The developmentally higher functioning of the females is reflected not only in premorbid competence scores but in symptom pictures that evince greater turning against the self and more paranoid coloration. The greater coping resources available at higher developmental levels should lead to better prognoses as evidenced by a later onset of disorder and a better outcome after the disorder becomes manifest.

Little research has examined gender differences within specific nonschizophrenic diagnostic groups (e.g., affective disorder, personality disorder). However, in the work thus far, males and females within specific nonschizophrenic diagnostic groups have not been found to differ in premorbid competence scores, age of onset of disorder, or age of first hospitalization. The issue of gender differences within various nonschizophrenic (e.g., affective disorder, anxiety disorder, personality disorder) diagnostic groups requires far greater research attention. One possibility is that fewer gender differences in premorbid competence or prognosis will appear within these groups because the symptom differences that define the diagnoses render patients within these groups relatively homogeneous with respect to developmental level. Thus, for example, while female affective disorder patients may outnumber males, males and females in this category may be similar in developmental level. The gender differences found with schizophrenic patients in premorbid competence, age of onset, and outcome of disorder may reflect the heterogeneity of individuals encompassed by that diagnostic category. This possibility generates the expectation that within subgroups of schizophrenic patients that are more homogeneous with respect to developmental level (as assessed by premorbid competence or developmental differences in symptomatology) males and females would not differ in age on first hospitalization or outcome.

While the gender differences discovered in schizophrenia can be interpreted as reflecting developmentally higher functioning in female patients, why females function at higher levels remains unclear. The basic principles of developmental theory do not address the issue of gender difference. With respect to schizophrenia, a number of interpretations have been advanced to account for the higher premorbid competence, later onset, and better outcome of female patients—variables that we interpret as reflecting developmentally higher functioning. These various interpretations have been carefully reviewed by Lewine (1981), Loranger (1984), Seeman (1982), and Zigler and Levine (1981a). One class of explanations involves biological factors that may either render female schizophrenic patients less vulnerable to disorder than males or provide greater protection to females. These biological explanations include possibilities that: (a) males may be more vulnerable than females either to schizophrenia or to stress more generally (Lewine, 1980, 1981; Seeman, 1982); (b) males and females may be differentially susceptible to different forms of schizophrenia with males more frequently manifesting a subtype characterized by poor premorbid competence, early onset, and typical rather than atypical schizophrenic symptoms (Lewine, 1981; Loranger, 1984; Seeman, 1982); and (c) certain biological characteristics may protect women against schizophrenia. Protective factors that have been considered are estrogens, which may exert an antidopaminergic effect (Loranger, 1984; Seeman, 1982), and greater cerebral bilaterality in women. As Seeman (1982) indicated, some evidence has been presented that schizophrenia is a left hemisphere disorder and that women, at least with regard to language functions, display greater bilaterality or less left hemispheric specialization than men. Less specialization in the left hemisphere may thus have a protective effect against schizophrenic disorder for women.

As was the case with symptomatology, the different socialization experiences of males and females can account for gender differences in premorbid competence.[1] Social interaction and academic work functioning comprise major variables on the Zigler-Phillips index and other measures of premorbid competence. These variables appear to be sensitive to the fulfillment of societal expectations by the individual. Women in our society may be subjected to far greater pressure for social conformity than men. These differences in socialization may be such that even when suffering from major disorder women display less disorganization and give evidence of better social adjustment than men. The higher premorbid competence of many female patients would in turn lead to differences in age of onset and first hospitalization and in outcome.

The earlier onset of schizophrenia in males could also reflect differences in the point in the life cycle where the two genders encounter particular life stressors capable of precipitating psychological disorder. In our society, late adolescence and early adulthood are critical and demanding periods for both sexes. During this time, young men and women both face strong societal expectations to form intimate attachments with members of the opposite sex and to obtain employment (or to engage in higher-level and thus more demanding educational efforts) in order to become autonomous and contributing members of our society. In light of the sex role traditions in our society, the pressure to meet these societal expectations may nevertheless be greater for young men than for young women. This possibility that psychosocial stressors may impinge earlier on males was discussed in Chapter 9 and has been considered also by Lewine (1980, 1981), Loranger (1984), Seeman (1982), and Zigler and Levine (1981a). By interfering with the performance of life tasks at a younger age, an earlier onset of disorder can lead to lower premorbid competence scores inasmuch as the individual is less likely to marry or to achieve occupational success or employment regularity.

These alternative explanations for the higher premorbid competence and better prognoses of female schizophrenic patients are not mutually exclusive. Indeed, as Sroufe and Rutter (1984) argued, the developmental perspective provides a framework for integrating biological with psychological and social influences.

Gender Differences: Summary and Conclusions

With respect to schizophrenia, a highly consistent body of evidence points to a generally higher developmental level of functioning in women than in men. This evidence includes gender differences in: (a) symptomatology; (b) the schizophrenia subtype diagnoses men or women receive; (c) premorbid competence scores; (d) age of onset and of first hospitalization; and (e) outcome. Some evidence has been presented that, within diagnostically heterogeneous nonschizophrenic samples selected with no gender restrictions, women display symptom pictures that reflect developmentally higher functioning and obtain higher premorbid competence scores than men. Epidemiological and clinical findings that women display depressive disorders more than men while men are more frequently diagnosed as personality disorder or alcoholic are certainly consistent with the view that women's symptomatology can be characterized as developmentally higher (reflecting turning against the self) than those symptoms (involving self-indulgence and turning against others) more frequently displayed by men. As discussed earlier in this section, given the typical ages and genders of affective disorder and personality disorder patients, it seems quite likely that, in a diagnostically heterogeneous sample selected with no gender restrictions, women would be found overall to be first hospitalized at an older age than men. While the number of studies is limited, to date, no evidence has suggested that within specific nonschizophrenic diagnostic groups (e.g., affective disorder or personality disorder) men and women differ in premorbid competence or age upon first hospitalization. Some evidence has pointed to gender differences in symptomatology within specific diagnostic groups and especially with regard to the personality disorder category. Gender differences in outcome for nonschizophrenic patients have seldom been examined.

An important area for further research concerns gender differences in nonschizophrenic patients on all these variables. Such research has major relevance for our work on the developmental approach to psychopathology. The emphasis in our work up to this time has been on common principles and characteristics that apply across diagnostic groups. Commonalities across diagnostic groups were emphasized because the utility of the developmental-level construct is presumed not to be limited to particular disorders but to extend to a broad range of adaptive and maladatpive forms of functioning. The research presented in this book has demonstrated the utility of this developmental approach. Nevertheless, the individual's developmental level represents only one of a number of factors that should influence manifestations of psychopathology. Other major classes of variables presumed to influence psychopathology are biological factors, including specific vulnerabilities to particular disorders, and a variety of environmental and experiential factors. Some of these variables should be specific to particular disorders. Others would, like the developmental-level construct, be expected to influence behavior more generally. The differentiation of those relationships that appear only with respect to certain disorders from those that appear across a broad spectrum of diagnostic categories can help to illuminate underlying processes. If a relationship (e.g., between gender and age of onset) were found to hold only for a particular disorder, further research would focus on underlying variables related to specific characteristics of that disorder. Such variables might be biological but could be social or environmental as well. If, for example, women were found to be older at onset of disorder only within the schizophrenia category, explanations specific to characteristics of that diagnostic group would include the possible antidopaminergic effect of estrogen and also the possibility that major stressors may occur in late adolescence, and the early twenties for men but in the mid-twenties for women. By contrast, if gender differences were found to appear across a spectrum of disorders, attention would be directed toward processes applicable to many types of individuals. Differences in the socialization histories of males and females would, for example, be expected to relate to gender differences across a variety of disorders.

The possibility that gender differences may be found in heterogeneous patient groups (e.g., schizophrenics with a range of subtype diagnoses or nonschizophrenic samples including patients with many different diagnoses) but not within more homogeneous groups (e.g., high social competence schizophrenics or affective disorder patients) was discussed previously. If this possibility is substantiated in further research, the higher developmental scores of women would seem to constitute a general pattern in psychopathology even though it might not be found in homogeneous patient groups. Alternative explanations for the developmentally higher status of women with respect to premorbid competence and developmental categorizations of symptomatology include broad biological differences between the genders as well as differences in the socialization histories and social role expectations for males and females. Men and women are biologically different. It is possible that the general organismic maturation rates of men and women differ and that gender differences in psychopathology might reflect the same biological factors that underlie the well-documented gender differences in vulnerability to prenatal complications and in the length of the life span.

An explanation with considerable appeal to us concerns sex differences in socialization and social role expectations. Females in our culture are more severely socialized than males, and social skills, social interaction, and caring for others are more prominently stressed in the social role definitions of women than in those of men. Traditionally, the expressive role has been stressed for women, whereas instrumental role functioning has been emphasized for men. To the degree that such socialization differences influence behavior, as they certainly must, and if further research on gender differences in psychopathology continues to uncover a general pattern of higher developmental scores for women, an interesting implication can be drawn. Societal efforts have been directed toward socializing boys and girls more similarly and toward defining male and female roles more androgynously. Often, this effort has emphasized or even implicitly favored characteristics of the male social role (e.g., playing with trucks and construction toys, participation in competitive team sports, certain aspects of adult business demeanor). The pattern of gender differences discovered in psychopathology may argue for a different emphasis. Rather than socializing females and defining their social roles in ways traditionally considered to be more masculine, greater emphasis might be given to socializing and defining male roles in a more traditionally female manner.

SOCIAL CLASS DIFFERENCES IN PSYCHOPATHOLOGY

An issue that has been raised in regard to the developmental approach to psychopathology is whether the predictive value of premorbid competence and also developmental categorizations of symptomatalogy derives solely or primarily from the overlap of these variables with socioeconomic status (SES) (Nuttall & Solomon, 1965, 1970; Raskin & Golob, 1966; Turner & Zabo, 1968; Zigler & Child, 1973). Education and occupational status (traditional indexes of SES) comprise two variables in the Zigler-Phillips premorbid competence measure. In addition, Phillips (1968a) and Zigler (1970b) have discussed a general pattern in our culture whereby expression in direct action and aggression turned outward may be more characteristic in lower SES groups, whereas turning against the self and an orientation toward expression in thought may more frequently characterize middle-class individuals. We are thus confronted with competing interpretations for the data presented in this book. One interpretation postulates that social class status is primarily responsible for the relationships discovered between premorbid competence, symptomatology, and outcome. The other interpretation is our view that differences in developmental level mediate the relationships discovered between premorbid competence and many major variables of interest in psychopathology.

The social class variable by its very nature is more conducive to sociological than to psychological analysis. The emphasis for the sociologist is on social forces external to the individual. When a psychologist is confronted with evidence that a sociological variable (e.g., social class or a particular dwelling zone within a city) is related to a psychological variable (e.g., a particular form of mental disorder), the psychologist does not feel that the relationship has been explained until the sociological variable is conceptualized as a set of psychological events that could cause the behavior being examined. The psychologist's concern is with uncovering social–psychological concomitants of sociological variables that are advanced as psychological mechanisms mediating the relationship between social status variables and resultant psychological events. A discovered relationship between social class and behavior is itself likely to be neutral with respect to directing the psychologist to particular social–psychological processes mediating it. Relationships established on the social level leave open a broad spectrum of possible mediating processes. As Dohrenwend and Dohrenwend (1965) expressed it, the data concerning social class differences in psychopathology provide "an important source of working hypotheses" (p. 63).

This section will first review relationships discovered between SES and such major variables of interest in psychopathology as prevalence of disorder, diagnosis, and premorbid competence. The implications of these findings will then be considered both with respect to our developmental formulation and more generally as a source of hypotheses whereby psychological variables important to the understanding of psychopathology can be discerned.

Research Findings

Studies with patient samples and surveys of the general population have both revealed an inverse relationship between social class status and psychiatric impairment (Dohrenwend & Dohrenwend, 1965, 1974; Hollingshead & Redlich, 1958; Leaf et al., 1984; Rose, 1955; Srole et al., 1962). Strongly influencing this relationship has been the particularly high rate of disturbance found in the lowest social class (Dohrenwend & Dohrenwend, 1965; Hollingshead & Redlich, 1958; Strauss, Kokes, Ritzler, Harder, & Van Ord, 1978).

This general relationship between SES and psychopathology is tempered, however, when particular diagnostic groups are examined. Consistent with the inverse relationship found overall, schizophrenia is heavily concentrated in lower-class groups, particularly the lowest social class (Beck, 1978; Dohrenwend & Dohrenwend, 1974; Dunham, 1976; Hollingshead & Redlich, 1958; King, 1978; Kohn, 1973; Strauss & Carpenter, 1981). Far less consistent relationships between social class and the presence of psychopathology have been found for other diagnostic groups. Strauss (1979) thus concluded that "most types of psychiatric disorder apparently are not related to social class level. Schizophrenia may be an important exception" (p. 399). Some evidence has suggested that personality disorder patients are more frequently of low social class status (Dohrenwend & Dohrenwend, 1974). However, Birtchnell (1971), reporting on a very large sample of male patients, uncovered a more complex pattern. While alcoholic and personality disorder patients were found more frequently in low SES groups, such patients differed from psychotics in that they were as likely to be members of the higher social classes (I and II) as were individuals in the general population. Neurotic patients overall have not been found to differ from the general population in social class distribution (Birtchnell, 1971; Dohrenwend & Dohrenwend, 1974), while neurotic depression is more frequently diagnosed in the upper social classes (Hollingshead & Redlich, 1958; Liem & Liem, 1978; Schwab et al., 1968).

Findings regarding the social class status of depressed individuals have been conflicting. A number of investigators have reported that depressed patients are higher ranking and more heterogeneous in social class status than are schizophrenic patients (Becker, 1974; Dunham, 1976; Kendler, 1982; Schwab et al., 1968) or that affective disorder diagnoses have not been found to be related to social class (Dohrenwend & Dohrenwend, 1974; Strauss, 1979). In a number of instances and particularly with respect to bipolar or manic-depressive disorder, a greater frequency of depression has been associated with higher social class levels (Hollingshead & Redlich, 1958; Schwab et al., 1968). However, other studies have found more frequent depression in lower rather than higher social class groups (Comstock & Helsing, 1976; Dohrenwend, 1975; Husaini & Neff, 1981; Srole et al., 1962; Warheit, Holzer, & Schwab, 1973).

Weissman and Myers (1978) provide data that may help to reconcile the disparate findings. They found that current rates of minor depression were higher in lower social class persons whereas bipolar disorders were highest at upper-class levels. As Weissman and Myers (1978) suggest, the relation to social class may vary with the type of depression considered. Consistent with this position, Schwab et al. (1968) reported that, whereas the depressive symptoms of lower-class individuals involved a sense of futility that can be seen as an exaggeration of the general characteristics and conditions of lower-class status, middle-class individuals displayed more typical depressive symptomatology. In line with the greater sense of futility noted by Schwab et al. (1968), more fatalism (Ross, Mirowsky, & Cockerham, 1983) and a more external locus of control (Husaini & Neff, 1981) have been found to characterize depression in lower- as compared with middle-class individuals. Methods for assessing depression may be differentially sensitive to modes of depressive expression in the different social classes. In studies using symptom rating scales (e.g., the Beck Depression Inventory), depression tends to be found more frequently in lower social class individuals (Schwab et al., 1968; Weissman & Myers, 1978). By contrast, when actual psychiatric diagnosis is utilized, including the use of semistructured research diagnostic instruments, higher rates of depression are found in middle- than lower-class individuals (Schwab et al., 1968; Weissman & Myers, 1978). As Schwab et al. (1968) noted, the major symptom scales (e.g., the Beck Depression Inventory and the Hamilton Rating Scale) were developed in work with lower-class patients. They may thus be more sensitive to manifestations of depression in such individuals. By contrast, the higher rates of diagnosed major depression in middle- and upper-class individuals may reflect the more typical depressive symptomatology displayed by such persons. In Chapter 4, we discussed the need for more fine-grained measures of developmental level in depressive symptomatology. The finding that individuals in different social classes differ in the depressive symptomatology they display underscores this need for more fine-grained analyses of symptom expression. Depression is common in human experience. Methods are needed for distinguishing the various ways this broad emotion is expressed and experienced by different groups.

The greater frequency of major affective disorder diagnoses in middle- and upper-class individuals could also reflect clinicians' biases. Physicians, being middle- and upper-class themselves, may more readily recognize depression in these social class groups as compared with lower-class individuals. However, Weissman and Myers (1978) found higher lifetime rates of depression for upper-class as compared with lower-class individuals in a community survey utilizing a semistructured research diagnostic instrument, the Schedule for Affective Disorders and Schizophrenia—Diagnostic Research Criteria (SADS-RDC) (Spitzer, Endicott, & Robins, 1975). Such data suggest that the higher rates of diagnosed depression in upper-class individuals may reflect more than biases of diagnosticians and may indicate actual differences in the symptom pictures displayed by upper- and lower-class individuals. A major contribution of the research diagnostic instruments has been the increase of reliability accomplished through the use of explicit criteria that minimize subjective judgment by the diagnostician (see Chapter 5). Finally, the relation between social class and depression may vary as a function of the time period assessed. Weissman and Myers (1978) found lifetime rates of major depression to be higher in the upper social classes whereas current rates of major depression, while not strongly related to social class, tended to be higher for low SES individuals. These authors suggest that the difference between current and lifetime rates may reflect the better access to treatment of upper-class individuals.

In summary, then, more psychiatric impairment has been found in lower as compared with upper social classes. However, different disorders appear to be differentially related to social class. The strongest relationship has been found between schizophrenia and low social class status, especially membership in the lowest social class. Personality disorders are prevalent in the lowest social class but are found at expected rates of frequency in upper-class individuals also. Neuroses have generally not been found to be related to social class, and some evidence suggests that neurotic depression may be more frequent in upper- than lower-class individuals. The findings regarding depression are inconsistent. Nevertheless, the psychiatric syndrome of depression has not been found to be associated with lower-class status to the degree found with schizophrenia. Further, some evidence suggests that diagnoses of major depression may be more common in upper- than lower-class individuals at least when lifetime rates are considered. (Minor depressions, assessed utilizing symptom rating scales, may, by contrast, be more common in lower classes.) These relationships between social class and diagnosis are somewhat similar to the premorbid competence–diagnosis relationships discussed in Chapter 5. Schizophrenic and personality disorder patients obtain low premorbid competence scores, whereas the scores of neurotic and particularly affective disorder patients are significantly higher. The question arises, then, as to whether the differences in diagnosis and also symptomatology (e.g., turning against the self versus turning against others) that we have interpreted as reflecting differences in developmental level might be explained more simply as correlates of social class status. In order to evaluate this possibility, the meaning of social class membership will be examined more closely. First, however, the findings presented in Chapter 3 concerning relationships between premorbid competence scores and social class status will be briefly summarized.

Findings concerning the relationship between premorbid adjustment (or the process–reactive distinction) in schizophrenia and socioeconomic status have been inconsistent. Lower SES has been found to be related to higher (Chapman & Baxter, 1963) and lower (Allon, 1971) premorbid adjustment scores. In other studies (McCreary, 1974; Raskin & Golob, 1966), no significant relationships appeared between premorbid competence and SES. The Zigler-Phillips social competence index includes educational and occupational attainment (traditional gauges of SES) as social competence variables. The question, therefore, is not whether this index overlaps with SES but whether the relationships discovered between premorbid competence and other variables of interest in psychopathology primarily reflect this overlap of the premorbid competence measure with SES. The factor-analytic findings reported in Chapter 3 suggest that this is not the case. More compatible with the data is the position that the premorbid competence measure, while including a factor of social class, is broader than SES.

Interpretation of Social Class Differences

In disentangling the complex relationships that have been discovered between social class status and psychopathology, one important issue is the degree to which the low SES of some psychiatric patients represents a consequence rather than a cause of disorder. If the individual's psychiatric disorder (or low competence) leads to downward social mobility, the person's low SES can be interpreted as reflecting social selection. Alternatively, the social causation position presumes that the conditions of lower-class life cause higher prevalences of disorder. Studies comparing the social class status of patients with that of their fathers have provided evidence for downward social mobility in low (process) but not in high (reactive) premorbid competence schizophrenic patients (McCreary, 1974) and more generally for schizophrenic and personality disorder patients in comparison to other diagnostic groups (Birtchnell, 1971; Dohrenwend & Dohrenwend, 1974; Dunham, 1976; Goldberg & Morrison, 1963; Wing, 1978; Wiersma et al., 1983).

Dunham concluded that his evidence supports "the proposition that schizophrenia accounts for one's class position rather than the class position accounting for schizophrenia" (p. 152). In contrast to this view, the data of Hollingshead and Redlich (1958) supported a social causation rather than a social selection position regarding schizophrenia. More commonly, workers have concluded that both social selection and social causation may contribute to the higher rates particularly of schizophrenia in lower-class individuals (Clausen & Kohn, 1959; Dohrenwend & Dohrenwend, 1965; Srole et al., 1962; Wing, 1978). Evidence of such downward mobility has been less evident for depressive patients (Dohrenwend & Dohrenwend, 1974; Wing, 1980) and has not been found for neurotic patients (Birtchnell, 1971; Goldberg & Morrison, 1963).

While social selection appears to provide only a partial explanation for the low social class status of many psychiatric patients, it is important to note that downward social mobility has been observed for those groups that in our research have been characterized by low premorbid competence scores (process schizophrenics and personality disorder patients) and has seldom been found for patients characterized by higher premorbid competence scores (reactive schizophrenics, neurotic, and affective disorder patients). The downward social mobility observed primarily in low premorbid competence groups suggests that social class of origin cannot alone account for the poor social attainments of these groups. As Zigler and Child (1969) suggested, one test of the social class versus the developmental argument would be to examine whether the magnitude of relationships to other variables (in this instance diagnosis, symptomatology, outcome, etc.) is strengthened or weakened when social class measures are substituted for developmental indexes. Because of the issue of downward social mobility due to psychiatric impairment or lower social competence, paternal or parental SES appears to be more appropriate than the patient's own SES as an indicator of social class influence (Klorman et al., 1977). Further research should thus be directed toward (a) the examination of relations between patients' premorbid competence scores and parental SES and (b) comparisons of the efficacy of premorbid competence scores versus assessments of parental SES as predictors of such criterion variables as symptomatology, paranoid–nonparanoid status in schizophrenia, age on first hospitalization, psychiatric outcome, and self-image disparity.

Going beyond the specific relevance of social class to issues in our own work, relationships discovered between social class status and variables in psychopathology seem best regarded as sources of working hypotheses (Dohrenwend & Dohrenwend, 1965). Social class needs to be reduced to a set of psychological events if it is to be meaningful for psychological research on mental disorder (Zigler & Child, 1969). This need has been variously described by many researchers. Strauss (1979) emphasized the need to "bridge the gap" by constructing "specific links between sociocultural phenomena and psychopathology" (p. 398) as manifested in the individual patient. Brown and Harris (1978) cautioned that "we require not better measures of social class but better theory about the reasons for results obtained by the use of measures we have" (p. 158). The question is what mediates the relationships observed between social class status and variables of interest in psychopathology. Numerous mediating factors have been proposed particularly in relation to the influence of social class status on schizophrenia. Mediating variables proposed include (a) social class differences in family communication style (Strauss, 1979); (b) more frequent rejection in the childhood histories of low SES individuals (King, 1978); (c) greater genetic vulnerability to schizophrenia especially in the lowest social class (Strauss, 1979; Zigler, 1970a); (d) social class differences in coping style, locus of control, and learned helplessness (Billings, Cronkite, & Moos, 1983; Husaini & Neff, 1981; Kohn, 1973; Liem & Liem, 1978; Strauss, 1979; Strauss & Carpenter, 1981); (e) more stressful and undesirable events in the lives of lower-class people (Myers et al., 1974; Strauss, 1979); and (f) fewer social supports and more disruption in the social networks of lower-class individuals (Billings et al., 1983; Strauss, 1979; Zubin & Steinhauer, 1981).

Variables involving coping effectiveness have been cited frequently as mediating the relationship between social class and psychopathology. The coping styles of lower-class individuals have been found to involve more avoidance responses and less active problem solving (Billings et al., 1983), more fatalism and an external locus of control (Husaini & Neff, 1981), and a conformist orientation (Kohn, 1973). By contrast, these various investigators found more active problem-solving strategies, a more internally oriented locus of control, and a self-directed orientation in middle-class subjects. While the circumstances of lower-class life should contribute substantially to a greater passivity, fatalism, and sense of helplessness, such an orientation impedes the ability to handle problems and stressful circumstances effectively. Husaini and Neff (1981) did not uncover a significant relationship between social class and number of stressful life events. In fact, their higher SES subjects tended to report more stressful life events. Based on their data, Husaini and Neff suggested that "social class differences in impairment may arise from the coping styles of certain social classes (as measured by locus of control) rather than from the differential prevalence of [stressful] life events" (p. 638). Other investigators have found either more stressors (Billings et al., 1983) or more negative or severe stressful events (Billings et al., 1983; Myers et al., 1974) in the lives of lower SES individuals. The reader need not choose between greater stress and less effective coping as factors contributing to the high rate of certain disorders in low SES individuals. As Kohn (1973) noted with respect to schizophrenia, less effective coping mechanisms, higher levels of genetic vulnerability, and more stressors combine to place low SES individuals at "triple jeopardy" (p. 74). Whether coping effectiveness is conceptualized as a consequence of social class status, a cause of the status due to downward (and upward) social mobility, or a variable to be examined in its own right independent of social class, the findings reviewed underscore the importance of competence for the understanding of psychopathology.

Social supports seem also inextricably bound to differences in competence or coping effectiveness. Myers, Lindenthal, and Pepper (1975), for example, found that individuals who reported few stressful events but nevertheless displayed high levels of symptomatology were more likely to be of lower-class status, unmarried, and dissatisfied with their jobs. By contrast, other subjects reported many stressful events but displayed few symptoms. These individuals tended to be of higher social class status, married, and satisfied with their jobs or housekeeping roles. Myers et al. (1975) interpret their results as indicating that social supports (marriage and job satisfaction) buffer the effects of stress in precipitating psychiatric impairment. While marriage and job satisfaction can be seen as major sources of social support, they can also be interpreted as indicators of the individual's competence in social functioning. Under most circumstances, more competent individuals construct lives that provide greater social support in terms of intimate relationships and job satisfaction. Such supports certainly strengthen the individual's ability to deal with stress. As with other issues concerning social class, the distinction of cause from consequence becomes difficult.

These alternative mediating variables are not mutually exclusive. Our assumption is that individuals are active agents who continually influence and are influenced by a constantly changing environment. Continual environmental change is due both to actual alterations in external circumstances and to changes in the individual's perception of and manner of coping with these circumstances. In order to understand how so broad a construct as social class influences the behavior of individuals, research must examine the manner in which specific correlates of social class influence people with particular characteristics at specific points in time. Intensive longitudinal research involving the close examination of small numbers of subjects has thus been recommended (King, 1978; Strauss, 1979). The benefit of such close scrutiny of person–environment interactions for the understanding of social class influences on psychopathology is exemplified in the work of Brown and Harris (1978). Overall these authors found more depression in working-class than in middle-class women. However, a closer examination of particular environmental circumstances revealed that the social class difference primarily reflected the very high rates of depression in one group of working-class women compared to all other groups. This group comprised working-class women with three or more children 14 years old and younger living at home.

Social Class Differences: Summary

An inverse relationship between social class status and psychopathology has been found for some disorders (e.g., schizophrenia) but not for others (e.g., neuroses). By and large, this inverse relationship to social class has been most strongly evident for disorders that are associated also with lower premorbid competence scores. Regarding the relationship of our premorbid competence measure to social class status, data suggest that while this measure includes a factor of social class it is broader than SES.

For those disorders found to be related to social class status, the issue is what mediates this relationship. Evidence of downward social mobility has been found primarily for diagnostic groups whose members also tend to obtain lower premorbid competence scores. One variable that may mediate the relationship between social class status and psychiatric impairment is coping style that has been found to differ across social class groups. Coping effectiveness may well be positively related to the degree of social support available to the individual. Given the position that individuals actively structure as well as react to environmental circumstances, a continuous and complex interaction between a variety of characteristics of the individual and particular and changing environmental conditions must be envisioned. Intensive longitudinal research may be required to uncover the particular combinations of variables that may account for relations between social class and psychopathology in specific groups of people.

REFERENCE NOTE

1. Other explanations for the higher premorbid competence scores of women were examined in Chapter 3. Since marital status is a major variable on most premorbid competence measures, one possibility is that being married requires higher competence for men than for women. Because this explanation was not supported by other data presented in Chapter 3, it is not considered here. Another possibility is that the manner in which occupation was scored on the original Zigler-Phillips index favored women because clerical and sales positions were assigned to the highest category. While this argument may pertain to the Zigler-Phillips index, it does not explain findings obtained with other premorbid competence measures. Neither can this argument account for the later age of initial hospitalization and the more favorable outcomes for schizophrenic women as compared with men. Thus this measurement issue, while important, is not considered here.

CHAPTER 12

Summary of the Work
and Directions
for Further Research

The developmental approach to psychopathology represents an effort to apply the principles of developmental theory to a wide range of phenomena in adult psychopathology. The theoretical underpinnings of this approach derive principally from Werner's organismic–developmental theory (Werner, 1948, 1957; Werner & Kaplan, 1963) although the work has been influenced by other developmental theorists as well. We conceptualize developmental level as a very broad construct presumed to mediate all behavior. The developmental-level construct is presumed to be as applicable to adult as to childhood functioning and to pertain equally to adaptive and maladaptive behavior. Consistent with the organismic–developmental position, we view the individual as an organized entity whose behavior and development can be understood only on the basis of organizational constructs and as an active agent who mediates and constructs as well as reacts to experiences. Development is viewed as a positive process involving the emergence of even greater adaptive abilities.

Our position assumes that there is a process of growth underlying psychological functioning. Even in adulthood, individuals can be viewed as functioning at different levels along an underlying developmental continuum. Rather than conceptualizing psychopathology as entailing regression in the sense of a backward movement to earlier developmental levels, we believe that individuals, after they have been designated "psychopathological," continue to maintain a position along the developmental continuum that is similar to the one that characterized their premorbid functioning. Like adaptive behavior, then, manifestations of psychopathology should reflect underlying differences in the individual's developmental level.

The designation of developmental levels in adult functioning has been a persistent problem. The dramatic changes in cognitive organization that characterize development from infancy into adolescence have not been found in adulthood. Thus cognitive indicators of developmental level have only limited applicability for adults. In delineating adult life stages, a number of workers have concentrated on changes in external circumstances that necessitate readaptations at successive points in the adult life cycle (the designation of successive adult life tasks). In contrast to this approach, our primary concern is with internal changes in the manner in which individuals structure and cope with experience. At the outset of the work, Zigler and Phillips (1960) felt that the developmental-level construct was too broad and contained too many facets to permit a direct, simple, and practical single measure. Instead they chose to measure the individual's premorbid social competence, which was conceptualized as a broad though imperfect benchmark of maturity level. This premorbid competence measure has been found to be positively correlated with Rorschach developmental-level scores and with maturity in moral reasoning as assessed by Kohlberg's test (Lerner, 1968; Quinlan et al., 1980).

Categorizations of symptomatology based on developmental principles have also been employed to indicate developmental level. One categorization involves the classification of symptoms as indicative of three role orientations: (a) self-deprivation and turning against the self; (b) self-indulgence and turning against others; and (c) avoidance of others. Inasmuch as it implies the introjection of societal standards and greater social guilt, the role orientation of turning against the self is conceptualized as representing a developmentally higher form than the other two role orientations. The second type of symptom categorization distinguishes symptoms involving expression in action from those involving expression in thought. This mode of symptom classification derives from the fundamental assumption in developmental thought that developmentally lower functioning is marked by immediate, direct, and unmodulated responses to external stimuli and internal need states whereas higher levels of development are characterized by the appearance of indirect, ideational, conceptual, and symbolic or verbal behavior patterns. Because of the consistency of the findings concerning developmental differences in self-image disparity, the magnitude of the disparity between real and ideal self-images can now be considered a third type of indicator of developmental level. Greater real–ideal self-image disparity is construed as developmentally higher because it involves (a) greater differentiation between aspects of the self-concept; and (b) a greater internalization of societal standards. The convergence of relationships discovered using each of these measures argues for their validity as indicators of the broad developmental-level construct.

SUMMARY OF THE RESEARCH

Our research utilizing these measures has extended to many major variables in psychopathology. Since this work has been described in detail throughout the major portion of the book, it will be summarized very briefly here. With respect to symptomatology, higher premorbid competence scores have been found to be related to the role orientation reflecting self-deprivation and turning against the self, to symptom expression in thought rather than action, and to symptom pictures that include delusions without accompanying hallucinations (Draguns et al., 1970; Glick et al., 1985; Mylet et al., 1979; Phillips et al., 1966; Phillips & Zigler, 1961, 1964; Sanes & Zigler, 1971; Zigler & Levine, 1983; Zigler & Phillips, 1960, 1962). While some workers have questioned whether symptom analysis provides meaningful information for the understanding of psychopathology, the developmental work suggests that when symptoms are conceptually organized and interpreted as reflections of a major underlying dimension such as developmental level they can elucidate much about the nature of people and contribute much to the understanding of psychopathology.

Both premorbid competence and symptom categorizations involving role orientation have been related to major diagnostic categories. In regard to premorbid competence, a consistent finding has been that affective disorder and neurotic patients obtain higher premorbid competence scores than do schizophrenic and personality disorder patients (Glick et al., 1985; Lewine et al., 1980; Zigler et al., 1979; Zigler & Phillips, 1961a). In contrast to the developmental categorizations of symptomatology, traditional psychiatric diagnosis represents an atheoretical mode of classification based on symptom manifestation. Our findings indicate that, while these two modes of classification are not identical, a considerable overlap exists. The role orientation of turning against the self is associated with affective disorder (manic-depressive) and neurotic diagnoses; the role orientation of turning against others is most frequently found in personality disorder patients; while avoidance of others most frequently characterizes schizophrenic patients (Phillips et al., 1968; Zigler & Phillips, 1961c). With respect to the action–thought continuum, expression in action characterizes the symptoms of personality disorder (character disorder) patients, whereas expression in thought predominates for schizophrenics (Phillips et al., 1968). The thought dominance in schizophrenic patients despite other evidence of their relatively low developmental functioning points to the need for more fine-grained developmental distinctions within the thought category. The findings that our developmental measures (premorbid competence and developmental categorizations of symptomatology) relate to the conventional categories of psychiatric diagnosis pose the possibility, at least with regard to DSM-I and DSM-II, that clinicians may implicitly employ developmental constructs in assigning diagnoses.

Subtypes within certain diagnostic categories have also been differentiated using our developmental measures. The essential–reactive distinction in alcoholism and paranoid–nonparanoid status in schizophrenia have both been found to be related to premorbid competence (Levine & Zigler, 1973, 1981; Sugerman et al., 1965; Zigler & Levine, 1973; Zigler et al., 1976, 1977). In addition to generally obtaining higher premorbid competence scores, paranoid as compared with nonparanoid schizophrenic patients display less disorganization on a variety of cognitive and perceptual measures and an older age at onset of disorder. The dissimilarities between paranoid and nonparanoid schizophrenic patients along with a number of commonalities discovered between paranoid and affective disorder (especially manic) patients have led us to propose an alternative view of paranoid schizophrenia. Rather than being a true schizophrenia, paranoid schizophrenia, or at least some forms of this subtype, might more fruitfully be conceptualized as a phenotypic expression of underlying depression.

Prognosis is broadly conceptualized as including age of onset of disorder and age upon first hospital admission as well as outcome following treatment. While developmentally higher functioning is not presumed to prevent the occurrence of psychopathology, individuals at higher maturity levels should possess greater adaptive resources resulting in improved prognosis. Consistent with this view, higher premorbid competence scores have been found to be related both to an older age upon first admission and to more favorable outcomes following treatment for patients in a variety of diagnostic groups (e.g., schizophrenia, affective disorder) (Marsh et al., 1981; Zigler et al., 1979; Zigler & Levine, 1981a; Zigler & Phillips, 1961d; Glick & Zigler, in press; Glick et al., 1985). The role orientation of turning against the self has also been found to be related to shorter initial hospitalizations (Phillips & Zigler, 1964).

In contrast to other positions, most notably that of C. Rogers (e.g., Rogers & Dymond, 1954), which have viewed a sizable self-image disparity as ominous in nature and a sign of maladjustment, our developmental position interprets increased self-image disparity as the natural concomitant of normal growth and development. The twofold rationale for this position was briefly indicated earlier in this chapter and discussed in detail in Chapter 10. Our developmental interpretation of self-image disparity has been substantiated in research with children and with adult psychiatric and nonpsychiatric (medical) patients. As noted earlier, the findings have been so consistent that we now employ magnitude of self-image disparity as an indicator of developmental level. A recent expansion of the developmental interpretation of self-image disparity (Glick & Zigler, 1985) conceptualizes relations between the real and ideal self-images on the basis of three levels of organization. This model allows for a possible reconciliation of the Rogerian and developmental positions.

DIRECTIONS FOR FURTHER RESEARCH

The work on the developmental approach to psychopathology has yielded a substantial body of data that interconnects a wide range of variables of major importance in psychopathology. These include premorbid competence, symptomatology, diagnosis including subtypes within schizophrenia and alcoholism, the age of onset and outcome of disorder, and aspects of the individual's view of self. The converging relationships discovered using different methods for assessing developmental level argue for the validity of these measures as gauges of that broad construct, the individual's underlying developmental level. The developmental formulation has allowed for the discovery of principles that cut across particular psychopathological syndromes. For example, the relation of premorbid competence to outcome has been found to apply not only to schizophrenia but to most major categories of functional disorder (e.g., affective disorder, personality disorder). Some aspects of the work have encompassed normal development as well as disordered functioning. The ability of research on psychopathology to inform us about normal development and of research on normal development to enhance knowledge about psychopathology is most clearly illustrated in the work on self-image disparity. Orientations toward expression in action versus thought also appear to pertain to adaptive functioning as well as symptom expression (Phillips & Zigler, 1961). A major dimension for the analysis of childhood behavior problems involves the distinction between internalizing and externalizing modes of expression (Achenbach, 1966; Achenbach & Edelbrock, 1978). Longitudinal research has revealed that this dimension of childhood behavior, which closely parallels our action–thought continuum, is related to mental health status in adulthood (Kohlberg et al., 1972; Santostefano & Baker, 1972). Finally, the developmental formulation has permitted the generation of hypotheses that are counterintuitive. The position that increased self-image disparity reflects higher developmental functioning rather than greater maladjustment represents such a counterintuitive hypothesis. This hypothesis has been tested extensively. The position that paranoid schizophrenia or at least some forms of this disorder may represent a defense against depression rather than being a subtype of schizophrenic disorder is a recent hypothesis derived from our developmental formulation. This hypothesis remains to be tested.

A considerable amount has been accomplished. In light of the goals envisioned at the outset of the work, much remains to be done. The formulation of a theory rather than a frame of reference requires (a) that each concept in the system be defined through reference to events or operations that take place in the physical rather than conceptual world, and (b) that the exact relationship of each concept to every other concept in the system be delineated. Only when both conditions are met can we claim that the work constitutes a theory. In contrast to a frame of reference, a theory must permit the derivation of hypotheses that are as open to disproof as to proof. Evaluated by this standard, many of the concepts in our formulation require more precise definition. In many instances, the exact nature of relationships between the concepts in our nomological network requires further specification. In addition, a number of fundamental issues in psychopathology have yet to be addressed. In this section, we will indicate a number of areas in which further work is needed.

Considerable evidence has been presented for the validity of our premorbid competence measure. Yet the concept of competence remains poorly understood. We still do not know why measures of this construct predict as well as they do. One direction for further research involves an examination of the relationship between our premorbid competence index and Loevinger's (Loevinger & Wessler, 1970) measure of ego development. Loevinger's test had not been devised when our work began. This measure is derived from developmental precepts similar to our own. Findings that scores on the Zigler-Phillips index are positively correlated with ego development as measured by Loevinger's test would further substantiate our position that premorbid competence can be employed as a benchmark of maturity level. Already, the premorbid competence index has been found to be related to Rorschach developmental-level scores (Lerner, 1968) and to maturity in moral reasoning as assessed by Kohlberg's test (Quinlan et al., 1980).

The understanding of premorbid competence would also be enhanced by a closer examination of interrelationships between our measure and other frequently employed premorbid competence scales. Several studies (Garfield & Sundland, 1966; Held & Cromwell, 1968; Levinson & Campus, 1978; McCreary, 1974; Meichenbaum, 1969) have indicated that the total scale scores of various measures of premorbid competence are significantly related. The reasons for these repeatedly demonstrated correlations remain obscure. Are they due to overlap in the content of items on the various scales or is the discovered correlation among scales mediated by a social desirability response set? Further progress in illuminating the premorbid competence construct requires that investigators move beyond the intercorrelation of total scale scores to factor analyses of the various scales' items themselves. While some beginning efforts have been made (Lorr, Wittman, & Schonberger, 1951; Nuttall & Solomon, 1965), further factor analyses of the items employed in the various premorbid competence scales are needed to elucidate common dimensions underlying the various measures of premorbid competence. A further issue of interest would be whether the factorial structure of these premorbid competence items would vary as a function of diagnosis and gender.

An expansion of the Zigler-Phillips index to include more items that assess social participation (e.g., friendships and social activities) is also recommended. As it now stands, marital status is the only item on the scale that reflects interpersonal competence. The majority of the items pertain to competence in instrumental role functioning.

Further effort is required to update, expand, and refine the developmental categorizations of symptomatology. The categorizations of symptoms based on role orientation and expression in action versus thought were established more than 25 years ago. Since that time, the symptom criteria defining diagnoses have been refined and changed. Some presenting symptoms included in the original categorizations are seldom recorded now, whereas other symptoms (e.g., thought broadcasting) that once were infrequently recorded are now used as diagnostic criteria and often noted in case history records.

In addition to changes in the symptoms typically noted for patients, sophisticated statistical techniques for deriving clusters of items have now been developed. For both these reasons, our symptom categories defining role orientation and expression in action versus thought need updating. A first step would be to repeat the procedure of Phillips and Rabinovitch (1958) and review the case record of a sizable group of randomly selected inpatients for all presenting symptoms recorded. With this accomplished, two approaches to the classification of symptoms could be taken. The first would be a conceptual approach. Here, the aim would be to classify the symptoms conceptually with respect to role orientation and along the action–thought continuum. The second approach to classification would be empirical, based on cluster analysis. One issue would be the degree of correspondence between the conceptually derived categories and the statistical clusters. With respect to role orientation, another question would be whether the statistically derived clusters would continue to reflect three role orientations. Utilizing the present role orientation categories, our analyses have tended to confirm only one major distinction—between the turning-against-the-self category, which has been associated with higher developmental levels, and the two categories of turning against others and avoidance of others, both of which have been related to developmentally lower levels of functioning. A final issue for investigation would be whether the relationships discovered between our original developmental symptom categories and diagnosis would be replicated using the revised categories and DSM-III diagnoses.

In addition to revision of the categories reflecting role orientation and symptom expression in action versus thought, further developmental work requires more fine-grained analyses of developmental differences in specific symptoms. One such symptom is delusions. Paranoid as compared with nonparanoid schizophrenia and the presence of delusions have been associated with developmentally higher functioning as reflected in premorbid competence scores. Nevertheless, many off-quadrant instances exist. Some low competence patients manifest delusions. We need, therefore, to go beyond the presence of the symptom itself to more fine-grained analyses that can differentiate delusions that reflect developmentally higher functioning from ones that reflect developmentally lower modes of organization. Developmental theorizing suggests that the delusions of low developmental individuals would be global, disorganized, and unmodulated whereas in high developmental individuals they would be more organized, articulated, and hierarchical. The availability of a more fine-grained method for analyzing developmental differences in delusions could help to separate paranoid schizophrenic patients into groups that are more homogeneous with respect to developmental level. In regard to the relationship between premorbid competence and paranoid–nonparanoid status in schizophrenia, the expectation would be that the relation to high social competence would be more robust for paranoid schizophrenic patients who evince developmentally higher forms of organization in their delusions. In advancing the view that paranoid schizophrenia might be conceptualized as a response to an underlying depressive mode, Zigler and Glick (1984) questioned whether this formulation would be applicable to all paranoid schizophrenics or only to a subgroup characterized by developmentally higher functioning. A method for categorizing paranoid delusions as developmentally higher or lower would help address this question.

Methods for distinguishing developmental differences in depressive symptomatology and also in aggressive symptoms (turning against others) are needed as well. Affective disorder diagnoses and symptom pictures reflecting turning against the self have been associated with higher premorbid competence (e.g., Glick et al., 1985; Zigler et al., 1979; Zigler & Phillips, 1960, 1961a, 1962). Yet depression is not confined to high developmental individuals. Children and mentally retarded individuals frequently manifest depression. The question, therefore, is how differences in developmental level may modify the manner in which depression is experienced and expressed. In contrast to depression, aggressive symptomatology (turning against others) and personality disorder diagnoses have been associated with low premorbid competence scores (e.g., Zigler & Phillips, 1960, 1961a, 1962). A method for distinguishing developmental differences in aggressive symptomatology would permit developmental subclassification within the personality disorder group and the turning-against-others symptom category.

Our interpretation of regression is that it represents a weakening of the structural ties by means of which developmentally lower responses and modes of organization are subordinated to and controlled by developmentally higher levels of organization (see Chapter 2). In severely disordered individuals, particularly some schizophrenic patients, these lower forms of organization are presumed to break loose from and thus operate independently of higher mediating structures. A major characteristic of developmentally lower functioning is the relative lack of differentiation both between response systems within the individual and in distinguishing self from others in interpersonal interactions. A number of specific observable behaviors would seem to reflect such a lack of differentiation. For example, if individuals were asked to open their eyes wide and, in responding, opened their mouths as well, this would suggest a lack of differentiation between motor responses within the individual. Various contagion effects in interpersonal situations would seem to reflect a lack of differentiation or a weakening of the boundaries between self and other. Examples of such contagion effects would be yawning when another person yawns or laughing in response to a recording of people laughing. Other behavioral measures could be devised as well. Given the disorganized thought and behavior frequently manifested by schizophrenic individuals, one would expect that as a group these patients would display less differentiated responses than other diagnostic groups (e.g., affective disorder patients). Yet, if psychopathology generally involves the weakening of ties to higher mediating structures, the responses of affective disorder patients with psychotic symptoms should also be less differentiated than those of nonpsychopathological (medical) patients. Given our position that individuals continue to maintain their position on the developmental continuum even after they are adjudged pathological, the expectation would be that, even within the patient groups just considered, high developmental individuals would respond in a more differentiated manner than their low developmental counterparts. These presuppositions could be tested utilizing three patient groups (schizophrenia, affective disorder, and medical patients) subdivided into high and low developmental subgroups on the basis of premorbid competence scores. On a battery of behavioral measures of response differentiation, both diagnosis and premorbid competence would be expected to be related to degree of response differentiation.

The developmental approach to psychopathology has implications for treatment, but these have not yet been explored in our research. The effectiveness of various treatment modalities would be expected to be related to developmental level. For high developmental individuals, who are presumed to be oriented toward expression in thought and to have greater resources for coping, intellectualizing forms of therapy (e.g., psychoanalytically oriented psychotherapy or cognitive behavioral therapy) would be expected to be most appropriate and effective. By contrast, individuals at lower developmental levels, who are presumed to be more oriented toward expression in direct action and to possess fewer resources for coping, would be expected to derive greater benefit from forms of treatment that emphasize behavior (action) and concrete reinforcement and that provide training and support for coping efforts. Behavior modification, social skills training, and residence in halfway houses might thus be most beneficial to individuals who function at lower developmental levels.

Another potential contribution of the developmental formulation to research on treatment is it provides a framework within which a variety of levels of favorable outcome can be envisioned. A limitation in many personality theories is that they define adaptive functioning and mental health in terms of ideal criteria that few people can meet. The definition of the self-actualized person is one example of such an idealized view of mental health. As we stated in Chapter 2, workers must remain aware of how difficult it can be for many individuals to meet such ordinary demands of society as earning one's living, caring for one's self, and forming appropriate social relationships. Our position sees people as functioning at different developmental levels. Thus different levels of coping or adaptation would be defined as constituting a favorable outcome for individuals at different developmental levels.

Finally, a number of broad conceptual issues remain to be addressed. While our work has demonstrated that differences in developmental level contribute to the overall variance on many major variables of interest in psychopathology, our position is that developmental level represents only one of a number of broad classes of variables that influence psychopathology. The evidence is persuasive that biological and genetic factors are major determinants of many psychiatric syndromes. The developmental approach to psychopathology subscribes to the diathesis-stress model of the etiology of mental disorder (Meehl, 1962; Watt, 1978; Zubin & Spring, 1977). Thus environmental stressors are viewed as interacting with biological and psychological variables in precipitating psychopathology. Even in regard to psychological variables, we do not assume that developmental level is the only dimension of importance for understanding psychopathology. Research is thus needed to examine the manner in which these other classes of variables interact with developmental level to influence whether and in what way psychopathology is manifested.

With respect to psychological characteristics, the individual's psychodynamics ought to interact and with and at times outweigh the importance of developmental level in determining behavior. Outcome for paranoid schizophrenics may exemplify the interaction of developmental and psychodynamic characteristics. In comparison to nonparanoid schizophrenics, paranoid schizophrenic patients generally display developmentally higher functioning. Yet their psychiatric outcomes may not be more favorable than those of nonparanoid schizophrenic patients (see Chapter 9). The absence of x more favorable outcome for paranoid schizophrenics may be due to the psychodynamic importance of paranoid delusions as a defense against depression. In order to ward off the pain of depression, paranoid schizophrenics may thus maintain their delusions despite generally higher developmental functioning. The importance of examining the interaction of psychodynamic with developmental variables is also apparent when we recognize that individuals who are similar in developmental level may nevertheless employ different mechanisms of defense against a particular underlying problem. For example, we have proposed that paranoia, mania, and alcoholism may each serve to protect the individual from the awareness of underlying depression. Given a common underlying problem (e.g., depression), the question that remains is why one individual may display mania while others may manifest paranoia, alcoholism, or depression itself. The inclusion of psychodynamic variables in our model should help to clarify issues such as this. Our efforts to date have focused on the influence of developmental level on psychopathology. Thus we have paid relatively little attention to psychodynamics and the role of ego defense mechanisms in determining behavior. Our formulation might be enriched if in future work we consider psychodynamic factors in relation to developmental level.

Biological factors and genetic predispositions must be regarded as major etiological determinants in psychopathology. The relation of these determinants to developmental variables requires far closer research attention. At a general level, cognitive–developmental psychology emphasizes the importance of biological determinants of behavior. Often, however, the broad acknowledgment of the importance of inherent characteristics is not followed by the close examination of how particular biological influences interact with specific psychological and environmental factors in determining particular behaviors. In addition to questions concerning the manner in which biological factors may predispose individuals to certain forms of psychopathology, an issue within our developmental approach is the role of biological factors in determining developmental level. The family history method of examining correspondences between a patient's disorder and the occurrence of signs of the disorder in first-degree relatives could be extended to the consideration of developmental variables. Instead of examining the frequency with which a patient and first-degree relatives display symptoms associated with a particular disorder (e.g., schizophrenia), the concordance between the patient and relatives could be examined with respect to developmental categorizations of symptomatology (e.g., tendencies toward expression in action vs. thought) or Rorschach developmental-level scores. Rorschach developmental level may be a particularly useful measure since the types of responses that comprise the developmental-level categories are specific to the Rorschach and unlikely to be learned. The relationship between biogenetic, psychological, and environmental factors is surely complex and remains baffling. By what route, for example, might genetic characteristics interact with the environment to affect behavior? One possibility is that an individual's genetic makeup leads the person to create a particular environment for himself or herself. In relation to the social environment, another possibility is that genetically determined characteristics evoke distinctive responses from others and elicit rather than create a special environment. An example here is that aggression is often met with aggression. With respect to psychopathology, genetic vulnerabilities may also interact with inherent characteristics related to developmental level to determine whether disorder will be manifested, and, if it is, what form the disorder might take. Concomitantly, inherent predispositions related both to mental disorder and to developmental level should interact with a variety of environmental factors in determining modes of adaptive or maladaptive functioning.

As was the case with biological determinants of behavior, cognitive–developmental psychologists, while giving considerable lip service to the importance of experiential determinants of behavior, often in practice pay insufficient attention to this class of variables. While we adhere to the diathesis-stress model of the etiology of mental disorder, work to date on the developmental approach to psychopathology has not examined environmental events that may trigger the onset of disorder. Our assumption has been that external stresses or demands precipitate disorder in both high and low developmental level individuals. Just how stressful such imposing events will seem is determined by the psychological resources that can be mustered by the individual when attempting to deal with them. It would be expected that the low developmental level individual, who has relatively limited psychological resources, would succumb to the stress involved in meeting those constant societal demands to form social relations and maintain employment. By contrast, individuals at higher developmental levels should have the psychological resources to meet these basic societal expectancies successfully but break down when confronted with circumscribed life events involving great personal stress or disappointment (e.g., loss of a loved one or a major financial reverse). Further research is needed to test this formulation regarding the interaction between precipitating events and the individual's developmental level.

The effort to apply developmental principles to adult psychopathology has been going on for more than 25 years. The heuristic value of the approach has now been demonstrated with respect to a wide range of variables of central concern in psychopathology. While much has been accomplished, the work remains incomplete. This book has served to bring the work together, and this final chapter to indicate major directions for the further refinement and expansion of the formulation.

References

Abraham, K. (1960). Notes on the psychoanalytic investigation and treatment of manic-depressive insanity and allied conditions. In K. Abraham (Ed.), *Selected papers on psychoanalysis* (pp. 137–156). New York: Basic.

Abrams, R., Taylor, M. A., & Gaztanaga, P. (1974). Manic-depressive illness and paranoid schizophrenia: A phenomenologic, family history, and treatment–response study. *Archives of General Psychiatry, 31*, 640–642.

Abramson, L. Y., & Sackeim, H. A. (1977). A paradox in depression: Uncontrollability and self-blame. *Psychological Bulletin, 84*, 838–851.

Achenbach, T. (1966). The classification of children's psychiatric symptoms: A factor-analytic study. *Psychological Monographs, 80* (6, Whole No. 615).

Achenbach, T., & Edelbrock, C. (1978). The classification of child psychopathology: A review and analysis of empirical efforts. *Psychological Bulletin, 85*, 1275–1301.

Achenbach, T., & Zigler, E. (1963). Social competence and self-image disparity in psychiatric and nonpsychiatric patients. *Journal of Abnormal and Social Psychology, 67*, 197–205.

Achenbach, T., & Zigler, E. (1968). Cue-learning and problem-learning strategies in normal and retarded children. *Child Development, 3*, 827–848.

Affleck, J. W., Burns, J. & Forrest, A. D. (1976). Long-term follow-up of schizophrenic patients in Edinburgh. *Acta Psychiatrica Scandinavica, 53*, 227–237.

Akiskal, H. S., & McKinney, W. T., Jr. (1973). Depressive disorders: Towards a unified hypothesis. *Science, 182*, 20–29.

Akiskal, H. S., & McKinney, W. T., Jr. (1975). Overview of recent research in depression: Integration of ten conceptual models into a comprehensive clinical frame. *Archives of General Psychiatry, 32*, 285–305.

Albee, G. W. (1969). Emerging concepts of mental illness and models of treatment: The psychological points of view. *American Journal of Psychiatry, 125*, 870–876.

Allen, T. E. (1967). Suicidal impulse in depression and paranoia. *International Journal of Psychoanalysis, 48*, 433–438.

Allon, R. (1971). Sex, race, socioeconomic status, social mobility, and process–reactive ratings of schizophrenics. *Journal of Nervous and Mental Disease, 153*, 343–350.

Allport, G. W. (1937). *Personality: A psychological interpretation*. New York: Holt, Rinehart & Winston.

Allport, G. W. (1955). *Becoming: Basic considerations for a psychology of personality*. New Haven, CT: Yale University Press.

Allport, G. W. (1961). *Pattern and growth in personality*. New York: Holt, Rinehart & Winston.

Altrocchi, J., Parsons, O. A., & Dickoff, H. (1960). Changes in self-ideal discrepancy in repressors and sensitizers. *Journal of Abnormal and Social Psychology, 61*, 67–72.

Amenson, C., & Lewinsohn, P. M. (1981). An investigation into the observed sex difference in prevalence of unipolar depression. *Journal of Abnormal Psychology, 90*, 1–13.

American Psychiatric Association. (1980). *DSM III: Diagnostic and statistical manual of mental disorders* (3rd ed.). Washington, DC: Author.

Anderson, S., & Messick, S. (1974). Social competency in young children. *Developmental Psychology, 10*, 282–293.

Andreasen, N. C., & Powers, P. S. (1976). Psychosis, thought disorder, and repression. *American Journal of Psychiatry, 133*, 522–526.

Angyal, A. (1941). *Foundations for a science of personality*. New York: Commonwealth Fund.

Arana, J. D. (1978). Schizophrenic psychoses. In G. Balis, L. Wurmser, E. McDaniel, & R. G. Grenell (Eds.), *Clinical psychopathology* (pp. 123–155). Boston: Butterworth.

Arieti, S. (1976). *Creativity: The magic synthesis*. New York: Basic.

Arieti, S., & Bemporad, J. (1978). *Severe and mild depression*. New York: Basic.

Astrachan, B. M., Harrow, M., Adler, D., Brauer, L., Schwartz, A., Schwartz, C., & Tucker, G. (1972). A checklist for the diagnosis of schizophrenia. *British Journal of Psychiatry, 121*, 529–539.

Aylward, E., Walker, E., & Bettes, B. (1984). Intelligence in schizophrenia: A review and meta-analysis of the research. *Schizophrenia Bulletin, 10*, 113–125.

Babigian, H. M., Gardner, E. A., Miles, H. C., & Romano, J. (1965). Diagnostic consistency and change in a follow-up study of 1215 patients. *American Journal of Psychiatry, 121*, 895–901.

Baldessarini, R. J., Finklestein, S., & Arana, G. W. (1983). The predictive power of diagnostic tests and the effect of prevalence of illness. *Archives of General Psychiatry, 40*, 569–573.

Baldwin, J. M. (1911). *Genetic epistemology: Vol. 3. Thought and things*. New York: Macmillan.

Baloh, R. W., & Honrubia, V. (1979). *Clinical neurophysiology of the vestibular system*. Philadelphia: F. A. Davis.

Baltes, P. B., & Schaie, K. W. (Eds.). (1973). *Life-span developmental psychology: Personality and socialization*. New York: Academic.

Bandura, A. (1969). *Principles of behavior modification*. New York: Holt, Rinehart & Winston.

Bandura, A. (1978). The self system in reciprocal determinism. *American Psychologist, 33,* 344–358.

Bannister, D. (1968). The logical requirements of research into schizophrenia. *British Journal of Psychiatry, 114,* 181–188.

Barnes, G. (1979). The alcoholic personality: A reanalysis of the literature. *Journal of Studies on Alcohol, 40,* 571–634.

Barron, F. (1969). *Creative person and creative process.* New York: Holt, Rinehart & Winston.

Bart, P. B. (1974). The sociology of depression. In P. Roman & H. Trice (Eds.), *Explorations in psychiatric sociology* (pp. 139–158). Philadelphia: F. A. Davis.

Bauer, S. R., & Achenbach, T. (1976). Self-image disparity, repression–sensitization, and extraversion–introversion. A unitary dimension? *Journal of Personality Assessment, 40,* 46–51.

Baumrind, D. (1975). The contributions of the family to the development of competence in children. *Schizophrenia Bulletin, 14,* 12–37.

Beck, A. T. (1967). *Depression: Clinical, experimental, and theoretical aspects.* New York: Harper & Row.

Beck, J. C. (1978). Social influences on the prognosis of schizophrenia. *Schizophrenia Bulletin, 4,* 86–101.

Becker, J. (1974). *Depression: Theory and research.* New York: Wiley.

Becker, W. (1956). A genetic approach to the interpretation and evaluation of the process–reactive distinction in schizophrenia. *Journal of Abnormal and Social Psychology, 53,* 229–236.

Becker, W. (1959). The process–reactive distinction: A key to the problems of schizophrenia. *Journal of Nervous and Mental Disease, 129,* 442–449.

Bem, D. J., & Allen, A. (1974). On predicting some of the people some of the time: The search for cross-situational consistencies in behavior. *Psychological Review, 81,* 506–520.

Bem, D. J., & Funder, D. C. (1978). Predicting more of the people more of the time: Assessing the personality of situations. *Psychological Review, 85,* 485–501.

Berger, E. M. (1955). Relationships among acceptance of self, acceptance of others, and MMPI scores. *Journal of Counseling Psychology, 2,* 279–284.

Berle, B., Pinsky, R., Wolf, S., & Wolf, H. (1952). A clinical guide to prognosis in stress diseases. *Journal of the American Medical Association, 149,* 1624–1628.

Bibring, E. (1953). The mechanism of depression. In P. Greenacre (Ed.), *Affective disorders* (pp. 13–48). New York: International Universities Press.

Billings, A., Cronkite, R., & Moos, R. (1983). Social–environmental factors in unipolar depression: Comparisons of depressed patients and nondepressed controls. *Journal of Abnormal Psychology, 92,* 119–133.

Bills, R. E. (1953). Rorschach characteristics of persons scoring high and low in acceptance of self. *Journal of Consulting Psychology, 17,* 36–38.

Bills, R. E. (1954). Self-concepts and Rorschach signs of depression. *Journal of Consulting Psychology, 18,* 135–137.

Bills, R. E., Vance, E. L., & McLean, O. S. (1951). An index of adjustment and values. *Journal of Consulting Psychology, 15,* 257–261.

Birtchnell, J. (1971). Social class, parental social class, and social mobility in psychiatric patients and general population controls. *Psychological Medine, 1,* 209–221.

Bland, R. C., & Orn, H. (1979). Schizophrenia: Diagnostic criteria and outcome. *British Journal of Psychiatry, 134,* 34–38.

Bland, R. C., & Orn, H. (1982). Course and outcome in affective disorders. *Canadian Journal of Psychiatry, 27,* 573–578.

Blashfield, R. K., & Draguns, J. G. (1976). Evaluative criteria for psychiatric classification. *Journal of Abnormal Psychology, 85,* 140–150.

Blashfield, R. K., & Morey, L. C. (1979). The classification of depression through cluster analysis. *Comprehensive Psychiatry, 20,* 516–527.

Blatt, S. J., & Allison, J. (1963). Methodological considerations in Rorschach research: The W response as an expression of abstractive and integrative strivings. *Journal of Projective Techniques, 27,* 267–278.

Blatt, S. J., Brenneis, C., Schimek, J., & Glick, M. (1976). Normal development and psychopathological impairment of the concept of the object on the Rorschach. *Journal of Abnormal Psychology, 85,* 364–373.

Blatt, S. J., D'Afflitti, J. P., & Quinlan, D. M. (1976). Experiences of depression in normal young adults. *Journal of Abnormal Psychology, 85,* 383–389.

Blatt, S. J., & Wild, C. (1976). *Schizophrenia: A developmental analysis.* New York: Academic.

Bleuler, E. (1950). *Dementia praecox* (J. Zinkin, Trans.). New York: International Universities Press.

Bleuler, M. (1974). The long-term course of the schizophrenic psychoses. *Psychological Medicine, 4,* 244–254.

Block, J., Buss, D. M., Block, J. H., & Gjerde, P. F. (1981). The cognitive style of breadth of categorization: Longitudinal consistency of personality correlates. *Journal of Personality and Social Psychology, 40,* 770–779.

Block, J., & Thomas, H. (1955). Is satisfaction with self a measure of adjustment? *Journal of Abnormal and Social Psychology, 51,* 254–259.

Blum, J. D. (1978). On changes in psychiatric diagnosis over time. *American Psychologist, 33,* 1017–1031.

Blum, J., & Levine, J. (1975). Maturity, depression, and life events in middle-aged alcoholics. *Addictive Behaviors, 1,* 37–45.

Bookbinder, L., & Gusman, L. (1964). Social attainment, premorbid adjustment, and participation in inpatient psychiatric treatment. *Journal of Clinical Psychology, 20,* 513–515.

Bornstein, R., & Matarazzo, J. (1982). Wechsler VIQ versus PIQ differences in cerebral dysfunction: A literature review with emphasis on sex differences. *Journal of Clinical Neuropsychology, 4,* 319–334.

Bowers, K. S. (1973). Situationism in psychology: An analysis and a critique. *Psychological Review, 80,* 307–336.

Bowers, M. B., & Astrachan, B. M. (1967). Depression in acute schizophrenic psychosis. *American Journal of Psychiatry, 123,* 976–979.

Bowman, K. M., & Raymond, A. F. (1931). A statistical study of delusions in the manic-depressive psychoses. *Proceedings of the Association for Research in Nervous and Mental Diseases* (Vol. 2). Baltimore: Williams & Wilkins.

Braginsky, B. M., Braginsky, D. D., & Ring, K. (1969). *Methods of madness: The mental hospital as a last resort.* New York: Holt, Rinehart & Winston.

Brandt, L. (1965). Studies of "dropout" patients in psychotherapy: A review of findings. *Psychotherapy: Theory, Research & Practice, 2,* 6–12.

Breakey, W. R., & Goodell, H. (1972). Thought disorder in mania and schizophrenia evaluated by Bannister's Grid Test for schizophrenic thought disorder. *British Journal of Psychiatry, 120,* 391–395.

Brim, O. G., Jr., & Kagan, J. (Eds.). (1980). *Constancy and change in human development.* Cambridge, MA: Harvard University Press.

Bromet, E., Harrow, M., & Kasl, S. (1974). Premorbid functioning and outcome in schizophrenics and nonschizophrenics. *Archives of General Psychiatry, 30,* 203–207.

Brown, G., & Bunney, W. E., Jr. (1978). Affective psychoses. In G. U. Ballis, L. Wurmser, E. McDaniel, & R. G. Grenell (Eds.), *Clinical Psychopathology* (pp. 179–204). Boston: Butterworth.

Brown, G., & Harris, T. (1978). *Social origins of depression: A study of psychiatric disorder in women.* New York: Free Press.

Brown, R. (1973). Schizophrenia, language, and reality. *American Psychologist, 28,* 395–403.

Brownfain, J. J. (1952). Stability of the self-concept as a dimension of personality. *Journal of Abnormal and Social Psychology, 47,* 597–606.

Buchsbaum, M. S., & Haier, R. J. (1983). Psychopathology: Biological approaches. *Annual Review of Psychology, 34,* 401–430.

Buss, A. H., & Lang, P. J. (1965). Psychological deficit in schizophrenia. I. Affect, reinforcement, and concept attainment. *Journal of Abnormal Psychology, 70,* 2–24.

Byrne, D. (1964). Repression–sensitization as a dimension of personality. In B. A. Maher (Ed.), *Progress in experimental personality research* (Vol. 1) (pp. 169–220). New York: Academic.

Byrne, D. (1961). The repression–sensitization scale: Rationale, reliability, and validity. *Journal of Personality, 29,* 334–349.

Cameron, N. (1963). *Personality development and psychopathology.* Boston: Houghton Mifflin.

Cancro, R. (1979). Genetic evidence for the existence of subgroups of the schizophrenic syndrome. *Schizophrenia Bulletin, 5,* 453–459.

Cantor, N., Smith, E. E., French, R., & Mezzich, J. (1980). Psychiatric diagnosis as prototype categorization. *Journal of Abnormal Psychology, 89,* 181–193.

Carey, G., & Gottesman, I. I. (1978). Reliability and validity in binary ratings. *Archives of General Psychiatry, 35,* 1454–1459.

Carlson, G. A., & Goodwin, F. K. (1973). The stages of mania: A longitudinal analysis of the manic episode. *Archives of General Psychiatry, 28,* 221–228.

Carpenter, W. T., Jr. (1976). Current diagnostic concepts in schizophrenia. *American Journal of Psychiatry, 133,* 172–177.

Carpenter, W. T., Jr., Bartko, J. J., Carpenter, C. L., & Strauss, J. S. (1976). Another view of schizophrenia subtypes: A report from the International Pilot Study of Schizophrenia. *Archives of General Psychiatry, 33,* 508–516.

Carpenter, W. T., Jr., & Stephens, J. H. (1979). An attempted integration of information relevant to schizophrenic subtypes. *Schizophrenia Bulletin, 5,* 490–506.

Carpenter, W. T., Jr., Strauss, J. S., & Bartko, J. J. (1973). A flexible system for the identification of schizophrenia: A report from the International Pilot Study of Schizophrenia. *Science, 182,* 1275–1278.

Carpenter, W. T., Jr., Strauss, J. S., & Muleh, S. (1973). Are there pathognomic symptoms in schizophrenia? *Archives of General Psychiatry, 28,* 847–852.

Carroll, B. J., Feinberg, M., Greden, J. F., Tarika, J., Albala, A. A., Haskett, R. F., James, N. N., Kronfol, Z., Lohr, N., Steiner, M., deVigne, J. P., & Young, E. (1981). A specific laboratory test for the diagnosis of melancholia. *Archives of General Psychiatry, 38,* 15–22.

Chapman, L., & Baxter, J. (1963). The process–reactive distinction and patient's subculture. *Journal of Nervous and Mental Disease, 136,* 352–359.

Chapman, L. J., Day, D., & Burstein, A. (1961). The process–reactive distinction and prognosis in schizophrenia. *Journal of Nervous and Mental Disease, 133,* 383–391.

Chapman, L. J., & Chapman, J. P. (1980). Scales for rating psychotic and psychotic-like experiences as continua. *Schizophrenia Bulletin, 6,* 476–489.

Chase, P. H. (1957). Self concepts in adjusted and maladjusted hospital patients. *Journal of Consulting Psychology, 21,* 495–497.

Chino, A., & Funabiki, D. (1984). A cross-validation of sex differences in the expression of depression. *Sex Roles, 11,* 175–187.

Cicchetti, D., & Pogge-Hesse, P. (1982). Possible contributions of the study of organic retardates to developmental theory. In E. Zigler & D. Balla (Eds.), *Mental retardation: The developmental difference controversy* (pp. 277–318). Hillsdale, NJ: Erlbaum.

Cicchetti, D., & Sparrow, S. (1981). Developing criteria for establishing interrater reliability of specific items: Applications to assessment of adaptive behavior. *American Journal of Mental Deficiency, 86,* 127–137.

Cisin, I. H., & Cahalan, D. (1968). Comparison of abstainers and heavy drinkers in a national survey. *Psychiatric Research Reports, 24,* 10–21.

Clausen, J. A., & Kohn, M. L. (1959). Relation of schizophrenia to the social structure of a small city. In B. Pasamanick (Ed.), *Epidemology of mental disorder* (pp. 69–94). Washington, DC: American Association for the Advancement of Science.

Clayton, P., Pitts, F. N., Jr., & Winokur, G. (1965). Affective disorder. IV. Mania. *Comprehensive Psychiatry, 5,* 313–322.

Clum, G. A. (1975). Intrapsychic variables and the patient's environment as factors in prognosis. *Psychological Bulletin, 82,* 413–431.

Cohen, J. (1968). Weighted kappa: Nominal scale agreement with provision for scaled disagreement or partial credit. *Psychological Bulletin, 70,* 213–220.

Colby, K. M. (1975). *Artificial paranoia: A computer simulation of paranoid processes.* New York: Pergamon.

Colby, K. M. (1976). Clinical implications of a simulation model of paranoid processes. *Archives of General Psychiatry, 33,* 854–857.

Colby, K. M. (1977). Appraisal of four psychological theories of paranoid phenomena. *Journal of Abnormal Psychology, 86,* 54–59.

Connecticut State Department of Mental Health (1972). *Inpatient statistics for year ending June 30, 1972.* Hartford: Connecticut State Department of Mental Health.

Comstock, G. W., & Helsing, K. J. (1976). Symptoms of depression in two communities. *Psychological Medicine, 6,* 551–563.

Cooper, J. E., Kendell, R. E., Gurland, B. J., Sharpe, L., Copeland, J. R. M., & Simon, R. (1972). *Psychiatric diagnosis in New York and London.* London: Oxford University Press.

Cowen, E. L., Heilizer, F., Axelrod, H. S., & Alexander, S. (1957). The correlates of manifest anxiety in perceptual reactivity, rigidity, and self-concept. *Journal of Consulting Psychology, 21,* 405–411.

Crago, M. (1972). Psychopathology in married couples. *Psychological Bulletin, 77,* 114–128.

Cromwell, R. L. (1975). Assessment of schizophrenia. *Annual Review of Psychology, 26,* 593–619.

Cromwell, R. L. (1984). Schizophrenia: A right and just war [Review of schizophrenia: The epigenetic puzzle]. *Contemporary Psychology, 29,* 112–115.

Cromwell, R. L., & Pithers, W. D. (1981). Schizophrenic/paranoid psychoses: Determining diagnostic divisions. *Schizophrenia Bulletin, 7,* 674–688.

Crown, S. (1975). "On being sane in insane places": A comment from England. *Journal of Abnormal Psychology, 84,* 453–455.

Davis, D. W., Cromwell, R. L., & Held, J. M. (1967). Size estimation in emotionally disturbed children and schizophrenic adults. *Journal of Abnormal Psychology, 72,* 395–401.

Davison, K., & Bagley, C. R. (1969). Schizophrenia-like psychoses associated with organic disorders of the central nervous system: A review of the literature. In R. N. Herrington (Ed.), *Current problems in neuropsychiatry* (pp. 113–184). London: Royal Medico-psychological Association.

DeBeauvoir, S. (1974). *The second sex.* New York: Random House.

Depue, R. A. & Monroe, S. M. (1978). The unipolar–bipolar distinction in depressive disorders. *Psychological Bulletin, 85,* 1001–1029.

DeWolfe, A. S. (1973). Premorbid adjustment and the sex of the patient: Implications of Phillips scale ratings for male and female schizophrenics. *Journal of Community Psychology, 1,* 63–65.

Dohrenwend, B. P. (1975). Sociocultural and socio-psychological factors in the genesis of mental disorder. *Journal of Health and Social Behavior, 16,* 365–392.

Dohrenwend, B. P., & Dohrenwend, B. S. (1965). The problem of validity in field studies of psychological disorder. *Journal of Abnormal Psychology, 70,* 52–69.

Dohrenwend, B. P., & Dohrenwend, B. S. (1969). *Social status and psychological disorder.* New York: Wiley.

Dohrenwend, B. P., & Dohrenwend, B. S. (1974). Social and cultural influences on psychopathology. *Annual Review of Psychology, 25,* 417–452.

Dohrenwend, B. P., & Dohrenwend, B. S. (1976). Sex differences and psychiatric disorders. *American Journal of Sociology, 81,* 1447–1454.

Dollard, J., & Miller, N. (1950). *Personality and psychotherapy.* New York: McGraw-Hill.

Donnelly, E. F., Murphy, D. L., & Scott, W. H. (1975). Perception and cognition in patients with bipolar and unipolar depressive disorders: A study in Rorschach responding. *Archives of General Psychiatry, 32,* 1128–1131.

Donovan, D., Radford, L., Chaney, E., & O'Leary, M. (1977). Perceived locus of control as a function of level of depression among alcoholics and nonalcoholics. *Journal of Clinical Psychology, 33,* 582–584.

Draguns, J. G., Phillips, L., Broverman, I. K., & Caudill, W. (1970). Social competence and psychiatric symptomatology in Japan: A cross-cultural extension of earlier American findings. *Journal of Abnormal Psychology, 75,* 68–73.

Dunham, H. W. (1976). Society, culture, and mental disorder. *Archives of General Psychiatry, 33,* 147–156.

Eisenthal, S., Harford, T., & Solomon, L. (1972). Premorbid adjustment, paranoid–nonparanoid status and chronicity in schizophrenic patients. *Journal of Nervous and Mental Disease, 155,* 227–231.

Eliseo, T. S. (1964). Delusions in process and reactive schizophrenics. *Journal of Clinical Psychology, 20,* 352.

Elkind, D. (1969). Piagetian and psychometric conceptions of intelligence. *Harvard Educational Review, 39,* 319–337.

Engel, N. (1959). The stability of the self-concept in adolescence. *Journal of Abnormal and Social Psychology, 58,* 211–215.

Epstein, S. (1980). The stability of behavior. II. Implications for psychological research. *American Psychologist, 35,* 790–806.

Erikson, E. H. (1950). *Childhood and society.* New York: Norton.

Erikson, E. H. (1968). *Identity: Youth and crisis.* New York: Norton.

Escalona, S. (1968). *The roots of individuality.* Chicago: Aldine.

Escalona, S. (1972). The differential impact of environmental conditions as a function of different reaction patterns in infancy. In J. Westman (Ed.), *Individual differences in children* (pp. 145–157). New York: Wiley.

Evans, J. R., Goldstein, M. J., & Rodnick, E. H. (1973). Premorbid adjustment, paranoid diagnosis, and remission: Acute schizophrenics treated in a community mental health center. *Archives of General Psychiatry, 28,* 666–672.

Eysenck, H. J. (Ed.). (1961). *Handbook of abnormal psychology.* New York: Basic.

Eysenck, H. J., Wakefield, J. A., Jr., & Friedman, A. F. (1983). Diagnosis and clinical assessment: The DSM-III. *Annual Review of Psychology, 34,* 167–193.

Fairbairn, W. R. D. (1954). *An object–relations theory of personality.* New York: Basic.

Farber, I. E. (1975). Sane and insane: Constructions and misconstructions. *Journal of Abnormal Psychology, 84,* 589–620.

Farina, A., Garmezy, N., & Barry, H., III (1963). Relationship of marital status to incidence and prognosis of schizophrenia. *Journal of Abnormal and Social Psychology, 67,* 624–630.

Farina, A., Garmezy, N., Zalusky, M., & Becker, J. (1962). Premorbid behavior and prognosis in female schizophrenic patients. *Journal of Consulting Psychology, 26,* 56–60.

Feder, C. (1968). Relationship between self-acceptance and adjustment, repression sensitization and social competence. *Journal of Abnormal Psychology, 73,* 317–322.

Feffer, M. H. (1959). The cognitive implications of role taking behavior. *Journal of Personality, 27,* 152–168.

Feffer, M. H. (1967). Symptom expression as a form of primitive decentering. *Psychological Review, 74,* 16–28.

Feighner, J., Robins, E., Guze, S., Woodruff, R., Winokur, G., & Munoz, R. (1972). Diagnostic criteria for use in psychiatric research. *Archives of General Psychiatry, 26,* 57–63.

Fenichel, O. (1945). *The psychoanalytic theory of neurosis.* New York: Norton.

Ferber, A., Kligler, D., Zwerling, I., & Mendelsohn, M. (1967). Current family structure: Psychiatric emergencies and patient fate. *Archives of General Psychiatry, 16,* 659–667.

Finney, J., & Moos, R. (1979). Treatment and outcome for empirical subtypes of alcoholic patients. *Journal of Consulting and Clinical Psychology, 47,* 25–38.

Fisher, S. (1964). Body image and psychopathology. *Archives of General Psychiatry, 10,* 519–529.

Fisher, S. (1966). Body image in neurotic and schizophrenic patients. *Archives of General Psychiatry, 15,* 90–101.

Flippo, J. R., & Lewinsohn, P. M. (1971). Effects of failure on the self-esteem of depressed and nondepressed subjects. *Journal of Consulting and Clinical Psychology, 36,* 151.

Flugel, J. C. (1954). Humor and laughter. In G. Lindzey (Ed.), *Handbook of social psychology* (Vol. 2) (pp. 790–734). Reading, MA: Addison-Wesley.

Forrest, A. D., & Hay, A. J. (1971). Sex differences and schizophrenic experience. *Acta Psychiatrica Scandinavica, 47,* 137–149.

Fowler, R. C., Liskow, B. I., Tanna, V. L., Lytle, L., & Mezzich, J. (1980). Schizophrenia—primary affective disorder discrimination. I. Development of data-based diagnostic index. *Archives of General Psychiatry, 37,* 811–814.

Freedman, A. M., Kaplan, H., & Sadock, B. (1972). *Modern synopsis of comprehensive textbook of psychiatry.* Baltimore: Williams & Wilkins.

Freedman, N., Cutler, R., Engelhardt, D., & Margolis, R. (1967). On the modification of paranoid symptomatology. *Journal of Nervous and Mental Disease, 144,* 29–36.

Freedman, N., Cutler, R., Engelhardt, D., & Margolis, R. (1970). On the modification of paranoid symptomatology. II. Stylistic considerations and the effectiveness of phenothiazines. *Journal of Nervous and Mental Disease, 150,* 68–76.

Freedman, R., & Schwab, P. J. (1978). Paranoid symptoms in patients on a general hospital psychiatric unit. *Archives of General Psychiatry, 35,* 387–390.

Freeman, H. E., & Simmons, O. G. (1963). *The mental patient comes home.* New York: Wiley.

Freeman, T., Cameron, J. L., & McGhie, A. (1966). *Studies on psychosis.* New York: International Universities Press.

Freud, A. (1967). *The ego and the mechanisms of defense* (rev. ed.). New York: International Universities Press.

Freud, S. (1924). Neurosis and psychosis. In *Collected papers.* London: Hogarth and Institute of Psychoanalysis, 1946.

Freud, S. (1957). *Mourning and melancholia* (J. Strachey, Ed. and Trans.). London: Hogarth. (Original work published 1917)

Freud, S. (1961). Neurosis and psychosis. In J. Strachey (Ed. and Trans.), *The standard edition of the complete psychological works of Sigmund Freud* (Vol. 19, pp. 148–153). London: Hogarth. (Original work published 1924)

Freudenberg, R., & Robertson, J. (1956). Symptoms in relation to psychiatric diagnosis and treatment. *Archives of Neurology and Psychiatry, 76,* 14–22.

Friedman, H. (1953) Perceptual regression in schizophrenia: An hypothesis suggested by use of the Rorschach test. *Journal of Projective Techniques, 17,* 171–185.

Fulton, J., & Lorei, T. (1967). Predicting length of psychiatric hospitalization from history records. *Journal of Clinical Psychology, 23,* 218–221.

Funabiki, D., Bologna, N. C., Pepping, M., & Fitzgerald, K. C. (1980). Revisiting sex differences in the expression of depression. *Journal of Abnormal Psychology, 89,* 194–202.

Garber, J. (1984). Classification of childhood psychopathology: A developmental perspective. *Child Development, 55,* 30–48.

Gardner, H. (1980). *Artful scribbles.* New York: Basic.

Garfield, S., & Sundland, D. (1966). Prognostic scales in schizophrenia. *Journal of Consulting Psychology, 30,* 18–24.

Garmezy, N. (1970). Process and reactive schizophrenia: Some conceptions and issues. *Schizophrenia Bulletin, 2,* 30–74.

Garmezy, N. (1971). Vulnerability research and the issue of primary prevention. *American Journal of Orthopsychiatry, 41,* 101–116.

Garmezy, N., Masten, A., Nordstrom, L., & Ferrarese, M. (1979). The nature of competence in normal and deviant children. In M. W. Kent & J. E. Rolf (Eds.), *The primary prevention of psychopathology: Promoting social competence and coping in children* (Vol. 3) (pp. 23–43). Hanover, NH: University Press of New England.

Garmezy, N., & Rodnick, E. H. (1959). Premorbid adjustment and performance in schizophrenia: Implications for interpreting heterogeneity in schizophrenia. *Journal of Nervous and Mental Disease, 129,* 450–466.

Garmezy, N., & Streitman, S. (1974). Children at risk: The search for the antecedents of schizophrenia. I. Conceptual models and research methods. *Schizophrenia Bulletin, 8,* 14–90.

Garner, W. R., Hake, H. W., & Eriksen, C. W. (1956). Operationism and the concept of perception. *Psychological Review, 63,* 149–159.

Garside, R. F., & Roth, M. (1978). Multivariate statistical methods and problems of classification in psychiatry. *British Journal of Psychiatry, 133*, 53–67.

Gerner, R. H. (1979). Depression in the elderly. In O. Kaplan (Ed.), *Psychopathology of aging* (pp. 97–135). San Francisco: Academic.

Gerstein, A. L., Brodzinsky, D. M., & Reiskind, N. (1976). Perceptual integration on the Rorschach as an indicator of cognitive capacity: A developmental study of racial differences in a clinic population. *Journal of Consulting and Clinical Psychology, 44*, 760–765.

Gibson, R. W. (1978). Planning a total treatment program for the hospitalized depressed patient. In J. O. Cole, A. F. Schatzberg, & S. H. Frazier (Eds.), *Depression: Biology, psychodynamics, and treatment* (pp. 229–242). New York: Plenum.

Gift, T. E., Strauss, J. S., Harder, D. W., Kokes, R. F., & Ritzler, B. A. (1981). Established chronicity of psychotic symptoms in first admission schizophrenic patients. *American Journal of Psychiatry, 138*, 779–784.

Gift, T. E., Strauss J. S., Ritzler, B. A., Kokes, R. F., & Harder, D. W. (1980). How diagnostic concepts of schizophrenia differ. *Journal of Nervous and Mental Disease, 168*, 3–8.

Gilligan, C. (1982). *In a different voice: Psychological theory and women's development.* Cambridge: Harvard University Press.

Gittelman-Klein, R., & Klein, D. (1968). Marital status as a prognostic indicator in schizophrenia. *Journal of Nervous and Mental Disease, 147*, 289–295.

Gittelman-Klein, R., & Klein, D. (1969). Premorbid asocial adjustment and prognosis in schizophrenia. *Journal of Psychiatric Research, 1*, 35–53.

Glatt, C. T., & Karon, B. P. (1974). A Rorschach validation study of the ego regression theory of psychopathology. *Journal of Consulting and Clinical Psychology, 42*, 569–576.

Glick, M., Marsh, A., & Zigler, E. (1984). *Premorbid social competence, socioeconomic status and psychiatric outcome.* Unpublished manuscript, Yale University, New Haven.

Glick, M., & Zigler, E. (in press). Premorbid social competence and psychiatric outcome in male and female nonschizophrenic patients. *Journal of Consulting and Clinical Psychology.*

Glick, M., & Zigler, E. (1985). Self-image: A cognitive–developmental approach. In. R. L. Leahy (Ed.), *The development of the self* (pp. 1–53). New York: Academic.

Glick, M., Zigler, E., & Zigler, B. (1985). Developmental correlates of age on first hospitalization in nonschizophrenic psychiatric patients. *Journal of Nervous and Mental Disease, 173*, 677–684.

Glueck, E., & Glueck, S. (1968). *Delinquents and nondelinquents in perspective.* Cambridge: Harvard University Press.

Goldberg, E. M., & Morrison, S. L. (1963). Schizophrenia and social class. *British Journal of Psychiatry, 109*, 785–802.

Goldfried, M. R., Stricker, C., & Weiner, I. B. (1971). *Rorschach handbook of clinical and research applications.* Englewood Cliffs, NJ: Prentice-Hall.

Goldman, A. E. (1962). A cognitive–developmental approach to schizophrenia. *Psychological Bulletin, 59,* 57–69.

Goldstein, M. (1978). Further data concerning the relation between premorbid adjustment and paranoid symptomatology. *Schizophrenia Bulletin, 4,* 236–241.

Goldstein, M., Held, J., & Cromwell, R. (1968). Premorbid adjustment and paranoid–nonparanoid status in schizophrenia, *Psychological Bulletin, 70,* 382–386.

Goldstein, R. H., & Salzman, L. F. (1965). Proverb word count as a measure of overinclusiveness in delusional schizophrenics. *Journal of Abnormal Psychology, 70,* 224–245.

Goldstein, S. G., & Linden, J. D. (1969). Multivariate classification of alcoholics by means of the MMPI. *Journal of Abnormal Psychology, 74,* 661–669.

Gomberg, E. S. (1968). Etiology of alcoholism. *Journal of Consulting and Clinical Psychology, 32,* 18–20.

Gomberg, E. S. (1974). Women and alcoholism. In V. Franks & V. Burtle (Eds.), *Women in therapy* (pp. 169–190). New York: Brunner/Mazel.

Gomberg, E. S. (1979). Problems with alcohol and other drugs. In E. S. Gomberg & V. Franks (Eds.), *Gender and disordered behavior* (pp. 204–240). New York: Brunner/Mazel.

Goodwin, D. W., Alderson, P., & Rosenthal, R. (1971). Clinical significance of hallucinations in psychiatric disorders. *Archives of General Psychiatry, 24,* 76–80.

Gottesman, I., & Shields, J. (1972). *Schizophrenia and genetics: A twin study vantage point.* New York: Academic.

Gottesman, I., & Shields, J. (1976). A critical review of recent adoption, twin, and family studies of schizophrenia: Behavioral genetics perspectives. *Schizophrenia Bulletin, 2,* 360–401.

Gottesman, I., & Shields, J. (1982). *Schizophrenia, the epigenetic puzzle.* New York: Cambridge University Press.

Gottesman, L. (1964). Forced choice word associations in schizophrenia. *Journal of Abnormal and Social Psychology, 69,* 673–675.

Goulet, L. R., & Baltes, P. B. (1970). *Life-span developmental psychology: Research and theory.* New York: Academic.

Gove, W. R. (1979). Sex differences in the epidemiology of mental disorder: Evidence and explanations. In E. S. Gomberg & V. Franks (Eds.), *Gender and disordered behavior* (pp. 23–68). New York: Brunner/Mazel.

Gove, W., & Tudor, J. (1977). Adult sex roles and mental illness. *American Journal of Sociology, 42,* 704–715.

Greenberg, R. P., & Cardwell, G. F. (1978). Rorschach developmental level and intelligence factors. *Journal of Consulting and Clinical Psychology, 46,* 844–848.

Grziwok, R., & Scodel, A. (1956). Some psychological correlates of humor preferences. *Journal of Consulting Psychology, 20,* 42.

Guerney, B., Jr., & Burton, J. L. (1963). Relationships among anxiety and self, typical peer, and ideal percepts in college women. *Journal of Social Psychology, 61,* 335–344.

Gunderson, J. G., Autry, J. H., III, Mosher, L. R., & Buschsbaum, S. (1974). Special Report: Schizophrenia. *Schizophrenia Bulletin, 9*, 16–54.

Gurney, C., Roth, M., Garside, R. F., Kerr, T. A., & Schapira, K. (1972) Studies in the classification of affective disorders: The relationship between anxiety states and depressive illness. II. *British Journal of Psychiatry, 12*, 162–166.

Gurucharri, C., Phelps, E., & Selman, R. L. (1984). Development of interpersonal understanding: A longitudinal and comparative study of normal and disturbed youth. *Journal of Consulting and Clinical Psychology, 52*, 26–36.

Guze, S. (1976). *Criminality and psychiatric disorders.* New York: Oxford University Press.

Haan, N. (1963). Proposed model of ego functioning: Coping and defense mechanisms in relation to IQ change. *Psychological Monographs, 77*, 1–23.

Hackett, T. P., & Adams, R. D. (1974). Grief reactive depression, manic-depressive psychosis, involutional melancholia and hypochondriasis. In M. M. Wintrobe, G. W. Thorn, R. D. Adams, E. Braunwald, K. J. Isselbacher, & R. G. Petersdorf (Eds.), *Harrison's principles of internal medicine* (7th ed.) (pp. 1887–1895). New York: McGraw-Hill.

Haier, R. J. (1980). The diagnosis of schizophrenia: A review of recent developments. *Schizophrenia Bulletin, 6*, 417–428.

Hamilton, M. (1969). Standardized assessment and recoding of depressive symptoms. *Psychiatria Neurologia, Neurochirugia, 72*, 201–205.

Hamlin, R. M., & Lorr, M. (1971). Differentiation of normals, neurotics, paranoids and nonparanoids. *Journal of Abnormal Psychology, 77*, 90–96.

Hammen, C. L., & Padesky, C. (1977). Sex differences in the expression of depressive responses on the Beck Depression Inventory. *Journal of Abnormal Psychology, 86*, 609–614.

Harder, D. W., & Ritzler, B. (1979). A comparison of Rorschach developmental-level and form-level systems as indicators of psychosis. *Journal of Personality Assessment, 43*, 347–354.

Harder, D. W., Strauss, J. S., Kokes, R. F., Ritzler, B. A., & Gift, T. E. (1980). Life events and psychopathology severity among first psychiatric admissions. *Journal of Abnormal Psychology, 89*, 165–180.

Harrow, M., Bromet, E., & Quinlan, D. (1974). Predictors of posthospital adjustment in schizophrenia: Thought disorders and schizophrenic diagnosis. *Journal of Nervous and Mental Disease, 158*, 25–36.

Harrow, M., & Grossman, L. (1984). Outcome in schizoaffective disorders: A critical review and reevaluation of the literature. *Schizophrenia Bulletin, 10*, 87–108.

Harrow, M., & Quinlan, D. (1977). Is disordered thinking unique to schizophrenia? *Archives of General Psychiatry, 34*, 15–21.

Harrow, M., Tucker, G., & Bromet, E. (1969). Short-term prognosis of schizophrenic patients. *Archives of General Psychiatry, 21*, 195–201.

Harter, S. (1978). Effectance motivation reconsidered: Toward a developmental model. *Human Development, 21*, 34–64.

Harter, S. (1983). Developmental perspectives on the self-system. In P. H. Mussen (Ed.), *Handbook of child psychology* (4th ed.). *Vol. 4. Socialization, personal-*

ity, and social development. (E. M. Hetherington, Ed.) (pp. 275–385). New York: Wiley.

Harter, S., & Zigler, E. (1974). The assessment of effectance motivation in normal and retarded children. *Developmental Psychology, 10,* 169–180.

Hartman, A. M. (1962). The apparent size of after-images in delusions and delusional schizophrenics. *American Journal of Psychology, 75,* 587–595.

Hartman, W., & Meyer, J. (1969). Long term hospitalization of schizophrenic patients. *Comprehensive Psychiatry, 10,* 122–127.

Hartmann, E. (1975). Dreams and other hallucinations: An approach to the underlying mechanism. In E. L. Siegel & J. West (Eds.), *Hallucinations: Behavior, experience, and theory* (pp. 71–79). New York: Wiley.

Hartmann, H. (1952). Mutual influences in the development of ego and id. *Psychoanalytic Study of the Child, 7,* 9–30.

Hartmann, H. (1958). *Ego psychology and the problem of adaptation.* New York: International Universities Press.

Hartmann, H. (1964). *Essays on ego psychology: Selected problems in psychoanalytic theory.* New York: International Universities Press.

Hauser, S. T. (1976). Loevinger's model and measure of ego development: A critical review. *Psychological Bulletin, 83,* 928–955.

Havener, P. H., & Izard, C. E. (1962). Unrealistic self-enhancement in paranoid schizophrenics. *Journal of Consulting Psychology, 26,* 65–68.

Hawk, A. B., Carpenter, W. T., & Strauss, J. S. (1975). Diagnostic criteria and five-year outcome in schizophrenia: A report from the International Pilot Study of Schizophrenia. *Archives of General Psychiatry, 32,* 343–347.

Hawks, D. V. (1964). The clinical usefulness of some tests of overinclusive thinking in psychiatric patients. *British Journal of Social and Clinical Psychology, 3,* 186–195.

Hay, A. J., & Forrest, A. D. (1972). The diagnosis of schizophrenia and paranoid psychosis: An attempt at classification. *British Journal of Medical Psychology, 45,* 233–241.

Heffner, P., Strauss, M. E., & Grisell, J. (1975). Rehospitalization of schizophrenics as a function of intelligence. *Journal of Abnormal Psychology, 84,* 735–736.

Heilbrun, A. B. (1971). Style of adaptation to perceived aversive maternal stimulation and selective attention to evaluative cues. *Journal of Abnormal Psychology, 77,* 340–344.

Heilbrun, A. B. (1972). Defensive projection in late adolescents: Implications for a developmental model of paranoid behavior. *Child Development, 43,* 880–891.

Heilbrun, A. B., & Bronson, N. (1975). The fabrication of delusional thinking in normals. *Journal of Abnormal Psychology, 84,* 422–425.

Heilbrun, A. B., & Madison, J. K. (1978). An analysis of structural factors in schizophrenic delusions. *Journal of Clinical Psychology, 34,* 326–329.

Heilbrun, A. B., & Heilbrun, K. S. (1977). Content analysis of delusions in reactive and process schizophrenia. *Journal of Abnormal Psychology, 86,* 597–608.

Held, J., & Cromwell, R. (1968). Premorbid adjustment in schizophrenia: The evaluation of a method and some general comments. *Journal of Nervous and Mental Disease, 146,* 264–272.

Helgason, T. (1964). Epidemiology of mental disorders in Iceland. *Acta Psychiatrica Scandinavica, 40* (Suppl. 173), 11–258.

Hemmendinger, L. (1953). Perceptual organizational development as reflected in the structure of Rorschach responses. *Journal of Projective Techniques, 17,* 162–170.

Hemmindinger, L., & Schultz, K. (1977). Developmental theory and the Rorschach method. In M. A. Rickers-Ovsiankina (Ed.), *Rorschach psychology* (pp. 83–111). Huntington, NY: Robert E. Kreiger.

Hempel, C. G. (1961). Introduction to problems of taxonomy. In J. Zubin (Ed.), *Field studies in the mental disorders* (pp. 3–50). New York: Grune & Stratton.

Henderson, A. S., Krupinski, J., & Stoller, A. (1971). The epidemiological aspects of adolescent psychiatry. In J. G. Howells (Ed.), *Modern perspectives in adolescent psychiatry* (pp. 183–208). New York: Brunner/Mazel.

Herron, W. G. (1962). The process–reactive classification of schizophrenia. *Psychological Bulletin, 59,* 329–343.

Hersch, C. (1957). Perceptual structure in creative artists: An analysis by means of the Rorschach test. *Dissertation Abstracts International, 18/01,* 296 (University Microfilms No. 00-23896)

Heston, L. L. (1966). Psychiatric disorders in foster home reared children of schizophrenic mothers. *British Journal of Psychiatry, 112,* 819–825.

Heston, L. L., & Denney, D. (1968). Interactions between early life experience and biological factors in schizophrenia. In D. Rosenthal & S. S. Kety (Eds.), *The transmission of schizophrenia* (pp. 363–376). Oxford: Pergamon.

Hetherington, E. M. (1964). Humor preferences in normal and physically handicapped children. *Journal of Abnormal and Social Psychology, 69,* 694–696.

Hetherington, E. M., & Wray, N. (1964). Aggression, need for social approval, and humor preferences. *Journal of Abnormal and Social Psychology, 68,* 685–689.

Higgins, J. (1964). The concept of process–reactive schizophrenia: Criteria and related research. *Journal of Nervous and Mental Disease, 138,* 9–25.

Hill, J. M. (1936). Hallucinations in psychoses. *Journal of Nervous and Mental Disease, 83,* 405–421.

Hillson, J. S., & Worchel, P. (1957). Self concept and defensive behavior in the maladjusted. *Journal of Consulting Psychology, 21,* 83–88.

Hirsch, J. (1973). Behavior genetics and individuality understood. In E. Zigler & I. L. Child (Eds.), *Socialization and personality development* (pp. 192–211). Reading, MA: Addison-Wesley.

Hirt, M., Cuttler, M., & Genshaft, J. (1977). Information processing by schizophrenics when task complexity increases. *Journal of Abnormal Psychology, 86,* 256–260.

Hoffmann, H., & Nelson, P. C. (1971). Personality characteristics of alcoholics in relation to age and intelligence. *Psychological Reports, 29,* 143–146.

Hogarty, G. E., Goldberg, S. C., Schooler, N. R., & Ulrich, R. F. (1974). Drug and sociotherapy in the aftercare of schizophrenic patients. II. Two year relapse rates. *Archives of General Psychiatry, 31*, 603–618.

Hollingshead, A., & Redlich, F. (1958). *Social class and mental illness*. New York: Wiley.

Holmes, T., Joffe, J., Ketchan, J., & Sheehy, T. (1961). Experimental study of prognosis. *Journal of Psychosomatic Research, 5*, 235–252.

Holt, R. R. (1963). *Manual for the scoring of primary process manifestations in Rorschach responses* (Draft 9). Unpublished manuscript, New York University.

Holzman, P. S., & Levy, D. L. (1977). Smooth pursuit eye movements and functional psychosis: A review. *Schizophrenia Bulletin, 3*, 15–27.

Hornstra, R., & Udell, B. (1974). Patterns of psychiatric utilization by diagnosed schizophrenics in the Kansas City area, *Schizophrenia Bulletin, 9*, 133–147.

Horowitz, M. J. (1975). Hallucinations: An information-processing approach. In E. L. Siegel & J. West (Eds.), *Hallucinations: Behavior, experience, and theory* (pp. 163–195). New York: Wiley.

Houston, F., & Royse, A. B. (1954). Relationship between deafness and psychotic illness. *Journal of Mental Science, 100*, 990–993.

Huber, G., Gross, G., & Schüttler, R. (1975). A long-term follow-up study of schizophrenia: Psychiatric course of illness and prognosis. *Acta Psychiatrica Scandinavica, 52*, 49–57.

Huber, G., Gross, G., Schüttler, R., & Linz, M. (1980). Longitudinal studies of schizophrenic patients. *Schizophrenia Bulletin, 6*, 592–605.

Hunter, M., Schooler, C., & Spohn, H. E. (1962). The measurement of characteristic patterns of ward behavior in chronic schizophrenics. *Journal of Consulting Psychology, 26*, 69–73.

Hurwitz, I. (1954). A developmental study of the relationship between motor activity and perceptual processes as measured by the Rorschach test. *Dissertation Abstracts International, 14/10*, 1085. (University Microfilms No. 00-09011)

Husaini, B. A., & Neff, J. A. (1981). Social class and depressive symptomatology. *Journal of Nervous and Mental Disease, 169*, 638–647.

Iacono, W. G., Peloquin, L. J., Lumry, A. E., Valentine, B. H., & Tuason, V. B. (1982). Eye tracking in patients with unipolar and bipolar affective disorders in remission. *Journal of Abnormal Psychology, 91*, 35–44.

Ianzito, B. M., Cadoret, R. J., & Pugh, D. D. (1974). Thought disorder in depression. *American Journal of Psychiatry, 131*, 703–707.

Inglis, J., & Lawson, J. (1982). Sex differences in the functional asymmetry of the damaged brain. *Behavioral Brain Sciences, 5*, 307–309.

Inhelder, B. (1957). Developmental psychology. *Annual Review of Psychology, 8*, 139–162.

Jacobs, M. A., Muller, J. J., Anderson, J., & Skinner, J. C. (1972). Therapeutic expectations, premorbid adjustment, and manifest distress levels as predictors of improvement in hospitalized patients. *Journal of Consulting and Clinical Psychology, 39*, 455–461.

Jacobs, M. A., Muller, J. J., Anderson, J., & Skinner, J. C. (1973). Prediction of improvement in coping pathology in hospitalized psychiatric patients: A replication study. *Journal of Consulting and Clinical Psychology, 40,* 343–349.

Jahoda, M. (1958). *Current concepts of positive mental health.* New York: Basic.

James, W. (1890). *Principles of Psychology.* New York: Holt.

Jansson, B. (1968). The prognostic significance of various types of hallucinations in young people. *Acta Psychiatrica Scandinavica, 44,* 401–409.

Jencks, C. (1979). *Who gets ahead?* New York: Basic.

Johannsen, W. J., Friedman, S. H., Leitshuh, T., & Ammons, H. (1963). A study of certain schizophrenic dimensions and their relationship to double alternative learning. *Journal of Consulting Psychology, 17,* 375–382.

Johannsen, W. J., Friedman, S. H., & Liccione, J. V. (1964). Visual perception as a function of chronicity in schizophrenia. *British Journal of Psychiatry, 110,* 561–570.

John, R., Mednick, S., & Schulsinger, F. (1982). Teacher reports as a predictor of schizophrenia and borderline schizophrenia: A Bayesian decision analysis. *Journal of Abnormal Psychology, 91,* 399–413.

Johnson, D. (1980). Cognitive organization in paranoid and nonparanoid schizophrenia (Doctoral dissertation, Yale University). *Dissertation Abstracts International, 41,* 25208A.

Jones, E. F., & Berglas, S. (1978). Control of attributions about the self through self-handicapping strategies: The appeal of alcohol and the role of underachievement. *Personality and Social Psychology Bulletin, 4,* 200–206.

Jones, M. C. (1968). Personality correlates and antecedents of drinking patterns in adult males. *Journal of Consulting and Clinical Psychology, 32,* 2–12.

Judson, A. J. & Katahn, M. (1964). Levels of personality organization and production of associative sequences in process–reactive schizophrenia. *Journal of Consulting Psychology, 28,* 208–213.

Kaden, S., & Lipton, H. (1960). Rorschach developmental scores and posthospital adjustment of married male schizophrenics. *Journal of Projective Techniques, 24,* 144–147.

Kagan, J. (1971). *Change and continuity in infancy.* New York: Wiley.

Kagan, J. (1980). Perspectives on continuity. In O. G. Brim, Jr., & J. Kagan (Eds.), *Constancy and change in human development* (pp. 26–74). Cambridge: Harvard University Press.

Kalin, N. H., Risch, S. C., & Janowsky, D. S. (1981). Use of the dexamethasone suppression test in clinical psychiatry. *Journal of Clinical Psychopharmacology, 1,* 64–69.

Kanfer, F. H. (1970). Self-regulation: Research, issues, and speculations. In C. Neuringer & J. L. Michel (Eds.), *Behavior modification in clinical psychology* (pp. 178–220). New York: Appleton-Century-Crofts.

Kanfer, F. H., & Saslow, G. (1969). Behavioral diagnosis. In C. M. Franks (Ed.), *Behavior therapy: Appraisal and status* (pp. 417–444). New York: McGraw-Hill.

Kantor, R., & Herron, W. (1966). *Reactive and process schizophrenia.* Palo Alto, CA: Science and Behavior Books

Kantor, R., Wallner, J., & Winder, C. (1953). Process and reactive schizophrenia. *Journal of Consulting Psychology, 17,* 157–162.

Kantor, S. J., & Glassman, A. H. (1977). Delusional depressions: Natural history and response to treatment. *British Journal of Psychiatry, 131,* 351–360.

Kaplan, B. (1967). Meditations on genesis. *Human Development, 10,* 65–87.

Kaplan, H. B., & Pokorny, A. D. (1969). Self-derogation and psychosocial adjustment. *Journal of Nervous and Mental Disease, 149,* 421–434.

Karlsson, J. L. (1966). *The biological basis of schizophrenia.* Springfield, IL: Thomas.

Karlsson, J. L. (1974). Inheritance of schizophrenia. *Acta Psychiatrica Scandinavica* (suppl.) *247,* 1–116.

Katz, P., & Zigler, E. (1967). Self-image disparity: A developmental approach. *Journal of Personality and Social Psychology, 5,* 186–195.

Katz, P., Zigler, E., & Zalk, S. (1975). Children's self-image disparity: The effects of age, maladjustment, and action–thought orientation. *Developmental Psychology, 11,* 546–550.

Kay, D. W., Cooper, A. F., Garside, R. F., & Roth, M. (1976). The differentiation of paranoid from affective psychoses by patients' premorbid characteristics. *British Journal of Psychiatry, 129,* 207–215.

Kazdin, A. L., Bellack, A. S., & Hersen, M. (Eds.). (1980). *New perspectives in abnormal psychology.* New York: Oxford University Press.

Kendell, R. (1975). *The role of diagnosis in psychiatry.* Oxford: Blackwell Scientific Publications.

Kendell, R., Brockington, I. F., & Leff, J. P. (1979). Prognostic implications of six alternative definitions of schizophrenia. *Archives of General Psychiatry, 36,* 25–31.

Kendell, R., & Gourley, J. (1970). The clinical distinction between affective psychoses and schizophrenia. *British Journal of Psychiatry, 117,* 261–266.

Kendler, K. S. (1982). Demography of paranoid psychosis (delusional disorder). *Archives of General Psychiatry, 39,* 890–902.

Kendler, K. S., & Davis, K. L. (1981). The genetics and biochemistry of paranoid schizophrenia and other paranoid psychoses. *Schizophrenia Bulletin, 7,* 689–709.

Kendler, K. S., Gruenberg, A. M., & Tsuang, M. T. (1984). Outcome of schizophrenic subtypes defined by four diagnostic systems. *Archives of General Psychiatry, 41,* 149–154.

Kendler, K. S., & Tsuang, M. T. (1981). Nosology of paranoid schizophrenia and the other paranoid psychoses. *Schizophrenia Bulletin, 1,* 594–610.

Keniston, K., Boltax, S., & Almond, R. (1971). Multiple criteria of treatment outcome. *Journal of Psychiatric Research, 8,* 107–118.

Kenrick, D. T., & Stringfield, D. O. (1980). Personality traits and the eye of the beholder: Crossing some traditional philosophical boundaries in the search for consistency in all of the people. *Psychological Review, 87,* 88–104.

Kety, S. S., Rosenthal, D., Wender, P. H., Schulsinger, F., & Jacobsen, B. (1975).

Mental illness in the biological and adoptive families of adopted individuals who have become schizophrenic: A preliminary report based on psychiatric interviews. In R. Fieve, D. Rosenthal, & H. Brill (Eds.), *Genetic research in psychiatry* (pp. 147–165). Baltimore: Johns Hopkins University Press.

Kimble, G., Garmezy, N., & Zigler, E. (1980). *Principles of general psychology* (5th ed.). New York: Wiley.

Kimble, G., Garmezy, N., & Zigler, E. (1974). *Principles of general psychology.* New York: Ronald Press.

King, L. M. (1978). Social and cultural influences on psychopathology. *Annual Review of Psychology, 29,* 405–433.

Kinsbourne, M. (1982). Hemispheric specialization and the growth of human understanding. *American Psychologist, 37,* 411–420.

Kirshner, L. A., & Johnston, L. (1983). Effects of gender on inpatient psychiatric hospitalization. *Journal of Nervous and Mental Disease, 171,* 651–657.

Kissell, S. (1965). A brief note on the relationship between Rorschach developmental level and intelligence. *Journal of Projective Techniques and Personality Assessment, 29,* 454–455.

Klerman, G. L. (1978). Affective disorders. In A. M. Nicholi, Jr. (Ed.), *The Harvard guide to modern psychiatry* (pp. 253–281). Cambridge: Harvard University Press.

Klorman, R., Strauss, J. S., & Kokes, R. F. (1977). Premorbid adjustment in schizophrenia. III. The relationship of demographic and diagnostic factors to measures of premorbid adjustment in schizophrenia. *Schizophrenia Bulletin, 3,* 214–225.

Knauth, P. (1975). *A season in hell.* New York: Harper & Row.

Knight, R. A., Roff, J. D., Barnett, J., & Moss, J. L. (1979). Concurrent and predictive validity of thought disorder and affectivity: A 22 year follow-up of acute schizophrenics. *Journal of Abnormal Psychology, 88,* 1–12.

Knight, R. P. (1937). The dynamics and treatment of chronic alcohol addiction. *Bulletin of the Menninger Clinic, 1,* 233–250.

Knights, A., & Hirsch, S. R. (1981). Revealed depression and drug treatment for schizophrenia. *Archives of General Psychiatry, 38,* 806–811.

Koestler, A. (1964). *The act of creation.* New York: Macmillan.

Kohlberg, L. (1964). Development of moral character and moral ideology. In M. L. Hoffman & L. W. Hoffman (Eds.), *Review of child development research* (Vol. 1) (pp. 383–431). New York: Russell Sage Foundation.

Kohlberg, L. (1969). Stage and sequence: The cognitive–developmental approach to socialization. In D. Goslin (Ed.), *Handbook of socialization theory and research* (pp. 347–480). New York: Rand McNally.

Kohlberg, L., LaCrosse, J., & Ricks, D. (1972). The predictability of adult mental health from childhood behavior. In B. Wolman (Ed.), *Manual of child psychopathology* (pp. 1217–1284). New York: McGraw-Hill.

Kohlberg, L., & Zigler, E. (1967). The impact of cognitive maturity on the development of sex-role attitudes in the years four to eight. *Genetic Psychology Monographs, 75,* 89–165.

Kohn, M. L. (1973). Social class and schizophrenia: A critical review and a reformulation. *Schizophrenia Bulletin, 7,* 60–79.

Kokes, R. F., Strauss, J. S., & Klorman, R. (1977). Premorbid adjustment in schizophrenia: Concepts, measures, and implications. II. Measuring premorbid adjustment: The instruments and their development. *Schizophrenia Bulletin, 3,* 186–213.

Kopfstein, J. H., & Neale, J. M. (1971). Size estimation in schizophrenic and nonschizophrenic subjects. *Journal of Consulting and Clinical Psychology, 36,* 430–435.

Korchin, S., Meltzoff, J., & Singer, J. (1951). Motor inhibition and Rorschach movement response. *American Psychologist, 6,* 344–345.

Kovacs, M., & Beck, A. T. (1978). Maladaptive cognitive structures in depression. *American Journal of Psychiatry, 135,* 525–533.

Kraepelin, E. (1921). *Manic-depressive insanity and paranoia.* Edinburgh: E. and S. Livingston.

Kringlen, E. (1980). Schizophrenia: Research in the Nordic countries. *Schizophrenia Bulletin, 6,* 566–578.

Kris, E. (1950). Notes on the development and on some current problems of psychoanalytic child psychology. *Psychoanalytic Study of the Child, 5,* 34–62.

Kris, E. (1952). *Psychoanalytic explorations in art.* New York: International Universities Press.

Kruger, A. K. (1954). Direct and substitute modes of tension reduction in terms of developmental level: An experimental analysis by means of the Rorschach test. *Dissertation Abstracts International, 14,* 1806. (University Microfilms No. 00-09, 013)

Krupinski, J., & Stoller, A. (1975). Changing patterns of psychiatric hospitalization in the past fifty years: A cohort study. *Australian and New Zealand Journal of Psychiatry, 9,* 231–239.

Kuhn, T. S. (1962). *The structure of scientific revolutions.* Chicago: University of Chicago Press.

Laing, R. D. (1967). *The politics of experience.* New York: Ballantine.

Lane, E. (1968). The influence of sex and race on process–reactive ratings of schizophrenics. *Journal of Psychology, 68,* 15–20.

Lane, J. (1955). Social effectiveness and developmental level. *Journal of Personality, 23,* 274–284.

Langer, J. (1969). *Theories of development.* New York: Holt, Rinehart & Winston.

Langer, J. (1970). Werner's comparative organismic theory. In P. H. Mussen (Ed.), *Carmichael's Manual of Child Psychology* (3rd ed.) (pp. 733–771). New York: Wiley.

Langfeldt, G. (1969). Schizophrenia: Diagnoses and prognosis. *Behavioral Science, 14,* 173–182.

Larson, C. A., & Nyman, G. E. (1970). Age of onset in schizophrenia. *Human Heredity, 20,* 241–247.

Leaf, P. J., Weissman, M. M., Myers, J. K., Tischler, G. L., & Holzer, C. E., III.

Social factors related to psychiatric disorder: The Yale Epidemiologic Catchment Area Study. *Social Psychiatry, 19*, 53–61.

Leahy, R. L. (1981). Parental practices and the development of moral judgment and self-image disparity during adolescence. *Developmental Psychology, 17*, 580–594.

Leahy, R., Balla, D., & Zigler, E. (1982). Role-taking, self-image, and imitation in retarded and nonretarded individuals. *American Journal of Mental Deficiency, 86*, 372–379.

Leahy, R. L., & Huard, C. (1976). Role taking and self-image disparity in children. *Developmental Psychology, 12*, 501–508.

Lenneberg, E. (1967). *Biological foundations of language*. New York: Wiley.

Leonhard, K. (1975). Prognosis of paranoid states in relation to the clinical features. *Acta Psychiatrica Scandinavica, 51*, 1975, 134–151.

Lerner, P. M. (1968). Correlation of social competence and level of cognitive perceptual functioning in male schizophrenics. *Journal of Nervous and Mental Disease, 146*, 412–416.

Lerner, P. M. (Ed.). (1975). *Handbook of Rorschach scales*. New York: International Universities Press.

Levine, D. (1959). Rorschach genetic level and mental disorder. *Journal of Projective Techniques, 23*, 436–439.

Levine, J. (1963). Humor and mental health. In A. Deutsch & H. Fishman (Eds.), *Encyclopedia of mental health* (Vol. 3) (pp. 786–799). New York: Franklin Watts.

Levine, J. (1968). Humor. In *International encyclopedia of the social sciences*. New York: Macmillan.

Levine, J. (1969). Psychodynamics of sexual humor. *Human Sexuality, 3*, 57–63.

Levine, J., & Abelson, R. (1959). Humor as a disturbing stimulus. *Journal of General Psychology, 60*, 191–200.

Levine, J., & Redlich, F. C. (1955). Failure to understand humor. *Psychoanalytic Quarterly, 24*, 560–572.

Levine, J., & Redlich, F. C. (1960). Intellectual and emotional factors in the appreciation of humor. *Journal of General Psychology, 62*, 25–35.

Levine, J., & Zigler, E. (1973). The essential–reactive distinction in alcoholism: A developmental approach. *Journal of Abnormal Psychology, 81*, 242–249.

Levine, J., & Zigler, E. (1976). Humor responses of high and low premorbid competence alcoholic and nonalcoholic patients to cartoons having different content themes. *Addictive Behaviors, 1*, 139–149.

Levine, J., & Zigler, E. (1981). The developmental approach to alcoholism: A further investigation. *Addictive Behaviors, 6*, 93–98.

Levinson, D. (1978). *The seasons of a man's life*. New York: Knopf.

Levinson, D. (1985, February). *The seasons of a woman's life*. Paper presented to the Psychology Department, Yale University, New Haven, CT.

Levinson, P., & Campus, N. (1978). A comparison of four scales that assess premorbid competence. *Journal of Nervous and Mental Disease, 166*, 204–208.

Lewin, K. (1936). *Dynamic theory of personality*. New York: McGraw-Hill.

Lewin, K. (1946). Behavior and development as a function of the total situation. In L. Carmichael (Ed.), *Manual of child psychology* (pp. 791–844). New York: Wiley.

Lewine, R. R. J. (1980). Sex differences in age of symptom onset and first hospitalization in schizophrenia. *American Journal of Orthopsychiatry, 50,* 316–322.

Lewine, R. R. J. (1981). Sex differences in schizophrenia: Timing or subtypes? *Psychological Bulletin, 90,* 432–444.

Lewine, R. R. J., Burbach, D., & Meltzer, H. (1984). Effect of diagnostic criteria on the ratio of male to female schizophrenic patients. *American Journal of Psychiatry, 141,* 84–87.

Lewine, R. R. J., Strauss, J. S., & Gift, T. E. (1981). Sex differences in age at first hospital admission for schizophrenia? Fact or artifact? *American Journal of Psychiatry, 138,* 440–444.

Lewine, R. R. J., Watt, N., & Fryer, J. H. (1978). A study of childhood social competence, adult premorbid competence, and psychiatric outcome in three schizophrenic subtypes. *Journal of Abnormal Psychology, 87,* 294–302.

Lewine, R. R. J., Watt, N. F., Prentky, R. A., & Fryer, J. H. (1978). Childhood behavior in schizophrenia, personality disorder, depression, and neurosis. *British Journal of Psychiatry, 132,* 347–357.

Lewine, R. R. J., Watt, N. F., Prentky, R. A., & Fryer, J. H. (1980). Childhood social competence in functionally disordered psychiatric patients and in normals. *Journal of Abnormal Psychology, 89,* 132–138.

Lewinsohn, P. M. (1967). Factors related to improvement in mental hospital patients. *Journal of Consulting Psychology, 31,* 588–594.

Lewinsohn, P. M., & Nichols, R. C. (1967). Dimensions of change in mental hospital patients. *Journal of Clinical Psychology, 23,* 498–502.

Lewis, H. B. (1979a). Guilt in obsession and paranoia. In C. E. Izard (Ed.), *Emotions in personality and psychopathology* (pp. 399–414). New York: Plenum.

Lewis, H. B. (1979b). Shame in depression and hysteria. In C. E. Izard (Ed.), *Emotions in personality and psychopathology* (pp. 371–396). New York: Plenum.

Lichtenberg, P. (1957). A definition and analysis of depression. *Archives of Neurology and Psychiatry, 77,* 516–527.

Lidz, T. (1978). A developmental theory. In J. Shershow (Ed.), *Schizophrenia: Science and practice* (pp. 69–95). Cambridge: Harvard University Press.

Liem, R., & Liem, J. (1978). Social class and mental illness reconsidered: The role of economic stress and social support. *Journal of Health and Social Behavior, 19,* 139–156.

Lipkin, K. M., Dyrud, J., & Meyer, G. C. (1970). The many faces of mania: Therapeutic trial of lithium carbonate. *Archives of General Psychiatry, 22,* 262–267.

Lipton, H., Kaden, S., & Phillips, L. (1958). Rorschach scores and decontextualization: A developmental view. *Journal of Personality, 26,* 291–302.

Loevinger, J. (1966). The meaning and measurement of ego development. *American Psychologist, 21,* 195–206.

Loevinger, J. (1976). *Ego development.* San Francisco: Jossey-Bass.

Loevinger, J., & Knoll, E. (1983). Personality: Stages, traits, and the self. *Annual Review of Psychology, 34*, 195–222.

Loevinger, J., & Wessler, R. (1970). *Measuring ego development* (Vol. 1). San Francisco: Jossey-Bass.

Loevinger, J., Wessler, R., & Redmore, C. (1970). *Measuring ego development* (Vol. 2). San Francisco: Jossey-Bass.

Lofchie, S. H. (1955). The performance of adults under distraction stress: A developmental approach. *Journal of Psychology, 39*, 109–116.

Long, B. H., Ziller, R. C., & Bankes, J. (1970). Self–other orientations of institutionalized behavior-problem adolescents. *Journal of Counseling and Clinical Psychology, 34*, 43–47.

Loranger, A. W. (1984). Sex difference in age at onset of schizophrenia. *Archives of General Psychiatry, 41*, 157–161.

Loranger, A. W., & Levine, P. M. (1978). Age at onset of bipolar affective illness. *Archives of General Psychiatry, 35*, 1345–1348.

Lorr, M., Klett, C. J., & McNair, D. M. (1963). *Syndromes of psychosis*. Oxford: Pergamon.

Lorr, M., Wittman, P., & Schonberger, W. (1951). An analysis of the Elgin Prognostic Scale. *Journal of Clinical Psychology, 7*, 260–263.

Lovinger, E. (1956). Perceptual contact with reality in schizophrenia. *Journal of Abnormal and Social Psychology, 52*, 87–91.

Lowe, G. R. (1973). The phenomenology of hallucinations as an aid to differential diagnosis. *British Journal of Psychiatry, 123*, 621–633.

Luborsky, L., Chandler, M., Auerbach, A., Cohen, J., & Bachrach, H. (1971). Factors influencing the outcome of psychotherapy: A review of quantitative research. *Psychological Bulletin, 75*, 145–185.

Luborsky, L., Todd, T. C., & Katcher, A. H. (1973). A self-administered social assets scale for predicting physical and psychological illness and health. *Journal of Psychosomatic Research, 17*, 109–120.

Lucas, C. J., Sainsbury, P., & Collins, J. G. (1962). A social and clinical study of delusions in schizophrenia. *British Journal of Psychiatry, 108*, 747–758.

Luria, A. R. (1961). *The role of speech in the regulation of normal and abnormal behavior*. London: Pergamon.

MacAndrew, C., & Geertsma, R. H. (1964). A critique of alcoholism scales derived from the MMPI. *Quarterly Journal of Studies on Alcohol, 25*, 68–76.

MacFadyen, H. W. (1975). The classification of depressive disorders. I. A review of statistically based classification studies. *Journal of Clinical Psychology, 3*, 380–401.

MacLusky, N., & Naftolin, F. (1981). Sexual differentiation of the central nervous system. *Science, 211*, 1294–1303.

Magaro, P. A. (1980). *Cognition in schizophrenia and paranoia*. Hillsdale, NJ: Erlbaum.

Magaro, P. A. (1981a). Editorial introduction: The paranoid as an emerging character. *Schizophrenia Bulletin, 7*, 586–587.

Magaro, P. A. (1981b). The paranoid and the schizophrenic: The case for distinctive cognitive style. *Schizophrenia Bulletin, 7,* 632–661.

Magnusson, D., & Endler, N. S. (1977). Interactional psychology: Present status and future prospects. In D. Magnusson & N. S. Endler (Eds.), *Personality at the crossroads* (pp. 3–31). Hillsdale, NJ: Erlbaum.

Maloney, M. P., & Ward, M. P. (1979). *Mental retardation and modern society.* New York: Oxford University Press.

Mannino, F., & Shore, M. F. (1974). Family structure, aftercare, and posthospital adjustment. *American Journal of Orthopsychiatry, 44,* 76–85.

Marks, L. (1975). On colored-hearing synesthesia: Cross-modal translations of sensory dimensions. *Psychological Bulletin, 82,* 303–331.

Marsh, A., Glick, M., & Zigler, E. (1981). Premorbid social competence and the revolving door phenomenon in psychiatric hospitalization. *Journal of Nervous and Mental Disease, 169,* 315–319.

Martin, E. M., & Chapman, L. J. (1982). Communicative effectiveness in psychosis-prone college students. *Journal of Abnormal Psychology, 91,* 420–425.

Maslow, A. H. (1954). *Motivation and personality.* New York: Harper & Row.

Maslow, A. H. (1968). *Toward a psychology of being* (2nd ed.). Princeton, NJ: Van Nostrand.

Maslow, A. H. (1970). *Motivation and personality* (2nd ed.). New York: Harper & Row.

Mason, C. F. (1956). Pre-illness intelligence of mental hospital patients. *Journal of Consulting Psychology, 20,* 297–300.

Mayer-Gross, E., Slater, E., & Roth, M. (1969). *Clinical psychiatry* (3rd ed.). London: Balliere, Tindall & Cassell.

McCabe, M. S. (1975). Demographic differences in functional psychoses. *British Journal of Psychiatry, 127,* 320–323.

McCabe, M. S. (1976a). Reactive psychoses and schizophrenia with good prognosis. *Archives of General Psychiatry, 33,* 571–576.

McCabe, M. S. (1976b). Symptom differences in reactive psychoses and schizophrenia with poor prognosis. *Comprehensive Psychiatry, 17,* 301–307.

McCabe, M. S., Fowler, R. C., Cadoret, R. S., & Winokur, G. (1971). Familial differences in schizophrenia with good and poor prognosis. *Psychological Medicine, 1,* 325–332.

McCabe, M. S., Fowler, R. C., Cadoret, R. J., & Winokur, G. (1972). Symptom differences in schizophrenia with good and poor prognosis. *American Journal of Psychiatry, 128,* 1239–1243.

McCormick, D. J., & Broekema, V. J. (1978). Cardiac rate and size estimation in schizophrenic and normal subjects. *Journal of Abnormal Psychology, 87,* 385–398.

McCreary, C. P. (1974). Comparison of measures of social competence in schizophrenics and the relation of social competency to socioeconomic factors. *Journal of Abnormal Psychology, 83,* 124–129.

McDowell, D., Reynolds, B., & Magaro, P. A. (1975). The integration defect in paranoid and nonparanoid schizophrenia. *Journal of Abnormal Psychology, 84*, 629–636.

McGaughran, L., & Moran, L. (1956). "Conceptual level" vs. "conceptual area" analysis of object-sorting behavior of schizophrenic and nonpsychiatric groups. *Journal of Abnormal and Social Psychology, 52*, 43–50.

McGaughran, L., & Moran, L. (1957). Differences between schizophrenic and brain damaged groups in conceptual aspects of object sorting. *Journal of Abnormal and Social Psychology, 54*, 44–49.

McGhee, P. E. (1974). Cognitive mastery and children's humor. *Psychological Bulletin, 81*, 721–730.

McGhie, A. (1970). Attention and perception in schizophrenia. In B. Maher (Ed.), *Progress in experimental personality research* (Vol. 5) (pp. 1–35). New York: Academic.

McGlashan, T. H. (1984). Testing four diagnostic systems for schizophrenia. *Archives of General Psychiatry, 41*, 141–144.

McGlashan, T. H., & Carpenter, W. T., Jr. (1976). Postpsychotic depression in schizophrenia. *Archives of General Psychiatry, 33*, 231–239.

McGlone, J. (1980). Sex differences in human brain asymmetry: A critical survey. *Behavioral and Brain Sciences, 3*, 215–263.

Mead, G. (1934). *Mind, self and society.* Chicago: University of Chicago Press.

Mednick, S. A., Schulsinger, F., Teasdale, T. W., Schulsinger, H., Venables, P. H., & Roch, D. R. (1978). Schizophrenia in high risk children: Sex differences in predisposing factors. In G. Serban (Ed.), *Cognitive defects and the development of mental illness* (pp. 169–197). New York: Brunner/Mazel.

Meehl, P. E. (1962). Schizotaxia, schizotypy, schizophrenia. *American Psychologist, 17*, 827–838.

Meehl, P. E. (1973). *Psychodiagnosis: Selected papers.* Minneapolis: University of Minnesota Press.

Meichenbaum, D. H. (1966). The effects of social reinforcement on the level of abstraction of schizophrenics. *Journal of Abnormal Psychology, 71*, 354–362.

Meissner, W. W. (1978). *The paranoid process.* New York: Jason Aronson.

Meissner, W. W. (1981). The schizophrenic and the paranoid process. *Schizophrenia Bulletin, 7*, 611–631.

Mendel, W. M. (1976). *Schizophrenia: The experience and its treatment.* San Francisco: Jossey-Bass.

Messer, S. B. (1976). Is this the age of depression? [Review of *Depression: Biology, psychodynamics, and treatment,* J. O. Cole, A. F. Schatzberg, & S. H. Frazier, Eds.]. *Contemporary Psychology, 24*, 311–312.

Michael, C. M., Morris, D. P., & Soroker, E. (1957). Follow-up studies of shy, withdrawn children. II. Relative incidence of schizophrenia. *American Journal of Orthopsychiatry, 27*, 331–337.

Michaels, J. J. (1964). The need for a theory of delinquency. *Archives of General Psychiatry, 10*, 182–186.

Miller, G., & Willer, B. (1976). Predictors of return to a psychiatric hospital. *Journal of Consulting and Clinical Psychology, 44*, 898–900.

Miller, W. R. (1976). Alcoholism scales and objective assessment methods: A review. *Psychological Bulletin, 83,* 649–674.

Millon, T. (1975). Reflections on Rosenhan's "On being sane in insane places." *Journal of Abnormal Psychology, 84,* 456–461.

Milner, B. (1974). Hemispheric specializations: Scope and limits. In F. O. Schmitt & F. G. Worden (Eds.), *The neurosciences: Third study program* (pp. 75–89). Cambridge: MIT Press.

Mintz, S., & Alpert, M. (1972). Imagery, vividness, reality testing and schizophrenic hallucinations. *Journal of Abnormal Psychology, 79,* 310–316.

Misch, R. (1954). The relationship of motoric inhibition to developmental level and ideational functioning: An analysis by means of the Rorschach test. *Dissertation Abstracts International, 14,*1810. (University Microfilms No. 00-09-016)

Mischel, W. (1968). *Personality and assessment.* New York: Wiley.

Mischel, W. (1973). Toward a cognitive social learning reconceptualization of personality. *Psychological Review, 80,* 252–283.

Mischel, W. (1977). The interaction of person and situation. In D. Magnusson, & N. S. Endler (Eds.), *Personality at the crossroads* (pp. 333–352). Hillsdale, NJ: Erlbaum.

Möller, H. J., Von Zerssen, D., Werner-Eilert, K., & Wüschner-Stockheim, M. (1982). Outcome in schizophrenic and similar paranoid psychoses. *Schizophrenia Bulletin, 8,* 99–108.

Montagu, A. (1974). *The natural superiority of women.* New York: Macmillan.

Montemayor, R., & Eisen, M. (1977). The development of self-conceptions from childhood to adolescence. *Developmental Psychology, 13,* 314–319.

Morey, L. C. (1984). *The concept of alcohol abuse.* Unpublished manuscript, Yale University, New Haven.

Morey, L. C., & Blashfield, R. K. (1981a). Empirical classifications of alcoholism: A review. *Journal of Studies on Alcohol, 42,* 925–937.

Morey, L. C., & Blashfield, R. K. (1981b). A symptom analysis of the DSM-III definition of schizophrenia. *Schizophrenia Bulletin, 7,* 258–268.

Morey, L. C., Skinner, H. A., & Blashfield, R. K. (1984). A typology of alcohol abusers: Correlates and implications. *Journal of Abnormal Psychology, 93,* 408–417.

Morey, L. C., Skinner, H. A., & Blashfield, R. K. (in press). Trends in the classification of abnormal behavior. In A. R. Ciminero, K. S. Calhoun, & H. E. Adams (Eds.), *Handbook of behavior assessment* (2nd ed.). New York: Wiley.

Morris, H. H., Jr., Escoll, P. J., & Wexler, R. (1956). Aggressive behavior disorders of childhood: A follow-up study. *American Journal of Psychiatry, 112,* 991–997.

Muscari, P. G. (1979). Language, reality, and schizophrenia. *Schizophrenia Bulletin, 5,* 334–340.

Myers, J., Lindenthal, J., & Pepper, M. (1974). Social class, life events, and psychiatric symptoms: A longitudinal study. In B. S. Dohrenwend & B. P. Dohrenwend (Eds.), *Stressful life events: Their nature and effects* (pp. 191–206). New York: Wiley.

Myers, J., Lindenthal, J., & Pepper, M. (1975). Life events, social integration, and psychiatric symptomatology. *Journal of Health and Social Behavior, 16,* 421–429.

Myers, J. K., & Roberts, B. H. (1959). *Family and class dynamics in mental illness.* New York: Wiley.

Myers, J. K., Weissman, M. M., Tischler, G. L., Holzer, C. E., III, Leaf, P. J., Orvaschel, H., Anthony, J. C., Boyd, J. H., Burke, J. D., Jr., Kramer, M., & Stoltzman, R. (1984). Six-month prevalence of psychiatric disorders in three communities. *Archives of General Psychiatry, 41,* 959–967.

Mylet, M., Styfco, S., & Zigler, E. (1979). The interrelationship between self-image disparity and social competence, defensive style, and adjustment status. *Journal of Nervous and Mental Disease, 167,* 553–560.

Nash, J. (1970). *Developmental psychology: A psychobiological approach.* Englewood Cliffs, NJ: Prentice-Hall.

Neale, J. M., & Cromwell, R. L. (1968). Size estimation in schizophrenics as a function of stimulus presentation time. *Journal of Abnormal Psychology, 73,* 44–48.

Neale, J. M., Davis, D., & Cromwell, R. L. (1971). Size estimation in schizophrenia: Some additional controls. *Perceptual and Motor Skills, 32,* 363–367.

Neale, J. M., & Kopfstein, J. H. (1973). Performance profiles of hospitalized patients. *Perceptual and Motor Skills, 36,* 739–744.

Neale, J. M., Kopfstein, J. H., & Levine, A. J. (1972). Premorbid adjustment and paranoid status in schizophrenia: Varying assessment techniques and the influence of chronicity. *Proceedings of the 80th Annual Convention of the American Psychological Association, 7,* 321–322.

Neale, J. M., & Oltmanns, T. F. (1980). *Schizophrenia.* New York: Wiley.

Nesselroade, J. R., & Reese, H. W. (Eds.). (1973). *Life-span developmental psychology: Methodological issues.* New York: Academic.

Neugarten, B. (1979). Time, age, and the life cycle. *American Journal of Psychiatry, 136,* 887–894.

Noam, G., Hauser, S., Santostefano, S., Garrison, W., Jacobson, A., Powers, S., & Mead, M. (1984). Ego development and psychopathology: A study of hospitalized adolescents. *Child Development, 55,* 184–194.

Noyes, R., Jr., Clancy, J., Hoenk, P. R., & Slymen, D. J. (1980). The prognosis of anxiety neurosis. *Archives of General Psychiatry, 37,* 173–178.

Nuttall, R. L., & Solomon, L. F. (1965). Factorial structure and prognostic significance of premorbid adjustment in schizophrenia. *Journal of Consulting Psychology, 29,* 362–372.

Nuttall, R. L., & Solomon, L. F. (1970). Prognosis in schizophrenia: The role of premorbid, social class, and demographic factors. *Behavioral Science, 15,* 255–264.

Nydas, J. (1963). The paranoid–masochistic character. *Psychoanalytic Review, 50,* 215–251.

Nyman, A. K. (1978). Non-regressive schizophrenia: Clinical course and outcome. *Acta Psychiatrica Scandinavica.* (Suppl. 272)

Odegaard, O. (1953). New data on marriage and mental disease: The incidence of psychosis in the widowed and the divorced. *Journal of Mental Science, 99*, 778–785.

Offord, D. R., & Cross, L. A. (1971). Adult schizophrenia with scholastic failure or low IQ in childhood. *Archives of General Psychiatry, 24*, 431–436.

Ohnmacht, F. W., & Muro, J. J. (1967). Self-acceptance: Some anxiety and cognitive style relationships. *Journal of Psychology, 67*, 235–239.

O'Neill, P., O'Neill, P., & Quinlan, D. M. (1976). Perceptual development on the Rorschach. *Journal of Personality Assessment, 40*, 115–121.

Orr, W. F., Anderson, R. B., Martin, M. P., and Philpot, D. F. (1955). Factors influencing discharge of female patients from a state mental hospital. *American Journal of Psychiatry, 111*, 576–582.

Ostow, M. (1973). Letter to the editor. *Science, 180*, 360–361.

Overall, J. E. (1971). Association between marital history and the nature of manifest psychopathology. *Journal of Abnormal Psychology, 78*, 213–221.

Overall, J. E., Hollister, L. E., Johnson, M., & Pennington, V. (1966). Nosology of depression and differential response to drugs. *Journal of the American Medical Association, 195*, 946–950.

Overall, J. E., & Patrick. J. (1972). Unitary alcoholism factor and its personality correlates. *Journal of Abnormal Psychology, 79*, 303–309.

Overton, W., & Reese, H. W. (1973). Models of development: Methodological implications. In J. R. Nesselroade & H. W. Reese (Eds.), *Life-span developmental psychology: Methodological issues* (pp. 65–86). New York: Academic.

Pao, P. (1979). *Schizophrenia disorders: Theory and treatment from a psychodynamic point of view.* New York: International Universities Press.

Pauls, D. L. (1972). *A genetic analysis of mental retardation and high intelligence.* Dissertation Abstracts International 33105, 1948. (University Microfilms No. 72-27, 789)

Paykel, E. S. (1981). Have multivariate statistics contributed to classification? *British Journal of Psychiatry, 129*, 357–362.

Payne, R., & Caird, W. K. (1967). Reaction time, distractibility, and overinclusive thinking in psychotics. *Journal of Abnormal Psychology, 72*, 112–121.

Payne, R., Matussek, P., & George, E. (1959). An experimental study of schizophrenic thought disorder. *Journal of Mental Science, 105*, 627–652.

Pepper, S. C. (1942). *World hypotheses.* Berkeley, CA: University of California Press.

Perris, C. (1966). A study of bipolar (manic-depressive) and unipolar recurrent depressive psychosis. *Acta Psychiatrica Scandinavica Supplement, 42* (194), pp. 9–152.

Phillips, D., & Zigler, E. (1980). Children's self-image disparity: Effects of age, socioeconomic status, ethnicity, and gender. *Journal of Personality and Social Psychology, 39*, 689–700.

Phillips, D., & Zigler, E. (1982). Real and ideal self-images in second- and fifth-grade children: Reliability, validity, and factorial structure. *Journal of Applied Developmental Psychology, 3*, 263–274.

Phillips, L. (1953). Case history data and prognosis in schizophrenia. *Journal of Nervous and Mental Disease, 117,* 515–525.

Phillips, L. (1968a). *Human adaptation and its failures.* New York: Academic.

Phillips, L. (1968b). A social view of psychopathology. In P. London & D. Rosenhan (Eds.), *Foundations of abnormal psychology* (pp. 427–459). New York: Holt, Rinehart & Winston.

Phillips, L., Broverman, I. K., & Zigler, E. (1966). Social competence and psychiatric diagnosis. *Journal of Abnormal Psychology, 71,* 209–214.

Phillips, L., Broverman, I. K., & Zigler, E. (1968). Sphere dominance, role orientation, and diagnosis. *Journal of Abnormal Psychology, 73,* 306–312.

Phillips, L., & Draguns, J. G. (1971). Classification of the behavioral disorders. *Annual Review of Psychology, 22,* 447–482.

Phillips, L., & Framo, J. L. (1954). Developmental theory applied to normal and psychopathological perception. *Journal of Personality, 22,* 464–474.

Phillips, L., Kaden, S., & Waldman, M. (1959). Rorschach indices of developmental level. *Journal of Genetic Psychology, 94,* 267–285.

Phillips, L., & Rabinovitch, M. (1958). Social role and patterns of symptomatic behavior. *Journal of Abnormal and Social Psychology, 57,* 181–186.

Phillips, L., & Zigler, E. (1961). Social competence: The action–thought parameter and vicariousness in normal and pathological behavior. *Journal of Abnormal and Social Psychology, 63,* 137–146.

Phillips, L., & Zigler, E. (1964). Role orientation, the action–thought dimension and outcome in psychiatric disorder. *Journal of Abnormal and Social Psychology, 68,* 381–389.

Piaget, J. (1951). Principle factors in determining evolution from childhood to adult life. In D. Rapaport (Ed.), *Organization and pathology of thought* (pp. 154–175). New York: Columbia University Press.

Piaget, J. (1954). *The construction of reality in the child* (M. Cook, Trans.). New York: Basic.

Piaget, J. (1960). *The psychology of intelligence.* Paterson, NJ: Littlefield, Adams.

Pitts, F. N., & Winokur, G. (1966). Affective disorder, Pt. 7 (Alcoholism and affective disorder). *Journal of Psychiatric Research, 4,* 37–50.

Pokorny, A., & Overall, J. (1970). Relationships of psychopathology to age, sex, ethnicity, education and marital status in state hospital patients. *Journal of Psychiatric Research, 7,* 143–152.

Pollack, M., Woerner, M. G., Goodman, W., & Greenberg, I. M. (1966). Childhood development patterns of adult hospitalized schizophrenic and nonschizophrenic patients and their siblings. *American Journal of Orthopsychiatry, 36,* 510–517.

Pope, H. Jr., & Lipinski, J. (1978). Diagnosis in schizophrenia and manic-depressive illness. *Archives of General Psychiatry, 35,* 811–828.

Pope, H., Jr., Lipinski, J., Cohen, B., & Axelrod, D. (1980). "Schizo-affective disorder": An invalid diagnosis? A comparison of schizoaffective disorder, schizophrenia, and affective disorder. *American Journal of Psychiatry, 137,* 921–927.

Popper, K. R. (1972). *The logic of scientific discovery.* London: Hutchinson.

Prentky, R. A., Lewine, R. R. J., Watt, N., & Fryer, J. H. (1980). A longitudinal study of psychiatric outcome: Developmental variables vs. psychiatric symptoms. *Schizophrenia Bulletin, 6,* 139–148.

Prentky, R. A., Watt, N. F., & Fryer, J. H. (1979). Longitudinal social competence and adult psychiatric symptoms at first hospitalization. *Schizophrenia Bulletin, 5,* 306–312.

Price, R. H., & Eriksen, C. W. (1966). Size constancy in schizophrenia. *Journal of Abnormal Psychology, 71,* 155–160.

Procci, W. R. (1976). Schizo-affective psychosis: Fact or fiction? *Archives of General Psychiatry, 33,* 1167–1178.

Prugh, D. G., Staub, E. M., Sands, H. H., Kirschbaum, R., & Lenihan, E. (1953). A study of the emotional reactions of children and families to hospitalization and illness. *American Journal of Orthopsychiatry, 23,* 41–79.

Quinlan, D. M., Rogers, L. R., & Kegan, R. G. (1980, April). *Developmental dimensions of psychopathology.* Paper presented at the convention of the Eastern Psychological Association, Hartford, CT.

Rabinowitz, M. (1966). The relationship of self regard to the effectiveness of life experiences. *Journal of Counseling Psychology, 13,* 139–143.

Radloff, L. (1975). Sex differences in depression: The effects of occupation and marital status. *Sex Roles, 1,* 249–265.

Radloff, L., & Rae, D. (1979). Susceptibility and precipitating factors in depression: Sex differences and similarities. *Journal of Abnormal Psychology, 88,* 174–181.

Raimy, V. C. (1948). Self-reference in counseling interviews. *Journal of Consulting Psychology, 12,* 153–163.

Rapaport, D. (1951). Toward a theory of thinking. In D. Rapaport (Ed.), *Organization and pathology of thought* (pp. 689–730). New York: Columbia University Press.

Rapaport, D. (1960). The structure of psychoanalytic theory: A systematic attempt. *Psychological Issues* [Monograph 6]. New York: International Universities Press.

Rappaport, M., & Hopkins, H. K. (1969). Drug effects on auditory attention in paranoid and nonparanoid schizophrenics. *Journal of Nervous and Mental Disease, 148,* 597–605.

Rappaport, M., Hopkins, H. K., & Hall, K. (1972). Auditory signal detection in paranoid and nonparanoid schizophrenics. *Archives of General Psychiatry, 17,* 747–752.

Rappaport, M., Silverman, J., Hopkins, H. K., & Hall, K. (1971). Phenothiazine effects on auditory signal detection in paranoid and nonparanoid schizophrenics. *Science, 174,* 723–725.

Rashkis, H., Cushman, J. F., & Landis, C. (1946). A new method for studying disorders of conceptual thinking. *Journal of Abnormal and Social Psychology, 41,* 70–74.

Raskin, A., & Golob, R. (1966). Occurrence of sex and social class differences in premorbid competence, symptom and outcome measures in acute schizophrenics. *Psychological Reports, 18,* 11–22.

Raush, H. (1952). Perceptual constancy in schizophrenia. *Journal of Personality, 21,* 176–187.

Redlich, F. C., Levine, J., & Sohler, T. P. (1951). A mirth response test: Preliminary report on a psychodiagnostic technique utilizing dynamics of humor. *American Journal of Orthopsychiatry, 21,* 717–734.

Reese, H. W., & Overton, W. F. (1970). Models of development and theories of development. In L. R. Goulet & P. B. Baltes (Eds.), *Life-span developmental psychology: Theory and research* (pp. 115–145). New York: Academic.

Retterstol, N. (1975). Nosological aspects of paranoid psychoses. *Psychiatrica Clinica, 8,* 20–30. (From *Psychological Abstracts,* 1975, *55,* Abstract No. 12436)

Riegel, K. (1973). Developmental psychology and society: Some historical and ethical considerations. In J. R. Nesselroade & H. W. Reese (Eds.), *Life-span developmental psychology: Methodological issues* (pp. 1–23). New York: Academic.

Ritson, B. (1971). Personality and prognosis in alcoholism. *British Journal of Psychiatry, 118,* 79–82.

Ritzler, B. (1981). Paranoia–Prognosis and treatment: A review. *Schizophrenia Bulletin, 7,* 710–728.

Ritzler, B., & Smith, M. (1976). The problem of diagnostic criteria in the study of paranoid subclassification of schizophrenia. *Schizophrenia Bulletin, 2,* 209–217.

Robins, E., Gentry, K., Munoz, R., & Marten, S. (1977). A contrast of the three more common illnesses with the ten least common in a study and 18-month follow-up of 314 psychiatric emergency room patients. II. Characteristics of patients with the three more common illnesses. *Archives of General Psychiatry, 34,* 269–281.

Robins, L. (1966). *Deviant children grown up.* Baltimore, MD: Williams & Wilkins.

Robins, L. (1970). Antecedents of character disorder. In M. Roff & D. F. Ricks (Eds.), *Life history research in psychopathology* (pp. 226–239). Minneapolis: University of Minnesota Press.

Roe, A. (1956). *The psychology of occupations.* New York: Wiley.

Roff, J. D. (1975). Long-term outcome for a set of schizophrenic subtypes. In R. D. Wirt, G. Winokur, & M. Roff (Eds.), *Life history research in psychopathology* (Vol. 4) (pp. 211–236). Minneapolis: University of Minnesota Press.

Roff, J. D., & Knight, R. (1978). Young adult schizophrenics: Prediction of outcome and antecedent childhood factors. *Journal of Consulting and Clinical Psychology, 46,* 947–952.

Roff, M., & Ricks, D. (Eds.). (1970). *Life history research in psychopathology* (Vol. I.). Minneapolis: University of Minnesota Press.

Rogers, A. H. (1958). The self concept in paranoid schizophrenia. *Journal of Clinical Psychology, 14,* 365–366.

Rogers, C. R. (1951). *Client-centered therapy.* Boston: Houghton Mifflin.

Rogers, C. R. (1961). *On becoming a person.* Boston: Houghton Mifflin.

Rogers, C. R., & Dymond, R. F. (Eds.). (1954). *Psychotherapy and personality change.* Chicago: University of Chicago Press.

Rolf, J. E. (1972). The academic and social competence of children vulnerable to schizophrenia and other behavior pathologies. *Journal of Abnormal Psychology, 80,* 225–243.

Romano, J. (1977). On the nature of schizophrenia: Changes in the observer as well as the observed (1932–1977). *Schizophrenia Bulletin, 4,* 532–559.

Rose, A. M. (Ed.). (1955). *Mental health and mental disorder.* New York: Norton.

Rosen, B., Klein, D. F., & Gittelman-Klein, R. (1969). Sex differences in the relationship between premorbid asociality and posthospital outcome. *Journal of Nervous and Mental Disease, 149,* 415–420.

Rosen, B., Klein, D., & Gittelman-Klein, R. (1971). The prediction of rehospitalization: The relationship between age of first psychiatric treatment contact, marital status and premorbid asocial adjustment. *Journal of Nervous and Mental Disease, 152,* 17–22.

Rosen, B., Klein, D., Levenstein, S., & Shahinian, S. (1969). Social competence and posthospital outcome among schizophrenic and nonschizophrenic psychiatric patients. *Journal of Abnormal Psychology, 74,* 401–404.

Rosenberg, M. (1965). *Society and the adolescent self image.* Princeton, NJ: Princeton University Press.

Rosenberg, M. (1979). *Concerning the self.* New York: Basic.

Rosenblatt, B., & Solomon, P. (1954). Structural and genetic aspects of Rorschach responses in mental deficiency. *Journal of Projective Techniques, 18,* 496–506.

Rosenhan, D. L. (1973). On being sane in insane places. *Science, 179,* 250–258.

Rosenhan, D. L. (1975). The contextual nature of psychiatric diagnosis. *Journal of Abnormal Psychology, 84,* 426–474.

Rosenthal, D. (1970). *Genetic theory and abnormal behavior.* New York: McGraw-Hill.

Rosenthal, D. (1971). *Genetics of psychopathology,* New York: McGraw-Hill.

Rosner, S., & Abt, L. E. (Eds.). (1970). *The creative experience.* New York: Grossman.

Ross, C. E., Mirowsky, J., & Cockerham, W. C. (1983). Social class, Mexican culture, and fatalism: Their effects on psychological distress. *American Journal of Community Psychology, 11,* 383–399.

Roth, M., Gurney, C., Garside, R. F., & Kerr, T. A. (1972). Studies in the classification of affective disorders: The relationship between anxiety states and depressive illnesses. *British Journal of Psychiatry, 121,* 147–161.

Rotter, J. (1954). *Social learning and clinical psychology.* New York: Prentice-Hall.

Roy, A. (1980). Depression in chronic paranoid schizophrenia. *British Journal of Psychiatry, 137,* 138–139.

Rubenstein, E., & Lorr, M. (1956). A comparison of terminators and remainers in outpatient psychotherapy. *Journal of Clinical Psychology, 12,* 345–349.

Rudie, R., & McGaughran, L. (1961). Differences in developmental experiences, defensiveness, and personality organization between two classes of problem drinkers. *Journal of Abnormal and Social Psychology, 62,* 659–665.

Russell, P. N., & Beekhuis, M. E. (1976). Organization in memory: A comparison of psychotics and normals. *Journal of Abnormal Psychology, 85,* 527–534.

Sacks, M., Carpenter, W. T., Jr., & Strauss, J. S. (1974). Recovery from delusions: Three phases documented by patient's interpretations of research procedures. *Archives of General Psychiatry, 30,* 117–120.

Salokangas, R. K. R. (1978). *Psycho-social prognosis in schizophrenia.* Turku, Finland: Turun Yliopisto.

Salokangas, R. K. R. (1983). Prognostic implications of the sex of schizophrenic patients. *British Journal of Psychiatry, 142,* 145–151.

Salzman, L. (1960). Paranoid state: Theory and therapy. *Archives of General Psychiatry, 2,* 679–693.

Sanes, J., & Zigler, E. (1971). Premorbid social competence, role orientation, and paranoid–nonparanoid status in schizophrenia. *Journal of Abnormal Psychology, 78,* 140–144.

Sanford, N. (1968). Personality and patterns of alcohol consumption. *Journal of Consulting and Clinical Psychology, 32,* 13–17.

Santostefano, S. (1970). The assessment of motives in children. *Psychological Reports, 26,* 639–649.

Santostefano, S. (1978). *A biodevelopmental approach to clinical child psychology.* New York: Wiley.

Santostefano, S., & Baker, H. (1972). The contribution of developmental psychology. In B. Wolman (Ed.), *Manual of child psychopathology* (pp. 1113–1153). New York: McGraw-Hill.

Sarbin, T. R., & Mancuso, J. C. (1980). *Schizophrenia: Medical diagnosis or moral verdict?* New York: Pergamon.

Sartorius, N., Jablensky, A., Stomgren, E., & Shapiro, R. (1978). Validity of diagnostic concepts across cultures: A preliminary report from the International Pilot Study of Schizophrenia. In L. C. Wynne, R. L. Cromwell, & S. Matthysse (Eds.), *The nature of schizophrenia: New approaches to research and treatment* (pp. 657–669). New York: Wiley.

Savage, C. W. (1975). The continuity of perceptual and cognitive experiences. In E. L. Siegel & J. West (Eds.), *Hallucinations: Behavior, experience, and theory,* (pp. 257–286). New York: Wiley.

Schaeffer, D. S. (1977). Scores on neuroticism pathology, mood, and Rorschach and diagnosis of affective disorder. *Psychological Reports, 40,* 1135–1141.

Schaffer, H. R., & Emerson, P. E. (1964). Patterns of response to physical contact in early human development. *Journal of Child Psychology and Psychiatry and Allied Disciplines, 5,* 1–13.

Schaie, K. W., & Gribbin, K. (1975). Adult development and aging. *Annual Review of Psychology, 26,* 65–96.

Scharfetter, C., & Nusperli, M. (1980). The group of schizophrenias, schizoaffective psychoses, and affective disorders. *Schizophrenia Bulletin, 6,* 586–591.

Scheff, T. J. (1974). The labeling theory of mental illness. *American Sociological Review, 39,* 444–452.

Schimek, J. (1974). Some developmental aspects of primary process manifestations in the Rorschach. *Journal of Personality Assessment, 38,* 226–229.

Schlossberg, A., & Rattok, Y. (1974). The autokinetic phenomenon in schizophrenics. *Israel Annals of Psychiatry and Related Disciplines, 12,* 138–144.

Schneider, K. (1959). *Clinical psychopathology.* New York: Grune and Stratton.

Schooler, N. R., Goldberg, S. C., Boothe, H., & Cole, J. O. (1967). One year after discharge: Community adjustment of schizophrenic patients. *American Journal of Psychiatry, 123,* 9.

Schuckit, M., Pitts, F. N., Jr., Reich, T., King, L. J., & Winokur, G. (1969). Alcoholism. I. Two types of alcoholism in women. *Archives of General Psychiatry, 20,* 301–306.

Schuckit, M. A., & Winokur, G. (1972). Short term follow up of women alcoholics. *Diseases of the Nervous System, 33,* 672–678.

Schwab, J., Brown, J., Holzer, C., & Sokolof, M. (1968). Current concepts of depression: The sociocultural. *International Journal of Social Psychiatry, 14,* 226–234.

Schwartz, C. C., Myers, J. K., & Astrachan, B. M. (1975). Concordance of multiple assessments of the outcome of schizophrenia. *Archives of General Psychiatry, 32,* 1221–1227.

Schwartz, D. (1963). A review of the "paranoid" concept. *Archives of General Psychiatry, 8,* 349–361.

Schwartz, D. (1964). The paranoid–depressive existential continuum. *Psychiatric Quarterly, 38,* 690–706.

Scott, W. (1958). Research definitions of mental health and mental illness. *Psychological Bulletin, 55,* 1–45.

Sedman, G. (1966). Comparative study of pseudohallucinations, imagery, and true hallucinations. *British Journal of Psychiatry, 112,* 9–17.

Seeman, M. V. (1982). Gender differences in schizophrenia. *Canadian Journal of Psychiatry, 27,* 107–111.

Seifert, J. A., Draguns, J. G., & Caudill, W. (1971). Role orientation, sphere dominance, and social competence as bases of psychiatric diagnosis in Japan: A replication and extension of American findings. *Journal of Abnormal Psychology, 78,* 101–106.

Seitz, V. Rosenbaum, L. K., & Apfel, N. H. (1985). Effects of family support intervention: A ten-year follow-up. *Child Development, 56,* 376–391.

Seligman, M. E. P. (1975). *Helplessness: On depression, development, and death.* San Francisco: Freeman.

Selman, R. L. (1980). *The growth of interpersonal understanding: Developmental and clinical analyses.* New York: Academic.

Selman, R. L., & Demorest, A. P. (1984). Observing troubled children's interpersonal negotiation strategies: Implications of and for a developmental model. *Child Development, 55,* 288–304.

Sexton, M. C. (1945). The autokinetic test: Its value in psychiatric diagnosis and prognosis. *American Journal of Psychiatry, 102,* 399–402.

Shagass, C., Roemer, R. A., & Amadeo, M. (1974). Eye tracking performance in psychiatric patients. *Biological Psychiatry, 14,* 245–261.

Shakow, D. (1963). Psychological deficit in schizophrenia. *Behavioral Science, 8,* 275–305.

Shanfield, S., Tucker, G. J., Harrow, M., & Detre, T. (1970). The schizophrenic patient and depressive symptomatology. *Journal of Nervous and Mental Disease, 151,* 203–210.

Sheehan, S. (1982). *Is there no place on earth for me?* New York: Random House.

Sheerer, E. T. (1949). An analysis of the relationship between acceptance of and respect for others in ten counseling cases. *Journal of Consulting Psychology, 13,* 169–175.

Siegel, E. L. (1953). Genetic parallels of perceptual structuralization in paranoid schizophrenia: An analysis by means of the Rorschach technique. *Journal of Projective Techniques, 17,* 151–161.

Siegel, E. L., & West, J. (1975). *Hallucinations: Behavior, experience and theory.* New York: Wiley.

Silverman, C. (1968). *The epidemiology of depression.* Baltimore, MD: Johns Hopkins University Press.

Silverman, J. (1964). Scanning-control mechanism and "cognitive filtering" in paranoid and nonparanoid schizophrenia. *Journal of Consulting Psychology, 28,* 385–393.

Silverstein, M. L., & Harrow, M. (1978). First-rank symptoms in the postacute schizophrenic: A follow-up study. *American Journal of Psychiatry, 135,* 1481–1486.

Siris, S. G., Harmon, G. K., & Endicott, J. Postpsychotic depressive symptoms in hospitalized schizophrenic patients. *Archives of General Psychiatry, 38,* 1122–1123.

Skinner, H. A. (1981). Toward the integration of classification theory and methods. *Journal of Abnormal Psychology, 90,* 68–87.

Skinner, H. A., Glaser, F. B., & Annis, H. M. (1982). Crossing the threshold: Factors in self-identification as an alcoholic. *British Journal of Addiction, 77,* 259–273.

Slater, E. (1943). The neurotic constitution. *Journal of Neurology and Psychiatry, 6,* 1–16.

Slater, E., & Roth, M. (1969). *Clinical psychiatry.* Baltimore: Williams & Wilkins Co.

Smith, M. B. (1974). *Humanizing social psychology.* San Francisco: Jossey-Bass.

Sneath, P. H. E., & Sokal, R. (1973). *Numerical taxonomy.* San Francisco: Freeman.

Snyder, S. (1961). Perceptual closure in acute paranoid schizophrenics. *Archives of General Psychiatry, 5,* 406–410.

Spitzer, R. L., & Endicott, J. (1968). DIAGNO: A computer program for psychiatric diagnosis utilizing the differential diagnostic procedures. *Archives of General Psychiatry, 18,* 746–756.

Spitzer, R. L., & Endicott, J. (1978). *Schedule for affective disorders and schizophrenia* (SADS) (3rd ed.). New York: Biometrics Research, New York State Psychiatric Institute.

Spitzer, R. L., Endicott, J., & Robins, E. (1975). Clinical criteria for psychiatric diagnosis and DSM-III. *American Journal of Psychiatry, 132,* 1187–1192.

Spitzer, R. L., & Fleiss, J. L. (1974). A reanalysis of the reliability of psychiatric diagnosis. *British Journal of Psychiatry, 125,* 341–347.

Spitzer, R. L., Forman, J., & Nee, J. (1979). DSM-III field trials. I. Initial interrater diagnostic reliability. *American Journal of Psychiatry, 136,* 815–817.

Spitzer, R. L., Williams, J. B. W., & Skodol, A. E. (1980). DSM-III: The major achievements and an overview. *American Journal of Psychiatry, 137,* 151–164.

Srole, L. (1975). Measurement and classification in sociopsychiatric epidemiology: Midtown Manhattan study (1954) and Midtown restudy II (1974). *Journal of Health and Social Behavior, 16,* 347–364.

Srole, L., Langer, T., Michael, S., Opler, M., & Rennie, T. (1962). *Mental Health in the Metropolis* (Vol. 1). New York: McGraw-Hill.

Sroufe, L. A., & Rutter, M. (1984). The domain of developmental psychopathology. *Child Development, 55,* 17–29.

Steffy, R. A., & Becker, W. C. (1961). Measurement of the severity of disorder in schizophrenia by means of the Holtzman inkblot test. *Journal of Consulting Psychology, 25,* 555.

Steinberg, H. R., Green, R., & Durell, J. (1967). Depression occurring during the course of recovery from schizophrenic symptoms. *American Journal of Psychiatry, 124,* 153–156.

Stephens, J. H. (1978). Long term prognosis and follow-up in schizophrenia. *Schizophrenia Bulletin, 4,* 25–47.

Stephens, J. H., Astrup, C., & Mangrum, J. C. (1966). Prognostic factors in recovered and deteriorated schizophrenics. *American Journal of Psychiatry, 122,* 1116–1121.

Stephens, J. H., Astrup, C., & Mangrum, J. C. (1967). Prognosis in schizophrenia. *Archives of General Psychiatry, 16,* 693–698.

Stock, D. (1949). An investigation into the interrelations between the self concept and feelings directed towards other persons and group. *Journal of Consulting Psychology, 13,* 176–180.

Stoffelmayr, B., Dillavou, D., & Hunter, J. (1983). Premorbid functioning and outcome in schizophrenia: A cumulative analysis. *Journal of Consulting and Clinical Psychology, 51,* 338–352.

Stoodt, J., & Balla, D. (1974). *Developmental and experiential determinants of the self-concept of younger children.* Unpublished manuscript, Yale University, New Haven, CT.

Strahl, M. O., & Lewis, N. D. C. (Eds.). (1972). *Differential diagnosis in clinical psychiatry: The lectures of Paul H. Hoch, M. D.* New York: Science House.

Strauss, J. S. (1969). Hallucinations and delusions as points on continua function. *Archives of General Psychiatry, 21,* 581–586.

Strauss, J. S. (1979). Social and cultural influences in psychopathology. *Annual Review of Psychology, 30,* 397–415.

Strauss, J. S., & Carpenter, W. T., Jr. (1974a). Characteristic symptoms and outcome in schizophrenia. *Archives of General Psychiatry, 30,* 429–434.

Strauss, J. S., & Carpenter, W. T., Jr. (1974b). The prediction of outcome in schizophrenia. II. Relationships between predictor and outcome variables. *Archives of General Psychiatry, 31,* 37–42.

Strauss, J. S., & Carpenter, W. T., Jr. (1977). Prediction of outcome in schizophrenia. III. Five year outcome and its predictors. *Archives of General Psychiatry, 34,* 159–163.

Strauss, J. S., & Carpenter, W. T., Jr. (1981). *Schizophrenia.* New York: Plenum.

Strauss, J. S., Carpenter, W. T., Jr., & Bartko, J. J. (1974). The diagnosis and understanding of schizophrenia. III. Speculations on the processes that underlie schizophrenic symptoms and signs. *Schizophrenia Bulletin, 11,* 61–69.

Strauss, J. S., & Gift, T. (1977). Choosing an approach for diagnosing schizophrenia. *Archives of General Psychiatry, 34,* 1248–1253.

Strauss, J. S., & Harder, D. W. (1981). The case record rating scale: A method for rating symptom and social function data from case records. *Psychiatry Research, 4,* 333–345.

Strauss, J. S., Kokes, R. F., Carpenter, W. T., Jr., & Ritzler, B. A. (1978). The course of schizophrenia as a developmental process. In L. C. Wynne, R. L. Cromwell, & S. Matthysse (Eds.), *The nature of schizophrenia: New approaches to research and treatment* (pp. 617–630). New York: Wiley.

Strauss, J. S., Kokes, R. F., Ritzler, B. A., Harder, D. W., & Van Ord, A. (1978). Patterns of disorder in first admission psychiatric patients. *Journal of Nervous and Mental Disease, 166,* 611–623.

Strauss, J. S., Loevsky, L., Glazer, W., & Leaf, P. (1981). Organizing the complexities of schizophrenia. *Journal of Nervous and Mental Disease, 169,* 120–126.

Strauss, M. E., Foureman, W. C., & Parwatikar, S. D. (1974). Schizophrenics' size estimations of thematic stimuli. *Journal of Abnormal Psychology, 83,* 117–123.

Strauss, M. E., Sirotkin, R. A., & Grisell, J. (1974). Length of hospitalization and rate of readmission of paranoid and nonparanoid schizophrenics. *Journal of Consulting and Clinical Psychology, 42,* 105–110.

Strauss, M. J. (1973). Behavioral differences between acute and chronic schizophrenia: Course of psychosis, effects of institutionalization, or sampling biases? *Psychological Bulletin, 79,* 271–279.

Sturm, I. E., & Lipton, H. (1967). Some social and vocational predictors of psychiatric hospitalization outcome. *Journal of Clinical Psychology, 23,* 301–307.

Sugerman, A., Reilly, D., & Albahary, R. (1965). Social competence and the essential–reactive distinction in alcoholism. *Archives of General Psychiatry, 12,* 552–556.

Sullivan, H. S. (1956). *Clinical studies in psychiatry.* New York: Norton.

Sullivan, P., Miller, C., & Smelser, W. (1958). Factors in length of stay and progress in psychotherapy. *Journal of Consulting Psychology, 22,* 1–9.

Sundberg, N. D., Snowden, L. R., & Reynolds, W. M. (1978). Toward assessment of personal competence and incompetence in life situations. *Annual Review of Psychology, 29,* 179–221.

Swanson, D., Bohnert, P., & Smith, J. (1970). *The paranoid.* Boston: Little, Brown.

Szasz, T. S. (1961). *The myth of mental illness: Foundations for a theory of personal conduct.* New York: Harper and Row.

Tamminga, C. A., & Carpenter, W. T., Jr. (1982). The DSM-III diagnosis of schizophrenic-like illness and the clinical pharmacology of psychosis. *Journal of Nervous and Mental Disease, 170,* 744–751.

Tanaka, J. S., & Bentler, P. (1983). Factor invariance of premorbid social competence across multiple populations of schizophrenics. *Multivariate Behavioral Research, 18,* 135–146.

Taylor, M. A. (1972). Schneiderian first-rank symptoms and clinical prognostic features in schizophrenia. *Archives of General Psychiatry, 26,* 64–77.

Taylor, M. A., & Abrams, R. (1973). The phenomenology of mania: A new look at some old patients. *Archives of General Psychiatry, 19,* 520–522.

Taylor, M. A., & Abrams, R. (1975a). Acute mania: Clinical and genetic study of responders and nonresponders to treatments. *Archives of General Psychiatry, 32,* 863–865.

Taylor, M. A., & Abrams, R. (1975b). Manic-depressive illness and good prognosis schizophrenia. *American Journal of Psychiatry, 132,* 741–742.

Taylor, M. A., & Abrams, R. (1981a). Gender differences in bipolar affective disorder. *Journal of Affective Disorders, 3,* 261–277.

Taylor, M. A., & Abrams, R. (1981b). Prediction of treatment response in mania. *Archives of General Psychiatry, 38,* 800–802.

Terkel, S. (1974). *Working.* New York: Random House.

Thomas, A., & Chess, S. (1977). *Temperament and development.* New York: Brunner/Mazel.

Thomas, A., Chess, S., & Birch, H. G. (1968). *Temperament and behavior disorders in children.* New York: New York University Press.

Thorne, F. (1953). Back to fundamentals. *Journal of Clinical Psychology, 9,* 89–91.

Toone, B. K., & Ron, M. (1977). A study of predictive factors in depressive disorders of poor outcome. *British Journal of Psychiatry, 131,* 587–591.

Torrey, E. F. (1981). The epidemiology of paranoid schizophrenia. *Schizophrenia Bulletin, 7,* 588–593.

Trapp, C. E., & James, E. B. (1937). Comparative intelligence ratings in the four types of dementia praecox. *Journal of Nervous and Mental Disease, 86,* 399–404.

Tsuang, M. T. (1979). "Schizoaffective disorder": Dead or alive? *Archives of General Psychiatry, 36,* 633–634.

Tsuang, M. T., Crowe, R. R., Winokur, G., & Clancy, J. (1978). Relatives of schizophrenics, manics, depressives, and controls: An interview study of 1331 first-degree relatives. In L. C. Wynne, R. Cromwell, & S. Matthysse (Eds.), *The nature of schizophrenia: New approaches to research and treatment* (pp. 52–58). New York: Wiley.

Tsuang, M. T., Dempsey, G. M., & Rauscher, F. (1976). A study of "atypical schizophrenia." *Archives of General Psychiatry, 33,* 1157–1160.

Tsuang, M. T., Fowler, R. C., Cadoret, R. J., & Monnelly, E. (1974). Schizophrenia among first-degree relatives of paranoid and nonparanoid schizophrenics. *Comprehensive Psychiatry, 15,* 295–302.

Tsuang, M. T., & Winokur, G. (1974). Criteria for subtyping schizophrenia: Clinical differentiation of hebephrenic and paranoid schizophrenia. *Archives of General Psychiatry, 31,* 43–47.

Tsuang, M. T., Woolson, R. F., Winokur, G., & Crowe, R. R. (1981). Stability of psychiatric diagnosis. Schizophrenia and affective disorders followed up over a 30- to 40-year period. *Archives of General Psychiatry, 38,* 535–539.

Tucker, J. A., Vuchinich, R. E., & Sobell, M. B. (1981). Alcohol consumption as a self-handicapping strategy. *Journal of Abnormal Psychology, 90,* 220–230.

Turner, R. J., & Zabo, L. J. (1968). Social competence and schizophrenic outcome: An investigation and critique. *Journal of Health and Social Behavior, 9,* 41–51.

Ullmann, L. P., & Eck, R. A. (1965). Inkblot perception and the process–reactive distinction. *Journal of Clinical Psychology, 21,* 311–313.

Ullmann, L. P., & Gurell, L. (1962). Validity of symptom rating from psychiatric records. *Archives of General Psychiatry, 7,* 130–134.

Ullmann, L. P., & Giovannoni, J. (1964). The development of a self-report measure of the process–reactive continuum. *Journal of Nervous and Mental Disease, 138,* 38–42.

Ullmann, L. P., & Krasner, L. (Eds.). (1965). *Introduction to case studies in behavior modification.* New York: Holt, Rinehart & Winston.

United States Department of Health and Human Services (1980). *Head Start in the 1980's: Review and Recommendations.* A report of the 15th Anniversary Head Start Committee. Washington, DC: Head Start Bureau.

United States Government Printing Office (1949). *Dictionary of occupational titles.* Washington, DC: Author.

United States Government Printing Office (1965). *Dictionary of occupational titles.* Washington, DC: Author.

Vaillant, G. E. (1962). The prediction of recovery in schizophrenia. *Journal of Nervous and Mental Disease, 135,* 534–543.

Vaillant, G. E. (1964). Prospective prediction of schizophrenic remission. *Archives of General Psychiatry, 11,* 509–518.

Vaillant, G. E. (1971). Theoretical hierarchy of adaptive ego mechanisms. *Archives of General Psychiatry, 24,* 107–118.

Vaillant, G. E. (1974). Natural history of male psychological health. II. Some antecedents of healthy adult adjustment. *Archives of General Psychiatry, 31,* 15–22.

Vaillant, G. E. (1975). Natural history of male psychological health. III. Empirical dimensions of mental health. *Archives of General Psychiatry, 32,* 420–426.

Vaillant, G. E. (1976). Natural history of male psychological health. V. The relationship of choice of ego mechanisms of defense to adult adjustment. *Archives of General Psychiatry, 33,* 535–545.

Vaillant, G. E. (1977). *Adaptation to life.* Boston: Little, Brown.

Vaillant, G. E. (1978). Natural history of male psychological health. VI. Correlates of successful marriage and fatherhood. *American Journal of Psychiatry, 135,* 653–659.

Vaillant, G. E. (1980). Natural history of male psychological health. VIII. Antecedents of alcoholism and "orality." *American Journal of Psychiatry, 137,* 181–186.

Van den Daele, L. (1968). A developmental study of ego ideals. *Genetic Psychology Monographs, 78,* 191–256.

Venables, P. H. (1964). Input dysfunction in schizophrenia. In B. A. Maher (Ed.), *Progress in experimental personality research (pp. 1–47). New York: Academic.*

Venables, P. H., & O'Connor, N. (1959). A short scale for rating paranoid schizophrenia. *Journal of Mental Science, 105,* 815–818.

Vincent, L., & Vincent, K. (1979). Ego development and psychopathology. *Psychological Reports, 44,* 408–410.

Vojtisek, J. E. (1976). The influence of an interpolated stimulus on the size estimation performance of schizophrenic subgroups. *Dissertation Abstracts International, 36,* 5290–5291.

von Zerssen, D., & Weyerer, S. (1982). Sex differences in rates of mental disorders. *International Journal of Mental Health, 1,* 9–45.

Vygotsky, L. S. (1962). *Thought and language.* Cambridge, MA: MIT Press.

Wachtel, P. (1973). Psychodynamics, behavior therapy, and the implacable experimenter: An inquiry into the consistency of personality. *Journal of Abnormal Psychology, 82,* 324–334.

Wadeson, H., & Carpenter, W. T., Jr. (1976). Subjective experience of schizophrenia. *Schizophrenia Bulletin, 2,* 302–316.

Wahl, O. (1977). Sex bias in schizophrenia research: A short report. *Journal of Abnormal Psychology, 86,* 195–198.

Walker, E., Bettes, B., Kain, E., & Harvey, P. (1985). Relationship of gender and marital status with symptomatology in psychotic patients. *Journal of Abnormal Psychology, 94,* 42–50.

Ward, N. G., Strauss, M. M., & Ries, R. (1982). The dexamethasone suppression test as a diagnostic aid in late onset paranoia. *Journal of Nervous and Mental Disease, 170,* 248–250.

Warheit, G. J., Holzer, C. E., & Schwab, J. J. (1973). An analysis of social class and racial differences in depressive symptomatology: A community study. *Journal of Health and Social Behavior, 14,* 291–299.

Warner, R. (1978). The diagnosis of antisocial and hysterical personality disorders. *Journal of Nervous and Mental Disease, 166,* 839–844.

Watson, C. G., & Baugh, V. S. (1966). Patterns of psychiatric patients on the revised Beta Examination. *Journal of Clinical Psychology, 22,* 188–190.

Watt, J. A. G., Hall, D. J., Olley, P. C., Hunter, D., & Gardiner, A. Q. (1980). Paranoid states of middle life: Familial occurrence and relationship to schizophrenia. *Acta Psychiatrica Scandinavica, 61,* 413–426.

Watt, N. (1978). Patterns of childhood social development in adult schizophrenics. *Archives of General Psychiatry, 35,* 160–165.

Watt, N., & Lubensky, A. (1976). Childhood roots of schizophrenia. *Journal of Consulting and Clinical Psychology, 44,* 363–375.

Watt, N., Stolorow, R., Lubensky, A., & McClelland, D. (1970). School adjustment and behavior of children hospitalized for schizophrenia as adults. *American Journal of Orthopsychiatry, 40,* 637–657.

Weckowitz, T. E. (1957). Size constancy in schizophrenic patients. *Journal of Mental Science, 103,* 475–486.

Weckowitz, T. E., & Blewett, D. B. (1959). Size constancy and abstract thinking in schizophrenic patients. *Journal of Mental Science, 105,* 909–934.

Weiner, I. B., & Del Gaudio, A. C. (1977). Psychopathology in adolescence: An epidemiological study. *Annual Progress in Child Psychiatry and Development, 10*, 471–488.

Weintraub, S., Neale, J., & Liebert, D. (1975). Teacher ratings of children vulnerable to psychopathology. *American Journal of Orthopsychiatry, 45*, 838–845.

Weintraub, S., Prinz, R., & Neale, J. (1978). Peer evaluations of the competence of children vulnerable to psychopathology. *Journal of Abnormal Child Psychology, 6*, 461–473.

Weissman, M., & Klerman, G. (1977). Sex differences in the epidemiology of depression. *Archives of General Psychiatry, 34*, 98–111.

Weissman, M., & Klerman, G. (1979). Sex differences and the epidemiology of depression. In E. S. Gomberg & V. Franks (Eds.), *Gender and disordered behavior* (pp. 381–425). New York: Brunner/Mazel.

Weissman, M., & Myers, J. K. (1978). Affective disorders in a U. S. urban community: The use of Research Diagnostic Criteria in an epidemiological survey. *Archives of General Psychiatry, 35*, 1304–1311.

Weissman, M., Myers, J. K., & Harding, P. S. (1978). Psychiatric disorders in a U.S. urban community. *American Journal of Psychiatry, 135*, 459–462.

Weissman, M., & Paykel, E. (1974). *The depressed woman.* Chicago: University of Chicago Press.

Weisz, J., Quinlan, D. M., O'Neill, P., & O'Neill, P. C. (1978). The Rorschach and structured tests of perception as indices of intellectual development in mentally retarded and nonretarded children. *Journal of Experimental Child Psychology, 25*, 326–336.

Werner, H. (1937). Process and achievement: A basic problem of education and developmental psychology. *Harvard Educational Review, 7*, 353–368.

Werner, H. (1948). *Comparative psychology of mental development.* New York: Follett.

Werner, H. (1957). The concept of development from a comparative and organismic point of view. In D. Harris (Ed.), *The concept of development: An issue in the study of human behavior* (pp. 125–148). Minneapolis: University of Minnesota Press.

Werner, H., & Kaplan, B. (1963). *Symbol formation: An organismic–developmental approach to language and the expression of thought.* New York: Wiley.

Werner, H., & Wapner, S. (1952). Toward a general theory of perception. *Psychological Review, 59*, 324–338.

West, L. J. (1975). A clinical and theoretical overview of hallucinatory phenomena. In R. K. Siegel & L. J. West (Eds.), *Hallucinations: Behavior, experience and theory* (pp. 287–311). New York: Wiley.

White, R. W. (1959). Motivation reconsidered: The concept of competence. *Psychological Review, 66*, 297–333.

Whitelock, P. R., Overall, J. E., & Patrick, J. H. (1971). Personality patterns and alcohol abuse in a state hospital population. *Journal of Abnormal Psychology, 78*, 9–16.

Wiersma, D., Giel, R., De Jong, A., & Slooff, C. J. (1983). Social class and schizophrenia in a Dutch cohort. *Psychological Medicine, 13*, 1–50.

Wilensky, H. (1959). Rorschach developmental level and social participation of chronic schizophrenics. *Journal of Projective Techniques, 23,* 87–92.

Williams, A. F., McCourt, W. F., & Schneider, L. (1971). Personality self-descriptions of alcoholics and heavy drinkers. *Quarterly Journal of Studies on Alcohol, 32,* 310–317.

Wilson, K. (1956). A distribution-free test of analysis of variance hypotheses. *Psychological Bulletin, 53,* 96–101.

Wing, J. K. (1970). A standard form of psychiatric present state examination and a method for standardizing the classification of symptoms. In E. H. Hare & J. K. Wing (Eds.), *Psychiatric epidemiology: An international symposium* (pp. 93–108). London: Oxford University Press.

Wing, J. K. (1978). The social context of schizophrenia. *American Journal of Psychiatry, 135,* 1333–1339.

Wing, J. K. (1980). Social psychiatry in the United Kingdom: The approach to schizophrenia. *Schizophrenia Bulletin, 6,* 556–565.

Wing, J., & Nixon, J. (1975). Discriminative symptoms in schizophrenia: A report from the International Pilot Study in Schizophrenia. *Archives of General Psychiatry, 32,* 853–859.

Wing, J., Nixon, J., von Cranach, M., & Strauss, A. (1977). Further developments of the "Present State Examination" and the Catego System. *Archiv fur Psychiatrie und Nervenkrankheiten, 244,* 151–160.

Winkler, R. C., & Myers, R. A. (1963). Some concomitants of self-ideal discrepancy measures of self-acceptance. *Journal of Counseling Psychology, 10,* 83–86.

Winokur, G. (1979). Familial (genetic) subtypes of pure depressive disease. *American Journal of Psychiatry, 136,* 911–913.

Winokur, G., & Clayton, P. (1967). Family history studies. II. Sex differences and alcoholism in primary affective illness. *British Journal of Psychiatry, 113,* 973–979.

Winokur, G., & Clayton, P. (1968). Family history studies. IV. Comparison of male and female alcoholics. *Quarterly Journal of Studies on Alcohol, 29,* 885–891.

Winokur, G., Clayton, P. J., & Reich, T. (1969). *Manic-depressive illness.* St. Louis: Mosby.

Winokur, G., & Crowe, R. (1983). Bipolar illness: The sex-polarity effect in affectively ill family members. *Archives of General Psychiatry, 40,* 57–58.

Winokur, G., Morrison, J., Clancy, J., & Crowe, R. (1974). Iowa 500: The clinical and genetic distribution of hebephrenic and paranoid schizophrenia. *Journal of Nervous and Mental Disease, 159,* 12–19.

Winokur, G., Rimmer, J., & Reich, T. (1971). Alcoholism. IV. Is there more than one type of alcoholism? *British Journal of Psychiatry, 118,* 525–531.

Wittenborn, J. (1977). Stability of symptom ratings for schizophrenic men. *Archives of General Psychiatry, 34,* 437–440.

Wittenborn, J., McDonald, D. C., & Maurer, H. S. (1977). Persisting symptoms in schizophrenia predicted by background factors. *Archives of General Psychiatry, 34,* 1057–1061.

Wittenborn, J., & Weiss, W. (1952). Patients diagnosed manic depressive psychosis-manic state. *Journal of Consulting Psychology, 16*, 193–198.

Wittman, P., & Steinberg, D. (1944). Follow-up of an objective evaluation and prognosis in dementia praecox and manic-depressive psychoses. *Elgin State Hospital Papers, 5*, 216–227.

Wittman, P. (1941). A scale for measuring prognosis in schizophrenia patients. *Elgin State Hospital Papers, 4*, 20–33.

Woerner, M. G., Pollack, M., Rogalski, C., Pollack, Y., & Klein, D. F. (1972). A comparison of the school records of personality disorders, schizophrenics, and their sibs. In M. Roff, L. N. Robins, & M. Pollack (Eds.), *Life history research in psychopathology* (Vol. 2) (pp. 47–65). Minneapolis: University of Minnesota Press.

Wohlwill, J. F. (1970). The age variable in psychological research. *Psychological Review, 77*, 49–64.

Wurmser, L. (1980). Review of *The Paranoid Process* by W. W. Meissner. *Journal of Nervous and Mental Disease, 168*, 319–320.

Wyatt, R. J., Termini, B. A., & Davis, J. (1971). Biochemical and sleep studies of schizophrenia: A review of the literature 1960–1970. Part I. Biochemical studies. *Schizophrenia Bulletin, 1*, 10–44.

Wylie, R. C. (1974). *The self-concept: A review of methodological considerations and measuring instruments* (Vol. 1, rev. ed.). Lincoln, NE: University of Nebraska Press.

Youkilis, H. D., & DeWolfe, A. S. (1975). The regression hypothesis and subclassifications of schizophrenia. *Journal of Abnormal Psychology, 84*, 36–40.

Young, J. P. R. (1972). Acute psychiatric disturbances in the elderly and their treatment. *British Journal of Clinical Practice, 16*, 513–516.

Zigler, E. (1963). Metatheoretical issues in developmental psychology. In M. Marx (Ed.), *Theories in contemporary psychology* (pp. 341–369). New York: MacMillan.

Zigler, E. (1969). Developmental versus difference theories of mental retardation and the problem of motivation. *American Journal of Mental Deficiency, 73*, 536–556.

Zigler, E. (1970a). The nature–nurture issue reconsidered. In H. C. Haywood (Ed.), *Socio-cultural aspects of mental retardation* (pp. 81–106). New York: Appleton-Century-Crofts.

Zigler, E. (1970b). Social class and the socialization process. *Review of Educational Research, 40*, 87–110.

Zigler, E., Balla, D., & Watson, N. (1972). Developmental and experiential determinants of self-image disparity in institutionalized and non-institutionalized retarded and normal children. *Journal of Personality and Social Psychology, 23*, 81–87.

Zigler, E., & Child, I. (1969). Socialization. In G. Lindzey & E. Aronson (Eds.), *The handbook of social psychology* (Vol. 3, 2nd ed.) (pp. 450–589). Reading, MA: Addison-Wesley.

Zigler, E., & Child, I. (Eds.). (1973). *Socialization and personality development*. Reading, MA: Addison-Wesley.

Zigler, E., Glick, M., & Marsh, A. (1979). Premorbid social competence and outcome among schizophrenic and nonschizophrenic patients. *Journal of Nervous and Mental Disease, 167,* 478–483.

Zigler, E., & Levine, J. (1973). Premorbid adjustment and paranoid–nonparanoid status in schizophrenia: A further investigation. *Journal of Abnormal Psychology, 82,* 189–199.

Zigler, E., & Levine, J. (1981a). Age of first hospitalization of male and female paranoid and nonparanoid schizophrenics: A developmental approach. *Journal of Abnormal Psychology, 90,* 458–467.

Zigler, E., & Levine, J. (1981b). Premorbid competence in schizophrenia: What is being measured? *Journal of Consulting and Clinical Psychology, 49,* 96–105.

Zigler, E., & Levine, J. (1983a). *Gender differences and symptomatology in schizophrenia.* Unpublished manuscript, Yale University, New Haven.

Zigler, E., & Levine, J. (1983b). Hallucinations vs. delusions: A developmental approach. *Journal of Nervous and Mental Disease, 171,* 141–146.

Zigler, E., Levine, J., & Gould, L. (1966). The humor response of normal, institutionalized retarded, and noninstitutionalized retarded children. *American Journal of Mental Deficiency, 71,* 472–480.

Zigler, E., Levine, J., & Gould, L. (1967). Cognitive challenge as a factor in children's humor appreciation. *Journal of Personality and Social Psychology, 6,* 332–336.

Zigler, E., Levine, J., & Zigler, B. (1976). The relation between premorbid competence and paranoid–nonparanoid status in schizophrenia: A methodological and theoretical critique. *Psychological Bulletin, 83,* 303–313.

Zigler, E. Levine, J., & Zigler, B. (1977). Premorbid social competence and paranoid–nonparanoid status in female schizophrenic patients. *Journal of Nervous and Mental Disease, 164,* 333–339.

Zigler, E., & Phillips, L. (1960). Social effectiveness and symptomatic behaviors. *Journal of Abnormal and Social Psychology, 61,* 231–238.

Zigler, E., & Phillips, L. (1961a). Case history data and psychiatric diagnosis. *Journal of Consulting Psychology, 25,* 258.

Zigler, E., & Phillips, L. (1961b). Psychiatric diagnosis: A critique. *Journal of Abnormal and Social Psychology, 63,* 607–618.

Zigler, E., & Phillips, L. (1961c). Psychiatric diagnosis and symptomatology. *Journal of Abnormal and Social Psychology, 63,* 69–75.

Zigler, E., & Phillips, L. (1961d). Social competence and outcome in psychiatric disorder. *Journal of Abnormal and Social Psychology, 63,* 264–171.

Zigler, E., & Phillips, L. (1962). Social competence and the process–reactive distinction in psychopathology. *Journal of Abnormal and Social Psychology, 65,* 215–222.

Zigler, E., & Trickett, P. (1978). IQ, social competence and evaluation of early childhood intervention programs. *American Psychologist, 33,* 789–798.

Zilboorg, G., & Henry, G. W. (1941). *A history of medical psychology.* New York: Norton.

Ziller, R. C., & Grossman, S. A. (1967). A developmental study of the self-social constructs of normals and the neurotic personality. *Journal of Clinical Psychology, 23,* 15–21.

Ziller, R. C., Megas, J., & DeCencio, D. (1964). Self-social constructs of normal and acute neuropsychiatric patients. *Journal of Consulting Psychology, 28,* 59–63.

Zimbardo, P., Andersen, S., & Kabat, L. (1981). Induced hearing deficit generates experimental paranoia. *Science, 212,* 1529–1531.

Zimet, C. N., & Fine, H. J. (1959). Perceptual differentiation and two dimensions of schizophrenia. *Journal of Nervous and Mental Disease, 129,* 435–441.

Zubin, J., Salzinger, K., Fleiss, J. L., Garland, B., Spitzer, R. L., Endicott, J., & Sutton, S. (1975). Biometric approach to psychopathology: Abnormal and clinical psychology—Statistical, epidemiological, and diagnostic approaches. *Annual Review of Psychology, 26,* 621–671.

Zubin, J., & Spring, B. (1977). Vulnerability—A new view of schizophrenia. *Journal of Abnormal Psychology, 86,* 103–126.

Zubin, J., & Steinhauer, S. (1981). How to break the logjam in schizophrenia: A look beyond genetics. *Journal of Nervous and Mental Disease, 169,* 477–492.

Zuckerman, M., Baer, M., & Monashkin, I. (1956). Acceptance of self, parents, and people in patients and normals. *Journal of Clinical Psychology, 12,* 327–332.

Zuckerman, M., & Monashkin, I. (1957). Self-acceptance and psychopathology. *Journal of Consulting Psychology, 21,* 145–148.

Author Index

Subject Index